Justin Winsor, Harward University

**A Record of the Commemoration, November fifth to eighth, 1886**

On the two hundred and fiftieth Anniversary of the Founding of Harvard College

Justin Winsor, Harward University

**A Record of the Commemoration, November fifth to eighth, 1886**
*On the two hundred and fiftieth Anniversary of the Founding of Harvard College*

ISBN/EAN: 9783337062514

Printed in Europe, USA, Canada, Australia, Japan

Cover: Foto ©ninafisch / pixelio.de

More available books at **www.hansebooks.com**

1636.     HARVARD UNIVERSITY.     1886.

A

# RECORD OF THE COMMEMORATION,

NOVEMBER FIFTH TO EIGHTH, 1886,

ON THE

## Two Hundred and Fiftieth Anniversary

OF THE

## FOUNDING OF HARVARD COLLEGE.

CAMBRIDGE, N.E.:
JOHN WILSON AND SON.
University Press.
1887.

The Court agree to give Four Hundred pounds towards a School or College, whereof two hundred pounds shall be paid the next year, and two hundred pounds when the work is finished, and the next Court to appoint where and what building. — RECORDS OF A GENERAL COURT OF THE COLONY OF MASSACHUSETTS BAY, *October 28, 1636, O. S. (Nov. 7, N. S.).*

---

*November 15, 1886.* — *Voted,* That Mr. WINSOR, the Librarian of the University, be requested to edit for the University a volume containing a full account of the Proceedings at the Two Hundred and Fiftieth Anniversary of the Founding of Harvard College. — RECORDS OF THE PRESIDENT AND FELLOWS.

# CONTENTS.

|  | PAGE |
|---|---|
| THE PREPARATION | 11 |
|    OFFICERS OF THE ALUMNI ASSOCIATION | 12 |
|    EXECUTIVE COMMITTEE | 13 |
|    FINANCE COMMITTEE | 14 |
|    CIRCULAR, SEPT. 1, 1886 | 15 |
|    COMMITTEE ON MUSIC | 17 |
|    ANNIVERSARY CHORUS | 17 |
|    GENERAL INFORMATION FURNISHED | 19 |
| LAW DAY (*Friday*) | 16 |
|    PREPARATIONS | 55 |
|    COMMITTEES | 56 |
|    LAW SCHOOL ASSOCIATION | 57 |
|    ITS OFFICERS | 58 |
|    COMMITTEE OF ARRANGEMENTS | 59 |
|    EXERCISES IN SANDERS THEATRE | 60 |
|       President Carter's Address | 60 |
|       Judge Holmes's Oration | 65 |
|    THE DINNER | 79 |
|       *Addresses by* — | |
|       President Carter | 79 |
|       Professor Langdell | 84 |
|       Hon. Samuel E. Sewall | 89 |
|       Hon. Thomas M. Cooley | 92 |
|       President Eliot | 96 |
|       General Alexander R. Lawton | 99 |
|       Hon. George O. Shattuck | 105 |
|       Mr. Frank W. Hackett | 107 |
|       Professor John C. Gray | 110 |
|       Hon. E. R. Hoar | 112 |
|    REGISTRATION OF MEMBERS | 115 |

# CONTENTS.

|  | PAGE |
|---|---|
| UNDERGRADUATES' DAY (*Saturday*) | 19 |
| BOAT RACE | 21 |
| SERVICES IN SANDERS THEATRE | 21 |
|     Oration by F. E. E. Hamilton | 123 |
|     Poem by F. S. Palmer | 132 |
|     Address by E. J. Rich | 135 |
|     Ode by L. McK. Garrison | 145 |
| FOOT-BALL GAME | 21 |
| RECEPTION BY PRESIDENT ELIOT | 22 |
|     Congratulations of Cambridge University | 22 |
|             " of Emmanuel College | 23 |
|             " of the University of Edinburgh | 24 |
|             " of the University of Heidelberg | 26 |
| REUNION OF GRADUATES OF THE LAWRENCE SCIENTIFIC SCHOOL | 26 |
| | |
| FOUNDATION DAY (*Sunday*) | 30 |
| MORNING SERVICE | 31 |
|     Sermon by F. G. Peabody | 149 |
| SYMPHONY CONCERT | 30, 31 |
| EVENING SERVICE | 31 |
|     Sermon by Phillips Brooks | 171 |
| LIST OF USHERS | 32 |
| | |
| ALUMNI DAY (*Monday*) | 32 |
| PROCESSION | 33 |
| RECEPTION OF PRESIDENT CLEVELAND | 34 |
| EXERCISES IN SANDERS THEATRE | 35 |
|     President Devens's Address | 193 |
|     Professor Lowell's Oration | 194 |
|     Dr. Holmes's Poem | 237 |
|     Conferring of Honorary Degrees | 38 |
| DINNER IN MEMORIAL HALL | 41 |
|     President Devens's Address | 250 |
|   *Speeches by* — | |
|     President Eliot | 261 |
|     Governor Robinson | 263 |
|     President Cleveland | 267 |
|     Hon. Robert C. Winthrop | 271 |
|     Professor Mandell Creighton | 276 |

## CONTENTS.

|  | PAGE |
|---|---|
| Dr. Charles Taylor | 280 |
| Right Hon. Sir Lyon Playfair | 282 |
| President Timothy Dwight | 285 |
| President James B. Angell | 289 |
| Francis R. Rives | 293 |
| Senator Hoar | 295 |
| Professor Lowell | 300 |
| Dr. Holmes | 302 |
| Professor Gildersleeve | 304 |
| (Letter of Dr. R. D. Hitchcock) | 304 |
| George William Curtis | 309 |
| Alexander Agassiz | 313 |
| Dr. Wier Mitchell | 315 |
| Professor J. B. Thayer | 319 |

| | |
|---|---|
| SERVICES OF THE CHIEF MARSHAL AND HIS ASSISTANTS | 43 |
| LIST OF MARSHALS | 44 |
| SERVICES OF THE SECRETARIES, THE FINANCE COMMITTEE, THE BURSAR AND OTHERS | 44 |
| RECEPTION IN HEMENWAY GYMNASIUM | 45 |
| TORCHLIGHT PROCESSION AND FIREWORKS | 46 |
| ENTERTAINMENT OF INVITED GUESTS | 48 |
| EXHIBITION OF RELICS | 50 |
| OLDEST GRADUATES | 51 |
| REGISTRATION OF GRADUATES, NON-GRADUATE OFFICERS, AND GUESTS | 327 |

A

# SKETCH OF THE COMMEMORATION.

### The Preparation and Proceedings.

IN March, 1886, the Directors of the Association of the Alumni chose Col. HENRY LEE Chief Marshal of a celebration to be held in commemoration of the founding of the College. The arranging for the jubilee fell in the first instance into his hands, in connection with the Executive Committee of the Association. A General Committee of Arrangements was then appointed to co-operate with the Executive Committee, including representatives of each Class from 1817 to 1886. Of this Committee Mr. HENRY B. ROGERS, of the Class of 1822, was made Chairman; and the Secretaries were Mr. HENRY PARKMAN, of the Class of 1870, and Mr. JOSIAH QUINCY, of the Class of 1880. Mr. Rogers resigning the chairmanship, Mr. WILLIAM GRAY, of the Class of 1829, was later chosen in his place.

In considering the question of the number likely to attend, it was found that there were 4,600 living graduates of the College proper alone; and of these there were 1,833 who had graduated within ten years; 2,474, within fifteen years; and 2,974, within twenty years. So that it appeared that almost two thirds of the whole number of Alumni had left College within twenty years, a large part of whom might be expected to come to Cambridge. There were also about 1,000 undergraduates who would be on the spot.

On May 22 the Committee of Arrangements chose an Executive Committee of nine. Col. Henry Lee, the Chief Marshal, was at a later day made its Chairman, — when also the Chairman of the Committee of Arrangements, Mr. Gray, and the President of the College were added to this Committee.

The officers and committees of the Alumni who served during the celebration were accordingly as follows: —

## OFFICERS OF THE ALUMNI ASSOCIATION.

*President.*
CHARLES DEVENS.

*Directors.*

| | |
|---|---|
| SAMUEL A. GREEN. | ARTHUR LINCOLN. |
| THEODORE LYMAN. | FRANCIS M. WELD. |
| HENRY S. RUSSELL. | JOHN D. WASHBURN. |

JAMES B. THAYER.

*Treasurer.*
S. LOTHROP THORNDIKE.

*Secretary.*
HENRY PARKMAN.

*Committee of Arrangements.*

| | | | |
|---|---|---|---|
| 1817. | GEORGE BANCROFT. | 1831. | GEORGE C. SHATTUCK. |
| 1818. | SIDNEY BARTLETT. | 1832. | HENRY WHEATLAND. |
| 1820. | WILLIAM H. FURNESS. | 1833. | MORRILL WYMAN. |
| 1821. | EDWARD G. LORING. | 1834. | SAMUEL M. FELTON. |
| 1822. | HENRY B. ROGERS. | 1835. | EBENEZER R. HOAR. |
| 1823. | WILLIAM AMORY. | 1836. | HENRY LEE. |
| 1824. | A. B. MUZZEY. | 1837. | CHARLES THEODORE RUSSELL. |
| 1825. | FREDERIC H. HEDGE. | 1838. | CHARLES DEVENS. |
| 1826. | ANDREW P. PEABODY. | 1839. | SAMUEL ELIOT. |
| 1827. | EPES S. DIXWELL. | 1840. | WILLIAM G. RUSSELL. |
| 1828. | ROBERT C. WINTHROP. | 1841. | THOMAS W. HIGGINSON. |
| 1829. | WILLIAM GRAY. | 1842. | THORNTON K. WARE. |
| 1830. | JOHN O. SARGENT. | 1843. | JOHN LOWELL. |

## SKETCH OF THE COMMEMORATION.

| | | | |
|---|---|---|---|
| 1844. | LEVERETT SALTONSTALL. | 1866. | EDWARD W. EMERSON. |
| 1845. | MANNING F. FORCE. | 1867. | EDWARD J. LOWELL. |
| 1846. | GEORGE F. HOAR. | 1868. | LEVERETT S. TUCKERMAN. |
| 1847. | WILLIAM C. ENDICOTT. | 1869. | HENRY W. PUTNAM. |
| 1848. | THOMAS CHASE. | 1870. | ROGER WOLCOTT. |
| 1849. | CHARLES R. CODMAN. | 1871. | CHARLES J. BONAPARTE. |
| 1850. | JOSEPH H. THAYER. | 1872. | JOHN F. ANDREW. |
| 1851. | GEORGE O. SHATTUCK. | 1873. | ROBERT GRANT. |
| 1852. | WILLIAM G. CHOATE. | 1874. | RICHARD H. DANA. |
| 1853. | ARTHUR T. LYMAN. | 1875. | AUGUSTUS HEMENWAY. |
| 1854. | EDWARD D. HAYDEN. | 1876. | GEORGE WALTON GREEN. |
| 1855. | ALEXANDER AGASSIZ. | 1877. | WILLIAM FARNSWORTH. |
| 1856. | CHARLES FRANCIS ADAMS, Jr. | 1878. | AUGUSTUS P. LORING. |
| 1857. | JOHN C. ROPES. | 1879. | I. TUCKER BURR. |
| 1858. | EDWARD G. PORTER. | 1880. | JOSIAH QUINCY. |
| 1859. | JOHN C. GRAY. | 1881. | EDW. D. BRANDEGEE. |
| 1860. | EDMUND WETMORE. | 1882. | EVERT J. WENDELL. |
| 1861. | HENRY P. BOWDITCH. | 1883. | CHARLES P. CURTIS, Jr. |
| 1862. | CHARLES C. SOULE. | 1884. | T. JEFFERSON COOLIDGE, Jr. |
| 1863. | CHARLES C. JACKSON. | 1885. | JAMES J. STORROW, Jr. |
| 1864. | ROBERT T. LINCOLN. | 1886. | WALTER PHILLIPS. |
| 1865. | CHARLES W. CLIFFORD. | | |

NOTE. — The first appointments for the Classes of 1825 and 1835 were S. K. Lothrop and Amos A. Lawrence; but those gentlemen died before the celebration took place. For the Class of 1848 the name of Henry Saltonstall was substituted for that of Mr. Chase, who chanced to be in Europe.

## EXECUTIVE COMMITTEE.

CHARLES DEVENS . . . . . . . . *President of the Alumni Association.*
CHARLES W. ELIOT . . . . . . . *President of the University.*
WILLIAM GRAY . . . . . . . . . *Chairman Committee of Arrangements.*

HENRY LEE.         EDWARD G. PORTER.
SAMUEL ELIOT.      ARTHUR LINCOLN.
JOHN C. ROPES.     HENRY W. PUTNAM.
       JAMES J. STORROW, Jr.

HENRY PARKMAN, JOSIAH QUINCY . . *Secretaries.*
HENRY LEE . . . . . . . . . . . *Chief Marshal.*

NOTE. — In the absence of President Devens, the Chief Marshal acted as Chairman.

In June it was decided to extend the celebration over three days, November 6, 7, and 8; to invite Professor JAMES RUSSELL LOWELL to deliver an address, and Dr. OLIVER WENDELL HOLMES to read a poem. It was also determined to make the President of the Association of Alumni the presiding officer of the third or Alumni day, and that invitations to guests be sent out in the name of that Association, and by the President of that Association and the Chief Marshal, after consultation with the President of the College. The students of the College, at the request of the Executive Committee of the Alumni Association, prepared to participate in the celebration by the appointment of the following committees of the three higher classes: —

| *Class of* 1887. | *Class of* 1888. | *Class of* 1889. |
|---|---|---|
| F. L. SNELLING. | M. H. CLYDE. | G. T. KEYES. |
| F. E. E. HAMILTON. | C. F. ADAMS, 3d. | T. WOODBURY. |
| F. S. COOLIDGE. | F. B. LUND. | |

Other details were arranged, and then, June 19, the Executive Committee of the General Committee of Arrangements was empowered to carry out the plans proposed. A Finance Committee was appointed to provide the means, which Committee consisted of the following members: —

JUDGE JOHN LOWELL, *Chairman.*

| | |
|---|---|
| AMOS A. LAWRENCE. | CHARLES C. JACKSON. |
| GEORGE O. SHATTUCK. | ROGER WOLCOTT. |
| ALEXANDER AGASSIZ. | CHARLES J. BONAPARTE, *Baltimore.* |
| MATTHEW F. FORCE, *Cincinnati.* | JOHN F. ANDREW. |
| ARTHUR T. LYMAN. | AUGUSTUS HEMENWAY. |
| ROBERT T. LINCOLN, *Chicago.* | G. W. GREEN, *New York.* |
| FRANCIS M. WELD, *New York.* | WILLIAM FARNSWORTH. |

During July and August the committee were arranging details, and on September 1 the following circular was sent to every Alumnus whose address could be obtained: —

## SKETCH OF THE COMMEMORATION.

CAMBRIDGE, MASSACHUSETTS, September 1, 1886.

The Two Hundred and Fiftieth Anniversary of the Foundation of Harvard University will be celebrated on the 6th, 7th, and 8th days of November next.

On Saturday the 6th, Undergraduates' Day, the Students of the University will celebrate the event by Literary Exercises in the morning, Athletic Sports in the afternoon, and a Torchlight Procession in the evening.

On Sunday the 7th, Foundation Day, the anniversary of the passage by the General Court of the Colony of Massachusetts Bay of the memorable vote —

"The Court agree to give Four Hundred Pounds towards a School or College, whereof Two Hundred Pounds shall be paid the next year, and Two Hundred Pounds when the work is finished, and the next Court to appoint where and what building," —

there will be Commemorative Exercises, under the direction of the College authorities, in Appleton Chapel, conducted in the morning by the Plummer Professor, Rev. FRANCIS G. PEABODY, and in the evening by the Rev. PHILLIPS BROOKS. On this day clerical graduates of the University are requested to refer, in their pulpits, if the circumstances permit, to this act of the infant colony and the benefits which have followed from it.

On Monday, November the 8th, Alumni Day, the graduates of all Departments of the University and guests will meet in Massachusetts Hall, at 10 A.M., and proceed thence to Sanders Theatre, under escort of the undergraduates, where an address will be made by JAMES RUSSELL LOWELL, LL.D., and a poem delivered by OLIVER WENDELL HOLMES, LL.D., and honorary degrees will be conferred by the University.

In the afternoon, the Association of the Alumni, composed of all graduates of the *College*, with their invited guests, will have a collation in Memorial Hall.

It is suggested that the members of Harvard Clubs in the various cities of the United States who are unable to attend the celebration at Cambridge should commemorate the day.

Tickets for the collation in Memorial Hall, at two dollars apiece, will be for sale on and after Tuesday, November 2, to graduates of the College, holders of honorary degrees from the University, and members of the Faculties of the Professional

Schools and of the College, and may be obtained either on personal application or by letter. No tickets will be reserved unless the price accompanies the order; and tickets ordered by letter will not be sent by mail, but will be reserved to be called for until half-past one P.M., on Monday, November 8.

For the exercises on Monday morning in Sanders Theatre, the gallery, containing four hundred seats, will be reserved for ladies, and tickets at two dollars apiece can be obtained by graduates of the University in the same manner as tickets for the collation are obtained by graduates of the College; but not more than two tickets will be sold to any one Alumnus.

Address, for tickets for ladies and for the collation, ALLEN DANFORTH, Bursar, Cambridge, Mass. Office hours, 9 A.M. to 1 P.M.

It was found necessary in carrying out the purpose of the committee in respect to tickets to prescribe some rules not included in this circular, — among which was to allow holders of honorary degrees the same rights as graduates in all cases, and to dispense with a charge for Sanders Theatre tickets for ladies, substituting therefor an assignment by lot, after some necessary reservations.

Later in September a movement was completed among the past members of the Law School which resulted in a determination to devote a fourth day, preceding the three days already designated, to a commemoration in connection with the law department of the University. The expected ceremonies were satisfactorily carried out on Friday the 5th, as described on a later page; and as they were not an integral part of the celebration as planned by the Alumni of the College, further mention of it is omitted here.

On October 13, it was determined by the Executive Committee of the Alumni to put the direction of the music for Alumni Day in the hands of the Chief Marshal; and in order to provide music for other days, a committee was appointed who organized the Anniversary Chorus.

## SKETCH OF THE COMMEMORATION. 17

### COMMITTEE ON MUSIC.

HENRY LEE HIGGINSON, *Chairman.*  ARTHUR FOOTE.
JOHN KNOWLES PAINE.                SIGOURNEY BUTLER.
GEORGE LAURIE OSGOOD.              SAMUEL ATKINS ELIOT, *Secretary.*
WARREN ANDREW LOCKE.               EUGENE RODMAN SHIPPEN.

### ANNIVERSARY CHORUS.

*First Tenors.*

1858. JOHN HOMANS, M.D.
1859. DANIEL FRANCIS FITZ.
1859. SAMUEL WOODS LANGMAID, M.D.
1864. RUSSELL NEVINS BELLOWS, A.M.
1864. JONATHAN DORR, A.M.
1864. CHARLES COOLIDGE READ, LL.B.
1865. HORATIO GREENOUGH CURTIS.
1866. GEORGE LAURIE OSGOOD.
1869. EDWARD BOWDITCH.
1869. NATHANIEL CHILDS.
1871. FRANCIS JACKSON.
1872. EDWARD GRAY.
1873. ROBERT WHEELER WILLSON.
1874. ARTHUR LITHGOW DEVENS.
1875. HENRY WHITE BROUGHTON, M.D.

1879. STEPHEN BLAKE WOOD.
1882. JAMES EDWARD WELD, LL.B.
1883. EDWARD TWISLETON CABOT.
1883. PERCIVAL JAMES EATON.
1883. HOWARD LILIENTHAL.
1885. CHARLES CARROLL KING.
1886. JOHNSTON MORTON.
1887. BYRON SATTERLEE HURLBURT.
1887. EMERY HERMAN ROGERS.
1888. FRED BATES LUND.
1889. GARDNER CUTTING BULLARD.
1889. HORACE DELANO EVERETT.
1889. JOHN DOUGLAS MERRILL.
1890. LUTHER DAVIS.

*Second Tenors.*

1858. CHARLES HENRY LEAROYD, A.M.
1859. JAMES SCHOULER.
1860. STEPHEN WILLIAM DRIVER, M.D.
1860. HENRY GEORGE SPAULDING.
1862. CHARLES BURNHAM PORTER, M.D.
1862. CHARLES PICKARD WARE.
1863. FRANCIS ALEXANDER MARDEN.
1866. WILLIAM PAINE BLAKE, LL.B.
1867. CLEMENT KELSEY FAY.
1867. FRANCIS HENRY LINCOLN.
1868. FRANK IZARD EUSTIS, A.M.

1869. FRANCIS GREENWOOD PEABODY, A.M.
1871. FRANCIS MERRIAM.
1871. GEORGE RICHARDS MINOT.
1872. PHILIP SIDNEY STONE.
1875. VINCENT YARDLEY BOWDITCH, M.D.
1877. SIGOURNEY BUTLER.
1880. ROBERT BACON.
1881. MORRIS HICKY MORGAN.
1882. JAMES WILLIAMS BOWEN.
1882. GUSTAVUS TUCKERMAN.
1883. JOSEPH DORR.

18    SKETCH OF THE COMMEMORATION.

1883. CHARLES WALTER GEROULD.
1883. WILLIAM DUNNING SULLIVAN.
1884. SAMUEL ATKINS ELIOT.
1885. EDWIN HOWARD.
1885. WILLIAM WARREN WINSLOW.
1886. WALTER HOWARD EDGERLY.
1886. CHARLES HENRY MINOT.

1887. GEORGE AUSTIN MORRISON.
1887. FREDERIC SHURTLEFF COOLIDGE.
1888. FRANKLIN GREENE BALCH.
1888. HENRY LOWELL MASON.
1888. CHARLES TILDEN SEMPERS.
1889. RICHARD CLARKE CABOT.
1889. DANIEL HARRY CLARK.

*First Bass.*

1857. EZRA DYER.
1858. JAMES AUGUSTUS RUMRILL.
1860. HORACE JOHN HAYDEN, A.M.
1864. MARSHALL MUNROE CUTTER.
1868. ROBERT APTHORP BOIT.
1871. THEODORE SUTRO, LL.B.
1872. ALBERT LAMB LINCOLN, LL.B.
1874. JOHN WOODFORD FARLOW, M.D.
1874. WILLIAM PEARSON WARNER.
1876. EMOR HERBERT HARDING, LL.B.
1877. MORRIS GRAY, LL.B.
1878. LOUIS BAILEY DEAN.
1879. ALVAH CROCKER.
1879. LOUIS BRANCH HARDING.

1880. FRANCIS BOWLER KEENE.
1880. FREDERIC BOUND HALL.
1883. MARSHALL HENRY CUSHING.
1883. CHARLES SUMNER HAMLIN, LL.B
1884. JOHN EDWARD HOWE.
1884. THOMAS MOTT OSBORNE.
1885. HENRY KIRKLAND SWINSCOE.
1886. ALAN GREGORY MASON.
1886. CROSBY CHURCH WHITMAN.
1887. WILLIAM SYLVESTER ALLEN.
1887. WILLIAM EDWARD FAULKNER.
1888. LOCKWOOD HONORÉ.
1888. SOLOMON LEWIS SWARTS.

*Second Bass.*

1858. OTIS PUTNAM ABERCROMBIE, LL.B.
1860. EDWIN JOHNSON HORTON, A.M.
1860. OLIVER FAIRFIELD WADSWORTH, M.D.
1862. ARTHUR REED.
1863. FRANCIS MARSH.
1864. EDWIN PLINY SEAVER, A.M.
1866. AMOS MORSE LEONARD, A.M.
1866. JAMES JACKSON PUTNAM, M.D.
1866. MELVIN AUG. UNDERWOOD, A.M.
1868. AUGUSTUS GEORGE BULLOCK, A.M.
1868. EDWARD EVERETT SPRAGUE.
1869. NATHANIEL SMITH.
1870. FRANCIS WALCOTT ROBINSON.
1871. ALBERT MALLARD BARNES.
1871. ALFRED STACKPOLE DABNEY.
1871. HORACE APPLETON LAMB.
1873. EDWARD SHERMAN DODGE.
1874. GEORGE OLIVER GEORGE COALE.

1874. RICHARD HENRY DANA, LL.B.
1876. FRANCIS SHALTER LIVINGOOD.
1877. GARDNER SWIFT LAMSON.
1877. JOHN BERTRAM WILLIAMS.
1879. WILMOT TOWNSEND COX, LL.B.
1880. JOHN LOTHROP WAKEFIELD.
1881. WILLIAM GOLD BRINSMADE.
1882. CHARLES FRANCIS MASON.
1883. SUMNER COOLIDGE.
1883. JAMES HAMLET BOLT EASTON.
1885. DONALD ELLIS WHITE.
1887. EUGENE RODMAN SHIPPEN.
1888. CHARLES CHOLLET.
1889. HERBERT HENRY DARLING.
1889. ALMON DANFORTH HODGES.
1889. WILLARD ROBERT KIMBALL.
1889. HENRY DIKE SLEEPER.

SKETCH OF THE COMMEMORATION. 19

The Executive Committee prepared a circular, which embraced the following

## GENERAL INFORMATION.

*Registration Room.* — An office under the charge of Mr. GEORGE R. NUTTER will be opened at No. 4 University Hall on Tuesday, the 2d of November, for the registration of names, the sale of tickets, the delivery of badges, and the communication of needed information as to the time and place and conditions of the successive ceremonies of the Festival; and all graduates and invited guests of the University attending the celebration are requested to register their names, residences, and temporary addresses.

A badge will be given at the Registration Room to every participant in the celebration. The badges will serve as means of identification, and are necessary to admit their wearers to the Oration in Sanders Theatre on Friday the 5th, to the Observatory and the Athletic Sports on the 6th, and to Appleton Chapel and Sanders Theatre on the 7th.

*Restaurant in Massachusetts Hall.* — During the Festival a Restaurant and Smoking-Room will be established in Massachusetts Hall for the entertainment of graduates and undergraduates of the University, and their friends.

*Museums.* — The Museum of Comparative Zoölogy, the Peabody Museum of American Archæology and Ethnology, and the Mineral Cabinet in Boylston Hall will be open on Friday, Saturday, and Monday from 9 to 5 o'clock, and on Sunday from 1 to 5 o'clock. The Botanic Garden will be open during the Anniversary.

It also presented the Official programme for Saturday, November 6, as follows: —

## UNDERGRADUATES' DAY.

9.30 A.M. *Boat Club Scratch Races.* ¼ mile course. (*a*) Upper class eight-oars. (*b*) Freshman eight-oars. (*c*) Single scull shells. (*d*) Single scull working-boats, or single canoes.

11.30 A.M. *Literary Exercises in Sanders Theatre.* (*a*) Prayer by Rev. A. P. PEABODY. (*b*) Oration by F. E. E. HAMILTON, '87. (*c*) Poem by F. S. PALMER, '87. (*d*) Address to Undergraduates,

E. J. RICH, '87. (c) Ode by L. McK. GARRISON, '88. Music by the Glee Club and Pierian Sodality.

The floor and lower gallery of the Theatre will be reserved for the Undergraduates. Tickets for seats in the upper gallery will be issued without charge to graduates; and a limited number of admission tickets will be distributed after the supply of reserved-seat tickets has been exhausted. Graduates may procure tickets upon application at No. 4 University Hall. Guests of the University will also be provided with reserved seats upon application at the same place.

3 P.M. *Championship Foot-Ball Game.* Harvard v. Wesleyan. Jarvis Field.

5 P.M. The President will receive any invited guests of the University who have reached Cambridge, at No. 5 University Hall. Members of the Academic Council are requested to be present.

8 P.M. Marching of torchlight procession from Hemenway Gymnasium through Cambridge Street, Broadway, Quincy Street, Harvard Street, Prospect Street, Main Street, Quincy Street, Broadway, College Yard, Harvard Street, Harvard Square, Garden Street, Mason Street, Brattle Street, Craigie Street, Concord Avenue, Waterhouse Street, North Avenue, and Jarvis Street, to Holmes Field.

9.30 P.M. Display of fireworks on Holmes Field.

Former students of the Lawrence Scientific School will meet at the School building at 6.30 P.M. Lunch at 7 P.M. Tickets (price, $1.00) may be obtained of Prof. W. S. CHAPLIN, 16 Prescott Street, Cambridge, or of Mr. G. R. NUTTER at the Registration Room at No. 4 University Hall. Former students are requested as soon as they arrive to register at the School building, as well as at University 4.

The Observatory will be open to visitors from 10 A.M. to 5 P.M., when the instruments will be exhibited and their uses explained. The entrance to the grounds is on Garden Street.

This programme was all carried out, except that a heavy rain, beginning in the afternoon and lasting through the evening, rendered necessary a postponement of the students' procession and fireworks. The evening was occupied with private receptions.

There was a fog in the early morning, but it began to lift shortly after nine o'clock, and the races were rowed in the presence of a large number of spectators. The account in the "Daily Crimson" shows that of the Senior crews the winning one was composed of, — *stroke*, Adams '88; *7*, Keyes '87; *6*, Coolidge '87; *5*, Davis '89; *4*, Ayer '87; *3*, Goodwin '89; *2*, Appleton '88; *bow*, Bowen '87; *coxswain*, Morse '87. The winning eight of the Freshmen were, — *stroke*, Crehore; *7*, Lothrop; *6*, E. Sturgis; *5*, Beecher; *4*, Barnes; *3*, Leonard; *2*, Pulsifer; *bow*, Darling; *coxswain*, Brown '88. Of the single sculls, Taylor '90 was the winner.

Shortly after eleven o'clock the four classes of Undergraduates met at their appointed places in the college yard, and forming in procession with the Seniors in advance, proceeded to Sanders Theatre. As the students entered the auditorium the Pierian Sodality began Mendelssohn's "Cornelius March." The students occupied, when seated, all parts of the theatre except the centre division of the first balcony, which was reserved for the officers of the college and for guests; and the second gallery, which was filled with the graduates and with friends of the undergraduates. Mr. Winthrop Wetherbee, the Chairman of the Literary Committee of the students, presided. After a prayer by the Rev. Dr. Peabody, the other services went forward as given in detail on a later page, the intervals between the speaking being filled with a rendering of "Eichberg's National Hymn" by the Glee Club, and with the "Berceuse of Gounod-Brand" by the Pierian Sodality; at the close of all, the whole audience stood and joined in singing the words of the ode which had just been read, to the tune of "Fair Harvard."

The foot-ball game in the afternoon was played with vigor, but with some difficulty owing to the wet condition of the ground, while the ardor of the spectators was somewhat dampened by the steady rain which fell throughout and prevented the completion of the game, as darkness came on.

In the afternoon at five o'clock President Eliot, assisted by the Faculties and officers of the various departments, received the invited guests in the Faculty room of the college in University Hall. It was an hour devoted to social converse merely, the only formalities being the presentation by Dr. Taylor of an address of Congratulation from the University of Cambridge, England, and by Dr. Creighton of similar felicitations from the authorities of Emmanuel College. The addresses of presentation were very brief, as were the responses of President Eliot.

The documents presented were as follows:—

*Academia Cantabrigiensis Cantabrigiae Transatlanticae salutem dicit plurimam:*

QUANTA cum voluptate epistolam illam nuperrime accepimus, in qua Academiae nobiscum et nomine et origine coniunctissimae sacra saecularia celebraturi, etiam nostram Academiam sacris illis interesse voluistis. Iuvat profecto diem illum faustum prope praesentem contemplari quem nuper illo die appropinquantem prospeximus quo vestris ex alumnis unum, virum litterarum laude insignem, titulo nostro honorifico ornavimus. Iuvat Academiam illam cuius professores illustres in senaculo nostro identidem salutavimus, ipsam litteris hisce vetera hospitii iura testantibus e longinquo saltem affari. Nos certe temporis et spatii intervallo iniquo exclusi, et negotiis Academicis impediti, non possumus qua voluissemus frequentia ludos illos vestros praesentes celebrare. Unum tamen nostro e numero delegimus qui nostro omnium nomine nostras omnium gratulationes legatus ad vos perferat. Non aliter vosmetipsi (iuvat recordari) e professorum vestrorum ordine insigni virum eximium Collegium illud antiquum non ita pridem salutatum misistis, unde profectus unus ex alumnis nostris, ducentesimo quinquagesimo abhinc anno, extra Britanniae terminos artiores Collegium primum illorum ad fructum condidit qui eadem ac nos utuntur lingua, eisdem ac nos litterarum monumentis antiquis gloriantur. Laetamur Academiam illam vestram quam velut filiam nostram non sine superbia contemplamur, ipsam tot Collegiis novis trans aequor Atlanticum quasi matrem exstitisse. Etenim flamma illa prima quam conditor ille vester trans oceanum secum pertulit, e vobis usque ad ulterioris oceani fluctus transmissa, aliud ex alio culmen igne novo deinceps accendit: —

ὑπερτελής τε πόντον ὥστε νωτίσαι. . .
σθένουσα λαμπὰς οὐδέπω μαυρουμένη. . .
ἤγειρεν ἄλλην ἐκδοχὴν πομποῦ πυρός.

Facem illam doctrinae utinam fratribus nostris Transatlanticis diutissime praetendatis, locique nomen non minus nobis quam vobis carum, plurima in saecula indies illustrius reddatis. Valete.
*Datum Cantabrigiae*
*pridie idus Octobres*
A.S. MDCCCLXXXVI.

*Collegium Emmanuelis Universitati Harvardianae S. P. D.:*

AEVI miliarii jam quarta pars decucurrit ex quo rei academicae transmarinae fundamenta posuit Harvardius ille, quem et vestrum et nostrum communi pietate veneramur. Quod hac oblata occasione incunabula Academiae vestrae in memoriam revocaturi, et labores tot tantorumque hominum optime meritorum idoneis laudibus cumulaturi, nos quoque in gratulationis consortium vocastis, jucundissimo officio obstrictos nunc iterum nos habetis. Adhuc in omnium auribus resonat viri illius omni nomine laudandi facundia quem ad nos et sollemnia nostra ante duo hos annos legastis, cum Collegium Emmanuelis trium saeculorum jam emensorum memoriae litaret. Quo lubentius socium nostrum carissimum Mandellium Creighton, quem vobis Clio sua jam antea commendaverat, salutis nuntium designavimus, ut paullisper unus vestrum fiat.

Veteri ut dicitur Angliae, quo tempore vetustate sua pridem videbatur laborare, regnante Elisabetha nova quaedam illuxerat juventus; quae ne servitio aliunde ingravescenti succumberet fundator noster cum ipse senesceret providebat. Eodem fere consilio, neque ita multo post, fundator vester intra juventam moribundus nascenti populo ingenitum esse scientiae divinae et humanae studium doctrinamque et pari incremento in posterum maturari volebat. Siquidem vero fines cuique saeculo impositos vel prudentioribus excedere non concessum est, fieri vix potuit ut quod fundatori utrique placuisset novitati condicionum sufficeret, verum ex primordiorum salubribus angustiis in exitus inopinatos quidem sed locupletes numine quodam caelesti contigit dilatari.

Neque patriae quidem nostrae neque Collegio finem operis jamjam imminere sperare liceat. Vobis saltem indies amplior patescit campus, quo in excolendo ad vestros nec non etiam ad nostros largissima messis redundet. Stat sigillo vestro inscripta Veritas illa cui inservire virorum academicorum et summa laus est et haud levis opera: vobis et veterem fovendam et exquirendam novam cum majorum vox tum hodierna rerum opportunitas committunt Veritatem. Valete.

*Dabamus Cantabrigiae,*
*die quinta Octobris*
MDCCCLXXXVI.

Addresses, which follow, were also received from the universities of Edinburgh and Heidelberg, but they were not formally presented: —

*To Harvard University, on the occasion of the Two Hundred and Fiftieth Anniversary of her Foundation, Greeting from the University of Edinburgh.*

To the President, Fellows, and Association of Alumni of the University of Harvard:

On the auspicious occasion of the two hundred and fiftieth anniversary of the foundation of Harvard University, we the undersigned, on behalf of her elder Scottish sister, the University of Edinburgh, hereby convey our most hearty greetings and our sincerest wishes for her continued prosperity. Having with the deepest interest traced the history of the "College of New Towne" from her birth in 1636 down to her full maturity as a university in 1886, we are profoundly impressed with her high merits and the world-wide influence she exercises in the domains of Philosophy, Science, and Literature. Conscious that our own as well as other universities have yet much to learn from the Founders, Patrons, and Professors of Harvard, we regard with admiration their wisdom, their munificence, and their public spirit; and we hope ere long to benefit by their noble example in the extension and improvement of our own University system.

Warmly sympathizing with the educational institutions of America, we have lately deemed it a high privilege to enroll several of their most famous representatives among our honorary graduates. Foremost among these we would mention His Excellency James Russell Lowell, delegate from Harvard University at our Tercentenary Festival, and Dr. Oliver Wendell Holmes, whose eloquence has recently delighted us and powerfully stimulated our academic life. With such representatives of Harvard University fresh in our memories, with their noble sentiments graven on our hearts, we the more cordially and earnestly wish their revered Alma Mater God-speed!

Regretting deeply that we are unavoidably prevented from sending a delegate in person to participate in your Festival, we shall nevertheless be with you in spirit.

JOHN INGLIS, *Chancellor.*
W. MUIR, *Principal.*
ROBERT FLINT, *S. T. P.*
W. Y. SELLAR,
 *Litt. Hum. Prof.*
S. H. BUTCHER,
 *Litt. Graec. Prof.*
A. CAMPBELL FRASER,
 *Log. and Met. Prof.*
A. R. SIMPSON,
 *Medic. Obstet. Prof.*
DOUGLAS MACLAGAN,
 *Med.-Forensis Prof.*
P. G. TAIT, *Phil. Nat. Prof.*
G. CHRYSTAL, *Prof. Math.*
JAS. MUIRHEAD,
 *Prof. Civ. Law.*
THOMAS R. FRASER,
 *Prof. Mat. Med.*
J. C. EWART, *Prof. Nat. Hist.*
THOMAS ANNANDALE,
 *Cl. Surg. Prof.*
MALCOLM C. TAYLOR,
 *Hist. Eccl. Prof.*

JULIUS EGGELING,
 *Prof. Lit. Sanscr., Phil. Comp.*
ROBERT WALLACE,
 *Prof. Agriculture.*
JAMES GEIKIE, *Prof. Geology.*
J. KIRKPATRICK, *Hist. Prof.*
JOHN CHIENE,
 *Prof. of Surgery.*
H. CALDERWOOD,
 *Mor. Phil. Prof.*
DON MACKINNON,
 *Litt. Celt. Prof.*
S. S. LAURIE,
 *Instit. Educ. Prof.*
D. L. ADAMS,
 *Linguar. Orient. Prof.*
NORMAN MACPHERSON,
 *Prof. Scots. Law.*
W. RUTHERFORD,
 *Instit. Med. Prof.*
J. SHIELD NICHOLSON,
 *Œcon. Pol. Prof.*
ALEX. CRUM BROWN,
 *Chem. Prof.*
WM. TURNER, *Anat. Prof.*

25th OCTOBER, 1886.

The Right Honorable Sir Lyon Playfair was subsequently authorized by telegram to represent the University of Edinburgh.

A telegraphic despatch from the Government of Italy accredited, as the representative of the Italian universities, Rodolpho Lanciani, Professor of Archæology in the University of Rome, Director of the Museo Urbano, and Director of the archæological excavations in Rome and in Italy.

The following communication was also received from a university to whose five hundredth anniversary, celebrated during the past summer, Harvard University had sent a delegate, in the person of Dr. J. R. Chadwick of the Medical Department:

HEIDELBERG, den 12 Oktober, 1886.

Der Harvard Universität sagen wir besten Dank für die Einladung zur Feier Ihres zweihundert und fünfzig jährigen Bestehens. Leider gestatten die Umstände nicht, Vertreter aus unserer Mitte zur persönlichen Theilnahme an dem schönen Feste zu entsenden, und so können wir nur auf diesem Wege unsern warmen Gefühlen für das Wohl und Gedeihen der stamm- und geistes verwandten Schwester Ausdruck verleihen. Möge Ihr Bestehen in dem zweiten Jahrtausends Viertel ein ebenso gesegnetes sein wie in dem ersten, möge die Wirksamkeit entsprechend dem Aufblühen Ihres Landes noch ausgedehnter werden, und möge insbesondere der Zusammenhang zwischen amerikanischer und deutscher Wissenschaft und Lehre in alle Zeit unwandelbar ausdauern und Frucht bringen.

*Prorector und Senat der Grossherzoglich Badischen Universität zu Heidelberg.*

T. BEKKER.

Another event of this day was the reunion of those who had been students of the Lawrence Scientific School. Nearly a month earlier (October 12) a few of the graduates of the School, living in or near Cambridge, met to consider the propriety of bringing the graduates, the teachers, and the former students of the School together at the time of the Harvard celebration. It was decided that a reunion should be called, and a committee was appointed to make preparation for it. This reunion was held in the building of the Lawrence Scientific School. A business meeting took place in the

## SKETCH OF THE COMMEMORATION. 27

afternoon in the Library of the School, which was called to order by Professor E. C. Pickering; Mr. Andrew McFarland Davis was appointed chairman, and Professor Albert R. Leeds secretary. Former members of the School were assembled in gratifying numbers, and the proposal that an Association of the alumni of the School should be formed met with general approval. Professor Simon Newcomb was elected president, Professor William M. Davis secretary, and Dr. Walter Faxon treasurer, of the Association; and a committee, consisting of Professors Nathaniel S. Shaler and Edward C. Pickering and Mr. Samuel H. Scudder, was appointed to act with these officers in perfecting the organization of the Association. The present position and future prospects of the School were the subject of brief discussion, and Messrs. E. C. Pickering, F. W. Clarke, A. Agassiz, J. Trowbridge, A. McF. Davis, and W. S. Chaplin were constituted a committee to report at a future meeting on the condition of the School and on the measures best adapted to increasing its prosperity.

The meeting then adjourned to a supper served in an adjacent lecture-room, and there spent the evening in informal discussion, in which a good number of those present took part. Mr. A. McF. Davis presided, and called on Professor Pickering, who opened the discussion and made a general statement of the questions to be considered. Professor Trowbridge advocated the establishment of fellowships for advanced students, and was ready to take a share in the accomplishment of this end. Professor Clarke desired that the alumni of the School should have the right to vote for the overseers who take part in its government, and thought that the Association could do good work in securing this franchise to its members. President Eliot explained the earlier conditions of the University which had led to the limitation of franchise in the election of overseers to the graduates of the college; but as those conditions had now disappeared, he thought the limitation was no longer necessary and might be withdrawn. Other speakers agreed as to the importance of such a change in giving recognition to a department of the University whose graduates were perhaps of small number, but who were none the less interested in the management and the progress of the University on that account. The change in the relation of the College towards the School, from earlier to later years, was also dwelt upon by several speakers, who recognized therein the chief cause of the decrease in the number of students in the School; but it was also contended that the expansion of scientific teaching in the College was in part an effect of the work done in the School, which should be remembered to its credit. Professor Davis deprecated the suggestion that the School should be developed as a separate organization in the line of advanced studies, for it would then run parallel to the growing graduate department of the College, and would court a repetition of the decadence that it has already suffered alongside of the College itself. Dr. Bowditch regretted the late entrance into practical life made by men who passed four years in college and three years in a professional school, and hoped that the time devoted to these courses might be in some way abridged.

Among others who addressed the meeting were Messrs. Brewer, Watson, Herschel, Hyatt, Niles, Drown, Perkins, Alden, and Chaplin.

The following list of persons present is prepared from the registration book opened at the meeting. The names are placed in order of the year of graduation or of attendance at the School in the capacity of teacher or special student: —

| | | |
|---|---|---|
| 1853. | CHARLES L. PIERSON . . . . . . . | Boston. |
| 1854. | WILLIAM AUGUSTUS BREWER, Jr. . . . | South Orange, N.J. |
| " | ANDREW McF. DAVIS . . . . . . . | Cambridge. |
| " | JOHN TAYLOR GILMAN NICHOLS . . . . | Cambridge. |
| 1855. | CHARLES S. HOMER, Jr. . . . . . . | New York. |

## SKETCH OF THE COMMEMORATION. 29

| 1856. | José F. Carret | Cambridge. |
| 1857. | Alexander Agassiz | Cambridge. |
| " | William Watson | Boston. |
| 1858. | Louis Arnold | West Roxbury, Mass. |
| " | Frank W. Preston | New Ipswich, N.H. |
| 1860. | James F. Babcock | Boston. |
| " | Clemens Herschel | Holyoke, Mass. |
| " | Edward S. Morse | Salem, Mass. |
| 1861. | Roberdeau Buchanan | Washington, D.C. |
| 1862. | Charles W. Eliot | Cambridge. |
| " | Alpheus Hyatt | Cambridge. |
| " | Frederick W. Putnam | Cambridge. |
| " | Andrew Robeson | Brookline, Mass. |
| " | Samuel H. Scudder | Cambridge. |
| " | Nathaniel S. Shaler | Cambridge. |
| 1863. | John Goddard Stearns | Brookline. |
| 1864. | Edwin A. Hildreth | Harvard, Mass. |
| 1865. | Thomas M. Drown | Boston. |
| " | Charles Dudley Lamson | Boston. |
| " | William H. Niles | Cambridge. |
| " | Maurice Perkins | Schenectady. |
| " | Edward C. Pickering | Cambridge. |
| " | John Trowbridge | Cambridge. |
| 1866. | Stephen P. Sharples | Cambridge. |
| 1867. | Francis W. Clarke | Washington, D.C. |
| 1868. | George Ira Alden | Worcester, Mass. |
| " | Dalton Fallon | Boston. |
| " | William J. Knowlton | Boston. |
| " | Edward R. Taylor | Cleveland, O. |
| 1869. | William M. Davis | Cambridge. |
| " | Albert R. Leeds | Hoboken, N.J. |
| " | Arthur C. Walworth | Newton Centre, Mass. |
| " | Winfield S. Chaplin | Cambridge. |
| 1871. | Thomas M. Chatard | Washington, D.C. |
| " | Charles E. Munroe | Newport, R.I. |
| 1872. | A. F. Noyes | Auburndale. |
| 1875. | Francis W. Dean | Cambridge. |
| " | John B. Marcou | Washington, D.C. |
| 1876. | Seth Perkins | Boston. |
| " | Edward D. Thayer | Worcester, Mass. |
| 1877. | William C. Hodgkins | Washington, D.C. |
| 1878. | James H. Stebbins, Jr. | New York. |
| 1881. | Robert Swift | Boston. |
| 1884. | William F. Booth | Poughkeepsie, N.Y. |
| " | Robert Tracy Jackson | Boston. |
| 1886. | James E. Humphrey | North Weymouth, Mass. |

The official programme for Sunday, the third day, read as follows: —

## FOUNDATION DAY.

On the 7th of November, 1636, the General Court of the Colony of Massachusetts Bay passed the following vote: —

"The Court agree to give Four Hundred Pounds towards a *School* or *College*, whereof Two hundred Pounds shall be paid the next year, and Two Hundred Pounds when the Work is finished, and the next Court to appoint where and what building."

There will be commemorative services in Appleton Chapel at 10.30 A.M. and 7.30 P.M.

The morning service will be conducted by President DWIGHT of Yale College, and Prof. C. C. EVERETT, Dean of the Harvard Faculty of Divinity. The Plummer Professor, Rev. FRANCIS G. PEABODY, will preach the sermon.

The evening service will be conducted by President McCOSH of Princeton, and Prof. FRANCIS G. PEABODY. The Rev. PHILLIPS BROOKS, D.D., will preach the sermon.

At both these services the music will be sung by the Anniversary Chorus of Graduates.

At each service the entire Chapel will be reserved until ten minutes before the hour for guests, graduates, and officers of the University, who will be admitted at the south side-door on showing their badges. Each gentleman may be accompanied by one lady.

At 10.20 and 7.20 the north side-door will be opened to admit undergraduates of the University. At 10.25 and 7.25 the front doors will be opened to admit the public.

The Boston Symphony Orchestra will play the following music in Sanders Theatre at 4 P.M.: —

| | |
|---|---|
| OVERTURE ("LEONORA") | *Beethoven.* |
| TOCCATA | *Bach.* |
| LARGO | *Haendel.* |
| SYMPHONY No. 4 | *Beethoven.* |

Section D of the lower gallery will be reserved for the invited guests of the University until ten minutes before four o'clock. Graduates of the University wearing Badges will be admitted to the rest of the theatre until ten minutes before four o'clock. Each gentleman may be accompanied by one lady. At five minutes before four o'clock the doors will be opened to the public, if any room remains.

The day was clear. The crowd of expectant auditors filled Appleton Chapel at the given hour, and the services in the morning were begun by a prelude on the organ by Mr. Locke, the college organist; and this was followed by the usual Latin commemoration hymn (the words by Prof. J. B. Greenough), sung by the Anniversary Chorus. The Rev. Dr. Charles Carroll Everett next read from the reading desk, while the audience joined in alternation, the first fifteen verses of the One Hundred and Fifth Psalm. The Gloria "We Praise Thee, O God," followed, when Dr. Everett read from the first chapter of Genesis and from the first book of Kings. The great chorus next rendered the "Exaudivit Dominus." From the pulpit President Dwight of Yale University read passages from the New Testament, and concluded with a prayer. The choir next sang the "Integer Vitæ," and afterward, with the audience joining, a hymn from the Chapel hymn-book.

The sermon by Prof. Francis G. Peabody followed, and after the "Sanctus" of Gounod by the chorus, and the singing of the fifty-fifth hymn, the morning service was closed.

The Symphony Concert in Sanders Theatre in the afternoon was conducted before an audience which completely filled the auditorium.

The evening service in Appleton Chapel began with the hymn "Machet die Thore weit," rendered by the Anniversary Chorus. The Rev. Prof. Francis G. Peabody then read the One Hundred and Forty-third Psalm; and then came the anthem, "All Glory, Laud, and Honor!" A graduate quartet consisting of Dr. S. W. Langmaid (Class of 1859), George L. Osgood (1866), G. S. Lamson (1877), and A. M. Barnes (1871) now sang "Into the Silent Land," to music written for the occasion by Mr. Arthur Foote. Luther's Hymn,

"A Mighty Fortress," came next; and then followed the sermon by the Rev. Phillips Brooks, D.D. After this the "Sanctus," written for the occasion by Mr. Osgood, was sung by the choir; and the services closed with the audience joining in singing the two hundred and fifteenth hymn of the Chapel hymn-book.

The following gentlemen served as ushers for the three Sunday gatherings: —

SENIORS.

EUGENE RODMAN SHIPPEN, *Chief Usher.*

FREDERIC SHURTLEFF COOLIDGE.   HENRY WILDER KEYES.
WILLIAM ENDICOTT, 3d.          AUGUSTUS NEAL RANTOUL.
JAMES MARSH JACKSON.           STEPHEN BERRIEN STANTON.
ROGER WOLCOTT KEEP.            WINTHROP WETHERBEE.

JUNIORS.

FRANKLIN GREENE BALCH.         LOCKWOOD HONORÉ.
ARTHUR PIERCE BUTLER.          HENRY LOWELL MASON.
JAMES MOTT HALLOWELL.

The official programme for the last day, Monday, November 8, was as follows: —

ALUMNI DAY.

The graduates of all departments of the University, and all gentlemen specially invited to be present, will assemble at Gore Hall, and at 9.30 A.M. will proceed to Sanders Theatre, where an Address will be made by JAMES RUSSELL LOWELL, LL.D., and a Poem delivered by OLIVER WENDELL HOLMES, LL.D., after which Honorary Degrees will be conferred by the President of the University.

*The business of the day renders an early start imperative, and all persons concerned are urged to be punctual.*

The upper gallery of Sanders Theatre will be reserved for ladies having tickets. They will be received at the south door from 9.30 to 10.15 A.M. and no later.

At 2 P.M. the members of the Association of the Alumni, together with their invited guests, will form in procession at Gore

Hall, and march to Memorial Hall to partake of a Collation and listen to brief addresses.

Tickets for the Collation in the Dining Hall at two dollars apiece will be for sale at the Registration Room, No. 4 University Hall, on and after Tuesday the 2d of November, to graduates of the College, holders of Honorary Degrees from the University, and members of the Faculties of the College, and of the Professional Schools; and they may be obtained, until the supply is exhausted, on personal application, or secured by letter enclosing the price of the ticket. Tickets ordered by letter will be reserved until 1.30 P.M. on Monday, November 8, and must be called for by the applicant in person.

For the accommodation of gentlemen entitled to buy tickets for the Collation who apply for them after the supply is exhausted, a lunch will be provided in the Hemenway Gymnasium at 2 P.M., tickets for which, at fifty cents apiece, can be obtained at the Registration Room. After the procession has entered the Dining Hall, the east and west galleries will be opened to gentlemen wearing badges who were entitled to buy tickets for the Collation.

From 8 until 11 o'clock P.M. a reception will be given by the Faculties of the University, in the Hemenway Gymnasium, to the graduates and invited guests of the University. Each graduate is entitled to a card of admission, which can be obtained in University Hall No. 4, after he has registered. A card will admit one gentleman with ladies. *The entrance will be by the south door, and the exit by the west door.*

The Alumni, as having charge of the fourth day of the celebration, which was of the most general interest, were favored with good weather. By nine o'clock the crowd within the college yard was very large, mainly of graduates, meeting often after long intervals, and extending congratulations one to the other. It was estimated that the procession, marching by twos, would extend from a half to three quarters of a mile; and in order to form the line within the college yard three sections were made of it, so that the guests and officers, with the older graduates (1811–1849), were formed in Gore Hall, the graduates of later years (1850–1879) in or near Sever

Hall, and the younger men (1880–1886) on the path from Cambridge Street to Gore Hall. The several sections of the procession were gathered in their respective places, and all waited for the arrival of the President of the United States. It was not till a few minutes after ten o'clock that the band of his escort was heard; and presently the mounted lancers appeared, followed by the President's carriage, which moved along between crowds of cheering spectators. The escort formed about the main entrance to the yard, and the way within being cleared, the carriage of the President, drawn by four white horses, entered the gate. At the same instant the bell in the opposite meeting-house began to ring, and the batteries arranged on the Common answered with continued salvos. As the carriage passed through the crowd of undergraduates, ranged in lines on either side, its progress was marked by the exuberant *rah-rah-rahs* of the students. On reaching Gore Hall, where the head of the procession was formed, President Cleveland was received by the Chief Marshal, who introduced him to the President of the University, and almost immediately gave him his allotted place in the line. The march through and around the yard then began, each division falling into line, till the whole procession was stretched out in this order: —

Band.
Chief Marshal and Aids.
President of the Association of the Alumni.
Orator and Poet of the Day.
Chaplains of the Day.
President and Fellows of Harvard College.
The Honorable and Reverend the Overseers.
His Excellency, the Governor of the Commonwealth, and the
President of the United States.
The Governor's Aids.
Members of the President's Suite.
United States Senators from Massachusetts.
His Honor the Lieutenant-Governor and the Adjutant-General.
President of the State Senate, and Speaker of the House of Representatives.
Secretary of the State Board of Education.

## SKETCH OF THE COMMEMORATION. 35

Their Honors the Mayors of the City of Cambridge and of the City of
Boston, preceded by the Sheriffs of Middlesex and Suffolk.
Delegates from other Institutions of Learning.
Other invited Guests of the University.
Professors and Assistant Professors of the College Faculty.
Faculty of Divinity, Faculty of Law.
Faculties of Medicine, Dental Medicine, and Veterinary Medicine.
Faculties of the Scientific Departments.
Other Officers of Instruction and Government in the University.
Professors of other Colleges and Universities.
Holders of Honorary Degrees from the University.
Pastors of the Churches of the six neighboring Towns of 1642.
Committee of Arrangements.
Alumni of Harvard College, and Graduates of the Professional Schools
of the same Year of Graduation.

The upper gallery of Sanders Theatre had been thrown open to ladies having tickets, at half-past nine o'clock, and before ten was filled, except one range of seats in the middle-front. In a few minutes Colonel Stearns and Colonel Walker of the Governor's staff — the President of the United States and his suite having been the guests of the State of Massachusetts while in Boston — entered, escorting Mrs. Cleveland to the central seat, which she took with the wife of the Secretary of War and the wife of the Mayor of Boston on her right, and on her left the wife of the President of the University and the wife of the Governor. The assembled ladies greeted their arrival with applause and the fluttering of handkerchiefs.

In due time the head of the procession reached the hall, and was distributed quietly but promptly by the marshals, till every available seat and standing-place was occupied.

It appearing that there were 4,500 living alumni of the college, and about 3,500 of the professional schools, who were not also graduates of the college, or in all about 8,000 persons entitled to attend the celebration, to say nothing of invited guests and the ladies, it was a perplexing problem from the start, inasmuch as the season precluded the use of a tent, how many Sanders Theatre could contain, which at an outside limit and filling every unoccupied spot with a standing auditor was not capable of accommodating more than from twenty-six to twenty-seven hundred persons. It finally proved that under the careful provisions of the Chief Marshal, after taking out 442 seats for ladies in the second gallery, the entire procession succeeded in entering the hall, making an audience in the mass, as well as could be counted, of about 2,500 persons; and as this number corresponds with the estimates upon which the arrangements were based, it is probable that the same calculations reveal the way in which this 2,500 were made up, namely, —

| | |
|---|---:|
| Graduates of the College from 1811 to 1849 | 200 |
| From 1850 to 1879 | 1,000 |
| From 1880 to 1886 | 600 |
| Guests, faculties, and officials | 300 |
| Graduates of Schools (not alumni) | 400 |
| Total | 2,500 |

The President and Fellows of the University occupied their accustomed seats in the rear of the stage. In front of them sat the Chief Marshal and the President of the Association of the Alumni. A space was left vacant in their immediate front about the desk. On the left of the stage, as the audience faced it, occupying a seat next to the edge, sat President Cleveland, adjoining him the Governor, then the Lieutenant-Governor, the President of the Board of Overseers, and the Orator. In the seats on the right of the desk facing the others, sat President Dwight of Yale University, Ex-President Hopkins of Williams College, Professor Dana of Yale, and Professor Leidy of the University of Pennsylvania, and beyond them the Poet. Behind these rows, on either side, the other guests of the University were given each his predetermined seat; and behind them, on the extreme parts of the stage, the Overseers took places on the left, and the

## SKETCH OF THE COMMEMORATION. 37

Faculties of the University in their gowns on the right. The professors wore also the Oxford cap for the first time for many years.

It was a little after eleven o'clock when the sheriff of Middlesex, according to an ancient custom, called the assembly to order. The President of the day, Judge Devens, then stepped to the desk and made a brief speech of congratulation. His welcome to the President of the United States was followed by prolonged cheers and applause, during which President Cleveland rose and repeatedly bowed to the assembly. Judge Devens closed by calling upon Professor F. G. Peabody to offer prayer, and during the invocation the audience stood.

The chorus stationed in the gallery over the stage then sang Gounod's "Domine Salvam Fac."

Judge Devens now advanced and welcomed the Orator to the desk, but said nothing, nor could Mr. Lowell say anything, for the continued applause which kept him standing and bowing till the audience seemed at last satisfied with the ovation which was given this eminent graduate and professor of the College. He wore the academic gown of his position; and when he was allowed to begin, he spoke with a quiet deliberation which characterized his delivery throughout. He was frequently interrupted by applause, particularly when he made reference to the President of the University, and to the representative of Emmanuel College; and at the close of his oration, when he took his seat it was amid the most enthusiastic and long-continued demonstrations of approval, which followed upon his reference to the President of the United States.

The Anniversary Chorus in the gallery now sang "The Heavens proclaim Him," to Beethoven's music, after which Dr. Holmes was given his place at the desk by the presiding officer in the same silent manner. The Poet wore the black gown with red facings, which was the distinctive dress of the medical Faculty. Dr. Holmes was frequently interrupted by applause, as the Orator had been, and sat down amid a renewal of these expressions of approbation and honor.

After the Chorus had given Luther's hymn, "A Mighty Fortress is our God," an expectant silence came upon the assembly. President Eliot then advanced from behind the bar where the Corporation sat, and taking seat in the ancient chair of the Presidents said: —

In the name of the University, by authority committed to me by the President and Fellows and the Board of Overseers, and in the favoring presence of the nation's Chief Magistrate and of all these applauding friends, I now proceed to confer the highest distinctions which it is in the power of universities to give, upon the following men who have won for themselves renown in letters, science, the learned professions, or the public service, and who have come hither to take part in this festival: —

GEORGE DEXTER ROBINSON, upright public servant, Governor of the beloved Commonwealth which founded, cherished, and still cherishes the University;

LUCIUS QUINTIUS CURTIUS LAMAR, teacher, orator, legislator, administrator;

GEORGE FRISBIE HOAR, antiquarian, orator, jurist, senator from Massachusetts;

CHARLES TAYLOR, mathematician, Semitic scholar, master of St. John's College, delegate from the University of Cambridge;

MANDELL CREIGHTON, senior fellow of Emmanuel College, professor of ecclesiastical history in the University of Cambridge, canon of Worcester, delegate from John Harvard's College, Emmanuel;

The Right Honorable Sir LYON PLAYFAIR, teacher of science, legislator, delegate from the University of Edinburgh;

TIMOTHY DWIGHT, teacher, preacher, New Testament scholar, President of Yale University and its delegate;

EZEKIEL GILMAN ROBINSON, metaphysician, theologian, orator, teacher, President of Brown University and its delegate;

## SKETCH OF THE COMMEMORATION.

JOSEPH LEIDY, anatomist, biologist, a leader and exemplar among American naturalists, professor of anatomy in the University of Pennsylvania and its delegate;

CHARLES KENDALL ADAMS, historical author and teacher, long professor of history in the University of Michigan, now President of Cornell University and its delegate;

MARK HOPKINS, professor of moral and intellectual philosophy in Williams College, author in ethics and philosophy, guide, friend, and teacher for two generations of students;

FREDERIC HENRY HEDGE, theologian, teacher of ecclesiastical history, master of German literature and of English style, orator;

EDWARDS AMASA PARK, professor of Christian theology in Andover Seminary, preacher, master of Congregational polity, theological veteran;

WILLIAM SEYMOUR TYLER, professor of Greek in Amherst College, student of philology, exponent of the humanities;

JONATHAN INGERSOLL BOWDITCH, patron of science, and especially of astronomical research, giver and inciter to giving, public-spirited citizen;

EDWARD ELBRIDGE SALISBURY, long professor of Arabic and Sanskrit in Yale University, pioneer among American scholars in these departments;

CHARLES DEANE, antiquary and historian, a master among students of American history;

JAMES DWIGHT DANA, professor of geology and mineralogy in Yale University, specialist and philosopher, author and teacher, leader and exemplar among American men of science;

JAMES HALL, director of the New York State Geological Cabinet, geologist and Nestor of American palæontologists;

ROSWELL DWIGHT HITCHCOCK, theologian, professor of ecclesiastical history, President of the Union Theological Seminary of New York;

HENRY DRISLER, professor of Greek in Columbia College, lexicographer;

LINCOLN FLAGG BRIGHAM, jurist, chief justice of the Superior Court of Massachusetts;

THOMAS MCINTYRE COOLEY, professor of law in the University of Michigan, judge, jurist, author, and teacher;

SPENCER FULLERTON BAIRD, secretary of the Smithsonian Institution, director of the National Museum, United States fish commissioner, promoter of zoölogical science;

BASIL LANNEAU GILDERSLEEVE, professor of Greek in Johns Hopkins University, editor, author, philologist;

ASAPH HALL, professor of mathematics in the United States Navy, mathematician, and astronomer;

SILAS WEIR MITCHELL, physician, physiologist, author;

HENRY LARCOM ABBOT, colonel of United States engineers, military engineer, mathematician and physicist, author and teacher;

GEORGE JARVIS BRUSH, professor of mineralogy and metallurgy in Yale University, chief officer of the Sheffield Scientific School, mineralogist;

SAMUEL PIERPONT LANGLEY, director of the Observatory at Allegheny City, mathematician, astronomer, and physicist;

JOHN WESLEY POWELL, director of the United States geological survey, soldier, geologist, administrator;

WALBRIDGE ABNER FIELD, jurist, justice of the Supreme Court of Massachusetts;

JOHN SHAW BILLINGS, surgeon in the United States army, student and teacher of public medicine, medical bibliographer;

RODOLFO LANCIANI, professor of archæology in the University of Rome, director of excavations for the government and the city and of the Museo Urbano, archæologist, representative of the department of public instruction in Italy;

OTHNIEL CHARLES MARSH, professor of palæontology in Yale University, collector, investigator, and author in palæontology; —

All these I create Doctors of Laws, and declare them entitled to all the rights, honors, and privileges of that degree.

WILLIAM DE WITT HYDE, student of philosophy and ethics, preacher, teacher, President of Bowdoin College and its delegate;

GEORGE PARK FISHER, professor of ecclesiastical history in Yale University, historical student, teacher, and author;

EGBERT COFFIN SMYTH, preacher, theologian, professor of ecclesiastical history in the Andover Theological Seminary;

## SKETCH OF THE COMMEMORATION.

ALEXANDER VIETS GRISWOLD ALLEN, professor of ecclesiastical history in the Episcopal Theological School at Cambridge, historian of Christian doctrine; —

These I create Doctors of Divinity, and declare them entitled to all the rights, honors, and privileges of that degree.

By authority committed to me by the President and Fellows, and the Board of Overseers, I also confer the degree of Doctor of Laws upon the following distinguished men, who are prevented by distance or infirmity from attending this Festival: —

MICHEL EUGÈNE CHEVREUL, French chemist and physicist, born in 1786, and still in activity;
THEODORE DWIGHT WOOLSEY, professor, college administrator, publicist;
JOHN GREENLEAF WHITTIER, poet.

After the conferring of the degrees, the Rev. Prof. Andrew Preston Peabody pronounced the benediction. The audience then dispersed.

The delay in the early part of the day, with the unexpected length of the exercises in Sanders Theatre, shortened the interval between the close of the ceremonies in Sanders Theatre and the reforming of the procession at Gore Hall; so that it was three o'clock instead of two, as planned, when the procession, moving by the shortest route, entered Memorial Hall, and began to fill the tables of the dining-hall. A contraction of the tables and the spaces between them allowed of 1,190 persons being seated, and a little before half-past three o'clock the tables were filled, and the doors closed.

Upon a dais extending along the northern side of the hall was the table of the President of the Association of the Alumni, with the guests and leading officers of the University. On his right was the President of the University, with

President Dwight of Yale, the foreign delegates, and others. On his left, the Governor of the Commonwealth, the President of the United States and the gentlemen of the Cabinet accompanying him, with the Hon. Robert C. Winthrop, the Orator and Poet, and others. The Rev. Dr. McKenzie was called upon to say grace, after which the repast went on. It was later interrupted by the entrance into the gallery of Mrs. Eliot, escorted by two marshals, and accompanied by Mrs. Cleveland and the ladies of her party, who came from the house of President Eliot, where a lunch following the services in Sanders Theatre had been given to Mrs. Cleveland and the ladies accompanying her. The entrance of this party into the gallery was the signal for applause and cheers from the occupants of the tables below, who all rose simultaneously as soon as the visitors were recognized.

A little later a rap brought the assembly to order, and President Devens opened the exercises with a speech, which with those that followed are given on a later page. There was music at intervals by a band in the western gallery, and twice the company joined in singing, — first the Hundredth Psalm, and next the familiar "Fair Harvard." The enthusiasm of the hour rose highest when Governor Robinson in his speech referred to President Cleveland, and when that distinguished guest rose to respond to a sentiment in his honor.

Shortly after his address, President Cleveland with his Cabinet being about to leave, — as engagements made for him in Boston required his return to that city, — President Devens presented to the company, with a few words of recognition in each case, the distinguished gentlemen accompanying Mr. Cleveland; but there was no time for them to do more than bow in acknowledgment of the cheers which greeted their names. Mrs. Cleveland left the gallery at the same time; and as she and her attending ladies passed out above, and as President Cleveland with the members of his Cabinet

## SKETCH OF THE COMMEMORATION. 43

left the hall below, the same rapturous cheering was redoubled from every part of the hall.

President Cleveland, conducted by the Chief Marshal and accompanied by Governor Robinson, was not readily recognized on emerging from the building, for it had become dark; but loud and prolonged cheers soon announced that the recognition was made by the immense crowd which had lingered on the outside of the Hall. The President, whose departure was announced by renewed salutes from the guns on the common, was driven at once to Boston; but Mrs. Cleveland was taken by Mrs. Eliot to her house, where for an hour or more the ladies of the invited guests and those of the families of officers of the University were presented to Mrs. Cleveland.

At the close of the speaking in the dining-hall President Devens said: "Brethren, as we are about to adjourn, I desire to express the thanks of the Committee of Arrangements to the marshals. It has been pleasant to recognize in the list so many names honored in the history of the University; and especially we desire to remember the Chief Marshal [applause and shouts], in whose veins flows the blood of John Cotton and Governor Bradstreet and other Puritan worthies, and you will agree with me that he has not lost any of the Puritan energy or spirit. I propose three cheers for Colonel Lee." The cheers were enthusiastically given, and the great company dispersed.

At this point that part of the celebration specially intrusted to the direction of the Alumni closed.

The management of the day had fortunately been committed to good hands. The Chief Marshal, HENRY LEE, had so carefully considered the elements which he was to combine, and had so weighed the chances, — in which the weather was not an unimportant factor, — that the results justified his plans. He was assisted by the following marshals: —

## SKETCH OF THE COMMEMORATION.

| | |
|---|---|
| CHARLES FOLSOM WALCOTT, '57. | CHARLES HOWLAND RUSSELL, '72. |
| A. J. C. SOWDON, '57. | ALFRED DWIGHT FOSTER, '73. |
| ALFRED STEDMAN HARTWELL, '58. | WENDELL GOODWIN, '74. |
| CHARLES FAIRCHILD, '58. | HENRY LEE MORSE, '74. |
| WILLIAM WILLARD SWAN, '59. | ROBERT HALLOWELL GARDINER, '76. |
| HENRY STURGIS RUSSELL, '60. | ELLIOT CABOT LEE, '76. |
| THOMAS SHERWIN, '60. | SIGOURNEY BUTLER, '77. |
| NORWOOD PENROSE HALLOWELL, '61. | STEPHEN BULLARD, '78. |
| ARTHUR AMORY, '62. | RICHARD MIDDLECOTT SALTONSTALL, '80. |
| FRANCIS LEE HIGGINSON, '63. | HENRY BAINBRIDGE CHAPIN, '80. |
| JOHN WINTHROP, '63. | ROBERT BACON, '80. |
| CHARLES COOLIDGE READ, '64. | GARDINER MARTIN LANE, '81. |
| THOMAS FRANKLIN BROWNELL, '65. | EDWARD WILLIAMS ATKINSON, '81. |
| THOMAS NELSON, '66. | OWEN WISTER, '82. |
| SAMUEL HOAR, '67. | EDWARD TWISLETON CABOT, '83. |
| CHARLES TAYLOR LOVERING, '68. | WILLIAM HENRY ASPINWALL, '83. |
| FREDERICK CHEEVER SHATTUCK, '68. | SAMUEL ATKINS ELIOT, '84. |
| FRANCIS HENRY APPLETON, '69. | THOMAS MOTT OSBORNE, '84. |
| GEORGE RICHARDS MINOT, '71. | JOHN ELIOT THAYER, '85. |
| GEORGE CASPAR ADAMS, '86. | |

Colonel Lee, November 10, addressing a letter to his marshals said: " You know, and I know, how much you had to do with the success of the day by carrying out my plans promptly and perfectly; and I desire herein to record my hearty thanks to each and all of you."

Mr. Henry Parkman, the chief secretary of the Executive Committee, and the Finance Committee, of which the treasurer Charles C. Jackson, and his faithful helper William Farnsworth were the main instruments, did not fail in their important functions. The Finance Committee through the treasurer received altogether from class subscriptions the sum of $7,330.50; from collation tickets, $2,176, and from lunch tickets, $144.50, — making a total receipt of $9,651; and after paying expenses there was a small balance, which was paid into the treasury of the Alumni Association.

The government of the University recorded their appreciation of the manner in which much of the detailed work in Cambridge was done, when at a later day they

*Voted*, That the thanks of the President and Fellows be given to Allen Danforth, Bursar of the University, for the highly satisfactory manner in which he performed the large amount of work, quite outside of his regular functions, which was thrown upon him in connection with the recent celebration.

The Committee of Arrangements held their last meeting Jan. 15, 1887, when they closed their labors, and voted to deposit their records among the University Archives in Gore Hall.[1] A committee, under the chairmanship of Mr. John C. Ropes, was directed to draft letters of thanks to be sent to all gentlemen whose countenance and endeavors had contributed to the successful progress of the celebration. These letters were duly sent; and they included recognition of the services of the Orator, the Poet, the President of the Alumni, the President of the University, the Chief Marshal, Mr. Henry L. Higginson (who had generously borne the expense of the concert), the Bursar of the College (who had exercised a large control over the arrangements in Cambridge), the Mayor of Cambridge (who had furnished the police), Charles C. Jackson and William Farnsworth (who had carried the burden of the financial management), and the two secretaries of the Committee.

During the early hours of the evening of the last day many of the alumni left Cambridge to attend reunions of their classes in Boston; but a large number remained to partake of the hospitalities of the combined Faculties of the University, who were announced to receive the invited guests and the alumni at Hemenway Gymnasium. The guests came and went during the evening, and it was near midnight when this last of the festivities was over. This reception was in charge of a Committee consisting of Professors J. LAWRENCE LAUGHLIN, JAMES B. GREENOUGH, JOHN TROWBRIDGE, JAMES B. THAYER, and HENRY P. BOWDITCH.

[1] They were received Feb. 5, 1887.

Meanwhile the undergraduates, who had not been able because of the rain to march with their torches and to display their fireworks on Saturday evening, were enjoying a postponed merriment out of doors.

Their procession started at about half-past eight, the Seniors leading, under the direction of H. W. Keyes, W. A. Brooks, and F. S. Coolidge, who were mounted as marshals. The class was dressed in long red gowns and black Oxford caps. They bore with them on a dray one of the cleverest bits of their pleasantry, — a model of the Harvard statue, supported by the burlesque personations of a butcher, a cooper, and a grocer, in allusion to the father and two step-fathers of John Harvard, who successively left their little fortunes to his mother, whence the accumulated property in the main passed to John Harvard, who with the moiety of it endowed the infant college. The group was called "Johnnie Harvard's Pa's." Upon this and the other groups and decorations of the procession was thrown a flood of light from a profusion of Roman candles and other fireworks. An old printing-press was carried upon a wagon, and served by an Indian, in allusion to the printing of Eliot's Indian Bible at the College Press; while two printer's devils, in red tights, with long tails, distributed little handbills, on one side of which was a fac-simile of the titlepage of the Indian Bible, and on the reverse these two stanzas:—

> By what means may a young man best
>   His life learne to amend?
> If that he make and keep God's word
>   And therein his time spend.
>
>                               PSALM cxix.
>
> Ye Indians who receive the word,
>   Come, read it one and all;
> You'll find it in ye Library
>   In Master Gore his Hall.
>
>         WOWAUS, *alias* JAMES PRINTER.

SKETCH OF THE COMMEMORATION.   47

The representatives of the different college newspapers came next. Those of "The Crimson" were all dressed in the costume adopted by their class, but with a quill over the ear and scissors dangling at the belt as insignia of their editorial station. Those who represented "The Lampoon" were dressed as jesters, with cap and bells and bawbles.

A squad of Puritans, with sugar-loaf hats and knee-breeches, came next; and they gave at times a peculiar cheer. A small body of students imitating the old "Washington Corps," with blue swallow-tailed coats and white small-clothes, followed. The Juniors, with C. F. Adams 3d, J. W. Appleton, and C A. Porter as marshals, wore red coats with blue facings, buff vests crossed by blue belts, buff knee-breeches and black hose, and black and buff cocked-hats. With this class was a group of past benefactors and notables of the college, among whom were Sam Adams, Count Rumford, Boylston, Gore, Hollis, Stoughton, Holworthy, Flint, and Quincy, together with the solitary Indian graduate, Caleb Cheeshahteaumuck, of the class of 1665.

A flambeaux corps led the Sophomores, who, under the direction of P. D. Trafford, J. T. Davis, and G. T. Keyes, followed, dressed as the "dudes of 1833," — a gray cutaway, plug hat, white vest, buff trousers, and white gaiters.

Then came the Commencement Day Police, — a reminder of an organization of the early part of the century, — with false beards, clubs, and plug hats.

An old-fashioned stage-coach, drawn by six horses, was filled inside and outside with a motley crowd, costumed in the dress of the middle of the last century.

The Freshmen, marshalled by H. H. Hunnewell, Jr., Arthur Amory, and James P. Hutchinson, wore the blue regimentals of the Civil War. Amid their ranks came the Navy Club, — a recollection of the first years of the present century, when an association of such a kind was made up of the lazier men in the class, with the laziest of all as high admiral. This supreme sluggard lay on a red divan, dressed in an admiral's uniform.

A colossal image of the Mott Haven Cup, drawn on a dray, supported by J. M. Hallowell of '88 and H. D. Hale of '88, came next.

The Drum Corps of the Law School in policeman's uniform, led by James A. Frye as drum-major, and "drumming for clients," as their transparency declared, preceded the students of that department, who, clad in the crimson gowns, the ermine and the wig of the English courts, were officered by Joseph Lee, H. B. Cabot, H. M. Williams, and R. D. Smith as marshals, and bore various transparencies of punning proclivities, as where "Circuity of Action" was represented by a corporal's arm around a trim maiden's waist.

The procession was two hours on the march, and the streets through which it passed were aglow with lanterns and Bengal-lights.

When reaching Jarvis Field there was a display of fireworks, principal among which was a representation of the statue of John Harvard, standing in the midst of a gorgeous temple.

The provisions made for the entertainment of the invited guests of the University will appear from the following statements, included in the report of the Committee of the Academic Council on Hospitality, — Professors JOHN WILLIAMS WHITE, WILLIAM E. BYERLY, and FRANK W. TAUSSIG.

| GUESTS. | HOSTS. |
|---|---|
| President C. K. ADAMS (*Cornell Univ.*) | Mr. WINSOR, the Librarian. |
| President J. B. ANGELL (*Univ. of Michigan*) | " " |
| President F. A. P. BARNARD (*Columbia College*) | Professor LAUGHLIN. |
| President S. C. BARTLETT (*Dartmouth College*) | Professor LYON. |
| President J. W. BEACH (*Wesleyan Univ.*) | GEORGE PUTNAM, Esq. |
| Dr. JOHN S. BILLINGS (*Surgeon U. S. A.*) | Dr. H. P. WOLCOTT. |
| President EZRA BRAINARD (*Middlebury College*) | Professor EMERTON. |

## SKETCH OF THE COMMEMORATION. 49

| GUESTS. | HOSTS. |
|---|---|
| Professor GEORGE J. BRUSH (*Yale Univ.*) | Professor COOKE. |
| President MATTHEW H. BUCKHAM (*Univ. of Vermont*) | Professor DAVIS. |
| President FRANKLIN CARTER (*Williams College*) | H. E. SCUDDER, Esq. |
| Professor GEORGE C. CHASE (*Bates College*) | Professor GREENOUGH. |
| Professor THOMAS M. COOLEY (*Univ. of Michigan*) | Professor LANGDELL. |
| Professor MANDELL CREIGHTON (*Emmanuel College, Cambridge, Eng.*) | { President ELIOT. <br> { Professor NORTON. |
| Professor JAMES D. DANA (*Yale Univ.*) | Professor COOKE. |
| President TIMOTHY DWIGHT (*Yale Univ.*) | Professor J. H. THAYER. |
| Professor GEO. P. FISHER (*Yale Univ.*) | President ELIOT. |
| President D. C. GILMAN (*Johns Hopkins Univ.*) | Professor TROWBRIDGE. |
| Professor ASAPH HALL (*U. S. Nat. Observatory*) | Professor BYERLY. |
| JAMES HALL (*Curator State Mus. of Nat. Hist., Albany*) | Professor LOVERING. |
| President R. D. HITCHCOCK (*Union Theol. Sem.*) | Professor J. H. THAYER. |
| President W. D. HYDE (*Bowdoin College*) | Professor PALMER. |
| Professor S. P. LANGLEY (*Allegheny Coll.*) | Professor PICKERING. |
| Professor JOSEPH LEIDY (*University of Penn.*) | Professor SMITH. |
| Professor O. C. MARSH (*Yale Univ.*) | Mr. AGASSIZ. |
| President JAMES MCCOSH (*College of New Jersey*) | Professor F. G. PEABODY. |
| Dr. SILAS WEIR MITCHELL (*Philadelphia*) | Mr. AGASSIZ. |
| Professor EDWARDS A. PARK (*Andover Theol. Sem.*) | Rev. Dr. MCKENZIE. |
| President G. D. B. PEPPER (*Colby Univ.*) | Professor GREENOUGH. |
| Major J. W. POWELL (*U. S. Geological Survey*) | Professor SHALER. |
| FRANCIS R. RIVES (*Delegate University of Va.*) | Professor AMES. |
| President E. G. ROBINSON (*Brown University*) | Professor A. P. PEABODY. |
| President G. W. SMITH (*Trinity College*) | Rev. WILLIAM LAWRENCE. |
| Professor EGBERT C. SMYTH (*Andover Theol. Sem.*) | Professor PALMER. |
| Rev. Dr. CHARLES TAYLOR (*Master of St. John's College, Cambridge, Eng.*) | President ELIOT. |

4

The following guests and delegates, whose presence was hoped for, but who were prevented from attending, were offered hospitality by the persons named: —

| Guests. | Hosts. |
|---|---|
| Professor Henry L. Chapman (*Bowdoin Coll.*) . | Professor Sheldon. |
| Henry C. Lea (*Philadelphia*) . . . . . . | Professor Lovering. |
| The Rev. Father Edw. H. Welch (*Holy Cross*) . | Rev. J. H. Allen. |
| President Julius H. Seelye (*Amherst Coll.*) . | Professor Palmer. |

Delegates sent by institutions not already mentioned received hospitality from the gentlemen named: —

| Guests. | Hosts. |
|---|---|
| Professor A. T. Kelsey (*Hamilton Coll.*) . . . | Professor Searle. |
| Professor C. H. F. Peters (*Hamilton Coll.*) . . | Mr. Edmands. |
| Nelson L. Robinson (*St. Lawrence Univ.*) . . | Professor Taussig. |
| Frederick S. Lee, Ph.D., (*St. Lawrence Univ.*) . | Professor Taussig. |
| Professor Maurice Perkins (*Union College*) . | Professor Asa Gray. |

During the celebration there was stretched across one end of the interior of Gore Hall the flag bearing the Seal of the College, which was displayed from the top of the pavilion in which the dinner was served at the celebration in 1836. In a case was shown the silver pitcher, lent by the owner, which was given to Mr. Thomas Boyd, the contractor for raising that pavilion.

There was also exposed to view the original Charter of the College, 1650, of which a reduced fac-simile is given in the present volume. The institution had been administered previous to that date under votes of the Legislature. The earliest Record Book of the College was opened at the page showing the first design for the College Seal, and a fac-simile of this page is given in the frontispiece of the present volume. The other illustrations of this volume are drawn from two views of the college yard, painted in 1821 by Alvan Fisher, and preserved in the Faculty Room in University Hall.

The only book of John Harvard's library, bequeathed in 1638 by him to the College, and of which a list is preserved

HARVARD COLLEGE, 1821, AFTER ALVAN FISHER.
(*Taken from the rear of the Old President's House.*)

HARVARD COLLEGE, 1821, AFTER ALVAN FISHER.
(Taken from the site of Memorial Hall.)

in the College Records, was also placed on exhibition. It is supposed to have been in the hands of a borrower at the time the College Library was burned in 1764, and so escaped destruction. It is Downame's "Christian Warfare against the Devil, World, and Flesh," in folio, London, 1634.

The Bible of President Dunster was likewise shown. It is the property of the College. This anniversary was also chosen by the Rev. Samuel Dunster, of Attleborough Falls, Mass., and his son Professor E. S. Dunster (class of 1856), now of the University of Michigan, — descendants of the first President, — to leave with the College Library various original letters and other manuscripts of Henry Dunster, as well as a silver porringer used by him and marked $^H_D{^E}$, — Henry and Elizabeth Dunster, his wife.

The oldest living graduate of the College at the time of the celebration sent the following message to his Alma Mater : —

"Dr. William Perry, of Exeter, Class of 1811, the oldest of the Harvard boys, sends his kindest greeting to the Alumni, and best wishes for the prosperity of old Harvard."

Dr. Perry has since died, Jan. 11, 1887, aged ninety-eight. He had been the senior of the graduates since the death, in 1882, of Joseph Head, of the Class of 1804. Mr. William R. Sever, of Kingston, of the same Class of 1811, is now the oldest living graduate of the College. He sent his autograph to be kept among those present at the Two Hundred and Fiftieth Anniversary.

# THE LAW SCHOOL DAY.

# THE LAW SCHOOL DAY.

NOVEMBER 5, 1886.

IN July, 1886, a few graduates of the Harvard Law School met in Boston to consider the advisability of forming an Association of the past members of the School. It was felt that such an organization, if effective, could, by promoting the interests and increasing the usefulness of the School, advance the cause of legal education; that the Association would be of benefit to its own members by promoting mutual acquaintance among them; and that the approaching two hundred and fiftieth anniversary of the founding of Harvard College presented a fitting occasion for inaugurating the Association. The meeting appointed a committee on organization, who entered into communication with past members of the School, resident in different parts of the United States and of the Dominion of Canada. The interest in the proposed Association proved to be general, and Sept. 23, 1886, a largely attended meeting was held in Boston at which the organization was perfected, and the following committees were appointed to arrange for an oration and a dinner to be given at Cambridge Nov. 5, 1886, and to nominate a list of officers for the Association. The meeting then adjourned to meet at Austin Hall in Cambridge, Nov. 5, 1886.

## THE LAW SCHOOL DAY.

### Committee of Arrangements.

ROBERT M. MORSE, Jr., '60, Boston, CHAIRMAN.

| | | |
|---|---|---|
| RODERICK E. ROMBAUER, LL.B. | '58 | St. Louis. |
| SOLOMON LINCOLN, LL.B. | '64 | Boston. |
| CHARLES C. BEAMAN | '65 | New York. |
| ROBERT T. LINCOLN | '65 | Chicago. |
| GEORGE G. CROCKER, LL.B. | '66 | Boston. |
| FRANK W. HACKETT | '66 | Washington. |
| HENRY M. ROGERS, LL.B. | '67 | Boston. |
| JAMES J. MYERS, LL.B. | '72 | Cambridge. |
| FRANCIS RAWLE, LL.B. | '71 | Philadelphia. |
| ORVILLE D. BAKER, LL.B. | '72 | Augusta, Me. |
| JOSEPH D. BRANNAN, LL.B. | '72 | Cincinnati. |
| WILLIAM W. VAUGHAN, LL.B. | '73 | Cambridge. |
| CHARLES J. BONAPARTE, LL.B. | '74 | Baltimore. |
| T. CARLETON ALLEN, LL.B. | '74 | Fredericton, N. B. |
| JABEZ FOX, LL.B. | '75 | Cambridge. |
| RICHARD H. DANA, LL.B. | '77 | Boston. |
| ABBOTT LAWRENCE LOWELL, LL.B. | '80 | Boston. |
| WARREN K. BLODGETT, JR., LL.B. | '81 | Cambridge. |
| WILLIAM SCHOFIELD, LL.B. | '83 | Cambridge. |
| SHERMAN HOAR | '84 | Waltham, Mass. |

### Committee on Nomination of Officers.

DARWIN E. WARE, LL.B., '55, Boston, CHAIRMAN.

| | | |
|---|---|---|
| EDWARD L. PIERCE, LL.B. | '52 | Boston. |
| ADDISON BROWN, LL.B. | '55 | New York. |
| ROBERT R. BISHOP, LL.B. | '57 | Boston. |
| MOORFIELD STOREY | '67 | Boston. |
| GEORGE V. LEVERETT, LL.B. | '69 | Boston. |
| JOHN WOODBURY | '83 | Boston. |

On the 11th of October, 1886, the following letter was issued by the Committee of Arrangements, in response to which about four hundred graduates and past members of the Harvard Law School attended the meeting and celebration of Nov. 5, 1886.

## HARVARD LAW SCHOOL ASSOCIATION.

Boston, Oct. 11, 1886.

Dear Sir, — At a meeting of about one hundred and fifty former members of the Harvard Law School, held in Boston September 23, preliminary steps were taken for the organization of the Harvard Law School Association.

At this meeting a Constitution was adopted, and it was voted that the first general meeting of the Association for the election of officers should be held Friday, November 5, at Cambridge, to be followed by an oration and a dinner on the same afternoon.

A Committee on Nominations and a Committee of Arrangements were appointed to prepare for the meeting in November. Lists of these committees and the Constitution are appended.

Louis D. Brandeis, of Boston, was chosen secretary, and Winthrop H. Wade, of Boston, was chosen treasurer, to hold office till the November meeting.

The Committee of Arrangements are now able to announce that the oration will be delivered on the afternoon of November 5, by Oliver Wendell Holmes, Jr., Justice of the Supreme Judicial Court of Massachusetts, LL.B., '66. After the oration the dinner will be served either in the new Law School Building or in Memorial Hall. James C. Carter, LL.B., '53, of the New York Bar, is expected to preside at the dinner, and there will be brief addresses by distinguished members of the Association and invited guests. The price of dinner tickets will be $2.50. The Committee earnestly request you to fill out and mail the enclosed postal card *at once*, and to send the names and addresses of as many graduates and former students of the Law School as you can to the same address.

The date, November 5, was fixed with especial reference to the celebration of the two hundred and fiftieth anniversary of the founding of Harvard College, to which the 6th, 7th, and 8th days of November are to be exclusively devoted.

The Committee hope that you may find it convenient at this time to revisit the scenes of your professional study, to meet your fellow-students, and to inspect Austin Hall, the present home of the Law School.

They respectfully suggest, also, that the prosperity of the Harvard Law School Association will largely depend upon the success of its first meeting; and it is the opinion of all those who have interested themselves in its formation, that the Association, if successful, will exert a powerful influence in increasing the prosperity and usefulness of the School.

The Committee ask, therefore, for the hearty co-operation of all, and especially of those who live at a distance from Boston, in order that all parts of the country may be well represented at the meeting.

By the Committee of Arrangements,

ROBERT M. MORSE, JR.,
*Chairman.*

## OFFICERS OF THE HARVARD LAW SCHOOL ASSOCIATION,

*Elected at the meeting in Cambridge, November 5, 1886.*

### President.

Hon. JAMES C. CARTER, LL.B., . . . . '53 . . . New York.

### Vice-Presidents.

Hon. WILLIAM PRESTON, LL.B. . . . . '38 . . . Kentucky.
Hon. WILLIAM M. EVARTS . . . . . '39 . . . New York.
Hon. MARCUS MORTON, LL.B. . . . . '40 . . . Massachusetts.
Hon. CHARLES S. BRADLEY . . . . . '41 . . . Rhode Island.
Hon. OGDEN HOFFMAN, LL.B. . . . . '42 . . . California.
Hon. ALEXANDER R. LAWTON, LL.B. . . '42 . . . Georgia.
Hon. JOHN A. PETERS . . . . . . '44 . . . Maine.
Hon. RUTHERFORD B. HAYES, LL.B. . . '45 . . . Ohio.
Hon. JOHN LOWELL, LL.B. . . . . . '45 . . . Massachusetts.
Hon. HENRY C. SEMPLE, LL.B. . . . . '45 . . . Alabama.
Hon. MANNING F. FORCE, LL.B. . . . '48 . . . Ohio.
Hon. ARTHUR W. MACHEN, LL.B. . . . '51 . . . Maryland.
Hon. ALFRED RUSSELL, LL.B. . . . . '52 . . . Michigan.
Hon. JAMES B. EUSTIS, LL.B. . . . . '54 . . . Louisiana.
Hon. JEREMIAH SMITH . . . . . . . '61 . . . New Hampshire.
Hon. GEORGE B. YOUNG, LL.B. . . . '63 . . . Minnesota.
Hon. ANDREW ALLISON, LL.B. . . . . '65 . . . Tennessee.
Hon. ROBERT T. LINCOLN . . . . . . '65 . . . Illinois.
Hon. JOHN H. OVERALL, LL.B. . . . '67 . . . Missouri.
Hon. HUGH MCDONALD HENRY, LL.B. . '73 . . . Nova Scotia.

## THE LAW SCHOOL DAY.  59

### Council.

**FOR FOUR YEARS.**

| | | |
|---|---|---|
| Hon. JAMES M. BARKER | '63 | Pittsfield, Mass. |
| JOHN L. THORNDIKE, LL.B. | '68 | Boston, Mass. |
| WILLIAM SCHOFIELD, LL.B. | '83 | Cambridge, Mass. |

**FOR THREE YEARS.**

| | | |
|---|---|---|
| THEODORE H. TYNDALE, LL.B. | '68 | Boston, Mass. |
| Hon. PATRICK A. COLLINS, LL.B. | '71 | Boston, Mass. |
| FREDERICK P. FISH | '76 | Cambridge, Mass. |

**FOR TWO YEARS.**

| | | |
|---|---|---|
| Hon. FRANK P. GOULDING | '66 | Worcester, Mass. |
| SAMUEL B. CLARKE, LL.B. | '76 | New York, N.Y. |
| ABBOTT LAWRENCE LOWELL, LL.B. | '80 | Boston, Mass. |

**FOR ONE YEAR.**

| | | |
|---|---|---|
| Hon. ARTHUR L. HUNTINGTON, LL.B. | '74 | Salem, Mass. |
| FREDERICK C. S. BARTLETT[1] | '77 | New Bedford, Mass. |
| SHERMAN HOAR | '84 | Waltham, Mass. |

### Treasurer.

| | | |
|---|---|---|
| WINTHROP H. WADE, LL.B. | '84 | Boston, Mass. |

### Secretary.

| | | |
|---|---|---|
| LOUIS D. BRANDEIS, LL.B. | '77 | Boston, Mass. |

The Committee of Arrangements having charge of the celebration of the day made choice of a chief-marshal, who selected his own aids:

**CHIEF-MARSHAL.**

| | | |
|---|---|---|
| ROGER WOLCOTT, LL.B. | '74 | Boston. |

**AIDS.**

| | | |
|---|---|---|
| CHARLES C. READ, LL.B. | '67 | Cambridge. |
| TIMOTHY J. DACEY, LL.B. | '71 | Boston. |
| AUSTEN G. FOX, LL.B. | '71 | New York. |
| HENRY G. PICKERING, LL.B. | '71 | Boston. |
| LAURISTON L. SCAIFE | '71 | Boston. |
| WILLIAM F. WHARTON, LL.B. | '73 | Boston. |
| EDWARD W. HUTCHINS, LL.B. | '75 | Boston. |
| GEORGE WIGGLESWORTH, LL.B. | '78 | Boston. |
| WILLIAM A. GASTON | '82 | Boston. |
| FELIX RACKEMANN | '83 | Milton. |
| HENRY E. WARNER, LL.B. | '85 | Cambridge. |
| WILLIAM A. HAYES, Jr., | '87 | Cambridge. |

[1] Died Dec. 26, 1886.

At the close of the business meeting, the Association marched to Sanders Theatre, where the addresses which follow were delivered.

## PRESIDENT CARTER'S ADDRESS.

GENTLEMEN OF THE HARVARD LAW-SCHOOL ASSOCIATION:

I BEG to make to you my most grateful acknowledgments for the distinguished honor you have conferred upon me in electing me to the office of president. I regard this association of my name with the Harvard Law School, and particularly with such a movement as this, as a most distinguished honor. I hail this gathering, composed not only of members and recent graduates of the school, but also containing so many men who are veterans in the profession. I hail the undertaking thus inaugurated, as full of the promise of opportunities for publishing more widely the privileges, the advantages, which we suppose the institution furnishes. I hail it also as calculated to draw more closely the ties between the school and its graduates, giving them opportunities for observing its methods, for extending criticism perhaps upon them, and in all suitable ways furnishing to it that aid and assistance which the graduates of any educational institution are always capable of affording it.

The Harvard Law School I think we may justly consider as occupying, perhaps we ought not to say the first, but certainly no second place among the institutions of the country devoted to legal education. And so far as I have had the opportunities for observing, and so far as I have had the means of knowing, I believe that in the methods which are pursued here are to be found, in some respects, greater advantages for the study of the law than are anywhere else exhibited. And I think that the institution at no time in the course of its history has been so well provided and so well adapted for purposes of a legal education as now.

This Law School in its origin shone, perhaps, with a lustre not altogether its own, but borrowed in some degree from the great forensic renown of the distinguished men who early became its professors. But it is no disparagement whatever to the great names of Story and Greenleaf — who will ever be held in reverent admiration by us — to say that it is not always those who have attained the highest places in the profession of the law, or the highest seats upon the bench, who are the best calculated to impart their knowledge to others. And at the same time it is true, that in the experience we have had for the last half century in legal education new methods have been found, which are better adapted to the purpose than those which were originally pursued.

I have sometimes heard criticism upon the School to the effect that it was too much given to the theoretical part of legal education, and consequently that its graduates came from it less fitted for the real business and work of a professional life. This impression I believe to be quite erroneous; and I think that the methods that are now pursued, so far as I understand them, are a vast improvement over those with which I was acquainted when I was a member of the School.

What is it that students go to a law school to learn? What is it to begin the study of what we call "the law"? What is this thing which we call "law," and with the administration of which we have to deal? Where is it found? How are we to know it? It is not found in that code which was proclaimed amid the thunders of Sinai. It is not immediately and directly found in the precepts of the Gospel. It is not found in the teachings of Socrates, or Plato, or Bacon. It is found, and it is alone found, in those adjudications, those judgments, which from time to time its ministers and its magistrates are called upon to make in determining the actual rights of men.

What was our former method of acquiring it? Going primarily to those judgments? No. For the most part the basis of legal education was in the study of text-books, the authors of which if they had acquired any knowledge of the law for themselves, must have obtained it by resorting to those original sources. We therefore got it at second hand. I think the result of all investigation concerning the methods by which any science may be best acquired and cultivated, has been to teach us to go to the original sources, and not to take anything at second hand.

Now, is this method open to the objection that the study of cases is apt to make the student a mere "case" lawyer? Not at all. The purpose is to study the great and principal cases in which are the real sources of the law, and to extract from them the rule which, when discovered, is found to be superior to all cases.

And this is the method which, as I understand it, is now pursued in this School. And so far as the practical question is concerned, whether it actually fits those who go out from its walls in the best manner for the actual practice of the law, I may claim to be a competent witness. It has been my fortune for many years to have charge of a considerably diversified legal practice; and the most I have had to regret is that it has overwhelmed me so much with mere business that I have had too little time for the close study of the law which my cases have involved.

It has been necessary for me to have intelligent assistants, and I have long since discovered that most valuable aid could be derived from the young graduates of this School. I have surrounded myself with them, partly for the reason that I have an affection for the place, and also because I have found them in possession of a great amount of actual acquirement, and — what is of more consequence — an accuracy and precision of method far superior to anything which the students of my day exhibited.

This method of studying the law by going to its original sources is no royal road, — no primrose path. It is full of difficulties. It requires struggle. If there is anything which is calculated to try the human faculties in the highest degree, it is to take up the complicated facts of different cases; to separate the material from the immaterial, the relevant from the irrelevant; to assign to each element its due weight and limitation, and to give to different competing principles and rules of law their due place in the conclusion that is to be formed. And I know, on the other hand, of no greater intellectual gratifications than those which follow from the solution in this way of the great problems of the law as they successively present themselves.

Gentlemen, we must always remain students of the law, and our truest pleasures are found in the devoted study of it for the sake of excellence alone. We are subject to many temptations which tend to divert us from the straight path. The love of notoriety, popular applause, newspaper fame, mere pecuniary success, all have a tendency to divert from what should be the true professional aim. But he who engages in the rivalries thus invited, will find himself outstripped in the race by the charlatan and quack. After all, the only solid satisfaction is that which comes to us from the approval and the applause of our own professional brethren, the witnesses of our labors, as the reward of a lifetime of effort. The mightiest of those names which adorn the earliest annals of our profession, —

> "Those ancient, whose resistless eloquence
> Wielded at will that fierce democratie,
> Shook the arsenal, and fulmin'd over Greece
> To Macedon and Artaxerxes' throne," —

won their proud pre-eminence only by climbing that same steep and toilsome ascent, beset with difficulty and conquered only by struggle, which lies before — or behind — each one of you.

But, gentlemen, I keep you too long from the distinguished speaker whom you have gathered together to hear. His name of itself is sufficient to awaken expectations. If the Law were a mistress no more jealous than Medicine, letters might now hope to receive a contribution from the son like those so often made by the renowned father. But the law will put up with no divided homage. The great lawyer, the great jurist, with difficulty gains "the lover's myrtle;" he must forever resign "the poet's bay."

"How sweet an Ovid was in Murray lost!"

But, gentlemen, I think we may all safely assure ourselves that when he comes to speak, whatever he may choose to say, our best attention will be richly rewarded. I have the honor to present to you, gentlemen, Mr. Justice HOLMES of the Supreme Judicial Court of Massachusetts.

## JUDGE HOLMES'S ORATION.

It is not wonderful that the graduates of the Law School of Harvard College should wish to keep alive their connection with it. About three quarters of a century ago it began with a Chief Justice of the Supreme Court of Massachusetts for its Royall professor. A little later, one of the most illustrious judges who ever sat on the United States Supreme Bench — Mr. Justice Story — accepted a professorship in it created for him by Nathan Dane. And from that time to this it has had the services of great and famous lawyers; it has been the source of a large part of the most important legal literature which the country has produced; it has furnished a world-renowned model in its modes of instruction; and it has had among its students future chief-justices and justices, and leaders of state bars and of the national bar, too numerous for me to thrill you with the mention of their names.

It has not taught great lawyers only. Many who have won fame in other fields began their studies here. Sumner and Phillips were among the bachelors of 1834. The orator whom we shall hear in a day or two appears in the list of 1840 alongside of William Story, and the Chief Justice of this State, and one of the Associate Justices, who is himself not less known as a soldier and as an orator than he is as a judge. Perhaps, without revealing family secrets, I may whisper that next Monday's poet also tasted our masculine diet before seeking more easily digested, if not more nutritious, food elsewhere. Enough. Of course we are proud of the Harvard Law School. Of course we love every limb of Harvard College. Of course we rejoice to manifest our brotherhood by the symbol of this Association.

I will say no more for the reasons of our coming together. But by your leave I will say a few words about the use and meaning of law schools, especially of our law school, and about its methods of instruction, as they appear to one who has had some occasion to consider them.

A law school does not undertake to teach success. That combination of tact and will which gives a man immediate prominence among his fellows, comes from nature, not from instruction; and if it can be helped at all by advice, such advice is not offered here. It might be expected that I should say by way of natural antithesis, that what a law school does undertake to teach is law. But I am not ready to say even that, without a qualification. It seems to me that nearly all the education which men can get from others is moral, not intellectual. The main part of intellectual education is not the acquisition of facts, but learning how to make facts live. Culture, in the sense of fruitless knowledge, I for one abhor. The mark of a master is, that facts which before lay scattered in an inorganic mass, when he shoots through them the magnetic current of his thought, leap into an organic order and live and bear fruit. But you cannot make a master by teaching. He makes himself by aid of his natural gifts.

Education, other than self-education, lies mainly in the shaping of men's interests and aims. If you convince a man that another way of looking at things is more profound, another form of pleasure more subtile than that to which he has been accustomed, — if you make him really see it, — the very nature of man is such that he will desire the profounder thought and the subtiler joy. So I say the business of a law school is not sufficiently described when you merely say that it is to teach law, or to make lawyers. It is to teach law in the grand manner, and to make great lawyers.

Our country needs such teaching very much. I think we should all agree that the passion for equality has passed far beyond the political or even the social sphere. We are not only unwilling to admit that any class or society is better than that in which we move, but our customary attitude towards every one in authority of any kind is that he is only the lucky recipient of honor or salary above the average which any average man might as well receive as he. When the effervescence of democratic negation extends its workings beyond the abolition of external distinctions of rank to spiritual things; when the passion for equality is not content with founding social intercourse upon universal human sympathy and a community of interests in which all may share, but attacks the lines of Nature which establish orders and degrees among the souls of men, — they are not only wrong, but ignobly wrong. Modesty and reverence are no less virtues of freemen than the democratic feeling which will submit neither to arrogance nor to servility.

To inculcate those virtues, to correct the ignoble excess of a noble feeling to which I have referred, I know of no teachers so powerful and persuasive as the little army of specialists. They carry no banners, they beat no drums; but where they are, men learn that bustle and push are not the equals of quiet genius and serene mastery. They compel others who need their help or who are enlightened by their teaching, to obedience and respect. They set the example themselves; for they furnish in the intellectual world a perfect type of the union of democracy with discipline. They bow to no one who seeks to impose his authority by foreign aid; they hold that science like courage is never beyond the necessity of proof, but must always be ready to prove itself against all challengers. But to one who has shown himself a master they pay the proud reverence of men who know what valiant combat means, and who reserve the right of combat against their leader even, if he should seem to waver in the service of truth, their only queen.

In the army of which I speak, the lawyers are not the least important corps. For all lawyers are specialists. Not in the narrow sense in which we sometimes use the word in the profession, — of persons who confine themselves to a particular branch of practice, such as conveyancing or patents, — but specialists who have taken all law to be their province; specialists because they have undertaken to master a special branch of human knowledge, — a branch, I may add, which is more immediately connected with all the highest interests of man than any other which deals with practical affairs.

Lawyers, too, were among the first specialists to be needed and to appear in America. And I believe it would be hard to exaggerate the goodness of their influence in favor of sane and orderly thinking. But lawyers feel the spirit of the times like other people. They like others are forever trying to discover cheap and agreeable substitutes for real things. I fear that the bar has done its full share to exalt that most hateful of American words and ideals, "smartness," as against dignity of moral feeling and profundity of knowledge. It is from within the bar, not from outside, that I have heard the new gospel that learning is out of date, and that the man for the times is no longer the thinker and the scholar, but the smart man, unencumbered with other artillery than the latest edition of the Digest and the latest revision of the Statutes.

The aim of a law school should be, the aim of the Harvard Law School has been, not to make men smart, but to make them wise in their calling, — to start them on a road which will lead them to the abode of the masters. A law school should be at once the workshop and the nursery of specialists in the sense which I have explained. It should obtain for teachers men in each generation who are producing the best work of that generation. Teaching should not stop, but rather should foster, production. The "enthusiasm of the lecture room," the contagious interest of companionship, should make the students partners in their teachers' work. The ferment of genius in its creative moment is quickly imparted. If a man is great, he makes others believe in greatness; he makes them incapable of mean ideals and easy self-satisfaction. His pupils will accept no substitute for realities; but at the same time they learn that the only coin with which realities can be bought is Life.

Our school has been such a workshop and such a nursery as I describe. What men it has turned out I have hinted already, and do not need to say; what works it has produced is known to all the world. From ardent co-operation of student and teacher have sprung Greenleaf on Evidence, and Stearns on Real

Actions, and Story's epoch-making Commentaries, and Parsons on Contracts, and Washburn on Real Property; and, marking a later epoch, Langdell on Contracts and on Equity Pleading, and Ames on Bills and Notes, and Gray on Perpetuities, and I hope we may soon add Thayer on Evidence. You will notice that these books are very different in character from one another, but you will notice also how many of them have this in common, — that they have marked and largely made an epoch.

There are plenty of men nowadays of not a hundredth part of Story's power who could write as good statements of the law as his, or better. And when some mediocre fluent book has been printed, how often have we heard it proclaimed, "Lo, here is a greater than Story!" But if you consider the state of legal literature when Story began to write, and from what wells of learning the discursive streams of his speech were fed, I think you will be inclined to agree with me that he has done more than any other English-speaking man in this century to make the law luminous and easy to understand.

But Story's simple philosophizing has ceased to satisfy men's minds. I think it might be said with safety, that no man of his or of the succeeding generation could have stated the law in a form that deserved to abide, because neither his nor the succeeding generation possessed or could have possessed the historical knowledge, had made or could have made the analyses of principles which are necessary before the cardinal doctrines of the law can be known and understood in their precise contours and in their innermost meanings.

The new work is now being done. Under the influence of Germany science is gradually drawing legal history into its sphere. The facts are being scrutinized by eyes microscopic in intensity and panoramic in scope. At the same time, under the influence of our revived interest in philosophical speculation, a thousand heads are analyzing and generalizing the rules of law and the grounds on which they stand. The law has got to be stated over again; and I venture to say that in fifty years we shall have it in a form of which no man could have dreamed fifty years ago. And now I venture to add my hope and my belief, that when the day comes which I predict, the professors of the Harvard Law School will be found to have had a hand in the change not less important than that which Story has had in determining the form of the text-books of the last half-century.

Corresponding to the change which I say is taking place, there has been another change in the mode of teaching. How far the correspondence is conscious I do not stop to inquire. For whatever reason, the professors of this school have said to themselves more definitely than ever before: We will not be contented to send forth students with nothing but a ragbag full of general principles, — a throng of glittering generalities like a swarm of little bodiless cherubs fluttering at the top of one of Correggio's pictures. They have said that to make a general principle worth anything you must give it a body; you must show in what way and how far it would be applied actually in an actual system; you must show how it has gradually emerged as the felt reconciliation of concrete instances, no one of which established it in terms. Finally, you must show its historic relations to other principles, often of very different date and origin, and thus set it in the perspective without which its proportions will never be truly judged.

In pursuance of these views there have been substituted for text-books more and more, so far as practicable, those books of cases which were received at first by many with a somewhat contemptuous smile and pitying contrast of the good old days, but which now, after fifteen years, bid fair to revolutionize the teaching both of this country and of England.

I pause for a moment to say what I hope it is scarcely necessary for me to say, — that in thus giving in my adhesion to the present methods of instruction I am not wanting in grateful and appreciative recollection (alas! it can be only recollection now) of the earlier teachers under whom I studied. In my day the dean of this school was Professor Parker, the ex-Chief Justice of New Hampshire, who I think was one of the greatest of American judges, and who showed in the chair the same qualities that had made him famous on the bench. His associates were Parsons, almost if not quite a man of genius, and gifted with a power of impressive statement which I do not know that I have ever seen equalled; and Washburn, who taught us all to realize the meaning of the phrase which I have already quoted from Vangerow, the "enthusiasm of the lecture-room." He did more for me than the learning of Coke and the logic of Fearne could have done without his kindly ardor.

To return, and to say a word more about the theory on which these books of cases are used. It has long seemed to me a striking circumstance that the ablest of the agitators for codification, Sir James Stephen, and the originator of the present mode of teaching, Mr. Langdell, start from the same premises to reach seemingly opposite conclusions. The number of legal principles is small, says in effect Sir James Stephen, therefore codify them; the number of legal principles is small, says Mr. Langdell, therefore they may be taught through the cases which have developed and established them. Well, I think there is much force in Sir James Stephen's argument, if you can find competent men and get them to undertake the task; and at any rate I am not now going to express an opinion that he is wrong. But I am certain from my own experience that Mr. Langdell is right; I am certain that when your object is not to make a bouquet of the law for the public, nor to prune and graft it by legislation, but to plant its roots where they will grow, in minds devoted henceforth to that one end, there is no way to be compared to Mr. Langdell's way. Why, look at it simply in the light of human nature. Does not a man remember a concrete instance more vividly than a general principle? And is not a principle more exactly and intimately grasped as the unexpressed major premise of the half-dozen examples which mark its extent and its limits than it can be in any abstract form of words? Expressed or unexpressed, is it not better known when you have studied its embryology and the lines of its growth than when you merely see it lying dead before you on the printed page?

I have referred to my own experience. During the short time that I had the honor of teaching in the school, it fell to me, among other things, to instruct the first-year men in Torts. With some misgivings I plunged a class of beginners straight into Mr. Ames's collection of cases, and we began to discuss them together in Mr. Langdell's method. The result was better than I even hoped it would be. After a week or two, when the first confusing novelty was over, I found that my class examined the questions proposed with an accuracy of view which they never could have learned from text-books, and which often exceeded that to be found in the text-books. I at least, if no one else, gained a good deal from our daily encounters.

My experience as a judge has confirmed the belief I formed as a professor. Of course a young man cannot try or argue a case as well as one who has had years of experience. Most of you also would probably agree with me that no teaching which a man receives from others at all approaches in importance what he does for himself, and that one who has simply been a docile pupil has got but a very little way. But I do think that in the thoroughness of their training and in the systematic character of their knowledge, the young men of the present day start better equipped when they begin their practical experience than it was possible for their predecessors to have been. And although no school can boast a monopoly of promising young men, Cambridge, of course, has its full proportion of them at our bar; and I do think that the methods of teaching here bear fruits in their work.

I sometimes hear a wish expressed by the impatient that the teaching here should be more practical. I remember that a very wise and able man said to a friend of mine when he was beginning his professional life, "Don't know too much law," and I think we all can imagine cases where the warning would be useful. But a far more useful thing is what was said to me as a student by one no less wise and able, — afterwards my partner and always my friend, — when I was talking as young men do about seeing practice, and all the other things which seemed practical to my inexperience, "The business of a lawyer is to know law." The professors of this law school mean to make their students know law. They think the most practical teaching is that which takes their students to the bottom of what they seek to know. They therefore mean to make them master the common law and equity as working systems, and think that when that is accomplished they will have no trouble with the improvements of the last half-century. I believe they are entirely right, not only in the end they aim at, but in the way they take to reach that end.

Yes, this school has been, is, and I hope long will be, a centre where great lawyers perfect their achievements, and from which young men, even more inspired by their example than instructed by their teaching, go forth in their turn, not to imitate what their masters have done, but to live their own lives more freely for the ferment imparted to them here. The men trained in this school may not always be the most knowing in the ways of getting on. The noblest of them must often feel that they are committed to lives of proud dependence, — the dependence of men who command no factitious aids to success, but rely upon unadvertised knowledge and silent devotion; dependence upon finding an appreciation which they cannot seek, but dependence proud in the conviction that the knowledge to which their lives are consecrated is of things which it concerns the world to know. It is the dependence of abstract thought, of science, of beauty, of poetry and art, of every flower of civilization, upon finding a soil generous enough to support it. If it does not, it must die. But the world needs the flower more than the flower needs life.

I said that a law school ought to teach law in the grand manner; that it had something more to do than simply to teach law. I think we may claim for our school that it has not been wanting in greatness. I once heard a Russian say that in the middle class of Russia there were many specialists; in the upper class there were civilized men. Perhaps in America, for reasons which I have mentioned, we need specialists even more than we do civilized men. Civilized men who are nothing else are a little apt to think that they cannot breathe the American atmosphere. But if a man is a specialist it is most desirable that he should also be civilized; that he should have laid in the out-

line of the other sciences as well as the light and shade
of his own; that he should be reasonable, and see
things in their proportion. Nay, more, that he should
be passionate as well as reasonable, — that he should
be able not only to explain, but to feel; that the
ardors of intellectual pursuit should be relieved by
the charms of art, should be succeeded by the joy of
life become an end in itself.

At Harvard College is realized in some degree the
palpitating manifoldness of a truly civilized life. Its
aspirations are concealed because they are chastened
and instructed; but I believe in my soul that they are
not the less noble that they are silent. The golden
light of the University is not confined to the undergraduate department; it is shed over all the schools.
He who has once seen it becomes other than he was,
forever more. I have said that the best part of our
education is moral. It is the crowning glory of this
Law School that it has kindled in many a heart an
inextinguishable fire.

At the conclusion of Judge Holmes's oration, the members
of the Association and their invited guests, preceded by the
band, marched to the Hemenway Gymnasium, where the
dinner took place.

# THE DINNER.

AT 2.35 P. M. the company, to the number of about four hundred, sat down to dinner. Hon. James C. Carter, of New York, President of the Harvard Law School Association, presided. Upon his right sat Judge Oliver Wendell Holmes, Jr., Prof. C. C. Langdell the Dane Professor, Gen. Alexander R. Lawton of Georgia, Hon. George O. Shattuck, Prof. James B. Thayer, Hon. E. Rockwood Hoar, Judge Thomas M. Cooley of Michigan, and Prof. James Barr Ames; on the left of the presiding officer were President Eliot, Hon. Samuel E. Sewall, Hon. R. M. Morse, Jr., Judge Nathaniel Holmes, Hon. Dorman B. Eaton, Hon. Darwin E. Ware, Prof. John C. Gray, Prof. William A. Keener, and Dr. Mandell Creighton of Emmanuel College, Cambridge, England. Before and between the speeches the Germania Orchestra rendered musical selections. At the close of the dinner President CARTER called the company to order.

## PRESIDENT CARTER'S ADDRESS.

GENTLEMEN, — I think we may felicitate ourselves upon the auspicious commencement of this association. At least, so far as it has gone it could not have been better. Our friend Judge Holmes spoke in his oration of the grand manner in which the law ought to be studied and taught. To me, who come back to Cambridge rarely, and whose recollections of this place are as it was — I won't say how many years ago, — everything seems to be grand. From what grander building could we have marched than from

Austin Hall? To what grander building could we have gone to listen to our oration than the one in which we heard it? What grander oration could we have had? In what grander building could we have our dinner than the one in which we are now assembled, — if it is possible for anything to be heard in it, which I somewhat doubt.

Well, gentlemen, here we are, a lot of lawyers collected together all by ourselves. It is a rare occasion. It is rare for an assembly to be composed exclusively of lawyers. You know what they used to say of the Roman augurs, that whenever they met each other in the street they used to smile. And if half of what is said of lawyers be true, we ought all of us to be on a broad grin now. The wits and satirists of all ages have sat down on us pretty heavily. We have been accused of being the fomenters of strife, of grinding the faces of the poor, of being mere sophists, of disregarding the truth, of dwelling upon the quips and quirks and trifles. There is no form of imposture which has not at some time or other been imputed to us. Well, now, I suspect that pretty much all the wit and point of that lies in its incongruity and its falsity.

Occasionally, unworthy members of the profession do of course appear; and the incongruity between those and what the profession is generally found to be, and what it ought to be, is so great as to become ludicrous. But when we look for the real estimate in which lawyers and the legal profession are held by the community at large, we have better evidence upon which to rely. I suppose three fourths at least of all the members of the Congress of the United States from the organization of the government have been lawyers. The statutes of the United States to-day, — are they not a monument of their learning, their devotion, their patriotism, and their skill? The great majority of the Legislatures in all the States of the Union are, and ever have been, composed of lawyers. The great executive officers and magistrates of the States are for the most part lawyers.

And what, let me ask, would the community do if the profession of the law were stricken from the pursuits of human life? If there are great pecuniary trusts to be reposed, to whom are they so frequently intrusted as to lawyers? And how rarely is the trust betrayed! Those last confidences which every one hugs to his bosom are freely and fully imparted to lawyers; and how seldom is that trust betrayed! Why, I remember, not very long ago, that a reverend gentleman — whose name, were I at liberty to mention it, you would at once recognize as that of one of the most eminent and distinguished of your divines — said to me that upon a certain occasion he was called upon by another to give advice upon a most important piece of conduct. He gave to it his best reflection, and came to his conclusion. But such was his sense of the importance of the business, and such he thought to be its difficulty, that he could not feel sufficiently assured of the correctness of his conclusion. He wished light from others. The question had nothing to do with property; nothing to do with any legal right. It was a purely moral question, but deeply affecting character, deeply affecting reputation. He did not go to the members of his own profession; he went neither to theologians nor to moralists. He went to a lawyer, and among lawyers to one whose name, were I at liberty to mention that, you would recognize as one of the most distinguished among you,— and not one of those who would be considered as of the spiritually minded sort, but a strictly business, professional lawyer. He submitted the problem to him, and received an answer confirming his own conclusion, but accompanied with reasons so luminous and so satisfactory that all doubt was banished from his mind. We have some right to say, therefore, that the teachings of the law, as they are pronounced by its highest ministers, inform us *quid sit pulchrum, quid rectum, quid turpe, quid utile, quid non* a good deal better than those of Chrysippus or Crantor.

Now, why is this? Surely not for the reason that lawyers are any better than other classes of men: no one of us surely will set up a pretence of that sort. It is, I imagine, because our pursuits, our thoughts, our labors have to do with the direct, the immediate, the tangible interests of mankind, — with property, with liberty, and with life. It is because upon the strength of our determination property passes from one hand to another, or the question is settled whether one shall occupy the cell of a penitentiary or breathe the air of freedom. It is because those all-important present interests have ever refused, and will forever refuse, to submit to any other determinations than those founded upon the everlasting basis of truth and right, or so much of that everlasting basis as can be apprehended and applied by the wisest and the best of our race.

Now, gentlemen, I have already made my speech over in yonder building, and I am not going to inflict upon you another. I find myself upon this elevated platform, and it looks to me for all the world as if this were a bench of judges here, and I the Chief Justice, and you members of the Bar. I shall therefore treat these gentlemen on my right and left as *puisne* justices, and I shall not consult them as to the order of proceedings here. They will of course speak when they are spoken to, and give their opinions when they are called upon. We have in the city in which my labors are spent what they call a short calendar, — and it is called on Friday, too, — and it means causes that take up very little time indeed, and it means causes for the most part that have no merits. I propose to take up that short calendar. From time to time I shall call those cases that are set down on it. The calendar was not made up by me, but by the clerk of the court. And I think — and you must all agree with me upon this occasion — that the first honors are due to that great school of the law to which we all of us, or most of us, owe so much. I shall, therefore, first present to you Professor LANGDELL, the Dane Professor.

84     THE LAW SCHOOL DAY.

Professor LANGDELL, upon arising, was received with prolonged applause and three rousing cheers. When permitted to proceed, he spoke as follows: —

PROFESSOR LANGDELL'S ADDRESS.

GENTLEMEN OF THE HARVARD LAW SCHOOL ASSOCIATION:

I am very grateful for this unexpected greeting. You will be surprised to learn that this is the second time that your President has called upon me to speak for the Harvard Law School. The first time was nearly seventeen years ago, when I was about to assume the duties of Dane professor. And I do not know that I can do better than begin now where I left off then. On that occasion I called attention to the anomalous condition of legal education in English-speaking countries, — the anomaly consisting in the fact that in those countries a knowledge of law had been acquired, as a rule, only by or in connection with its practice and administration, while in all the rest of Christendom law has always been taught and studied in universities. And I ventured to express the opinion, that the true interests of legal education in this country required that in this respect we should not follow longer in the footsteps of England, but should bring ourselves into harmony with the rest of the civilized world.

Since that time I have not concerned myself with legal education outside of the Harvard Law School; but I have tried to do my part towards making the teaching and the study of law in that School worthy of a university; towards making the venerable institution of which we are celebrating the two hundred and fiftieth anniversary a true university, and the Law School not the least creditable of its departments; in short, towards placing the Law School, so far as differences of circumstances would permit, in the position occupied by the Law Faculties in the universities of continental Europe. And what I say of myself in this respect I may, with at least equal truth, say of all my associates.

To accomplish these objects, so far as they depended upon the Law School, it was indispensable to establish at least two things: first, that law is a science; secondly, that all the available materials of that science are contained in printed books. If law be not a science, a university will best consult its own dignity in declining to teach it. If it be not a science, it is a species of handicraft, and may best be learned by serving an apprenticeship to one who practises it. If it be a science, it will scarcely be disputed that it is one of the greatest and most difficult of sciences, and that it needs all the light that the most enlightened seat of learning can throw upon it. Again, law can only be learned and taught in a university by means of printed books. If, therefore, there are other and better means of teaching and learning law than printed books, or if printed books can only be used to the best advantage in connection with other means, — for instance, the work of a lawyer's office, or attendance upon the proceedings of courts of justice, — it must be confessed that such means cannot be provided by a university. But if printed books are the ultimate sources of all legal knowledge; if every student who would obtain any mastery of law as a science must resort to these ultimate sources; and if the only assistance which it is possible for the learner to receive is such as can be afforded by teachers who have travelled the same road before him, — then a university, and a university alone, can furnish every possible facility for teaching and learning law. I wish to emphasize the fact that a teacher of law should be a person who accompanies his pupils on a road which is new to them, but with which he is well acquainted from having often travelled it before. What qualifies a person, therefore, to teach law is not experience in the work of a lawyer's office, not experience in dealing with men, not experience in the trial or argument of causes, — not experience, in short, in using law, but experience in learning law; not the experience of the Roman advocate or of the Roman prætor, still less of the Roman procurator, but the experience of the Roman juris-consult.

My associates and myself, therefore, have constantly acted upon the view that law is a science, and that it must be learned from books. Accordingly, the Law Library has been the object of our greatest and most constant solicitude. We have not done for it all that we should have been glad to do, but we have done much. Indeed, in the library of to-day one would find it difficult to recognize the library of seventeen years ago. We have also constantly inculcated the idea that the library is the proper workshop of professors and students alike; that it is to us all that the laboratories of the university are to the chemists and physicists, all that the museum of natural history is to the zoölogists, all that the botanical garden is to the botanists.

From what I have already said it easily follows, first, that a good academic training, especially in the study of language, is a necessary qualification for the successful study of law; secondly, that the study of law should be regular, systematic, and earnest, not intermittent, desultory, or perfunctory; thirdly, that the study should be prosecuted for a length of time bearing some reasonable proportion to the magnitude and difficulty of the subject. Accordingly, to secure the first of these objects, we have established an examination for admission for such as are not graduates. To secure the third, we have made three years of study necessary in all cases for a degree. To secure the second, we have done several things. First, we have established a course of study which we require to be pursued in the prescribed order. Secondly, we have established annual examinations to be held at the end of each year in the work of that year. Thirdly, we require every candidate for a degree to pass his examinations in the studies of the first year at the end of his first year as a condition of being admitted into the second year, and in the studies of the second year as a condition of being admitted into the third year; and we do not permit any one to pass his examinations in the studies of any year unless he has been regularly admitted into that year at the beginning of the year.

In other words, we do not permit any one to pass examinations in any studies except those of the year to which he belongs. Fourthly, we have increased the amount of instruction, in the last seventeen years, from ten hours a week to thirty-six hours a week. This enables us to give the whole of the three years' course every year, thus giving to each class its appropriate instruction.

The result of all these measures is that the School is strictly divided into three classes, each class doing the work which belongs to its year, and every man having the strongest possible inducements to do his work *as* it should be done and *when* it should be done.

Let it not be supposed that we are unmindful of the work of our predecessors; we should indeed be ungrateful if we were. We do not forget that they began with nothing, while we have enjoyed the fruits of all their labors. We do not wish to disguise the fact that we could not have done our work, had we not had the labors of our predecessors to build upon as a foundation.

Nor are we unmindful of the support and encouragement which we have constantly received from the President of the University. He has never hesitated, wavered, or faltered when any responsibility was to be assumed or work to be done.

Lastly, we are not unmindful of the support we have received from the students of the School, both while they were in the School and since they have left it. Without their support and co-operation, the various measures to which I have referred (many of which could not have been expected to be popular measures) could never have been maintained. It has been in a great degree the eagerness with which they have always encountered difficulties, the ability with which they have followed the subtlest lines of reasoning, and detected the slightest flaws or sophistries in argument, and the persistence with which they have refused to be satisfied so long as any doubt remained in their minds to be cleared up, that has given to the instructors such success as they have achieved. Finally, it is almost wholly to their testimony, both while in the School and after leaving it, that the School is indebted for such public recognition as it has received.

THE PRESIDENT: Gentlemen, the origin of our School does not go back into the remotest antiquity. I rather supposed myself to be about the oldest graduate; but I find that there are others here who surpass me in that particular. We are fortunate in having among us a gentleman who entered the School at its very origin, and who, having passed through a long career of usefulness in his profession, remains at a green old age to take satisfaction in our present enterprise. I beg to present to you Hon. SAMUEL E. SEWALL.

Mr. Sewall received a very enthusiastic greeting, at the conclusion of which he said:—

## HON. SAMUEL E. SEWALL.

MR. PRESIDENT,— It gives me the highest pleasure to meet so large an assembly of lawyers, especially when they are engaged in so noble a work as the

improvement of legal education, and assisting the
Harvard Law School. When I look back upon my
early entrance upon the profession, I see that the
state of law at that time, especially the remedial part
of it, was wretched. I seem to have lived in the dark
ages. The first principle was that no man, excepting
in certain special cases, could be a witness for himself.
That was the strong principle on which the law was
based. And no person that had the slightest interest
in a case could be a witness for the party to be bene-
fited by his testimony. The first principle, at that
time, of remedial law was, in England and all over
the United States, to exclude one of the best means
of obtaining evidence and getting at truth. Wise
men seemed to think, in those days, that to exclude
any sort of evidence was to assist at getting at the
truth, because all men were liars.

That, you know, is all changed. Then the next
miserable thing in our law was the state of pleading.
The artificial logical system, by which it was supposed that justice was promoted, proved in practice a
complete failure; and every person who practised at
that time will admit, I think, that it was a terrible
period. Either a plaintiff or defendant might be
driven out of court upon a point of pleading which
had nothing to do with the real merits of the action
or the defence. Now, I repeat, that was a wretched
state of things.

Then, also, we may look a little further. We find
that the Supreme Court had not full equity jurisdiction. Their equity jurisdiction was exceedingly

meagre; and it frequently happened that a man had a good case in law, — that is, had a right which was recognized by all the courts, — but the remedies of the common law were entirely insufficient to vindicate those rights. He could not get an injunction in many cases; he could not bring an action to enforce the specific performance of a contract; and in many ways in which the direct remedies of equity would be useful the common law refused to act. This was acknowledged by the courts, and has all been remedied since by our Supreme Court gaining full equity jurisdiction.

Then there is another thing which at that time was very bad. We had no Court of Insolvency. Frequently nothing was done when a man failed; but a scramble of the creditors to attach his property ensued. If he made an assignment, the assignment was not always just, — that is, it did not put all the creditors upon an equality. There has been no remedy known for this except an insolvency system. A national bankrupt act would be more perfect if we could get one; but, so far as the State goes, our insolvency system is a very good one.

All these defects in legal remedies have, as you know, been to a great extent removed.

I might go further, and specify other branches of the law that have been improved; but I do not think it would be just to trespass upon your time in that way. It seems to me indeed, that, taking it altogether, the present state of the law in Massachusetts, as amended by statute, is as great an improvement upon the old system as that magnificent Austin Hall is over the humble place in which I studied law.

There is one branch of the law, however, which has been greatly expanded since I began practice, and that is the abstruse doctrine of fees and retainers, which has been studied with great success, not only in this State, but, I believe, still more in our sister State of New York. In that State, indeed, the researches of the profession have really thrown a golden light on this subject.

THE PRESIDENT: I will not at this time enter into any controversy with my venerable friend in regard to New York practices. I must allow him to have his way in that particular; besides, I suspect there is great truth in it. That comity, gentlemen, which is taught by the law, and which I hope will always be practised, advises us, and for other reasons it is entirely agreeable, that we should hear, if possible, some gentlemen of the legal profession in other parts of the country. We now have with us a distinguished gentleman from Michigan. I beg to introduce to you Hon. THOMAS M. COOLEY, late Chief Justice of Michigan.

Judge Cooley, on rising, was greeted with applause. He said: —

## HON. THOMAS M. COOLEY.

COMING from a distant State to look in upon Harvard in the day of its festivity, I have something of that feeling which we may suppose would have thrilled the explorer, Ponce de Leon, if in his search for the fountain of youth he had found the myth a reality, and been permitted a sight of the waters of perennial renovation. For here, indeed, we stand in the presence of a true fountain of perpetual youth. Empires will be built up and be overthrown, but Harvard goes on forever, with a perpetual renewal of lusty youth, and a perpetual taking on of new vigor and new capabilities. For Harvard there is neither fear of time, nor doubt of time's beneficence; and while trees grow and waters run, this school of learning will be noting the vicissitudes of nations, as they rise and fall, and calmly teaching the moral of their story to the youth of successive generations.

But the Law School of Harvard, which more immediately receives our attention to-day, has a life and a vigor of its own, which has impressed the political institutions of the country more than most of us perhaps have realized. You who have gathered in this hall for good fellowship and pleasant reminiscence, though yourselves a part of its strength and its greatness, will very naturally have the Law School in mind in its personal rather than its general aspects; but one who unfortunately cannot claim the personal relation, but who nevertheless for many years has observed how Harvard, by its teachings and by the leadership of strong minds, has built itself into the political institutions of the land, making every commonwealth and every municipality the better for its sound law and wholesome constitutional doctrine, must be permitted to look beyond the membership, and to say a word of results which have been the most striking and impressive of all its grand realities. Those who are of the brotherhood may take delight in the men who, in the forum or the senate, have made the Law School famous; but one who is not of the household may as an American indulge his patriotic pride in contemplating what it has done for the whole country, and in confident anticipation of what it will do hereafter. Its beneficent influence has not been bounded by State lines, or limited to sectional divisions. The most adventurous pioneer who penetrates the remote wilderness is likely, if his rights are brought in controversy, to find them determined on the authority of Harvard's great teachers; and the political philosopher who studies the constitutional unity in diversity which the founders of the Republic hoped for but did not live to realize, will remember that the teachings of the Harvard Law School led steadily up to the great consummation, and that there went out from it an influence, born not less of conviction than of sentiment, which in the hour of national peril was as necessary to unity as the army itself. Indeed, it was the firm belief in the Federal Constitution as an instrument of indissoluble union that made an invincible army possible; so that it is no small part of the just renown of Harvard that its legal oracles perceived the truth from the first, and maintained the faith, and taught it until it became irresistible.

It has been my fortune to be to some extent in various ways a teacher of the law; and in what I have done in that field I have taken pleasure in seeking wisdom from Harvard, and in accepting its guidance, — whether in presenting the principles of right which lie at the foundation of our inherited institutions, or in pointing out the necessary dependence of true liberty upon steady administration of law, or in inculcating the nobility of the lawyer's calling, which should be at once the effective instrument of justice and of true benevolence. If my efforts have not been in vain, I have done something to make the fact obvious, that, aside from physical needs, the State is most of all dependent for the happiness of its people upon a clear recognition and ready acceptance of the rules which determine and protect our rights. The sense of security, upon which public content not less than public liberty depends, must spring mainly from a steady administration of just laws; and we fail to appreciate the dignity of our profession if we look for it either in profundity of learning or in forensic triumphs. These, however striking and notable, are only means to the great end for which the profession exists. Its reason for being must be found in the effective aid it renders to justice, and in the sense it gives of public security through its steady support of public order.

These are commonplaces, but the strength of the law lies in its commonplace character; and it becomes feeble and untrustworthy when it expresses something different from the common thoughts of men. Harvard in the past has been a great school of the common law; and it will be a great school of a nobler common law in the future, as the common law improves with an improving and elevating humanity. So may it be! And we in the distant West, whether between the great lakes, or on the boundless prairies, or over the snow-crowned mountains, will bare our heads to it reverently as we behold it still "nourishing a youth sublime," while its "centuries behind it like a fruitful land repose."

THE PRESIDENT: Of course we are all of the opinion that the Law School is by far the most important department of the University; but at the same time we must not forget that the University does exist, and should be noticed on this occasion. Allow me, therefore, to present to you President ELIOT.

PRESIDENT ELIOT.

As President Eliot rose he was greeted with tremendous applause and "Fair Harvard." After the applause had subsided, he said: —

MR. PRESIDENT AND GENTLEMEN, — Formerly it was not the custom for the President of Harvard College to have anything to do with the professional schools. I remember the first time I went into Dane Hall after I was elected President. It was in the autumn of 1869, a few weeks after the term began. I knocked at a door, which many of you remember, — the first door on the right after going through the outside door of the Hall, — and, entering, received the usual salutation of the ever genial Governor Washburn, "Oh, how are you? Take a chair," — this without looking at me at all. When he saw who it was, he held up both his hands with his favorite gesture, and said, "I declare, I never before saw a President of Harvard

College in this building!" Still, all precedent to the contrary notwithstanding, I did propose to make myself acquainted with the needs and plans of all the departments, and particularly of the Law School as one of the most important. Then and there I took a lesson under one of the kindest and most sympathetic of teachers.

The next winter Professor Parsons, one of the veterans of the School, resigned, and the Dane professorship became vacant. Then I remembered that when I was a junior in college, in the year 1851–1852, and used to go often in the early evening to the room of a friend who was in the Divinity School, I there heard a young man who was making the notes to "Parsons on Contracts" talk about law. He was generally eating his supper at the time, standing up in front of the fire and eating with good appetite a bowl of brown bread and milk. I was a mere boy, only eighteen years old; but it was given to me to understand that I was listening to a man of genius. In the year 1870 I recalled the remarkable quality of that young man's expositions, sought him in New York, and induced him to become Dane professor. So he became Professor Langdell. He then told me, in 1870, a great many of the things he has told you this afternoon: I have heard most of his speech before. He told me that law was a science: I was quite prepared to believe it. He told me that the way to study a science was to go to the original sources. I knew that was true, for I had been brought up in the science of chemistry myself; and one of the first rules of a conscientious student of science is never to take a fact or a principle out of second-hand treatises, but to go to the original memoir of the discoverer of that fact or principle. Out of these two fundamental propositions, — that law is a science, and that a science is to be studied in its sources, — there gradually grew, first, a new method of teaching law; and secondly, a reconstruction of the curriculum of the School.

So, with great patience, in the course of fifteen or sixteen years, chiefly, as Professor Langdell has pointed out, by the steady devotion of the professors to a policy of thoroughness, and through the zeal and intelligence with which that policy has been apprehended and adopted by the most successful students of the School, — gradually, as I say, building on all that was good in the past, this School has been converted into a scientific school of law without losing its best qualities as a practical school of law. I have witnessed no change in the University during the last seventeen years which is more satisfactory to all those who have taken part in it, or more important with reference to the ultimate interests of the community, than this development.

I need not say that I have seen four professors added to the Faculty since Professor Langdell's accession; and if genius be a remarkable capacity for work, they are all men of genius.

Gentlemen, in the presence of this distinguished assembly of lawyers it would be unbecoming in me, who am the only layman present, to say more. No University event has been more agreeable to me during the last seventeen years than the institution of this Association. For it tells all of us who have our hearts in this School and earnestly desire its future prosperity, that the School is to receive that without which no professional school can greatly prosper, — the cordial support of the profession which it feeds.

THE PRESIDENT: I think, gentlemen, that it was always one of the passions, so to speak, of those who have presided over the destinies of the Law School to cultivate the sentiment of the unity of our nation. Some of them passed away before that fearful conflict came which rent it in twain. I think, however, it is a most fortunate circumstance that we inaugurate the present movement with a reunited land, which gives us the advantage of hearing from those former members of the School who came from the South, — a pleasure of which we might otherwise be deprived. And I now have the pleasure of introducing to you Gen. ALEXANDER R. LAWTON, of Georgia, who graduated from the Law School in 1842.


## GEN. ALEXANDER R. LAWTON.

As General Lawton rose, Mr. Roger Wolcott proposed "three cheers for General Lawton, of Georgia," which were vigorously given, and were followed by loud applause. When this had subsided, General LAWTON said: —

IT seems that my place in the "short calendar" has been reached. I promise to keep within the time prescribed. You will doubtless discover also that my part is in keeping with that other characteristic ascribed to the short calendar by our President, — "there is very little in it."

When I was kindly invited to join with those who had been members of the Harvard Law School in forming this Association, I was much impressed by a sentence in the address of your presiding officer at the preliminary meeting, as reported in a newspaper which reached me at the same time. "Fortunately," said he, "there is now no serious danger of a physical disruption of this great government, but possibly of a chemical disintegration for want of that connection and association with and knowledge of each other which lead to mutual confidence and affection," — and gave that as a good reason for thus calling us together. I believe it was the gentleman on my right [turning to Hon. George O. Shattuck] who uttered this sentiment, and I heartily indorse and respond to every word of it. It seems to me that, next to the promotion of the highest order of legal education, the very object for which we should come together is to supply that deficiency and avert that danger.

How much better do we of the North and the South really know each other now than we did twenty-five years ago, before the great collision took place! We have learned by contact; and the world now knows, as matter of history, that it was not all temper and ebullition on the one side, nor all calculation and money-loving on the other, — as many on both sides had believed. The great struggle has demonstrated that sentiment existed and controlled in the highest degree in this colder region, where money-loving and money-getting were supposed by some to have absolute sway, — that under a warmer sun heroic endurance of suffering, of loss, of poverty, of disappointment, was exhibited to an extent rarely if ever seen before in the history of war, where ebullitions of temper and momentary displays of courage were believed to constitute the great gifts of that people. I invade not the domain of politics, and only allude to sectional strife that we may discover how much has been accomplished by actual association, better knowledge, and even physical contact with each other, — though much of that contact may have occurred on the field of battle.

Having learned more fully to appreciate the differences caused by origin, climate, early training, occupation, and other belongings, we now know that it is not possible, nor indeed desirable, in a country with such an area as this — thirty-eight States and numerous Territories — for all to be alike in feelings, views, habits, and manners. Thank God! we can now come together without explanation or apology, and confidently expect that these minor differences will not merely be tolerated but appreciated, in order that, where unity and concentration are of greatest importance, we may the more readily move on together in solid phalanx.

For my part, gentlemen, having enjoyed the advantages of the Harvard Law School in the last days of Story and Greenleaf, you will pardon me if I am not only loyal to their memories, but also to their methods of teaching, from which I derived not only such sincere pleasure, but so large a part of whatever professional training I ever received. Without referring, except in praise, to your present methods of instruction, in this presence, I stand by the men and the methods of that day. Unlike the distinguished gentleman on my left [Judge Cooley], I am moved by pleasant memories and "personal experience" amid these surroundings, and cannot refer to them without emotion. What a privilege to sit under the teachings of Story and Greenleaf! No man with intellect or soul could fail to appreciate it. I speak not here of those grander gifts and attainments which gave to Story his worldwide reputation; but who that ever felt their influence can forget his genial manner, happy temper, and charming methods of beguiling you into a love of the law? Some of you have seen him preside at a Moot Court, when he would say, "Gentlemen, this is the High Court of Errors and Appeals from all other courts in the world;" then he would add, "Tell me not of the last decided case having overruled any great principle, — not at all. Give me the *principle*, even if you find it laid down in the Institutes of Hindu Law." Pardon me for enjoying the conviction that such methods were not vicious, even though antiquated! I well remember in what terms of exalted praise the Chief Justice of England spoke of Greenleaf, at an entertainment where it was my fortune to be present. He declined to regard his fame as all belonging to us, but said that England claimed him as well, and that "wherever there is an English-speaking people living under English law, Greenleaf is recognized as high authority." It was through these men — their example and their teachings — that I was brought into loving association with Harvard and its surroundings. I can never forget and only desire to perpetuate them. I travel not far out of this line of thought when I add, that the advantages of Harvard in all its departments are most happily affected by social surroundings and a literary atmosphere. The most cultivated community in America adds all its attractions to the sterner opportunities within college walls, and these unite to reach the happiest results.

In attaching so much importance to this "face to face" instruction, we may be met by the scholar with a protest. "Come with me to the library," he says; "there learn from books, through which the great, the wise, the gifted of earth, not as they lived in material forms with the frailties of our common humanity about them, but as in moments of purest inspiration and sublimest achievement made their thoughts and themselves immortal." I still venture to insist on the greater advantages of that method of instruction, where the voice and eye and ear all combine to stimulate and enlighten, and the human countenance, with its magnetic power, leads on to affection, desire, and accomplishment.

One word more, and I take my seat. Gentlemen of the legal profession, during that period of darkness familiarly known as the "reconstruction period" the first ray of light to illumine it was flashed forth from the judicial department of the government. When that South-land was under military-proconsular government, and divided into "Districts Number One, Two, Three," we trembled for the autonomy of the States, and feared lest the lines of State authority had become so dim that they might nevermore be seen by that unhappy people. Then it was that out of our profession, in a case at law earnestly argued and solemnly decided, the Supreme Court of the United States electrified the country and gladdened our hearts by the announcement that this is "an indissoluble Union of indestructible States." Who so bold as to seriously dispute it, after the highest Court in the land, with the recent past in view, thus proclaimed the fundamental law of this dual government? Nothing is so powerful to convince or restrain as a formal judicial decision reached through regular channels. Nothing that Congress could have said, no utterances from pulpit or public meeting, could have been so comforting or reassuring in that hour of suffering and uncertainty. And thus are we permitted to claim for our noble profession the first rank in the final disposition of great and pressing questions.

Brethren of the Bar, what event can make us feel more proud of our profession?

I fear that I have been beguiled by my theme to break my promise and forget the limit of time assigned me. May we often meet again as we do to-day! I came with happy memories of Harvard and its belongings, in the long-gone past. I shall now go away with relations to it made still happier and more tender by the events and recollections of to-day.

THE PRESIDENT: Gentlemen, the great and principal object, after all, of a legal education is to minister to the actual business of life, and to create a profession the members of which in the actual business of life shall be able to bear their part.

And it is very important that that class of men should correctly appreciate and be correctly appreciated by this School. I am going to call upon a gentleman who is a representative of that class. I beg to present Hon. GEORGE O. SHATTUCK, of Boston.

## HON. GEORGE O. SHATTUCK.

GENTLEMEN OF THE HARVARD LAW-SCHOOL ASSOCIATION :

THE Bar took no part in laying the foundations of Harvard College. We can make no claim here to-day by reason of that service. Although some of the men — those eminent and sagacious men — who promoted the founding of this college had read law in England, the atmosphere was not favorable to the practice of the law, and in 1636 there were no lawyers in the infant colony. It was most unfortunate for the colony. No man can read the gloomy records of the seventeenth century without regret that those dismal years of poverty and theological strife were not illumined by the gladsome light of jurisprudence. So feeble were the beginnings, that Harvard College had arrived at the age of more than fifty years before she gave birth to one properly educated lawyer. Judge Benjamin Lynde is believed to have been the first. It was not until after the Revolution, after the college had arrived at the ripe age of one hundred and forty-eight years, that she admitted a lawyer to her councils to take part as a member of the corporation. The man who received this honor was John Lowell, and from that day to this the name has been illustrious in the annals of the college; and if I may quote the opinion of Dr. Walker, given twenty-five years ago, it ought to stand first among the benefactors of Harvard College and of the city of Boston.

From that day, when the college first received the wise counsel of one of our brethren, the Bar has never been without a strong representation in its management. For a century the Bar has given its best to the college. In the corporation have been Theophilus Parsons, Christopher Gore, Charles Jackson, Harrison Gray Otis, Joseph Story, Lemuel Shaw, Benjamin R. Curtis, Charles G. Loring, George T. Bigelow, and others among the living whom I will not name. Christopher Gore was for many years the largest benefactor of the college. Since the overseers have been elected by the alumni, the majority of that body have been bred to the law. Some of them, it is true, have wandered from its rugged paths into the more inviting fields of literature and politics, but I can safely say that the great educational movement of the last ten years has been supported by our profession; and if any wholesome limitations have been placed on the autocratic power which with so much wisdom and vigor now rules the college, our fraternity have had a large share in imposing them. And while our profession has thus by slow and painful steps climbed to its place of power and influence in the University, and has rendered it some service, who can tell what the University has done for us? Even before it recognized the members of our profession and admitted them to its management, it had given us Otis, Adams —

Samuel and John — and the Quincys, the great leaders of the Revolution. But why do our hearts warm with gratitude to-day? It is not because the college has done much for our profession; it is not that it has given us a few great lights, more or less illustrious; but it is because we, with the thousands who have been within its walls, feel that we have lived better, richer, and stronger lives because in the days of our youth we sat in her seats, and listened to her words of wisdom.

THE PRESIDENT: I have in mind one of our enthusiastic members who has carried the renown of Harvard to a distance from home. I think you will like to hear from him on this occasion. If he is here I would like to introduce to you FRANK W. HACKETT, Esq., of the Washington Bar.

### FRANK W. HACKETT.

MR. PRESIDENT, — Believing that I possess a fair share of that diffidence which is the crowning glory of our profession, I hardly know what to do. Under ordinary circumstances I should have carefully refrained from any response whatever, and should have sought by disappearing to avoid answering your very flattering and unmerited introduction. But, sir, I will carry out the suggestion which you have so happily made, that you are upon the bench as a Chief Justice. I shall take the liberty of using a term which is much more familiar to me than that of president, and I shall address you as "Your Honor."

I feel upon this occasion, if your Honor please, that I have been retained by my brethren around me here to argue their case in response to what we have heard from the bench. We are a pretty good-natured set of fellows, but we are not accustomed to be talked at for two hours without being given some chance to reply. Although I feel myself wholly unequal to such a task, I feel it my duty at least to undertake it. I was reminded, when considering the solid chunks of wisdom which have come from that quarter, of the opening speech with which a young limb of the law addressed the court early in his career. He said: "Your Honors do not sit there like marble statues, to be wafted about by every idle breeze." Let me remind you that you have an advantage, because you have been sitting with your backs to the clock, whereas it has been staring us in the face.

Lawyers are equal to every occasion. Although accustomed to speak in the court-house, they seem to do quite as well in the gymnasium. I never have had an opportunity myself to speak or eat in a gymnasium before, but it seems a very comfortable sort of place. I am struck with the fact that they have very appropriately located me alongside of the heavy weights. I am totally unaware of the reason why I have been called up. I did prepare a speech some twenty years ago, but not having been called upon at that time, or since, it has become I fear a little antique. However, being on my feet, I want to explain one thing. I am given to understand that the city where I live has a pretty bad reputation. I want to explain why I found the atmosphere of Boston altogether too pure for me, and so emigrated to Washington.

My classmate, of whom I never was so proud as at this moment, happily alluded in his oration this morning to the necessity of practical education in a law school. Now I want you distinctly to understand that a few of us got a practical education here that was somewhat unique. I doubt whether many of you gentlemen present have had an opportunity to study criminal law in the dock. That great blessing was conferred on me. I will make a short story of it. Passing innocently through the college grounds one night (these fellows, by the way, invariably happen to be innocent!), by some complication I found myself at the station house. I never had given much attention to the subject of bail, but it became to me then a very practical question. It was two o'clock in the morning before I found my way to my domicile. I had received a pressing invitation that night to meet Judge Ladd at nine o'clock the next morning. I was there; and a large part of the Law School honored me by their presence on that occasion. A cruel and unusual punishment was inflicted by Mr. Justice Ladd in the shape of a moral lecture of about half an hour. That night was the turning point of my career. I emigrated.

That I may not convey a wrong impression, I want to state, before I sit down, that we have some people there of whom we are proud. When I started out on a collecting expedition — the first business of that nature that I have had for some time — among the Harvard Law School graduates, although they are not numerous, I could not help being struck with the character that they exhibited. We have on our rolls an Associate Justice of the Supreme Court of the United States; two Cabinet Officers; the Chief Justice of the Court of Claims; a Judge of the Supreme Court of the District of Columbia; an Assistant Attorney-General of the United States, and an Assistant Secretary of the Treasury; and — modesty forbids my making further mention. The rest of us, I believe, are not altogether unknown.

THE PRESIDENT: I have down on the calendar here a professor who has protested against being called upon; but I must follow out the programme, and present to you Professor JOHN C. GRAY. His known antipathy to the perpetuities will at least insure us a short speech.

Professor Gray was received with hearty applause.

### PROFESSOR JOHN C. GRAY.

MR. CHAIRMAN AND GENTLEMEN, — I certainly understood from his Honor that I was not to be called upon. Nearly everything that can be said about the School has been said, and there really is nothing for me to add.

Mr. Justice Holmes hit what I think is the merit of the School, so far as it has any merit, that we try to teach the law in a large manner, but not, on that account, in any the less practical way. If any gentlemen present doubt about the practical merit of our teaching, or if they have any friends who doubt about it, I would commend to them the little tract on which our examination papers are printed at the end of every year. If they will look over those papers, — I do not say it of every question, perhaps not of every paper, — but if they will look at those papers taken together, they will see that the questions relate not to fancy or to merely theoretical points; they will see that any man who can answer all these papers — as many students whom we turn out every year can answer them — is well fitted to meet the real questions which arise in practice.

When a doubt occurs to me whether sometimes, as is the danger in academic teaching, we are not getting too far away from the world around us, I think of these papers, and feel satisfied that what we teach closely touches real life.

When I was a law student I read twenty or thirty text-books through: I fear little of them remained in my mind. I had to begin again with the study of particular cases and learn my law in that way. We try to save our students that experience, and start them in the way of practical learning three years earlier than if, as is so often the case, they had to acquire such learning after they have been admitted to the Bar.

THE PRESIDENT: Well, now, gentlemen, the shades of night are closing about us. I had intended calling upon a very old friend of the University and this School, but he has protested against it. But perhaps Judge HOAR will now play —

[At this point the President glanced towards Judge Hoar, who was looking at him with a countenance apparently expressive of great displeasure. The company noticed this little by-play, and broke into loud laughter and applause. Whereupon the President resumed :]

I was going to say that perhaps Judge HOAR will play the office of crier, and adjourn the court; but he may extend his remarks if he desires.

Judge Hoar was received with most enthusiastic applause.

## HON. E. R. HOAR.

I EXPECTED, Mr. President, that you were calling me up as a reminiscence, — a capacity which, on reflection, after what I have heard to-day, I am tolerably well qualified to fill. I feel a good deal like the old friend of mine who went to a public dinner on one occasion, and they said he was a most remarkable old gentleman; that before dinner he remembered General Washington, and that after dinner he remembered Christopher Columbus.

I was reminded, by what was said by our orator to-day, that I have personally known every instructor in the law at this University from the beginning. I knew, as a boy, Chief Justice Parker. I knew Professor Stearns very well, as a boy and as a young man. I had the pleasure of some acquaintance with that model teacher, whose light went out too early for this institution and for the society around him, — John Hooker Ashmun, whose epitaph at Mt. Auburn contains that summary of the character of a great lawyer: "He had the beauty of accuracy in his understanding, and the beauty of uprightness in his character." I was here, sharing with the gentleman from Georgia on my left, who has addressed you, in the instruction of Story and Greenleaf; and I left the Law School to go into the office of one who subsequently became one of your most valuable instructors, Emory Washburn. My relations to this institution are therefore very strong and tender. I have had the pleasure twice before of attending a dinner of the graduates of the institution and members of the Law School. I do not suppose that many of the younger part of this audience know that such a thing ever occurred before. But it was tried on two occasions; and I hope this third experiment will differ from those in this, — that you will not allow it to die out for want of speedy repetition.

I cannot say that in our day we used to have the School divided quite so accurately into three distinct classes as Professor Langdell insists that it now is. He put me in mind a little of what a friend of mine, who was a lawyer in this neighborhood, told me when, the year before he began his studies as a lawyer, he went to a neighboring theological institution (not in Cambridge) for the purpose of studying theology, although he intended afterward to be a lawyer. I asked him what sort of folks he found there to associate with. Well, he said, that school was carefully divided into three classes. The first had piety without talents; the second had talents without piety; and the third had neither.

It is too late to go on and make a speech. Yet as one of the side judges, to carry out the figure of the presiding officer, I will simply say that I concur in the opinion that he delivered in another place, and entirely concur in the opinion that he expressed here, — that he would better not say a great deal more, and that his example be generally followed by his associates. If I am to close the meeting, I think I prefer to do it, instead of in the ordinary phrase of a crier, by pronouncing a benediction in words which have frequently, through my long professional career, experience, and acquaintance, been brought to my mind as the chief consolation and reward of lawyers, — " Blessed are the peacemakers."

THE PRESIDENT: If you are inclined to give one cheer for the Harvard Law School and the Harvard Law School Association, our marshal will lead.

The cheers were given with a will, and the gathering broke up at 5:15 P. M.

NAMES REGISTERED.

# REGISTERED AT THE LAW SCHOOL.

## NOVEMBER 5, 1886.

THE names without occupation are almost entirely those of lawyers, though a few signers failed to fill out the blank in respect to this point.

Abbot, Edwin Hale, *Counsellor and Trustee of Railways* . . . . . . . . . . . . . . Milwaukee, Wis.
Allen, Thomas Carleton, *Clerk Supreme Ct., N. B.* Fredericton, N. B.
Angell, Elgin Adelbert . . . . . . . . . Cleveland, O.
Appleton, John Henry . . . . . . . . . Cambridge.
Avery, Edward . . . . . . . . . . . . Boston.
Ayers, George David . . . . . . . . . Malden.
Babson, Thomas McCrate . . . . . . . Boston.
Bachelder, Thomas Cogswell . . . . . . South Boston.
Bailey, Harrison . . . . . . . . . . . Fitchburg.
Bailey, Hollis Russell . . . . . . . . . Boston.
Ball, George Homer . . . . . . . . . . Worcester.
Barnes, Charles Maynard . . . . . . . Boston.
Bartlett, Charles Hammat . . . . . . . Bangor, Me.
Batchelder, Samuel . . . . . . . . . . Cambridge.
Baum, James Henry, *Pottery Business* . . . East Liverpool, O.
Bendelari, Giorgio Anacleto Corrado, *Professor Modern Languages, Yale University* . . . . New Haven, Conn.
Bent, Samuel Arthur . . . . . . . . . . Boston.
Bicknell, Edward . . . . . . . . . . . Boston.
Biddle, Edward John, "*Newspaperman*" . . . St. Louis, Mo.
Bishop, Robert Roberts . . . . . . . . Newton.
Blackmar, Wilmon Whilldin . . . . . . Boston.
Blodgett, Warren Kendall, Jr. . . . . . . Boston.
Bolles, Frank, *Secretary Harvard College* . . . Cambridge.
Bonaparte, Charles Joseph . . . . . . . Baltimore, Md.
Bouvé, Walter Lincoln . . . . . . . . . Hingham.
Bradford, George Hillard . . . . . . . Roxbury.
Bradish, Frank Eliot . . . . . . . . . Boston.
Brooks, James Willson, *Business* . . . . . Cambridge.
Brown, Howard Kinmonth . . . . . . . Framingham.
Brown, William Bailey Clark, *Student Harvard Law School* . . . . . . . . . . . . Independence, Mo.

Brown, William Reynolds, *Real Estate* . . . . New York, N. Y.
Brown, John Merrill . . . . . . . . . . Boston.
Brush, Abraham Stephens . . . . . . . . Boston.
Buffum, Walter Nutting . . . . . . . . . Boston.
Bullard, John Richards . . . . . . . . . Dedham.
Burnham, Telford . . . . . . . . . . . Chicago, Ill.
Casas, William Beltran de las . . . . . . . Malden.
Caverly, Robert Boody, *Writing of Books* . . . Lowell.
Child, Linus Mason . . . . . . . . . . Boston.
Churchill, Asaph . . . . . . . . . . . Boston.
Churchill, Charles Marshall Spring . . . . . Milton.
Clifford, Charles Warren . . . . . . . . . New Bedford.
Clifford, Walter . . . . . . . . . . . . New Bedford.
Cole, John Hanun . . . . . . . . . . . New York, N. Y.
Cook, Frank Gaylord . . . . . . . . . . Cambridge.
Coolidge, Joseph Randolph, *Retired* . . . . . Boston.
Coolidge, William Henry . . . . . . . . Natick.
Crocker, George Glover . . . . . . . . . Boston.
Cummings, Samuel Wells, *Real Estate* . . . . Boston.
Cushing, Livingston . . . . . . . . . . Weston.
Cushman, Archibald Falconer . . . . . . . New York, N. Y.
Dacey, Timothy John . . . . . . . . . . Boston.
Dana, James . . . . . . . . . . . . . Boston.
Dana, Richard Henry . . . . . . . . . . Boston.
Danforth, Henry Gold . . . . . . . . . . Rochester, N. Y.
Davis, Charles Thornton, *Student* . . . . . . Newton.
Davis, Edward Livingston . . . . . . . . Worcester.
Davis, Simon . . . . . . . . . . . . . Boston.
Deming, Horace Edward . . . . . . . . . New York, N. Y.
Denniston, Arthur Clark . . . . . . . . . Philadelphia, Pa.
Dewey, George Tufts . . . . . . . . . . Worcester.
Dickson, Joseph . . . . . . . . . . . . St. Louis, Mo.
Du Bois, Loren Griswold . . . . . . . . . Boston.
Dudley, Sanford Harrison . . . . . . . . Cambridge.
Duff, William Frederick . . . . . . . . . Boston.
Duggan, Roland Augustus . . . . . . . . Atlantic.
Dunbar, Charles Franklin, *Prof. Harv. Univ.* . . Cambridge.
Dyer, Micah, Jr. . . . . . . . . . . . . Dorchester (Boston).
Eaton, Dorman Bridgman . . . . . . . . New York, N. Y.
Eaton, George Herbert . . . . . . . . . Lawrence.
Ela, Richard, *Agent Standard Turning Works* . . Cambridge.
Ellis, Ralph Waterbury . . . . . . . . . Springfield.
Elting, Irving . . . . . . . . . . . . . Poughkeepsie, N. Y.
Emery, Samuel Hopkins, Jr. . . . . . . . . Concord.
Emery, Woodbury, *Post-Office* . . . . . . . Boston.
Emery, Woodward . . . . . . . . . . . Cambridge.
Ensign, Charles Sidney . . . . . . . . . Newton.

## NAMES REGISTERED. 117

| | |
|---|---|
| Estabrook, George William | Boston. |
| Everett, William, *Schoolmaster* | Quincy. |
| Farley, James Phillips, Jr. | Beverly Farms. |
| Fisher, Horace Newton, *Consul of Chili* | Boston. |
| Fox, Austen George | New York, N. Y. |
| Fox, Jabez | Cambridge. |
| Fuller, Henry Weld | Boston. |
| Gaston, William Alexander | Boston. |
| Gould, John Melville, *Lawyer and Librarian* | Newton. |
| Gove, William Henry | Salem. |
| Grant, Ronald Cameron | St. John, N. B. |
| Gray, Morris | Chestnut Hill. |
| Gray, Reginald | Boston. |
| Green, James | Worcester. |
| Gregory, Charles Augustus | Chicago, Ill. |
| Gregory, Francis Brooke | Fredericton, N. B. |
| Grinnell, Charles Edward | Boston. |
| Griswold, Freeman Clark | Greenfield. |
| Hackett, Frank Warren | Washington, D. C. |
| Hale, Abraham Garland Randall | Rock Bottom. |
| Hamlin, Charles Sumner | Roxbury. |
| Harding, Emor Herbert | Boston. |
| Hardon, Henry Winthrop | New York, N. Y. |
| Hartwell, Alfred Stedman | South Natick. |
| Haskins, David Greene, Jr. | Cambridge. |
| Hathaway, Amos Lawrence | Boston. |
| Hemenway, Charles Morrison | Somerville. |
| Hoar, Samuel | Concord. |
| Hoar, Sherman | Waltham. |
| Holden, Joshua Bennett | Boston. |
| Holway, Melvin Smith | Augusta, Me. |
| Homer, Thomas Johnston | Roxbury. |
| Howe, Archibald Murray | Cambridge. |
| Howland, William Russell | Cambridge. |
| Hudson, Woodward | Concord. |
| Hulse, Samuel Vaughan | Newark, N. J. |
| Huntington, Arthur Lord | Salem. |
| Hutchins, Edward Webster | Boston. |
| Hutchinson, Gardiner Spring, *Merchant* | New York, N. Y. |
| Ingalsbe, Grenville Mellen | Sandy Hill, N. Y. |
| Jacobs, Justin Allen, *City Clerk* | Cambridge. |
| James, George Abbot | Nahant. |
| Jones, Arthur Earl | Cambridge. |
| Jones, Leonard Augustus, *Lawyer and Author* | Boston. |
| Keasbey, Edward Quinton | Newark, N. J. |
| Kendall, Robert Bruce | Chicago, Ill. |
| Kent, Edward, *Student of Law* | New York, N. Y. |

Keyes, Charles Gilman . . . . . . . . . Jamaica Plain.
Keyes, Prescott . . . . . . . . . . . . Concord.
Kidder, Camillus George . . . . . . . . . New York, N. Y.
Knowlton, Thomas Oaks . . . . . . . . . New Boston, N. H.
Ladd, Babson Savilian . . . . . . . . . Boston.
Lathrop, John . . . . . . . . . . . . Boston.
Lawrence, George Porter . . . . . . . . Cambridge.
Lawrence, Rosewell Bigelow . . . . . . . Medford.
Lawrence, William Badger . . . . . . . Medford.
Levy, Harry Milton, *Merchant* . . . . . . . Cincinnati, O.
Lincoln, Arthur . . . . . . . . . . . . Boston.
Lincoln, Solomon . . . . . . . . . . . Boston.
Loring, Augustus Peabody . . . . . . . . Boston.
Loring, William Caleb . . . . . . . . . Boston.
Lothrop, Arthur Prescott . . . . . . . . Taunton.
Lowell, Abbott Lawrence . . . . . . . . Boston.
Lowell, John . . . . . . . . . . . . . Chestnut Hill.
McClure, Edward Woodbridge . . . . . . Concord.
McCoy, Walter Irving . . . . . . . . . . New York, N. Y.
McDaniel, Samuel Walton . . . . . . . . Cambridge.
McInnes, Edwin Guthrie . . . . . . . . . Malden.
McIntire, Charles John . . . . . . . . . Cambridge.
McIntire, Fred . . . . . . . . . . . . Somerville.
Mack, Alfred . . . . . . . . . . . . . Cincinnati, O.
Mack, Julian William, *Student Harvard Law School* Cincinnati, O.
McKeever, Henry Francis . . . . . . . . Boston.
Mansfield, Ex Sumner . . . . . . . . . Brookline.
Marrett, Lorenzo . . . . . . . . . . Cambridgeport.
Merrill, Charles Benjamin . . . . . . . . Portland, Me.
Milliken, Frank Albion . . . . . . . . . New Bedford.
Minot, Laurence, *Student* . . . . . . . . Boston.
Minot, Robert Sedgwick . . . . . . . . . Boston
Morison, John Holmes . . . . . . . . . Boston.
Morse, Nathan . . . . . . . . . . . . Boston.
Morse, Robert McNeil, Jr. . . . . . . . . Boston.
Morton, Marcus, Jr. . . . . . . . . . . Andover.
Motte, Ellis Loring . . . . . . . . . . Boston.
Munroe, William Adams . . . . . . . . . Cambridge.
Myers, James Jefferson . . . . . . . . . Cambridge.
Nettleton, Edward Payson . . . . . . . . Boston.
Nickerson, George Augustus . . . . . . . Boston.
Norcross, Grenville Howland . . . . . . . Boston.
Norcross, Otis . . . . . . . . . . . . Boston.
Norris, Samuel, Jr. . . . . . . . . . . . Bristol, R. I.
Ordronaux, John . . . . . . . . . . . Roslyn, N. Y.
Otis, Albert Boyd . . . . . . . . . . . Boston.
Otterson, James F. J. . . . . . . . . . . Marlborough.

## NAMES REGISTERED. 119

| | |
|---|---|
| Parkman, Henry | Boston. |
| Parmenter, James Parker | Arlington. |
| Parmenter, William Hale, *Shoe Manufacturer* | Boston. |
| Patterson, Rev. George Herbert, *Rector, Berkeley School* | Providence, R. I. |
| Payson, Edward Payson | Boston. |
| Pellew, George | Boston. |
| Phillips, Willard Quincy | Paris, France. |
| Pickering, Henry Goddard | Boston. |
| Pierce, Edward Peter | Fitchburg. |
| Pinney, George Miller | New York, N. Y. |
| Poor, Albert | Boston. |
| Prentiss, John | Boston. |
| Putnam, Henry Ware | Boston. |
| Rackemann, Charles Sedgwick | Boston. |
| Rackemann, Felix | Boston. |
| Rand, Edward Lathrop | Cambridge. |
| Rawle, Francis | Philadelphia, Pa. |
| Raymond, Robert Fulton | New Bedford. |
| Read, Charles Coolidge | Cambridge. |
| Reardon, John Joseph | Holyoke. |
| Reed, Charles Montgomery | Boston. |
| Reed, Frederick | Boston. |
| Reed, Joseph Wheeler | Maynard. |
| Richards, William Reuben | Boston. |
| Richardson, William Minard | Cambridge. |
| Riley, Thomas | Boston. |
| Robinson, Nelson Lemuel | Canton, N. Y. |
| Ropes, John Codman | Boston. |
| Sampson, Alden, *Literature* | New York, N. Y. |
| Saunders, Charles Gurley | Boston. |
| Sears, Philip Howes | Boston. |
| Sewall, Samuel Edmund | Melrose. |
| Simmons, John Franklin | Abington. |
| Smith, Henry Augustus | Roxbury. |
| Smith, Robert Dickson | Boston. |
| Smith, William Henry Leland, *Retired* | Boston. |
| Spaulding, John | Boston. |
| Spelman, Henry Munson | Cambridge. |
| Stackpole, Joseph Lewis | Boston. |
| Starbuck, Henry Pease | New York, N. Y. |
| Starr, Benjamin Charles | Cleveland, O. |
| Stevens, Charles Frank | Worcester. |
| Storer, John Humphreys, *Real Estate* | Boston. |
| Sullivan, Cornelius Patrick | Boston. |
| Sullivan, Jeremiah Henry, *Clerk* | East Cambridge. |
| Sullivan, Richard | Boston. |

| | |
|---|---|
| Suter, Hales Wallace | Boston. |
| Swift, Henry Walton | Boston. |
| Taussig, Frank William, *Professor Harv. Univ.* | Cambridge. |
| Thacher, Stephen | Boston. |
| Thayer, Albert Smith | New York, N. Y. |
| Thompson, Lucian Bisbee | Boston. |
| Thorndike, Samuel Lothrop | Cambridge. |
| Tiffany, Francis Buchanan | Boston. |
| Tompson, Edward William Emery | Brookline. |
| Towne, Trueman Benjamin | Boston. |
| Tuttle, William Henry Harrison | Arlington. |
| Tyler, John Ford | Boston. |
| Underwood, Adin Ballou | Boston. |
| Van Slyck, Cyrus Manchester | Providence, R. I. |
| Vaughan, William Warren | Boston. |
| Wadsworth, Alexander Fairfield | Boston. |
| Wakefield, John Lathrop | Dedham. |
| Wales, George Worcester | Burlington, Vt. |
| Ware, Charles Eliot, Jr. | Fitchburg. |
| Warner, Henry Eldridge | Cambridge. |
| Warner, Joseph Bangs | Cambridge. |
| Waterhouse, Frank Shepard | Portland, Me. |
| Wendell, Barrett, *Instructor in Harvard College* | Boston. |
| Wenzell, Henry Burleigh | St. Paul, Minn. |
| Weston, Melville Moore | Boston. |
| Wharton, William Fisher | Boston. |
| White, Moses Perkins | Cambridge. |
| Wigglesworth, George | Boston. |
| Willard, Joseph | Boston. |
| Wilson, Frank | Sanford, Me. |
| Wilson, John Thomas | Winchester. |
| Winkler, Alexander, *Student Harvard Law School* | Cincinnati, O. |
| Winslow, John | Brooklyn, N. Y. |
| Wood, Stephen Blake | Roxbury. |
| Woodruff, Thomas Tyson | Boston. |
| Worthington, Erastus, *Clerk of Courts* | Dedham. |
| Young, Alexander, *Literature* | Boston. |

# THE UNDERGRADUATES' DAY.

THE Students of the College assembled in Sanders Theatre, and after a prayer by the Rev. ANDREW PRESTON PEABODY, D.D., listened to the following addresses and poems.

THE

# UNDERGRADUATES' DAY.

November 6, 1886.

## ORATION.

BY FRANKLIN ELMER ELLSWORTH HAMILTON.

Class of 1887.

THE anniversary which we are met this morning to observe is one of extraordinary significance. We commemorate the quarter-millennium of a University which, "first among equals," has striven to give form to American education; we commemorate the triumph of Puritan life, and the widening success of that struggle of Puritanism which, running through eight generations, would perfect a form of education distinctively Puritan, yet wholly American. We commemorate the progress of that idea of liberality in education which, cherished first and most ardently at Harvard, has passed from her to every kindred American institution. While commemorating the work of Harvard University, we foresee the inevitable fulfilment of her hopes, and therefore celebrate the natal day of a University at once the oldest and the newest in the land. Newest, I say, as well as oldest; for

Harvard University from the days of Increase Mather has maintained as a fundamental principle that a University founded "for Christ and the Church," and holding the motto "Truth," ought in no wise to depart from the path marked out in that famous resolve, *Libere philosophari*, made so early in her history. It has been her endeavor during more than two centuries to think without bigotry, and to train men who not only shall think but also shall act in that spirit of advance which seeks to keep pace with the spirit of the age.

It is wise, upon an occasion like this, that we should seek instruction rather in the past than in the present. And through these two and a half centuries we are carried back into the morning of our national life, back into those sober religious days of sturdy New England Puritanism, where we find ourselves with men who in the spirit of their Cromwell have determined to secure forever on these quiet shores a retreat from "The King's return to his own again." For "it was," as our own poet says, "the drums of Naseby and Dunbar that gathered the minute men on Lexington Common; it was the red dint of the axe in Charles's block that marked ONE in our era." What marvel, then, that we see these men of duty, — with their motto "faith in God, faith in man, faith in work," — "taking orders for a college at Newtown," and appropriating for its establishment "a year's rate of the whole colony," that, so runs the record, "the Commonwealth may be furnished with knowing and understanding men, and the churches with an able ministry." Yet this was "the first occasion on which a people ever taxed *themselves* to found a place of education."

Follow the life and work of that little seminary during those first years of poverty and suffering, dependent for very existence upon a precarious benevolence, and tossed upon every sea of political and religious controversy that rocked the province. Though led at times into error, and once — during the frenzy of the Salem Witchcraft — even tempted to persecution, still she remains true to the motto on her walls, raising higher and higher the standard of the literature of the country, and sending forth from her doors larger and wiser men. Long before the resistance to the Stamp Act, before the fearless voice of Patrick Henry rang out, before Faneuil Hall had thrown open its doors to an eloquent patriotism, a graduate of Harvard in his Commencement Thesis "announced the whole doctrine of the Revolution" in words that sounded like a tocsin through the land. And as if in answer to the summons, there passed from the college halls in quick succession an Otis, a Warren, a John Hancock, a Quincy, and a younger Adams.

We are told that at the period of the Revolution even the undergraduates caught the inspiration of the times, and that their declamations and forensic disputes breathed the uncompromising spirit of liberty. With the enthusiasm of the hour, they voted unanimously to take their degrees clothed only in the manufactures of their native land; and when Washington, on Cambridge green, took command of the

American army, the students forsook the college in a body that its halls might shelter the patriot troops. Pass through the transept of this Hall, raised as a memorial to those sons of Harvard who fell in the last war, and there, on the tablets upon the walls, read a Mother's proud testimony to the patriotism of her twelve hundred and thirty-two volunteers, who as one man followed their flag to the front, and trace her tribute to the memory of her three hundred and sixty-one martyrs who gave their lives for the cause. Nor let us forget at this hour and in this place that the gray covered as devoted hearts as the blue, and that many a soldier of the South who fell on the field of battle claimed Harvard as his Alma Mater.

Thus it has ever been in the history of the University. In the necessitous provincial days fostering a spirit of fortitude; in the early crisis of Independence inspiring to patriotism; in the hour of national trial admonishing to duty, — she has always taught her students to study, not only the wisdom of the past, but also the lessons of the present and the more perplexing problems of the future. And for this reason, if for no other, Harvard stands where she does to-day, as the representative University of the representative Republic. The reforms of which she is a leading exponent are simply the necessary outcome of the call of a nation for an enlargement of the higher education. Constantly has the University, down through the long list of her honored faculties, endeavored to meet the educational needs of the country; and it has been this endeavor which has assured to Harvard the eminent success that she now enjoys. Thus, although an outgrowth of Puritanism, she nevertheless has sought to become a cosmopolitan University in a country by no means Puritan; and though surrounded and often restrained by conservative influences of the most positive character, she has struggled continually not to be conservative. And as the school at Newtown, founded originally as a Theological Seminary, soon became in compliance with the country's need a college, so later when it was discovered, to the amazement of many, that all education is not comprehended in

*Lingua, Tropus, Ratio, Numerus, Tonus, Angulus, Astra,*

the college broadened into a university, — a university so extensive that in her instruction to-day we see the most recent sciences placed upon an equality with mathematics and the classics.

The University now has reached another great epoch in her work, with the adoption of reforms as startling to the present conservative conception of education as they may appear destructive to the time-honored significance of the academic degree. But much of this alarm arises from the failure of the American college in the past to keep pace with the nation's spirit and growth. The attempt upon the part of Harvard to meet the demands of a growing people very naturally has given much occasion for criticism. The origin of such criticism, however, is by no means recent. We read that "many godly men of the Province," even in the seventeenth century, "conceived a great sorrow" from a like cause. And even earlier, the one Indian youth, whom tradition recalls as having received a degree by the side of his Puritan brothers, doubtless heard the same question discussed.

But the very criticism of a progressive institution evidences the necessity for education in the future to meet the demands of an advancing, practical life. Is it not high time that a country like our own, which has given to the world such signal triumphs of non-collegiate training in the pursuits of industry, and has witnessed in mechanics and engineering the proudest attainments of inventive genius, should offer to her sons a university training adapted to fit them as well for a life of manly work as for a life of cultivated leisure? The call for collegiate students to interest themselves less in what concerns them as mere catalogues of books than in that which concerns them as "men, and leaders of men," was heard, in this very Hall, in that scathing arraignment of the American scholar which is finding in the broadening claims of education its justification and confirmation.

It was the hope of the founders of the University that "so long as New England or America hath a name on the earth's surface," the fame and fruit of their work should be "blessed." Two centuries and a half have passed away since the college, which in the words of one of her most famous presidents now stands

"... like a Pharos founded on a rock,"

was planted, at the promptings of weakness, in a new land among a free people. On this anniversary morning we know how she has stood during successive generations, as inflexible in purpose as when a humble Puritan "School of the Prophets" she listened to the preaching of her first president, the devout Dunster. She has trained clergymen, schoolmasters, soldiers, statesmen, mechanics. Through her quarter-millennium they have entered her doors, received her instruction, and passed on to their work. And, as in the beginning, these walls re-echo still the footsteps of the ambitious pressing on toward the future. Would that, if but for a moment, we might recall the departed of good and great Harvard's line, that we might conjure from the "doggerel dirge and Latin epitaph" some fitting memorial to the many who have gathered in these halls and lingered among the shadows of these elms! But, no; they are forgotten. Of John Harvard himself the most meagre traditions remain, and only his munificence to our University preserves from oblivion his name. "He died upon a date misstated upon his monument, — a monument which does not mark his grave!"

Looking back through this quarter-millennium, can we not see that the work of the University has been the work of a people, — a work marked at times, it is true, by prejudice and intolerance, at times by liberality and magnanimity; now betraying feeble struggles and powerful temptations, now recalling waves of enthusiasm "on whose crumbling crests we sometimes see nations lifted for a gleaming moment"? Can we not see how her influence has grown from her work? Consider for a moment that influence. Each generation as it has passed has bequeathed to the University some ample accumulation of wealth, some new lesson of "Truth" learned, some old problem of life solved. Nobly has she repaid her bequests! Not the Commonwealth of Massachusetts alone, but the whole country, through State and Territory, has been furnished from her graduates "with knowing and understanding men, and the churches with an able ministry." In 1699 it was truly, if somewhat quaintly, said to the General Court by the Earl of Bellamont, while Governor of Massachusetts, "It is a very great advantage you have above other provinces, that your youth are not put to travel for learning, but have the Muses at their doors." For this advantage, keeping pace with the increase of population and wealth, has given to the State of Massachusetts a foremost place in refinement and learning, and to her metropolis a classic name. The influence of Harvard has been fundamental, for she has promoted a freedom of thought; through her call for an earnest individuality she has inspired her sons to more courageous persistence as pioneers of intellectual reforms. In the privations of poverty the instruction at Harvard has always encouraged a noble ambition and effort, as in prosperity it has lent new meaning to affluence and culture. In sectarian disputes and political reformations, during "the vicissitudes of the infant settlements," through the perilous struggles of a patriotic resistance to injustice, amid the fires of a civil strife testing a great social principle, Harvard University, whether tried by penury or endangered by a prosperous growth, has stood throughout a conscientious champion of "Truth" and a fearless preacher "for Christ and the Church."

Some future orator, on some distant anniversary, will recall, perhaps, this day. I charge him to forget not, in the gratulations of that occasion, the Puritan founders of Harvard. Let their memory as a widening influence through his words reach on and out like the light of the setting sun, though they themselves have passed from us and risen on another and sublimer life. But if there is yet one lesson to be drawn from this hour it is surely this, — that the future history of Harvard, like the voice of our widest usefulness, calls to us, as the students of a great University, for the best work and noblest living; to make, as says Carlyle, some nook of God's creation a little fruitfuller, some human hearts a little manfuller. And as Harvard, at once the oldest and the newest, — Harvard first among equals, but ever *first*, — passes from us into the future, let us recall again those burning words spoken so recently to us here: "Your country needs a new enthusiasm. To whom but to you, her young men, shall she look to give it her? You are the trustees of posterity. On whom else shall she call to wake the deep slumber of careless opinions; to startle the torpor of an immoral acquiescence; to kindle burning aspirations; to set noble examples; to cleanse the Augean stables of politics and trade; to shame false ideals of life; to deepen the lessening sense of the sacredness of marriage; to make your Press nobler and less frivolous; to make the aims of society more earnest;

to make homes pure; to make life simple; to defy the petty and arrogant tyrannies of the thing which calls itself public opinion; to trample on the base omnipotence of gold? She calls to you! Will you hear her voice, or will you too make, like the young ruler, the great refusal?"

## POEM.

### BY FRANCIS STERNE PALMER.

#### CLASS OF 1887.

LONG years ago, the stern New England rock
   A wizard smote, and straightway forth did gush —
Here in this wilderness that felt the shock —
   A fountain, filling all the forest's hush
With joy. Our College was that woodland spring;
   The Puritan it was who there made flow
A fount that in the years to come should swing
   Its mighty tide through all the land, and show
How great is truth to conquer wrong and woe.

More than two centuries with frost and snow
   Of fierce New England winters now have gone;
The stream grows hoar with time, and yet its flow
   Is still as young as on its birthday's dawn, —
As young as youth eternal, a fountain still
   Of youth, new and fresh, yesterday, to-day,
To-morrow; flowing, changing at its will:
   Though men sometime its course would turn or stay,
   Still with the nation's life it makes its way.

Our stream to-day its narrow banks o'erflows;
   Deserted ruins on its course appear
That tell where once the towers of temples rose;
   And yet its waters still are fresh and clear
With purity, and savor of the spring
   Rock-born, and of the forest-flowing rill:
And still those youths are here who first did bring
   Their sober minds unto the college mill,
   Though now they do not go in ruff or frill.

Behold the modern Puritan! His talk
   Is all of matters grave, his face sedate;
He moves, and 't is a most majestic stalk!
   His flashing eye could rule a troubled state;
He yearns to serve his country, and meanwhile
   For college offices has no distaste;
And yet, forsooth, let him provoke no smile:
   'T is only sad that in our age he 's placed,
   And that so much stern virtue goes to waste.

And those young princes of the native race
   Whom our forefathers vainly tried to tame,
Does haze that fills the distant years efface
   Their savage splendor, or is it wont to flame
Across the sober tints of college life,
   When some young magnate of the West arrays
Himself in gorgeousness, his dress all rife
   In bright, barbaric hues, and so essays
   The war-dance, and the tomahawk displays?

Our College in the years that saw her young,
   And like young mothers full of love and care
And foolish fear, around her children flung
   Her arms too close, nor granted them that share
Of trust and freedom they with justice craved;
   But growing wiser as the years went by,
She loosed the petty irksome bonds, and saved
   Their love for her, and taught them to descry
   In her a friend and not a crafty spy.

## THE UNDERGRADUATES' DAY.

Many brave hopes Fair Harvard's fountain fed,
   And great achievements on its stream were borne;
Men who in stirring times the State have led,
   And names by poets, thinkers, workers, worn, —
All these were ours, and our bright list adorn.


*One* name the fountain claims its own and keeps:
   Life's river may not bear that name away;
Joyous and loving as sunshine which leaps
   About the stream and gilds its dancing spray,
This one the true embodiment doth seem
   Of youth eternal; and while the fountain's play
Doth last, his ever kindly wit shall gleam
   Within its pools, the while his laughing voice
   Doth make the murm'ring waters to rejoice.


No need to tell his name, for you all know it, —
Our Doctor, Autocrat, and Poet.


The shining sun not always maketh bright
   Our stream; there was a time when war swept o'er
The shudd'ring land, when face to face met Right
   And Wrong; and then the river onward bore
Its tide of youth and hope, all dark and stained
   With blood shed by its bravest and its best.
The later Puritan, whose heart regained
   Its ancient zeal, opposed his stubborn breast,
   And by his side were heroes of the West.


The gilded youth were also there to show
   Good metal lay beneath the outward dross;
And all went forth against the country's foe,
   Nor did they heed of life and limb the loss,
But were the foremost in the fierce affray;
   And many died, and dying so, died well,
And Harvard hon'ring all, and fain to pay
   Her debt of love to those who fought and fell,
   Hath built a stately Hall her love to tell.

Pray Heaven that war may never come again
   To fill the nation's heart with grief and hate!
But strife will come, and with it woe and pain;
   And bloodless battles will be fought as great
As those of war, and men will freely spend
   Their lives to add unto the truth some light;
And in this strife must Harvard join and lend
   Her learning and her zeal to those that fight
Against all evil things and to uphold the right.

Old Harvard's stream must ever onward sweep,
   Still wid'ning, blessing, lab'ring, singing, strong
With youth, joyous with hope, and broad and deep
   With wisdom gathered from the years which throng
Its past; and yet 'midst all this honor fair
   And power which to its age and works belong,
It still must keep and guard with fondest care
   The purity of that clear fount which gushed
From out the rock when all was new and forest-hushed.

## ADDRESS TO UNDERGRADUATES.

### BY EDGAR JUDSON RICH.

#### Class of 1887.

Fellow-Students, — In this age of Darwinianism and Spencerianism, when it is the fashion for writers and orators to trace the growth of the infinitely complex from the inconceivably simple, an occasion like this would be sadly incomplete without an attempt to apply the principles of evolution to some appropriate object. And on this occasion, when we the unweaned children are gathered together to celebrate the two hundred and fiftieth birthday of our revered mother, what more grateful service could we render her than to show how much better and wiser than her elder children are we, her latest born. Let then the "Evolution of the Harvard Student" be the burden of my remarks.

It must be remembered that the Harvard student and the rest of mankind sprang from the same stalk; that the separation did not take place until about the year 1636, when our branch of the family rose into ethereal heights in the vain hope that sometime it might be able to commune with the gods of high Olympus in their own tongue.

Consider this Harvard student for a moment functionally. He appears to us under three distinct forms: first, as a creature addicted to study — in a moderate degree; secondly, as a creature supposed to pray; and thirdly, — about which, in those early times at least, there can be no conjecture, — as a creature most prone to transgression. We will now trace out his evolution along each of these principal lines of development, beginning with the last.

Our early fathers were firm believers in the total depravity of mankind. If at any time a brother's faith in this doctrine seemed weak, he was exhorted to look at the young men of the college, upon whose souls the Devil still held tenacious grip. Upon the college authorities responsibility bore heavily. It was an axiom with them, that if there was a choice between right and wrong, the student would always do wrong;

if there was no wrong to be done within easy reach, he would go out of his way to find it, — as if to prove the truth of the fundamental theological dogma of the day. The college exercised great ingenuity in attempting to anticipate the student. A list of all conceivable offences was drawn up, and the penalty for each affixed. Some offences were punishable with expulsion, some with suspension, some with flogging, some with cuffing; a list of fifty-two minor offences with fines, ranging from a penny for tardiness at prayers to £2 10s. for absence from town a month without leave. Flogging was administered by the President, in the presence of faculty and students. In order to realize the picturesqueness of this performance, imagine such a case of discipline brought down to our time, and this place the scene of the punishment. The members of the faculty are ranged on the platform, and you, the students, are summoned to witness and to take warning. The culprit is brought forward. Our worthy President invokes divine blessing; then, with all solemnity, flogs or cuffs the student, as the nature of his offence demands; and, finally, petitions the Almighty to give the offender a new heart, and to bring him into the fold of the righteous.

The system of fines is still more amusing. We can picture to ourselves the mischief-loving student going through a mental calculation in order to ascertain in what way a given sum of money invested in fines would yield the greatest return in fun: whether he should get drunk, or thrash a fellow-student, or lie to the Dean, or cut a recitation, or swap jack-knives without the consent of the proctor, — all of these offences being punishable by the same fine, one shilling and sixpence.

These absurd methods of punishment gradually died out; but it was not until about the time of the Revolution that flogging fell entirely into desuetude, and it was some time in the present century before the system of fines was wholly discontinued. The faculty became less autocratic and more rational in their government. It dawned upon them by degrees that a student might have an iota of reason and common-sense. And as years rolled on, as the student became less of a child in age, greater freedom of action was allowed him. The liberal form of government did not reach its ideality, however, until the year 1885, when the conference committee, — peace be to its ashes! — was established. But this much-abused conference committee has not lived in vain, if it has only shown that there is little or nothing in Harvard College requiring the attention of such a body. Its very uselessness indicates the ideal condition of college discipline.

Let us now look at the student on another side of his nature, — the religious side; and here we will attempt to trace briefly his evolution and his growth. Founded as our college was by the stern Puritan for the purpose largely of educating men for the Christian ministry, we should naturally expect that the spiritual needs of the student would receive the most careful attention. Presidents and professors were chosen with regard to their theological views; the curriculum was shaped to meet the religious wants of the student. Religious exercises were frequent and compulsory; prayers were held twice a day, and absence from service was punished with a fine. At the morning service, held in winter by candle-light, the student was obliged to read a portion of the Old Testament out of the Hebrew into the Greek; and at evening prayers, a portion of the New Testament out of the English into the Greek. One marvels that under such a stultifying system of worship a student emerged from college with a spark of religious fervor in him! But, like prescribed Latin and Greek, prescribed religion was slowly abandoned, until, at the beginning of this memorable year in Harvard's annals, the last vestiges of an antiquated and unnatural system have disappeared.

These changes, which we choose to call growth, are trumpeted abroad by hostile critics as a departure which brings with it the decay of religious life at Harvard. It *is* the death-blow to compulsory religion, but it is the signal for the re-awakening of true religion. To-day there is in this college a greater respect for religion, a purer and nobler religious life, than there was two hundred years ago, when religion was secondary to theology; than one hundred years ago, when religion was tempered with fear; than fifty years ago, when religion was subservient to policy; than yesterday, when religion by reason of its compulsion was fast losing its hold upon the students. The attitude of the religious papers upon this question is deserving of the severest censure. Their utterances are maliciously false; they display a temper becoming the bigoted sectarian, but not the humble Christian. Let them know, and all the world besides, that religion is not dead at Harvard; that on the contrary, under a voluntary system, it is entering upon a new and purer life.

Those who would enforce religion mistake the nature of religion, and more especially the nature of the persons upon whom they would enforce it. The most and the best which a college can do for the spiritual wants of the student, is to give him *opportunities* of listening to the great teachers of the land. And what college has done more in this direction than Harvard?

But we have not yet considered the student in the light in which he is usually regarded by the outside world, — that is, as a cultivated, learned, and wise man. Let us then see in what ways he has acquired this culture, learning, and wisdom at different periods in the history of the college. In the laws of the college, printed in 1646, we find the following, referring to the qualifications for admission: "When any scholar is able to read Tully, or such like classical Latin author, *ex tempore*, and make and speak true Latin in verse and prose, and decline the paradigms of nouns and verbs in the Greek tongue, then may he be admitted into the college; nor shall any claim admission before such qualifications." Thus, during almost the entire first century of our college's existence, a student need only talk gibberish Latin, write doggerel Latin verse, show some familiarity with Greek grammar, in order to gain admission to the first institution of learning in the land! But woe unto the student who found himself here without a pretty thorough training in those meagre requirements! Once under the authority of the college he could not, by a vigorously enforced statute, use his mother tongue except in public declamation. If he could not give in choice Latin a reasonable excuse for failure at recitation, he suffered double penalties; if he failed to ask in Latin for food at the commons, he went away hungry. But the students had the satisfaction of knowing that the inflictors of this refined torture were themselves sometimes put to the test. It is related that an honored president of this University, once desiring the ejection of a dog which had strayed into evening prayers, called out in angry tone, "Exclude canem, et, et — shut the door!"

After four years spent in learning a few cant conversational Latin phrases, and in acquiring a smattering of Greek and of Hebrew, the student was ready to receive his first degree. If, upon examination, it were found that he could " read the original of the Old and New Testament into the Latin tongue and resolve them logically," he became by the authority of the college a Bachelor of Arts.

What can be said in defence of a curriculum so narrow, so ill-suited to make men educated, much less useful? This,— that at a time when natural phenomena were just beginning to be investigated with intelligence, when our literature was but in its infancy, when philosophy had hardly emerged from scholasticism, when history was yet unwritten, our college offered to her children the best that the age could give. And we are proud to say that this is a policy which our Alma Mater has ever followed. As science advanced, as philosophy became infused with an interest more human, as literature was written and history recorded, she gladly opened her doors to the new light, and gave her children a glimpse of a world of learning hitherto unknown. Gradually the ancient requirements were modified and broadened, until now the college offers to the student a course of study the best calculated of any in the land to make her graduates educated, intelligent, and useful men. Those who leave her doors now are not pedantic mincers of elegant Latin phrases, nor *dilettante* and captious lookers-on in a world of action, but men possessed of a knowledge which can rectify wrong and accomplish results, — men who become powers in the religious, the social, and the political worlds.

But the question suggests itself, May not our college in thus broadening its curriculum, and in giving almost absolute freedom of choice in the selection of studies, have gone too far? This is not the time to criticise flippantly, or to air personal whims; but I know that I voice the sentiments of hundreds of undergraduates and of graduates, when I say that our college has made some serious mistakes. If it be the chief purpose of a college course to give a liberal education, — and that I conceive is its purpose, — there must be certain studies essential to such an education. Latin, as an indispensable aid to the study of law, of medicine, and of science, as the basis of almost all modern languages, as the very sap of the English language, should be required of every scholar seeking admission to college. But the elements of the language once mastered, I confess it seems like mere pedantry to pursue the study further; for the discipline which Latin gives has already been largely acquired; and as to its literature — see to it that you have first become familiar with the infinitely grander literature of your own language. Relegate Latin to the preparatory schools, but insist upon it there.

Again, there are studies universally admitted as essential to a liberal education which should be pursued after the student has entered college. In the place formerly occupied by prescribed Greek, Latin, and mathematics, let us have prescribed philosophy, political economy, and English literature, and also history and science, if the elements of these subjects cannot be required for admission. All these studies need not occupy half of the college course; and the indisputable advantages of an elective system would not be lost. In answer to these criticisms I know it can be said that where the option lies between Greek and Latin, Latin will almost invariably be chosen; and that those studies which we would prescribe are now, as a matter of fact, pursued by a large majority of students. But there will be those who will know nothing of Latin, and there will be those who will be ignorant of those other essential subjects; and then there will be men graduated from this college who will not be liberally educated.

But perhaps we criticise too severely, when we consider what stupendous strides our college has made towards attaining an ideal system of education. She has outstripped all rivals, who, while criticising her vehemently for every advance, are finally compelled to follow tardily in her footsteps.

A word to close. With all this advance in methods of discipline; with this enlarging and quickening of the religious life; with this tremendous progress in the curriculum work, — with all this, has there been a corresponding advance in the manhood of the student? For this, after all, is the test of the efficiency of every educational system. If self-reliance, sincerity, earnestness, are elements of manhood, then there has been advance; for there never was a time when students were more self-reliant, more sincere, more earnest, than they are to-day; and this year will go down to posterity as a year memorable, not so much because it marks the quarter-millennium of the existence of the college, as because it marks the culmination of an educational policy the equal of which to produce true manhood cannot be found in this land, or in any other land.

# ODE.

### BY LLOYD McKIM GARRISON.

#### CLASS OF 1888.

MOTHER, peerless, immortal, our lips but repeat
 The words so oft spoken before,
As we timidly, rev'rently, kneel at thy feet
 And ask for thy blessing once more.
Our fathers rejoiced at thy dawn overcast;
 We exult in thy radiant day;
So, our sons and their sons, when our glories are past,
 And our names as forgotten as they:

For though mountain and river should part thee for aye
 From the child thou hast reared at thy knee,
The niche that he keeps in his heart is too high
 To be filled by another than thee.
The centuries fade, like a mist from the glass;
 We are gone, — why, we know not, nor where;
Yet as ever we wearily halt as we pass,
 We behold thee still young and still fair.

# FOUNDATION DAY.

There were two services in Appleton Chapel, — in the morning, when the Rev. FRANCIS G. PEABODY, Plummer Professor of Christian Morals, delivered the sermon; and in the evening, when the Rev. PHILLIPS BROOKS, D.D., made the discourse.

# FOUNDATION DAY.

Sunday, November 7, 1886.

---

## A SERMON.

BY THE REV. FRANCIS GREENWOOD PEABODY,

*Plummer Professor of Christian Morals.*

---

Even so would he have removed thee out of a strait into a broad place. — *Job* xxxvi. 16.

THERE is but one note to strike throughout our worship to-day. It is the note of thanksgiving. We are here simply to thank our God for the wonderful and increasing multitude of blessings through which our University has been led, — for the blessings which she has been permitted to receive, and the blessings which she has been able to bestow. We thank God for his influence on the hearts of our ancestors, so moving them that they waited neither for days of prosperity nor peace to found this college, but, fearing God's displeasure visited upon ignorance more than they feared their own poverty or their savage enemies, set apart "a year's rate of the whole colony" to establish a place of learning. We thank God that we can fairly join with the historian of the University in believing that "for a like spirit under like circumstances history will be searched in vain." We thank God for the marvellous contrasts of the present and the past, for the strange deliverances from perilous controversies, for the widening of the intellectual horizon and the increase of spiritual liberty which have been witnessed here. We thank God to-day that by ways which the wisdom of our ancestors could not have conceived, and from which their hearts would have recoiled, we have been brought "out of a strait into a broad place."

It is not for to-day, or for a service of worship, to trace in detail the story of these heroic beginnings and this dramatic growth. We are all waiting with a great expectation for this story as it will be told to-morrow in lyric prose and eloquent verse. But, after all, the most striking and central part of this history remains the peculiar property of this day and of our service of worship. For the story of those early days, though it abounds in political and intellectual interest, is in its central element nothing else than a chapter of religious history. Its hopes and heroisms are those of the religious life; its controversies and dissensions are those of the theologians. We remember to-day that the college was founded for the specific purpose of rearing fit persons for the Christian ministry, or, as the first appeal for help announced, "that the Commonwealth may be furnished with knowing and understanding men, and the churches with an able ministry." This specific purpose directed the whole early history which we commemorate. In the first list of college regulations, — called, as now seems curious, "the liberties" of the college, — the first rules are these: "Every scholar shall consider the main end of his life and study to know God and Jesus Christ. Every one shall so exercise himself in reading the Scriptures twice a day, that they be ready to give an account of their proficiency. And all sophisters and bachelors shall publicly repeat sermons in the hall whenever they are called forth." Such was the college from within; and when, somewhat later, there was doubt in the community as to its administration, and ten articles were proposed for a visitation of its affairs, seven of these articles had exclusive reference to its religious and moral condition. "Whether the Holy Scriptures be daily read in the hall, and how often expounded? How are the Saturday exercises performed, and are the great concerns of their souls duly inculcated in the youths?"

What, then, do we see in this primitive Puritan college? We see one central characteristic, whose dignity even these narrow and mechanical regulations cannot hide. It is an institution founded by men in whom the sense of God is the controlling impulse, and to whom his glory is the end of education. When the families of the colony brought out of their poverty their offerings to the college, — the one of five shillings, and the other of a few sheep, and the other the fourth part of a bushel of corn, or "something equivalent thereto," — it was not as an offering to culture, but as an offering to religion and for a holy end. It was the widow casting her mite into the treasury of the temple for the sake of the faith which she desired to have fitly preached.

It is, therefore, a fortunate coincidence that our day of commemoration falls upon our day of worship, and that we are called, first of all, to take up our great theme in the language of religion. The University has wisely invited her graduates, wherever they are serving her to-day in the Christian ministry, to direct their thoughts toward this history of their college; and we rejoice to think how the whole continent is this morning girdled with these prayers of filial love. A University with such a history can never be indifferent or neutral to the problems of faith and duty. She may change her methods, but never her desire. She has had set before her by her founders an ideal of education as a work to do in the sight of God, — education under religious responsibility; education as a means to character. We thank God for this; and we survey this history aright only when we look at it, first of all, in the spirit of worship and under the power of prayer.

Let us then dismiss from our minds to-day the other aspects of this history, and consider only the relations of the University to the moral and religious life. Let us trace the wonderful contrasts which present themselves in this central concern, — the gains, the losses, and the lessons of religious faith which are to be seen in this great transition from "a strait into a broad place." Let us set over against each other the way of the higher life, as it seems to have been in a Puritan college and as it ought to be in a modern university.

The Puritan State out of which our college sprang presents a curious paradox. On the one hand, it is among the most heroic, devout, and fruitful incidents of history; on the other hand, it is among the most hopeless, Quixotic, and fruitless dreams of religious enthusiasm. Its spirit was the sense of responsibility to God in every detail of social and political life; its form was the illusory scheme of a State based on the Old Testament. In its spirit, we can compare it only with that intimate recognition of a living God which makes Hebrew history sacred history. In its form, we must compare it with those visionary communities which have been so confidently proposed, from the days of Plato's Republic to the days of Brook Farm. Thus, the Puritan State was at once a conspicuous failure and a magnificent success. The Puritan failed in the purpose on which he had set his heart; and he would look with bewilderment, if not with horror, on the community which he himself created. Yet the very qualities in him which made him sure to fail are the very qualities which have been perpetuated, and which it would be our social ruin to lose.

It is easy to trace the elements of this strange contradiction. On the one hand stands the form of Puritanism. These men meant to build a State which should reproduce the theocracy of the Hebrews. They seemed to themselves a chosen people, driven forth into a new land with no guidance but that of Jehovah. "They guided their legislation," as one historian has said, "with a Jewish austerity, and reinforced their authority by Old Testament texts." Repeating thus the theocracy of the Hebrews, they were bound to repeat the intolerance of the Hebrews. It was a question between serving God and serving Baal. The logic of their situation sent Roger Williams to Rhode Island and the Quakers to the gallows. If the State was but the instrument of the Church, then the limitation of the franchise to church members became a matter of course. "In England," says John Cotton, "none but members of the Church of England are intrusted with the management of affairs; in Popish countries, none but such as are Catholics; in Turkey, none but men devoted to Mahomet. Yea! these very Indians that worship the Devil will not be under the government of any sagamores but such as join with them in the observance of their 'powwows' and idolatries. So that it seems to be a principle imprinted in the minds of men, that such a form of government as best serves to establish their religion should be established in the civil state." Thus, the limited franchise might be an inexpedient measure, but it was an inevitable one. It was the corollary of the unfaltering conviction that the will of God had been revealed in a peculiar way. "Thus stands the case," said Governor Winthrop, "between God and us. We are entered into a covenant with him for this work. We have taken out a commission."

It is evident that a commonwealth like this, though it might be a lofty dream, was a dream impossible of realization. Like the charge at Balaklava, it was magnificent, but it was predestined to defeat. It might be consistent for church members alone to vote, but the time soon would come when it would be impossible. The choice had to be made between yielding the form and wrecking the State; and the form was yielded. Thus it happens that those who could not secure to us what they wanted to secure, yet secured to us something infinitely more precious. The limitation of the vote passed away, but the vote remained. The Puritan meant to give us church suffrage: he really gave us the free ballot. He meant to found a peculiar people: he really founded a free State.

Such was the form of the Puritan State. It was set in "a strait place." The principles which it held could not fairly disclose themselves until the form was broken. Puritanism came over like one of the hyacinth bulbs which this generation imports. It was a colorless, gnarly, flowerless thing; and those who brought it never seemed to have realized the beauty and fragrance which might issue from it. Kept in the box which brought it over, it was as unpromising a plant as ever crossed the ocean. Set forth in the sunshine of freedom and in congenial soil, it has brought forth a flower which a Puritan might have thought almost too fair. Even within the form, as it first appeared, lay this potency for large results. Half-hidden beneath this narrowness of expression, there already worked a spirit as different from dogmatic intolerance as a blossom is from a bulb: it is a spirit of the most straightforward and simple piety. There never was a Christian congregation founded whose covenant was simpler or more adapted to all time than the covenant made six weeks after the landing of Governor Winthrop, and still inscribed upon the walls of the First Church of Boston. There never was a nobler exposition of the principles of Christian society than in Winthrop's discourse written upon his voyage. It removes the whole community "out of a strait into a broad place." "The only way to avoid shipwreck," he says, "and to provide for our prosperity is to follow the counsel of Micah, 'to do justly, to love mercy, and to walk humbly with our God.' For this work we must be knit together as one man. We must uphold a familiar commerce together, in all meekness, gentleness, patience, and liberality. So shall we keep the unity of the spirit in the bond of peace. We shall find that the God of Israel is among us, so that men shall say of succeeding plantations, 'The Lord made it like to that of New England.'"

What, then, might happen when a community like this, with this conflict within itself of an impracticable scheme and a noble ideal, felt the duty laid upon it of founding a college? There might lie before the college either the way of the Puritan form or the way of the Puritan spirit. The college might develop along the line of intolerance and narrowness, or along the line of a simple sense of responsibility to God. Nothing could seem more uncertain than the way which the college might take. It becomes at once the centre of controversy between the ecclesiastics and the liberal-minded. Its history becomes of dramatic interest. We wonder how soon it will be overwhelmed with dogmatic tests, or administered out of party interests. We see it led to the very brink of these fatal issues. It startles us to think what kind of a college we might have inherited, if certain words then accepted by all had crept into its charter, or if, as so nearly, Cotton Mather had succeeded his father as president. "I am informed," he says in his wrath, "that yesterday the six men who call themselves the corporation of the college met, and, contrary to the epidemical expectation of the country, chose a modest young man, of whose piety (and little else) every one gives a laudable character. I always foretold these two things of the corporation: first, that if it were possible for them to steer clear of me, they will do so; secondly, that if it were possible for them to act foolishly, they will do so."

Thus from the very outset the peril of bigotry beset the college. Its officials were judged, not according to their learning, but according to their orthodoxy. The first president was indicted by the grand jury, convicted, and dismissed from his position and his house in the dead of winter, being sent forth without a home, with his wife sick, and, as he says, "his youngest child extremely so," not because he was not a virtuous, humble, and learned man, but because, as Cotton Mather said, he had fallen "into the briers of anti-pædo-baptism." The second president did not, indeed, like Dunster, hold that only adults should be baptized. His heresy consisted in believing that in baptism sprinkling was insufficient, and that the infant should be washed all over, — "an opinion," says the historian, "not tolerable in this cold region, and impracticable in certain seasons of the year." It was for such a conviction as this that President Chauncy suffered all his long life, finally representing to the General Court "that he was without land to keep a horse or a cow upon, or habitation to be dry or warm in; whereas, in English universities, the president is allowed diet as well as stipend according to his wants." And it was no doubt his view of baptism which made the committee of the General Court report on this petition, "that they conceived the country has done honorably toward the petitioner, and that his parity with English colleges is not pertinent." Here is the way in which the college seemed at first inevitably led, — the way of doctrinal tests and sectarian animosity. It was "a strait place" to which it seemed directed, — a place of contention, first between the various factions of one sect, and then no less between the prevailing sect and the vigorous movement of Anglicanism. It is safe to say that if this way of development had been taken, we should have little to celebrate to-day. But, by a guidance which seems miraculous at such a time, the college was led of God "out of a strait into a broad place." It seems fairly incredible that at the very time when the orthodoxy of its officers was thus suspected, and the religious opinions of its students a constant matter of concern, there should not appear in any charter of the college a single word of doctrinal test or sectarian tendency. The first constitution of the college dedicates it to "piety, morality, and learning." The charter of 1650 announces as its object "the education of the English and Indian youth of this country in knowledge and godliness;" and in 1643 the college seal was adopted, with its motto "Veritas" written across the open books. Piety, morality, godliness, and truth, — these are the four great words which mark the earliest official utterances of this college to religion. Discuss and bicker as its governors might concerning its temporary affairs, it seems as if they were sobered and lifted in their thought when they dealt with the permanent conditions of the institution, with the same sense of awful responsibility toward these young souls which has kept every administration of the college ever since above all suspicion of sectarian purpose or strategy. We are led in these utterances out of the temporary form of Puritanism into the higher spirit of Puritanism. The incidents of the college were determined by the one: its continuous development was determined by the other. Piety, morality, godliness, and truth, — to these ends, for which our ancestors founded this institution and made room for it in the "strait place" of their struggling life, — to these ends we dedicate her life once more to-day. We know, as they knew, that she can serve the State only as she rears her students in piety and morality. We know, as they knew, that her permanent prosperity must come through her increase of godliness; and we believe, with a completeness which perhaps they could not have confessed, that the first religious duty of a university is loyalty to truth.

Such is the story of religion in its official and organic relation to the college. It is a history of strange deliverances. Superficially looked at, it might not seem a story which ministers could tell with satisfaction; for it must be admitted to be a story of the continuous decline of clerical influence. Slowly the government of the college passed from the hands of the ministers; slowly it grew less and less a theological school. But in reality no greater service could be done by an institution of learning to the Christian ministry than by taking the institution out of the ministers' hands. It was the only way of permitting to the ministry its share in the growth of the world's thought. It was the only way in which the college could be changed from rearing a strait ministry to the more noble task of rearing a broad ministry. Those who believe in religion must believe that it does not ask of a university a peculiar or exclusive care, but that it asks only a fair chance for welcome and for discipline. Once more, the Puritan builded better than he knew. He failed in his absorbing scheme of a seminary peculiarly devoted to Biblical instruction; but he laid the foundation of a type of religion much more likely to endure than his own, whose corner-stones, placed by his own hands, are piety, morality, godliness, and truth.

But, after all, these official and organic aspects of the college are less interesting to us to-day than are its lessons concerning personal and individual life. That which concerns us in our worship is not so much the institution as the souls which compose it. Let us turn from the college as a whole to the story of its students' lives. What are the transitions which we there notice? How has it been with this army of young men? Has student life in these days anything yet to learn of faith or duty of those primitive times? These are the questions which interest us to-day. It is the spiritual history of the college which we are tracing, and that is a matter of personal character and individual faith.

The first thing that is noteworthy in this history of personal character is the fact that the same depressing judgments were then passed upon student life which we are in the habit of hearing now. To a certain class of minds their own age always appears an age of peculiar degeneracy. Many persons feel this now about our college, many persons always have felt so, and the gossip of one hundred and fifty years ago might almost be taken as the gossip of to-day. Thus, Cotton Mather writes of children who left home "with some gospel symptoms of piety, and quickly lose all, and neither do nor hear any more such things as they had before they went from home;" and, again, of "young ministers who are the gifts of Christ in the service of our churches, who declare that before they came to be what they are they found it necessary to lay aside the sentiments which they brought from the college with them." He inquires, like some modern critic of the elective system, "whether the pupils, having learned what is expected of them (which to the more acute sparks requires very little preparation), all the rest of the time is not, in a manner, their own, and little care to make them deserve the name of students?" So, also, Rev. Ezekiel Rogers, of Rowley, dying in 1661, suspects that the golden age is passed. "I tremble to think," he writes, "what will become of the glorious work we have done when the ancients shall be gathered with their fathers. I fear grace and blessing will die with them. We grow worldly everywhere. Every one for himself, little care for the public good."

The next thing to notice is that such complaints and despondency were quite as much justified then as now. Although the tutors chastised at discretion, and the students twice a day practised reading of the Scriptures, "accompanied by theoretical observations on its language and logic," complaints of immorality were by no means rare. It was not a time to which one may look back as one of strenuous morality. It was a time in which such offences as blasphemy, thieving, card-playing, and extravagance are noted in the college books. Thus the golden age of college morality is not to be sought for in its distant past. Nor does such searching of the records give us any reason to deplore the tendencies of the present. The ethics of our college show on the whole a continuous gain. The more one studies our history the more likely he is to believe that the moral tone among us was never higher than it is to-day. The more these young men have been trusted, the more they have justified our trust; the more they have been left free, the better has been our college discipline. The observing world catches sight of the scum which floats on the surface of college life, and calls it unclean; but the nearer one gets to the mass of student life to-day, the surer he grows that the heart of it is sound. He does not pine for the good old times, for he sees the assurance of a much manlier morality in the tendencies and standards which prevail among us now.

But issuing from these details of morality, we are brought into one great contrast of the spiritual life of a Puritan student with the spiritual life of a young man to-day, which sums up all that I wish to say. It is the contrast between life considered as an obligation and life considered as an opportunity, between life regulated by the uniform method of superimposed authority and life opening out into an infinite variety of equal privileges. I need not emphasize this contrast. Life as an obligation made the Puritan what he was. It fixed the method of study here. God demanded a definite type of student life, and it must be forthcoming. If our founders had been told that this was "a strait place," they would have quickly retorted, "Strait is the gate that leadeth unto life, and broad the way that leadeth unto death." Now, on the other hand, there lies before us the sense of life as an opportunity. It marks the university as against the college system. Instead of uniformity, complexity; instead of a straight and narrow way, an endless variety of paths. It is no longer the choice between a strait and a broad path: it is the choice between a highway and a way which one makes for himself. Under the

Puritan method the young man stands looking along a turnpike road; he pays his toll and his path is defined. Under the modern method he stands looking up at the mountain of the scholar's life; and it is for him to make his own way upward, threading as he may through the underbrush to the fair prospect at the summit.

When this contrast thus presents itself, our first mood is one of unqualified congratulation. The gains in such a transition are obvious. It is the deliverance "out of a strait into a broad place." But what it becomes us to-day to remember is this: that the contrast is not one born of opposition, but one reached by growth. It is not possible for an institution or for any individual within it to value life as an opportunity until he has valued it as an obligation. It is not possible, either historically or personally, to outgrow the Puritan limitation until the Puritan position has itself been held. First, the qualities of Puritanism; then, larger qualities which Puritanism did not know, — such must be the order of growth alike in the community and in each soul.

Such, for instance, is every man's experience about education. On the one hand, he must confess that the great transition of his intellectual life was when he passed from thinking of study as an obligation to thinking of it as an opportunity. Then it was that the guidance of his work was changed from a superimposed, authoritative, external direction to a voluntary, spontaneous, inward impulse. Then it was that he passed from the studies of a boy to the studies of a man. Yet, on the other hand, any student knows that except in rare cases of peculiar genius one does not come to value the opportunities of study unless he has been trained in the obligations of study. The method of the boy precedes the method of the man. First, the discipline of authority; then, the discovery that one may discipline himself. Let a young man come into the atmosphere of university life without this sense of obligation, and he rarely reaches the sense of opportunity. He has no background of Puritan discipline, and the time which to many marks an intellectual regeneration is a time frittered away.

So it is in the development of the moral life. It is, indeed, a glad transition when the sense of moral obligation passes into that of moral opportunity, and the duties of life are accepted as its privileges. Yet it is none the less true that in the soul, as in the Bible, the law must precede the gospel. The higher grades of spontaneous virtue are rooted in the disciplined sense of duty. They do not outgrow duty: they grow out of it. To reach them independently is but trying to gather the fruits of life without nourishing the roots of life. "Perfect love casteth out fear," says a nobler spirit than that of the Puritans; but no less truly replies the Puritan, "The fear of the Lord is the beginning of wisdom."

Or look at this contrast in what we may call our view of life. It was a hard, stern view which prevailed among the Puritans, fostered by their struggles, their poverty, and their creed. But what a courage, endurance, and optimism it bred! These men never despaired of their country or their race, or of the final purposes of God. And what, on the other hand, is this other curious phenomenon which we now witness among the cultivated, — this refined and gentle pessimism, this faith that the world is bad, and this enervating reliance on the solaces of art amid the wreck of hope, as though, while things must be evil, it was comforting that they were still beautiful? It is, once more, because so many men are now thrown into the midst of the opportunities of life before they have felt the obligations of life. What they need is a wholesome reinforcement of Puritan discipline, a healthier friction with reality. Strangely enough, it is not easy conditions of life which make men have faith in life: it is hard conditions. The Hebrews set forth into poverty and homelessness, and develop a glorious optimism. Greece maintains herself in a continuous struggle against overwhelming odds, and begins, not the philosophy of despair, but the philosophy of hope. Pessimism, on the other hand, is not the outcome of hardship and struggle: it is the outcome of ease; it is the philosophy of Sybarites. They believe in the badness of a world they have not tried. Trial is their redemption. They fall back upon the holiness of beauty, because they have not tested the beauty of holiness. If we would regain faith in the world, it must be not by multiplying luxury, but by returning to simplicity. The Puritan view of life has its lesson still to teach amid the multiplying and dissipating resources of the modern world; and where shall that lesson be taught and heeded, if not through increased simplicity and diminished ostentation in a Puritan college like this?

But, more than all, let us observe this same transition in the religious world. The one great and happy change in a soul or in a world is when it issues from thinking of religion as an obligation, and comes to see it is an opportunity. It is not a change which is even yet universal. We still hear much of "supporting religion," of "standing up for Jesus," as though religion were a poor, weak thing, against which we must build our scaffoldings to buttress and sustain it. But the fact is that we do not support religion, — it supports us. "Thou bearest not the root, but the root thee." Its mass sustains our props; and when we remove the scaffoldings of obligation, and, standing off, observe the structure in its own fairness, then for the first time comes the full glow of the religious life. Religion stands there, not as an institution to be supported, but as an opportunity to be accepted. It is like a great cathedral rising in the midst of a busy town, with its daily persuasions to the soul. Such is the higher aspect of the religious life, of which the Puritan teaching knew but little. Yet, once more, the pressing peril of religion to-day lies in its divorce from the religion of the past. The opportunities of religion are but enervating influences unless they grow out of its obligations. Among the essays of Mr. Hutton, there is one which deals with what he calls the "Hard Church." It is the body of those whose faith is rigid, dogmatic, authoritative, obligatory. Certainly, the Puritans belonged to the hard church; and we may be grateful that a gentler age has come. But a kindred peril besets the modern world. It is the danger of falling into the ranks of what we must call the "soft church," — soft, because instead of faith it has a mush of sentiment, with no vertebrated thought or rigid ethics, with the nature of a mollusk rather than the nature of a man. The hard church sees the obligations of religion, and fails to see its gentler graces. The soft church sees the opportunities of religion, but builds on no rock of obligation. It is tolerant toward other beliefs, because it has no strong belief of its own. It is broad, but thin. It calls itself liberal, when it is only spiritually indolent, and is liberal only because it is soft. The soft church thinks religion is to be had without effort, — that while a man has to work to be rich or learned, he ought, somehow, to get his religion easily. It is fond of quoting that God can be had for the asking, as though that asking for God did not mean all the wrestling and waiting which the Puritan religion knew so well. Oh for some renewal of a more strenuous faith amid this world of religious opportunity which opens so easily before us in our day! If a man would build up into these higher opportunities, he must build down to the substructure of the sense of obligation. He must discipline himself to await his summons, or the summons will come to him in vain. He must endure hardness as a good soldier of Jesus Christ, or the soft church will claim him as its own.

Thus it is that the morals and faith of the Puritans stand in relation to the morals and faith of to-day.

We have passed from the domain of the Puritan scheme, and we are grateful. We thank God that we are brought " out of a strait into a broad place." Yet the way of life before us is not that of reaction, — it is that of evolution. There never was a time which needed more a background of the Puritan spirit. We need in our business morals a sterner sense of the fear of God. We need in our home life a renewed simplicity. We need in our religion a revival of discipline and responsibility. It is the Puritan calling to us across centuries, and summoning us to the readjustment of the present with the past.

And, finally, where shall this profoundest problem of the time be most fitly solved? In what kind of a community is it likely that faith shall thus grow large, continuous, and stable? The Puritan had his answer to this question. He believed that when men desired to advance the kingdom of God in a community, the best thing they could do was to found a college. We, too, reaching across the gulf of years, join hands with the Puritans in this belief. We know that what threatens religious truth is not — as many vainly cry — increase of learning, but increase of ignorance. We know that when minds are truly learned, they become not self-asserting or self-sufficient, but humble and tolerant in the presence of that unfathomed mystery into which all their learning opens. We know that the soft church is made up of the undisciplined minds, the superficial theologians, the self-sufficiency of ignorance. Just as we know that the first glimpse of learning has turned many minds from religion, so we know that it is by the higher learning that religious conviction must be restored. If scholarship must change prevailing conceptions, it is for a higher scholarship to bring in a new reverence. The atmosphere of a true university should be an atmosphere pervaded by the sanctity of all learning honestly pursued. A college dedicated to Truth ought to be the servant of Christ and of his Church.

Thus, then, in the name and in the service of religion, we praise and honor our University. We thank God that her way has been removed from a strait place and broadened toward a larger destiny. The fathers built their little skiff and launched it in circumscribed and familiar waters, and it served them well; but an unheeded current bore it slowly down toward the tide and the scent of the sea. Their sons enlarged and strengthened it, and ventured forth beyond the headlands in brief and timid voyages of discovery. For us, the skiff has been transformed into a mighty vessel; and all the oceans of research are open to it and all the continents of knowledge wait beyond, and its dependence is no longer on the changeful winds which blow upon it, but on a motive power which is within itself. God give it many a prosperous voyage, and make it the bearer of many an honest man on many a manly errand!

# SERMON.

### BY THE REV. PHILLIPS BROOKS, D.D.,

*Rector of Trinity Church, Boston.*

---

JESUS CHRIST, THE SAME YESTERDAY, TO-DAY, AND FOR EVER. — *Hebrews* xiii. 8.

THERE is no finer effort of the imagination than that which, at times like this, clothes a great institution with personality, and makes it live in all the fulness of intelligence and affection and will. It is not an uncommon power. The finest powers are not those which are exceptional and rare, but those which belong in general to all humanity, and constitute the proof-marks of its excellence. In every age the member of the body of Christ has seen the great expression of Christ's life of which he was a part stand forth sublime and gracious as Mother-Church. In every time of national peril and preservation the patriot has been able to cry out to his beloved land standing before him in personal distinctness, —

> "O Beautiful! my Country! ours once more!
> Smoothing thy gold of war-dishevelled hair
> O'er such sweet brows as never other wore!"

In every period of her history the College has been a true person, a very Alma Mater to her children.

The vividness of such personification must be great in proportion to the prominence and distinctness of human life in the institution which thus assumes personality. Not the railroad or the factory, things of machinery, but the church or the college, things of men, stand forth like great human beings and accept their titles when we call them *he* or *she*. And just because she has human life within her in its most vivid and eager and critical time and shape, does a college most readily and thoroughly become the subject of this mysterious and beautiful process by which out of the confused and tumultuous experiences of uncounted men there issues as we gaze upon them one great image, which is, strangely, at once the aggregate and embodiment of them, and also something greater than them all, — their protector and nurse, their teacher, friend, and mother. It is out of the infinite human experience and pathos of this place, — it is out of the way in which these buildings and these grounds have been the scenes of so much human life for these two hundred and fifty years; of struggles and hopes and fears and aspirations; of doubts and dreads; of men's conflicts with themselves, and of men's coming to the knowledge of themselves; of solitudes and associations; of gainings of faith and of losings of faith; of triumphs and of despairs; of temptations and of ecstasies, — it is out of all this hovering like a great cloud over, rising like a great exhalation from, the long history of Harvard College and its generations of men, that slowly, mysteriously, but at last very clearly, there shapes itself as we look, as the great outcome of the whole, a majestic being which we call the College, with human features and capacities, with eyes to smile or frown on us, with a mouth to praise us or rebuke us, with a heart to love us, with a will to rule us and to fix standards for our life.

It is that embodiment of the College as a gigantic gracious personality that is most present with her children who have come up to her festival. She sits like Jerusalem upon her hills, "the mother of us all." It is that personal presence which is with us here to-night. What I want to do in the time which I may occupy with this sermon, is to remind myself and you that this great being whom we reverence and love must stand in some conscious relation and obedience to universal being, must feel her life included in some larger life, or else she fails of her best growth and good; and to see how that larger life in which hers must be inclosed, and out of which it is to be fed, is expressed in these words out of the old Epistle to the Hebrews, "Jesus Christ, the same yesterday, to-day, and for ever."

The necessity of which I speak is universal. There is no life which fulfils itself entirely and worthily except as it is inclosed within the grasp of a life larger than its own. Such inclosure may be represented as an obedience to which the life is bound, a service which it is compelled to render, — or, more truly, as the existence within an element which is its natural supply and food. Just think how numerous the illustrations are. Each man must feel about him the grasp of the total humanity to which he belongs: if he does not, he becomes unhuman. Each truth must be aware of the great whole of truth of which it utters a fragment: if it does not, it becomes untrue. Each star must quiver with the movement of the system, or it is a mere waif and stray of brilliance, living at random in the sky. Each article of faith must feel the creed around it. Each class in the community must live in the larger life of the community, which is above all classes and embraces all. Each nation must be part of the federation of the world. Each age in history must be conscious of all human history in whose embrace it is held, and of the vast eternity in which all the history of this world, all time, swims as a cloud swims in the limitless sky. The Christian in the church, the citizen in the state, the institution in the commonwealth, — everywhere you have this principle of elemental life; the principle that every life except the greatest lives in its element, the partial in the universal, the temporary in the eternal; that, whether they be actively conscious of it or not, all things that really live are feeding themselves out of a great atmosphere of larger life which surrounds them, and to which they must forever keep themselves open. The part which knows itself and lives in obedience and receptivity to its great whole is strong. The part which calls itself a whole, and shuts itself up against the inflow of that universal which is "ever green," grows dry and barren and desolate, and dies.

Of how many dying lives of men and institutions is the secret here! All false partisanship, all barren specialism, all intellectual and spiritual selfishness, is but the effort of the part to take itself out of the embrace of the whole. The healthy partisanship is always reaching out toward the universal interests and methods. The healthy specialism is always bathing itself in the absolute and universal truth.

And now it is the privilege of festival times like those which our college is to keep to-morrow, that in them the part finds and feels anew its deep relations to the whole of things. That which the clash and clamor of detail, the necessary absorption of busy life in its own operations, has shut out and silenced, presses in and makes itself heard. The universal claims the special. The Infinite and Eternal makes itself known to the temporary and the finite. The planet stops one second to wonder at its own mysterious life, and then the thrill of the suns comes pouring in upon it. The one enthusiastic study pauses for an instant, and in that quiet moment it feels the grasp of all knowledge warm around it. In its great anniversary days the city bathes itself in the higher loyalty, the broader patriotism, of the State. On his birthday, when he stops his work to gather up his life, the man knows himself more than the individual; the whole humanity to which he belongs grows clear to him.

Nor is this something which belongs only to the day of anniversary observance; it comes with the lapse of history itself. Every institution which healthily lives is always in the very process of its life freeing itself more and more from slavery to its partial and temporary connections, and entering into broader relations with the true element of its existence. All healthy action and movement tends to more and more liberated and enlarged relation to the intended conditions and elemental supply of the thing which acts and moves. There is no truer sign of the divine presence in, the divine care of, the world than that. The Church of Christ begins almost as a Jewish institution. It is wrapt around with Jewish prejudices; it treads at every step on the lines of Jewish exclusiveness. But it lives, it moves, it does its work; and by and by it has found out for itself, and it is asserting before the world, that its field is universal human nature, that the true element of its existence is a sympathy as broad as human kind. A man begins on some limited occupation. His care and interests are shut in to the little thing that he is doing. He thinks of himself only as the shoemaker or tailor. Is it not good, is it not beautiful, to see how as he faithfully does his one thing year after year his relation to other things that other men are doing but which he will never do, and to the whole of life in which his thing and all those other things are included, opens around him and becomes real to him, and he comes more and more to be not only the shoemaker and tailor, but the man? If that broadening is not always going on, he is not working faithfully. So every true action in any sphere makes real the larger spheres in which we live. Long service of any master makes us feel the higher masteries, and sets us free to serve them. The longer we live truly in time the more we breathe the breath of eternity. The more largely we work in our specialty, the more we enter into the sense of the divineness of all work, the more we are the brothers of all workers everywhere.

It would be terrible if it were not so. It is terrible that it is not so to hosts of workers in their drudgeries. Alas for the man who is not growing into broader sympathy with men the longer that he does his special work! Alas for the institution that does not feel all life clamorous and profuse about it, the longer that it goes on building its little corner or laying its bit of the foundation of the great structure! Each has missed the best result of living, which is that life enlarges itself by its own healthy action, — *solvitur ambulando*, — and grows more conscious and more receptive of the true element of its existence the longer and more faithfully it does its work.

I have dwelt long on these first principles, because in them I find the key of the meaning of this college festival. All thankfulness for the past, all hope for the great future, depends I think on this, — on whether the University which we profoundly love has grown towards, and shall continually grow more and more into, a full obedience to the great masteries, a full acceptance of the great elemental influences and supplies on which all life must feed, into the fuller and fuller relation to God and universal human life which can alone make her and keep her what she ought to be. Let us see, with a hurried glance at some points in her history, whether there is any light upon the question which must rest heavily on many of her children's minds.

First, then, it is hard to realize, although history clearly tells us of it, how definite and limited and special was the foundation of Harvard College. It lay like a round, compact ball of light in the intention of its founders. It had no relations with any region of human life except its own. To make ministers of a certain faith and of a certain order, — that faith conceived of as the final expression of the truth of God; that order accepted as the appointed means for men's salvation, — to create certain types of experience and to protect an acknowledged system of church discipline, this was the end for which the college was established. Learning was valued, but it was valued for this end. Never was there a system more clearly conceived, more definitely limited, than that New England Puritanism. The great world of humanity lay around it unfelt, unregarded. All secular interests were absorbed into it, and where they could not be absorbed were ignored or denounced. Like a rock in a great sea, resting upon its own foundations, beaten upon by waves of which it took no manner of account, so stands the Puritanism of the seventeenth century, and the Harvard College which it built in the midst of the multifarious and restless history of man.

The history of the college since that time of its foundation has been the story of a constant opening of this intense and limited and narrow life to the great human world by which it was surrounded.

The years have brought perpetual enlargement. That narrowness and specialness of the seventeenth century Puritanism has shown how healthy it was even in its isolation, by the capacity which it has developed to blend once more with larger human life, and make itself more and more truly human.

There are four periods coming almost at the beginning and in the middle of each century, almost exactly fifty years apart, which seem to me to mark the stages of this outward pulsation of our college life, this feeling of and response to humanity around it. They have all taken the form of special controversies, but their spirit was larger and deeper than their form.

At the beginning of the eighteenth century came the struggle about church discipline. There was a bursting open of the tight, compact body of technical sainthood. Increase Mather, the great exponent of the genius and nature out of which the college sprang, published on the 1st of March, 1700, his "Order of the Gospel Justified." "Sundry ministers of the Gospel in New England" replied to him. The real question was, who should be counted true subjects of the Christian sacraments? When Increase Mather and his son Cotton were defeated, it was a sign that the earnestness which existed in human life at large had made itself felt within the church, and that the hard close envelope of church discipline had broken open.

Fifty years later came another contest, resulting in a new enlargement. In 1736 there was a "great awakening" or revival of religion in Northampton, where Jonathan Edwards was preaching his intense and earnest gospel. In 1740 George Whitfield came like a great wind of God across the land. The college life was stirred. The sober souls grew fearful of enthusiasm. President Holyoke preached against Pharisaism; and Dr. Wigglesworth, the Hollis Professor, wrote a strong letter to the great English Evangelist, protesting against his aspersions on the college piety. It is not necessary to take sides in the old dead dispute; certainly it is not necessary for us to praise in full what no doubt was a very lukewarm condition of religious zeal, — but we may well rejoice in the occurrence as a breaking open of what had been a very hard and tight idea of religious experience. It was a protest in behalf of the variety and spontaneity of spiritual life; it was a claiming of its rights for the soul of man. So it was in the region of experience a true enlargement of the deep life of the college.

The nineteenth century began with a more serious convulsion. In 1805 the Rev. Henry Ware was chosen, after a long struggle, to the Hollis Professorship of Divinity. Once more, we need not commit ourselves to his theology, nor to that which for many years after remained the ruling theology of the University, in order to recognize that in that act and all which was connected with it there was a true breaking open of the shell of dogma and a participation by the college thought in the more universal currents which were sweeping through the world. It was an opening of the truth to the more general influence of Truth. It was as if a skin-full of water which had been floating in the ocean had burst, and the water in it had flowed out and the water of the mighty ocean had flowed in.

All these enlargements were within the sphere of what is technically called theology. Need I remind you of how in these more recent days, in the third and fourth quarters of this nineteenth century, technical theology itself has broken open and mingled itself with life. New sciences have claimed that they too have revelations to give us of the will and ways of God. The actual life of men, the problems of the personal soul, the perplexities of social life, — these, as well as the abstractions of the intellect, have proved their power to waken doubt and to inspire faith. You cannot separate theology any longer by sharp lines from psychology and sociology. The open doors of the college chapel into which no man henceforth is driven, from which no man is excluded, in and out of which men pass spontaneously and freely, give a true symbol of the way in which theology and life — what men have loved to call the sacred, and what men have dared to call the profane — flow freely in and out of one another.

These, very hurriedly suggested, are the four. The enlargement of Discipline, the enlargement of Experience, the enlargement of Dogma, the enlargement of Life, — these are the successive openings of the envelopes which have inclosed the thought and action of the college, until at last it stands free to draw its inspiration from, and to exercise its influence upon, the whole activity of man.

What meaning shall we see in all this? No doubt it is possible enough to see no meaning, or to see low meanings, in it. Possible enough to see no meaning, to think of it all as a long dynasty of accidents, — chance killing chance, and taking possession of the vacant throne. If that is all, then nobody can guess the future from this past: on into utter recklessness or back into a darker and severer superstition than any from which she has escaped, either way, this chance-governed, ungoverned world of ours may go. Possible to give it all a low meaning; possible enough to see in it nothing but the casting off of restraint after restraint, in order that at last all traces of connection with the supernatural shall disappear, and the slavery and degradation of pure secularism shall be complete, — until at last religion and the mystery of life shall be forever dissipated, and the thin, hard, and colorless relic which is left shall lie staring upon us in the glare of the electric light which men choose to call by the great name of science.

Either of these ways of looking at it all is possible. But there is yet another and a higher possibility. There may be in all this progress of enlargement which we have traced a richer and more gracious meaning. It may signify — we believe that it does signify — the partial gradually reconciling itself to the universal; the temporary, little by little, fulfilling itself with the eternal. There was a discipline of

the Christian Church larger than the discipline of
the Puritans, in which the discipline of the Puritans
had floated as the part floats in the whole. The
discipline of the Puritans felt that; was pressed on,
was tempted by it, and at last broke open in the
attempt to find it. Experience was larger than Whitfield, Dogma was larger than Calvin, Life was larger
than Theology; and so one after another, in these
which are the concentric spheres within which human
nature lives, the successive openings of the partial
into the universal, and the temporary into the eternal, came. Not less but more mysterious and rich
and religious is the little floating part when it hears
the vast whole on every side of it calling with deep
voice, and opens its small existence and is first filled
and then absorbed by the complete, which is greater
than its partialness.

And now I know that you have felt how I have
been circling about my text, and just upon the point
of touching it. What is this whole, after which all
the partial life of our great College has been reaching, toward which she has been enlarging herself
all these two hundred and fifty years? What is
this universal and eternal power within which these
and all the temporary struggles of mankind are included? We open the Sacred Book, we turn to the
majestic letter written centuries ago to members of
the great sacred nation, and there we find our answer: "Jesus Christ, the same yesterday, to-day,
and for ever."

And what and who is Jesus Christ? In reverence and humility let us give our answer. He is the meeting of the Divine and Human, — the presence of God in humanity, the perfection of humanity in God; the divine made human, the human shown to be capable of union with the divine; the utterance therefore of the nearness and the love of God, and of the possibility of man. Once in the ages came the wondrous life, once in the stretch of history the face of Jesus shone in Palestine, and his feet left their blessed impress upon earth; but what that life made manifest had been forever true. Its truth was timeless, the truth of all eternity. The love of God, the possibility of man, — these two which made the Christhood, — these two, not two, but one, had been the element in which all life was lived, all knowledge known, all growth attained. Oh, how little men have made it, and how great it is! Around all life which ever has been lived there has been poured forever the life of the loving deity and the ideal humanity. All partial excellence, all learning, all brotherhood, all hope has been bosomed on this changeless, this unchanging Being which has stretched from the forgotten beginning to the unguessed end. It is because God has been always, and been always good, and because man has been always the son of God, capable in the very substance of his nature of likeness to and union with his Father, — it is because of this that nobleness has never died, that truth has been sought and found, that struggle and hope have always sprung anew, and that the life of man has always reached to larger and to larger things.

This is the Christian truth of Christ. "In Him was life, and the life was the light of men." This is the truth of man's redemption. As any man or any institution feels and claims around its life, as the element in which it is to live, the sympathy of God and the perfectibility of man, that man or institution is redeemed; its fetters and restraints give way, and it goes forward to whatever growth and glory it is in the line of its being to attain.

It is the duty of an anniversary to test and recognize the relation in which a man or a venerable college stands to this element of the Christhood, to the goodness of God and the greatness of man, as making together the atmosphere of life. Think then about the history of our college as we hurriedly traced it. Is its true explanation here? Has all this constant enlargement of its life been moving towards the great truths of the goodness of God and the sublime capacity of man? It must be so. Our progress of these two centuries and a half would be a terrible mockery if it were not so, — if, whether we are conscious of it or not, we had not been always advancing towards a deeper, warmer, truer certainty of the divine love surrounding us, and a profounder assurance of the unexhausted capacity of man whose faculties were finding training here.

"Whether we are conscious of it or not," I say; for one of the assurances which comes to us most clearly at a time of festival like this, is that our history has been under diviner guidance and has moved toward nobler ends than we have understood. The college has been in greater, holier hands than she has known. Alas for the college, if these two hundred and fifty years have meant for her no more than she has been able to see that they were meaning! In many ways it seems as if she had been strangely and specially unable to read the deeper meanings of her history. Our college is not quick to believe the highest things about herself. Our Harvard way is, as a whole, to read life on its negative side more than on its positive. We think of such enlargements as I have depicted rather as escapes from bigotry and superstition than as possible entrances into deeper faith. We dwell more on the exposure of error than on the discovery of truth in spiritual things. We are more afraid of believing something which we ought not to believe, than of not believing something which we ought to believe. We distrust the enthusiasms of faith. As we loose our ship from any moorings of the past to sail out into any great uncertain ocean of the future, we are more ready to listen to the malarial voices which cry to us from the shore, "Begone, Begone!" than to hear the great deep with its unbounded inspirations bidding us, "Come on, Come on!" Who of us does not know this temper of our good mother, and how sedulously she instils it into her children?

Therefore it is that more than most institutions our University has lived under greater forces and for greater ends than she has habitually acknowledged to herself. Therefore it is that in her commemorative season our University is specially bound to look deep into her own life, to look broadly across her own history, and to see with unhesitating eyes what diviner significance than she has known has been in her. If when she only said to herself that she was training boys to make their living, giving them good habits, showing them how to study, now and then by the way discovering a bit of truth which had not been known before, now and then by the way casting out a bit of error which had been proved untrue, — if all the time when she has been seeming to herself to be doing only this, God has been bearing testimony in her to the nearness of His love and to the divineness of manhood as His child, — now at her festival, when she gathers all her history up into her consciousness and stands in awe before herself, now is the time for her to boldly recognize her own profounder meaning, to own the Christhood within which she has lived, and to give her whole future up to it for government and help and blessing. My friends, brethren in the love and care of our great mother, let us do that for her. Let us demand of her to do that for herself to-day.

What does it mean, to do that? How can she do that, does she ask? Let her remember, let her know, that Christ is law as well as truth; Christ is righteousness as well as revelation. The Christhood which is yesterday, to-day, and forever is the perpetual utterance of the unchanging ordinance of God that only through the doing of the right does man come to the knowledge of the true. Let then the college which seeks the highest truth in Christ accept the necessity of righteousness as the sole doorway and avenue to it. We miss this great conviction in too much of our University history. In the multitude of our police regulations, in the thoroughly economical view of conduct which a great community begets, we feel too rarely the great inspiration of righteousness as opening the way to truth, of character as the medium through which light can flow. "Blessed are the pure in heart, for they shall see God,"—are those words too lofty, too transcendent, to write on the new portal of the college yard? Would they be but a mockery of the baser thoughts of life, the lower ideas of learning, which the yard contains? Alas for the college if that be so! for only when a great University cultivates character and insists on righteousness, because so only can she know the real truth concerning the divine and human, concerning God and man, only then has she claimed her place within that power which bridges the eternities; only then has she really given herself to Jesus Christ, the same yesterday, today, and forever.

To such a University, cultivating righteousness as the medium of faith, must come great privileges. We love to think that she must become a great home of reconciliations. In her calm and lofty air the friends of whom the world would make foes must meet and own their friendship. Science and religion, faith and reason, individuality and society, conservatism and radicalism, poverty and wealth, the past and the future, — these must join hands and walk in peace with one another in a city of scholars, where not in the base spirit of compromise, but in the higher atmosphere of universal and eternal truth and duty, the essential unity of all good things shall be made manifest and clear.

I hope that I have made clear the thought of the college which was upon my heart when I began to speak. Let me put that thought in a single word as I close. Behind all life, before all life, above all life, below all life is Christ. As the world lives in the sky, so all life lives in Him. He is the power and love of God and the divine capacity in man, not held as truths, but folded in personal inspiration around the life which lives in them. All progress, all enlargement of any institution consists in nearer and freer and more spiritual approach to Him. His method of drawing lives to Him is the method of enlightenment through righteousness. We are thankful for all the righteous life of the past. We pray for honesty, uprightness, purity, courage in the future, because through these the college must more and more cease to be an isolated struggle in a special field. More and more it must become a part of the great onward movement of the purposes of God, — a part of the great everlasting development of man into the measure of the stature of the fulness of Christ.

How can we better close than with these words out of this same Epistle to the Hebrews : " We are made partakers of Christ if we hold the beginning of our confidence steadfast unto the end." There is no break in such a history as ours. To ever larger duty, to ever larger truth, the old college goes forth under the perpetual inspirations of faith in God and faith in man. Those two together make the faith of Christ. May He who has been our master from the far-off beginning, be our master, ever more and more acknowledged, ever more and more obeyed, on even to the distant end!

# THE ALUMNI DAY.

THE main features of this day were the services in Sanders Theatre in the forenoon, and the dinner, with the addresses, in the afternoon.

# THE ALUMNI DAY.

NOVEMBER 8, 1886.

―――•―――

I.

## The Services in Sanders Theatre.

THE President of the Association of the Alumni advanced and spoke as follows: —

### OPENING ADDRESS.

BY THE HONORABLE CHARLES DEVENS.

MR. PRESIDENT, BRETHREN OF THE ALUMNI:

I congratulate you that we are assembled in such full numbers on this interesting occasion and in the presence of the authorities of the University, who unite with us in its celebration.

Together on this day we are entitled to enjoy the history and the memories of the past two hundred and fifty years during which our cherished institution has had its life, and hopefully to anticipate for it an ever-widening sphere of usefulness in the years which are to come.

On your behalf, and on that of all present, I welcome most cordially the honored President of the United States, and the members of his cabinet who accompany him; his Excellency the Governor of the Commonwealth; the delegates from other universities and colleges; and the other distinguished guests who honor us by their presence.

Without preface, I will ask your attention to the literary exercises which have been arranged. Neither orator nor poet will need any introduction from me to you.

At their conclusion, the President of the University will make certain announcements from his ancient academic chair, to which I am sure you will gladly listen.

In your name, Brethren, I invite the Rev. Prof. FRANCIS G. PEABODY to commence our day with prayer.

After the prayer and singing, the Orator and Poet each took his place in turn at the desk.

## ORATION.

### BY JAMES RUSSELL LOWELL.

*Professor in the University.*

IT seems an odd anomaly, that, while respect for age and deference to its opinions have diminished and are still sensibly diminishing among us, the relish of antiquity should be more pungent, and the value set upon things merely because they are old should be greater in America than anywhere else. It is merely a sentimental relish; for ours is a new country in more senses than one, and like children when they are fancying themselves this or that, we have to play very hard in order to believe that we are old. But we like the game none the worse, and multiply our anniversaries with honest zeal, as if we increased our centuries by the number of events we could congratulate on having happened a hundred years ago. There is something of instinct in this; and it is a wholesome instinct, if it serve to quicken our consciousness of the forces that are gathered by duration and continuity, — if it teach us that, ride fast and far as we may, we carry the Past on our crupper, as immovably seated there as the black Care of the Roman poet. The generations of men are braided inextricably together, and the very trick of our gait may be countless generations older than we.

I have sometimes wondered whether as the faith of men in a future existence grew less confident, they might not be seeking some equivalent in the feeling of a retrospective duration, if not their own, at least that of their race. Yet even this continuance is trifling and ephemeral. If the tablets unearthed and deciphered by geology have forced us to push back incalculably the birthday of man, they have in like proportion impoverished his recorded annals, making even the Platonic year but as a single grain of the sand in Time's hour-glass, and the inscriptions of Egypt and Assyria modern as yesterday's newspaper. Fancy flutters over these vague wastes like a butterfly blown out to sea, and finds no foothold. It is true that if we may put as much faith in heredity as seems reasonable to many of us, we are all in some

transcendental sense the coevals of primitive man, and
Pythagoras may well have been present in Euphorbus
at the siege of Troy. Had Shakespeare's thought
taken this turn when he said to Time, —

> "Thy pyramids built up with newer might
> To me are nothing novel, nothing strange;
> They are but dressings of a former sight."

But this imputed and vicarious longevity, though it
may be obscurely operative in our lives and fortunes,
is no valid offset for the shortness of our days, nor
widens by a hair's breadth the horizon of our memories. Man and his monuments are of yesterday, and
we, however we may play with our fancies, must content ourselves with being young. If youth be a defect,
it is one that we outgrow only too soon.

Mr. Ruskin said the other day that he could not live
in a country that had neither castles nor cathedrals;
and doubtless men of imaginative temper find not only
charm but inspiration in structures which Nature has
adopted as her foster-children, and on which Time has
laid his hand only in benediction. It is not their antiquity, but its association with man, that endows
them with such sensitizing potency. Even the landscape sometimes bewitches us by this glamour of a
human past; and the green pastures and golden slopes
of England are sweeter both to the outward and to
the inward eye that the hand of man has immemorially
cared for and caressed them. The nightingale sings
with more prevailing passion in Greece that we first
heard her from the thickets of a Euripidean chorus.
For myself, I never felt the working of this spell so

acutely as in those gray seclusions of the college quadrangles and cloisters at Oxford and Cambridge, conscious with venerable associations, and whose very stones seemed happier for growing old there. The chapel pavement still whispered with the blessed feet of that long procession of saints and sages, and scholars and poets, who are all gone into a world of light, but whose memories seem to consecrate the soul from any ignobler companionship.

Are we to suppose that these memories were less dear and gracious to the Puritan scholars, at whose instigation this college was founded, than to that other Puritan who sang the "dim religious light," the "long-drawn aisle and fretted vault," which these memories recalled? Doubtless all these things were present to their minds, but they were ready to forego them all for the sake of that truth whereof, as Milton says of himself, they were members incorporate. The pitiful contrast which they must have felt between the carven sanctuaries of learning they had left behind and the wattled fold they were rearing here on the edge of the wilderness, is to me more than tenderly — it is almost sublimely — pathetic. When I think of their unpliable strength of purpose, their fidelity to their ideal, their faith in God and in themselves, I am inclined to say with Donne that

"We are scarce our fathers' shadows cast at noon."

Our past is well-nigh desolate of æsthetic stimulus. We have none, or next to none, of these aids to the imagination, of these coigns of vantage for the tendrils of memory or affection. Not one of our older buildings is venerable, or will ever become so. Time refuses to console them. They all look as if they meant business, and nothing more. And it is precisely because this college meant business, business of the gravest import, and did that business as thoroughly as it might with no means that were not niggardly except an abundant purpose to do its best, — it is precisely for this that we have gathered here to-day. We come back hither from the experiences of a richer life, as the son who has prospered returns to the household of his youth, to find in its very homeliness a pulse, if not of deeper, certainly of fonder, emotion than any splendor could stir. "Dear old mother," we say, "how charming you are in your plain cap and the drab silk that has been turned again since we saw you! You were constantly forced to remind us that you could not afford to give us this and that which some other boys had; but your discipline and diet were wholesome, and you sent us forth into the world with the sound constitutions and healthy appetites that are bred of simple fare."

It is good for us to commemorate this homespun past of ours; good, in these days of a reckless and swaggering prosperity, to remind ourselves how poor our fathers were, and that we celebrate them because for themselves and their children they chose wisdom and understanding and the things that are of God rather than any other riches. This is our Founders' Day, and we are come together to do honor to them all: first, to the Commonwealth which laid our corner-stone; next, to the gentle and godly youth from whom we took our name, — himself scarce more than a name; and with them to the countless throng of benefactors, rich and poor, who have built us up to what we are. We cannot do it better than in the familiar words: " Let us now praise famous men and our fathers that begat us. The Lord hath wrought great glory by them through his great power from the beginning. Leaders of the people by their counsels, and by their knowledge of learning meet for the people; wise and eloquent in their instructions. There be of them that have left a name behind them that their praises might be reported. And some there be which have no memorial, who are perished as though they had never been. But these were merciful men whose righteousness hath not been forgotten. With their seed shall continually remain a good inheritance. Their seed standeth fast, and their children for their sakes."

This two hundred and fiftieth anniversary of our college is not remarkable as commemorating any memorable length of days. There is hardly a country in Europe but can show us universities that were older than ours now is when ours was but a grammar-school, with Eaton as master. Bologna, Paris, Oxford were already famous schools when Dante visited them (as I love to think he did) six hundred years ago. We are ancient, it is true, on our own continent,—ancient even as compared with several German universities more renowned than we. But it is not primarily the longevity of our Alma Mater upon which we are gathered here to congratulate her and each other. Kant says somewhere, that, as the records of human transactions accumulate, the memory of man will have room only for those of supreme cosmopolitical importance. Can we claim for the birthday we are keeping a significance of so wide a bearing and so long a reach? If we may not do that, we may at least affirm confidently that the event it records and emphasizes is second in real import to none that has happened in this western hemisphere. The material growth of the colonies would have brought about their political separation from the Mother Country in the fulness of time, without that stain of blood which unhappily keeps its own memory green so long. But the founding of the first English college here was what saved New England from becoming a mere geographical expression. It did more; for it insured, and I believe was meant to insure, our intellectual independence of the Old World. That independence has been long in coming, but it will come at last; and are not the names of the chiefest of those who have hastened its coming written on the roll of Harvard College?

I think this foundation of ours a quite unexampled thing. Surely never were the bases of such a structure as this has become, and was meant to be, laid by a community of men so poor, in circumstances so unprecedented, and under what seemed such sullen and averted stars. The colony, still insignificant, was in danger of an Indian war; was in the throes of that Antinomian controversy which threatened its very existence, — yet the leaders of opinion on both sides were united in the resolve that sound learning and an educated clergy should never cease from among them or their descendants in the commonwealth they were building up. In the midst of such fears and such tumults Harvard College was born, and not Marina herself had a more blusterous birth or a more chiding nativity. The prevision of those men must have been as clear as their faith was steadfast. Well they knew and had laid to heart the wise man's precept, "Take fast hold of instruction; let her not go; for she is thy life."

There can be little question that the action of the General Court received its impulse and direction from the clergy, men of eminent qualities and of well-deserved authority. Among the Massachusetts Bay colonists the proportion of ministers, trained at Oxford and Cambridge, was surprisingly large; and if we may trust the evidence of contemporary secular literature, such men as Higginson, Cotton, Wilson, Norton, Shepard, Bulkley, Davenport, to mention no more, were in learning, intelligence, and general accomplishment far above the average parson of the country and the church from which their consciences had driven them out. The presence and influence of such men were of inestimable consequence to the fortunes of the colony. If they were narrow, it was as the sword of righteousness is narrow. If they had but one idea, it was as the leader of a forlorn hope has but one, and can have no other, — namely, to do the duty that is laid on him, and ask no questions. Our Puritan ancestors have been misrepresented and maligned by persons without imagination enough to make themselves contemporary with, and therefore able to understand, the men whose memories they strive to blacken. That happy breed of men who both in Church and State led our first emigration, were children of the most splendid intellectual epoch that England has ever known. They were the coevals of a generation which passed on in scarcely diminished radiance the torch of life kindled in great Eliza's golden days. Out of the new learning, the new ferment alike religious and national, and the new discoveries with their suggestion of boundless possibility, the alembic of that age had distilled a potent elixir either inspiring or intoxicating, as the mind that imbibed it was strong or weak. Are we to suppose that the lips of the founders of New England alone were unwetted by a drop of that stimulating draught? — that Milton was the only Puritan who had read Marlow and Shakespeare, and Ben Jonson and Beaumont and Fletcher? I do not believe it, whoever may. It was from the natural sympathy of a gentleman and scholar with gentlemen and scholars, that holy George Herbert wrote, —

> "Religion stands a-tiptoe in this land,
> Ready to part for the American strand."

Did they flee from persecution to become themselves persecutors in turn? This means only that they would not permit their holy enterprise to be hindered or their property to be damaged even by men with the most pious intentions, and as sincere, if not always so wise, as they. They would not stand any nonsense, as the phrase is, — a mood of mind from which their descendants seem somewhat to have degenerated. They were no more unreasonable than the landlady of Taylor the Platonist, in refusing to let him sacrifice a bull to Jupiter in her back-parlor. The New England Puritans of the second generation became narrow enough, and puppets of that formalism against which their fathers had revolted. But this was the inevitable result of that isolation which cut them off from the great currents of cosmopolitan thought and action. Communities as well as men have a right to be judged by their best. We are justified in taking the elder Winthrop as a type of the leading emigrants; and the more we know him the more we learn to reverence his great qualities, whether of mind or character. The posterity of those earnest and single-minded men may have thrown the creed of their fathers into the waste-basket, but their fidelity to it and to the duties they believed it to involve is the most precious and potent drop in their transmitted blood. It is especially noteworthy that they did not make a strait-waistcoat of this creed for their new college. The more I meditate upon them, the more I am inclined to pardon the enthusiasm of our old preacher, when he said that God had sifted three kingdoms to plant New England.

The Massachusetts Bay Colony itself also was then and since without a parallel. It was established by a commercial company, whose members combined in themselves the two by no means incongruous elements of religious enthusiasm and business sagacity, — the earthy ingredient, as in dynamite, holding in check its explosive partner, which yet could and did explode on sufficient concussion. They meant that their venture should be gainful, but at the same time believed that nothing could be long profitable for the body wherein the soul found not also her advantage. They feared God, and kept their powder dry because they feared Him and meant that others should. I think their most remarkable characteristic was their public spirit; and in nothing did they show both that and the wise forecast that gives it its best value more clearly, than when they resolved to keep the higher education of youth in their own hands and under their own eye. This they provided for in the college. Eleven years later they established their system of public schools, where reading and writing should be taught. This they did partly, no doubt, to provide feeders for the more advanced schools, and so for the college; but even more, it may safely be inferred, because they had found that the polity to which their ends — rough-hew them as they might — must be shaped by the conditions under which they were forced to act, could be safe only in the hands of intelligent men, or, at worst, of men to whom they had given a chance to become such.

In founding the college they had three objects: first, the teaching of the Humanities and of Hebrew, as the hieratic language; second, the training of a learned as well as godly clergy; and third, the education of the Indians, that they might serve as missionaries of a higher civilization and of a purer religion, as the necessary preliminary thereto. The third of these objects, after much effort and much tribulation, they were forced to abandon. John Winthrop, Jr., in a letter written to the Honorable Robert Boyle in 1663, gives us an interesting glimpse of a pair of these dusky catechumens. "I make bold," he says, "to send heere inclosed a kind of rarity. . . . It is two papers of Latin composed by two Indians now scollars in the colledge in this country, and the writing is with their own hands. . . . Possibly as a novelty of that kind it may be acceptable, being a reall fruit of that hopefull worke y$^t$ is begū amongst them, . . . testifying thus much that I received them of those Indians out of their own hands, and had ready answers frō them in Latin to many questions that I propounded to them in y$^t$ language, and heard them both express severall sentences in Greke also. I doubt not but those honorable *Fautores Scientiarum* [the Royal Society] will gladly receive the intelligence of such *vestigia doctrinæ* in this wilderness amongst such a barbarous people." Alas, these *vestigia* became only too soon *retrorsum!* The Indians showed a far greater natural predisposition for disfurnishing the outside of other people's heads than for furnishing the insides of their own. Their own wild life must have been dear to them; the forest beckoned just outside the college door, and the first blue-bird of spring whistled them back to the woods. They would have said to the President, with the gypsy steward in the old play, when he heard the new-come nightingale, — "Oh, sir, you hear; I am called." At any rate, our college succeeded in keeping but one of these wild creatures long enough to make a graduate of him, and he thereupon vanishes into the merciful shadow of the past. His name — but as there was only one Indian graduate, so there is only one living man who can pronounce his unconverted name; and I leave the task to Dr. Hammond Trumbull.

I shall not attempt, even in brief, a history of the college. It has already been excellently done. A compendium of it would be mainly a list of unfamiliar names, and Coleridge has said truly that such names " are non-conductors; they stop all interest."

The fame and usefulness of all institutions of learning depend on the greatness of those who teach in them, —

> Queis arte benigna,
> Et meliore luto finxit præcordia Titan,—

and great teachers are almost rarer than great poets. We can lay claim to none such (I must not speak of the living), unless it be Agassiz, whom we adopted, but we have had many devoted, and some eminent. It has not been their fault if they have not pushed farther forward the boundaries of knowledge. Our professors have been compelled by the necessities of the case (as we are apt to call things which we ought to reform, but do not) to do too much work not properly theirs, and that of a kind so exacting as to consume the energy that might have been ample for higher service. They have been obliged to double the parts of professor and tutor. During the seventeenth century we have reason to think that the college kept pretty well up to the standard of its contemporary colleges in England, so far as its poverty would allow. It seems to have enjoyed a certain fame abroad among men who sympathized with the theology it taught, — for I possess a Hebrew Accidence, dedicated some two hundred years ago to the "illustrious academy at Boston in New England," by a Dutch scholar whom I cannot help thinking a very discerning person. That the students of that day had access to a fairly good library may be inferred from Cotton Mather's "Magnalia," though he knew not how to make the best use of it, and was a very nightmare of pedantry. That the college had made New England a good market for books is proved by John Dunton's journey hither in the interests of his trade. During the eighteenth and first quarter of the nineteenth centuries, I fancy the condition of things here to have been very much what it was in the smaller English colleges of the period, if we may trust the verses which Gray addressed to the goddess Ignorance. Young men who were willing mainly to teach themselves might get something to their advantage, while the rest were put here by their parents as into a comfortable quarantine, where they could wait till the gates of life were opened to them, safe from any contagion of learning, except such as might be developed from previous infection. I am speaking of a great while ago. Men are apt, I know, in after life to lay the blame of their scholastic shortcomings at the door of their teachers. They are often wrong in this, and I am quite aware that there are some pupils who are knowledge-proof; but I gather from tradition, which I believe to be trustworthy, that there have been periods in the history of the college when the students might have sung with Bishop Golias, —

> Ili nos docent, sed indocti;
> Ili nos docent, et nox nocti
> Indicat scientiam.

Despite all this, it is remarkable that the first two American imaginative artists, — Allston in painting, and Greenough in sculpture, — were graduates of Harvard. A later generation is justly proud of Story.

We have a means of testing the general culture given here towards the middle of the last century in the *Gratulatio* presented by Harvard College on the accession of George III. It is not duller than such things usually are on the other side of the water, and it shows a pretty knack at tagging verses. It is noteworthy that the Greek in it, if I remember rightly, is wholly or chiefly Governor Bernard's. A few years earlier, some of the tracts in the Whitfield controversy prove that the writers had got here a thorough training in English at least. They had certainly not read their Swift in vain.

But the chief service, as it was the chief office, of the college during all those years was to maintain and hand down the traditions of how excellent a thing learning was, even if the teaching were not always adequate by way of illustration. And yet so far as that teaching went, it was wise in this, — that it gave its pupils some tincture of letters as distinguished from mere scholarship. It aimed to teach them the authors, — that is, the few great ones (the late Professor Popkin, whom the older of us remember, would have allowed that title only to the Greeks), — and to teach them in such a way as to enable the pupil to assimilate somewhat of their thought, sentiment, and style, rather than to master the minuter niceties of the language in which they wrote. It struck for their matter, as Montaigne advised, who would have men taught to love virtue instead of learning to decline *virtus*. It set more store by the marrow than by the bone that encased it. It made language, as it should be, a ladder to literature, and not literature a ladder to language. Many a boy has hated, and rightly hated, Homer and Horace the pedagogues and grammarians, who would have loved Homer and Horace the poets had he been allowed to make their acquaintance. The old method of instruction had the prime merit of enabling its pupils to conceive that there is neither ancient nor modern on the narrow shelves of what is truly literature. We owe a great debt to the Germans, — no one is more indebted to them than I; but is there not danger of their misleading us in some directions into pedantry? In his preface to an Old French poem of the thirteenth century, lately published, the editor informs us sorrowfully that he had the advantage of listening only two years and a half to the lectures of Professor Gaston Paris, in which time he got no further than through the first three vowels. At this rate, to master the whole alphabet, consonants and all, would be a task fitter for the centurial adolescence of Methuselah than for our less liberal ration of years. I was glad my editor had

had this advantage, and I am quite willing that Old French should get the benefit of such scrupulosity; but I think I see a tendency to train young men in the languages as if they were all to be editors, and not lovers of polite literature. Education, we are often told, is a drawing out of the faculties. May they not be drawn out too thin? I am not undervaluing philology or accuracy of scholarship; both are excellent and admirable in their places. But philology is less beautiful to me than philosophy, as Milton understood the word; and mere accuracy is to truth as a plaster-cast to the marble statue, — it gives the facts, but not their meaning. If I must choose, I had rather a young man should be intimate with the genius of the Greek dramatic poets than with the metres of their choruses, though I should be glad to have him on easy terms with both.

For more than two hundred years, in its discipline and courses of study, the college followed mainly the lines traced by its founders. The influence of its first half century did more than any other, perhaps more than all others, to make New England what it is. During the one hundred and forty years preceding our War of Independence it had supplied the schools of the greater part of New England with teachers. What was even more important, it had sent to every parish in Massachusetts one man, — the clergyman, — with a certain amount of scholarship, a belief in culture, and generally pretty sure to bring with him or to gather a considerable collection of books, by no means wholly theological. Simple and godly men were they, the truest modern antitypes of Chaucer's Good Parson, receiving much, sometimes all, of their scanty salary in kind, and eking it out by the drudgery of a cross-grained farm where the soil seems all backbone. If there was no regular practitioner, they practised without fee a grandmotherly sort of medicine, probably not much more harmful (*O, dura messorum ilia*) than the heroic treatment of the day. They contrived to save enough to send their sons through college, to portion their daughters, — decently trained in English literature of the more serious kind, and perfect in the duties of household and dairy, — and to make modest provision for the widow, if they should leave one. With all this, they gave their two sermons every Sunday of the year, and of a measure that would seem ruinously liberal to these less stalwart days, when scarce ten parsons together could lift the stones of Diomed which they hurled at Satan with the easy precision of lifelong practice. And if they turned their barrel of discourses at the end of the Horatian ninth year, which of their parishioners was the wiser for it? Their one great holiday was Commencement, which they punctually attended. They shared the many toils and the rare festivals, the joys and the sorrows, of their townsmen as bone of their bone and flesh of their flesh, for all were of one blood and of one faith. They dwelt on the same brotherly level with them as men, yet set apart from and above them by their sacred office. Preaching the most terrible of doctrines, as most of them did, they were humane and cheerful men, and when they came down from the pulpit seemed to have been merely twisting their "cast-iron logic" of despair, as Coleridge said of Donne, "into true-love-knots." Men of authority, wise in counsel, independent (for their settlement was a life-tenure), they were living lessons of piety, industry, frugality, temperance, and, with the magistrates, were a recognized aristocracy. Surely never was an aristocracy so simple, so harmless, so exemplary, and so fit to rule. I remember a few lingering survivors of them in my early boyhood, relics of a serious but not sullen past, of a community for which in civic virtue, intelligence, and general efficacy I seek a parallel in vain: —

> "rusticorum mascula militum
> Proles . . . docta . . .
> Versare glebas et severæ
> Matris ad arbitrium recisos
> Portare fustes."

I know too well the deductions to be made. It was a community without charm, or with a homely charm at best, and the life it led was visited by no Muse even in dream. But it was the stuff out of which fortunate ancestors are made, and twenty-five years ago their sons showed in no diminished measure the qualities of the breed. In every household some brave boy was saying to his mother, as Iphigenia to hers, —

Πᾶσι γάρ μ' Ἕλλησι κοινὸν ἔτεκες οὐχὶ σοὶ μόνῃ.

Nor were Harvard's sons the last. This hall commemorates them, but their story is written in headstones all over the land they saved.

To the teaching and example of those reverend men whom Harvard bred and then planted in every hamlet as pioneers and outposts of her doctrine, Massachusetts owes the better part of her moral and intellectual inheritance. They, too, were the progenitors of a numerous and valid race. My friend Dr. Holmes was, I believe, the first to point out how large a proportion of our men of light and leading sprang from their loins. The illustrious Chief Magistrate of the Republic, who honors us with his presence here to-day, has ancestors italicized in our printed registers, and has shown himself worthy of his pedigree.

During the present century, I believe that Harvard received and welcomed the new learning from Germany at the hands of Everett, Bancroft, and Ticknor, before it had been accepted by the more conservative universities of the Old Home. Everett's translation of Buttmann's Greek Grammar was reprinted in England, with the "Massachusetts" omitted after "Cambridge," at the end of the preface, to conceal its American origin. Emerson has told us how his intellectual life was quickened by the eloquent enthusiasm of Everett's teaching. Mr. Bancroft made strenuous efforts to introduce a more wholesome discipline and maturer methods of study, with the result of a rebellion of the Freshman Class, who issued a manifesto of their wrongs, written by the late Robert Rantoul, which ended thus: "Shall FREEMEN bear this? FRESHMEN are freemen!" They, too, remembered Revolutionary sires. Mr. Bancroft's translation

of Heeren was the first of its kind, and it is worth
mention that the earliest version from the prose of
Henry Heine into English was made here, though
not by a graduate of Harvard. Ticknor also strove
earnestly to enlarge the scope of the collegiate courses
of study. The force of the new impulse did not last
long, or produce, unless indirectly, lasting results.
It was premature; the students were really school-
boys, and the college was not yet capable of the
larger university life. The conditions of American
life, too, were such that young men looked upon
scholarship neither as an end nor as a means, but
simply as an accomplishment, like music or dancing,
of which they were to acquire a little more or a little
less (generally a little less), according to individual
taste or circumstances. It has been mainly during
the last twenty-five years that the college, having
already the name but by no means all the resources
of a university, has been trying to perform some at
least of the functions which that title implies.

> "Now half appears
> The tawny lion, pawing to get free."

Let us, then, no longer look backward, but forward, as our fathers did when they laid our humble
foundations in the wilderness. The motto first proposed for the college arms was, as you know, *Veritas*,
written across three open books. It was a noble one,
and, if the full bearing of it was understood, as daring
as it was noble. Perhaps it was discarded because an
*open* book seemed hardly the fittest symbol for what
is so hard to find, and, if ever we fancy we have found

it, so hard to decipher and to translate into our own language and life. Pilate's question still murmurs in the ear of every thoughtful, and Montaigne's in that of every honest, man. The motto finally substituted for that — *Christo et Ecclesiæ* — is, when rightly interpreted, substantially the same; for it means that we are to devote ourselves to the highest conception we have of truth and to the preaching of it. Fortunately, the Sphinx proposes her conundrums to us one at a time, and at intervals proportioned to our wits.

Joseph de Maistre says that "un homme d'esprit est tenu de savoir deux choses: 1°, ce qu'il est; 2°, où il est." The questions for us are, In what sense are we become a university? And then, if we become so, What and to what end should a university aim to teach, now and here in this America of ours, whose meaning no man can yet comprehend? And when we have settled what it is best to teach, comes the further question, How are we to teach it? Whether with an eye to its effect on developing character or personal availability, — that is to say, to its effect in the conduct of life, — or on the chances of getting a livelihood? Perhaps we shall find that we must have a care for both, and I cannot see why the two need be incompatible; but if they are, I should choose the former term of the alternative.

In a not remote past, society had still certain recognized, authoritative guides, and the college trained them as the fashion of the day required. But

"Damnosa quid non imminuit dies?"

That ancient close corporation of official guides has been compelled to surrender its charter. We are pestered with as many volunteers as at Niagara, and as there, if we follow any of them, may count on paying for it pretty dearly. The office of the higher instruction, nevertheless, continues to be as it always was, the training of such guides; only it must now try to fit them out with as much more personal accomplishment and authority as may compensate the loss of hierarchical prestige.

When President Walker, it must be now nearly thirty years ago, asked me in common with my colleagues what my notion of a university was, I answered: "A university is a place where nothing useful is taught; but a university is possible only where a man may get his livelihood by digging Sanscrit roots." What I meant was that the highest office of the somewhat complex thing so named was to distribute the true "bread of life," — the *pane 'degli angeli*, as Dante called it, — and to breed an appetite for it; but that it should also have the means and appliances for teaching everything, as the mediæval universities aimed to do in their *trivium* and *quadrivium*. I had in mind the ideal and the practical sides of the institution, and was thinking also whether such an institution was practicable, and if so, whether it was desirable, in a country like this. I think it eminently desirable; and if it be, what should be its chief function? I choose rather to hesitate my opinion than to assert it roundly. But some opinion I am bound to have, either my own or another man's, if I would be in the fashion, though

I may not be wholly satisfied with the one or the other. Opinions are "as handy," to borrow our Yankee proverb, "as a pocket in a shirt," and, I may add, as hard to come at. I hope, then, that the day will come when a competent professor may lecture here also for three years on the first three vowels of the Romance alphabet, and find fit audience, though few. I hope the day may never come when the weightier matters of a language, — namely, such parts of its literature as have overcome death by reason of their wisdom and of the beauty in which it is incarnated; such parts as are universal by reason of their civilizing properties, their power to elevate and fortify the mind, — I hope the day may never come when these are not predominant in the teaching given here. Let the Humanities be maintained undiminished in their ancient right. Leave in their traditional pre-eminence those arts that were rightly called liberal; those studies that kindle the imagination, and through it irradiate the reason; those studies that manumitted the modern mind; those in which the brains of finest temper have found alike their stimulus and their repose, taught by them that the power of intellect is heightened in proportion as it is made gracious by measure and symmetry. Give us science, too; but give first of all, and last of all, the science that ennobles life and makes it generous. I stand here as a man of letters, and as a man of letters I must speak. But I am speaking with no exclusive intention. No one believes more firmly than I in the usefulness, I might well say the necessity, of variety in study, and of opening the freest scope possible to the prevailing bent of every mind when that bent shows itself to be so predominating as to warrant it. Many-sidedness of culture makes our vision clearer and keener in particulars. For, after all, the noblest definition of science is that breadth and impartiality of view which liberates the mind from specialties, and enables it to organize whatever we learn, so that it become real knowledge by being brought into true and helpful relation with the rest.

By far the most important change that has been introduced into the theory and practice of our teaching here by the new position in which we find ourselves, has been that of the elective or voluntary system of studies. We have justified ourselves by the familiar proverb that "one man may lead a horse to water, but ten can't make him drink." Proverbs are excellent things, but we should not let even proverbs bully us. They are the wisdom of the understanding, not of the higher reason. There is another animal, which even Simonides could compliment only on the spindle-side of his pedigree, and which ten men could not lead to water, much less make him drink when they got him thither. Are we not trying to force university forms into college methods too narrow for them? There is some danger that the elective system may be pushed too far and too fast. There are not a few who think that it has gone too far already. And they think so because we are in process of transformation, still in the hobbledehoy period, — not having ceased to be a college, nor yet having reached the full manhood of a university, so that we speak with that ambiguous voice, half bass, half treble, or mixed of both, which is proper to a certain stage of adolescence. We are trying to do two things with one tool, and that tool not specially adapted to either. Are our students old enough thoroughly to understand the import of the choice they are called on to make; and if old enough, are they wise enough? Shall their parents make the choice for them? I am not sure that even parents are as wise as the unbroken experience and practice of mankind. We are comforted by being told that in this we are only complying with what is called the Spirit of the Age, — which may be, after all, only a finer name for the mischievous goblin known to our forefathers as Puck. I have seen several Spirits of the Age in my time, of very different voices and summoning in very different directions, but unanimous in their propensity to land us in the mire at last. Would it not be safer to make sure first whether the Spirit of the Age — who would be a very insignificant fellow if we docked him of his capitals — be not a lying spirit, since such there are? It is at least curious that while the more advanced teaching has a strong drift in the voluntary direction, the compulsory system, as respects primary studies, is gaining ground. Is it indeed so self-evident a proposition as it seems to many, that "You may" is as wholesome a lesson for youth as "You must"? Is it so good a fore-schooling for Life, which will be a teacher of quite other mood, making us learn, rod in hand, precisely those lessons we should not have chosen? I have, to be sure, heard the late President Quincy (*clarum et venerabile nomen!*) say that if a young man came hither and did nothing more than rub his shoulders against the college buildings for four years, he would imbibe some tincture of sound learning by an involuntary process of absorption. The founders of the college also believed in some impulsions towards science communicated *à tergo*, but of sharper virtue, and accordingly armed their president with that *ductor dubitantium* which was wielded to such good purpose by the Reverend James Bowyer at Christ's Hospital in the days of Coleridge and Lamb. They believed with the old poet that whipping was "a wild benefit of nature," and could they have read Wordsworth's exquisite stanza, —

> "One impulse from a vernal wood
> Can teach us more of man,
> Of moral evil and of good,
> Than all the sages can," —

they would have struck out "vernal" and inserted "birchen" on the margin.

I am not, of course, arguing in favor of a return to those vapulatory methods; but the birch, like many other things that have passed out of the region of the practical, may have another term of usefulness as a symbol after it has ceased to be a reality.

One is sometimes tempted to think that all learning is as repulsive to ingenuous youth as the multiplication table to Scott's little friend Marjorie Fleming, though this be due in great part to mechanical methods of teaching. "I am now going to tell you," she writes, "the horrible and wretched plaege that my multiplication table gives me; you can't conceive it.

The most Devilish thing is 8 times 8 and 7 times 7; it is what nature itself can't endure." I know that I am approaching treacherous ashes which cover burning coals, but I must on. Is not Greek, nay, even Latin, yet more unendurable than poor Marjorie's task? How many boys have not sympathized with Heine in hating the Romans because they invented Latin grammar? And they were quite right; for we begin the study of languages at the wrong end, at the end which Nature does not offer us, and are thoroughly tired of them before we arrive at them, if you will pardon the bull. But is that any reason for not studying them in the right way? I am familiar with the arguments for making the study of Greek especially a matter of choice or chance; I admit their plausibility and the honesty of those who urge them. I should be willing also to admit that the study of the ancient languages without the hope or the prospect of going on to what they contain would be useful only as a form of intellectual gymnastics. Even so they would be as serviceable as the higher mathematics to most of us. But I think that a wise teacher should adapt his tasks to the highest, and not the lowest, capacities of the taught. For those lower also they would not be wholly without profit. When there is a tedious sermon, says George Herbert, —

"God takes a text and teacheth patience," —

not the least pregnant of lessons. One of the arguments against the compulsory study of Greek, — namely, that it is wiser to give our time to modern languages and modern history than to dead languages and ancient history,— involves, I think, a verbal fallacy. Only those languages can properly be called dead in which nothing living has been written. If the classic languages are dead, they yet speak to us, and with a clearer voice than that of any living tongue.

> "Graiis ingenium, Graiis dedit ore rotundo
> Musa loqui, præter laudem nullius avaris."

If their language is dead, yet the literature it enshrines is rammed with life as perhaps no other writing, except Shakespeare's, ever was or will be. It is as contemporary with to-day as with the ears it first enraptured; for it appeals not to the man of then or now, but to the entire round of human nature itself. Men are ephemeral or evanescent, but whatever page the authentic soul of man has touched with her immortalizing finger, no matter how long ago, is still young and fair as it was to the world's gray fathers. Oblivion looks in the face of the Grecian Muse only to forget her errand. Plato and Aristotle are not names, but things. On a chart that should represent the firm earth and wavering oceans of the human mind, they would be marked as mountain ranges, forever modifying the temperature, the currents, and the atmosphere of thought, — astronomical stations whence the movements of the lamps of heaven might best be observed and predicted. Even for the mastering of our own tongue, there is no expedient so fruitful as translation out of another; how much more when that other is a language at once so precise and so flexible as the Greek! Greek literature is also the most fruitful comment on our own. Coleridge has told us with what profit he was made to study Shakespeare and Milton in conjunction with the Greek dramatists. It is no sentimental argument for this study that the most justly balanced, the most serene, and the most fecundating minds since the revival of learning have been steeped in and saturated with Greek literature. We know not whither other studies will lead us, especially if dissociated from this; we do know to what summits, far above our lower region of turmoil, this has led, and what the many-sided outlook thence. Will such studies make anachronisms of us, unfit us for the duties and the business of to-day? I can recall no writer more truly modern than Montaigne, who was almost more at home in Athens and Rome than in Paris. Yet he was a thrifty manager of his estate, and a most competent mayor of Bordeaux. I remember passing once in London where demolition for a new thoroughfare was going on. Many houses left standing in the rear of those cleared away bore signs with the inscription, "Ancient Lights." This was the protest of their owners against being built out by the new improvements from such glimpse of heaven as their fathers had, without adequate equivalent. I laid the moral to heart.

I am speaking of the college as it has always existed and still exists. In so far as it may be driven to put on the forms of the university, — I do not mean the four Faculties merely, but in the modern sense, — we shall naturally find ourselves compelled to assume the method with the function. Some day we shall offer here a chance, at least, to acquire the *omne scibile.* I shall be glad, as shall we all, when the young American need no longer go abroad for any part of his training, — though that may not be always a disadvantage, if Shakespeare was right in thinking that

"Home-keeping youths have ever homely wits."

I should be still gladder if Harvard might be the place that offered the alternative. It seems more than ever probable that this will happen, and happen in our day. And whenever it does happen, it will be due, more than to any and all others, to the able, energetic, single-minded, and yet fair-minded man who has presided over the college during the trying period of transition, and who will by a rare combination of eminent qualities carry that transition forward to its accomplishment without haste and without jar, — *ohne Hast, ohne Rast.* He more than any of his distinguished predecessors has brought the University into closer and more telling relations with the national life, in whatever that life has which is most distinctive and most hopeful.

But we still mainly occupy the position of a German gymnasium. Under existing circumstances, therefore, and with the methods of teaching they enforce, I think that special and advanced courses should be pushed on, so far as possible, as the other professional courses are, into the post-graduate period. The opportunity would be greater because the number would be less, and the teaching not only more thorough but more vivifying, through the more intimate relation of teacher and pupil. Under those conditions the voluntary system will not only be possible, but will come of itself; for every student will know what he wants and where he may get it, and learning will be loved, as it should be, for its own sake as well as for what it gives. The friends of university training can do nothing that would forward it more than the founding of postgraduate fellowships and the building and endowing of a hall where the holders of them might be commensals, — remembering that when Cardinal Wolsey built Christ Church at Oxford his first care was the kitchen. Nothing is so great a quickener of the faculties, or so likely to prevent their being narrowed to a single groove, as the frequent social commingling of men who are aiming at one goal by different paths. If you would have really great scholars, and our life offers no prizes for such, it would be well if the University could offer them. I have often been struck with the many-sided versatility of the Fellows of English colleges who have kept their wits in training by continual fence one with another.

During the first two centuries of her existence, it may be affirmed that Harvard did sufficiently well the only work she was called on to do, perhaps the only work it was possible for her to do. She gave to Boston her scholarly impress, to the Commonwealth her scholastic impulse. To the clergy of her training was mainly intrusted the oversight of the public schools; these were, as I have said, though indirectly, feeders of the college, for their teaching was of the plainest. But if a boy in any country village showed uncommon parts, the clergyman was sure to hear of it. He and the squire and the doctor, if there was one, talked it over, and that boy was sure to be helped onward to college; for next to the five points of Calvinism our ancestors believed in a college education,— that is, in the best education that was to be had. The system, if system it should be called, was a good one, a practical application of the doctrine of natural selection. Ah! how the parents — nay, the whole family — moiled and pinched that their boy might have the chance denied to them! Mr. Matthew Arnold has told us that in contemporary France, which seems doomed to try every theory of enlightenment by which the fingers may be burned or the house set on fire, the children of the public schools are taught in answer to the question, "Who gives you all these fine things?" to say, "The State." Ill fares the State in which the parental image is replaced by an abstraction. The answer of the boy of whom I have been speaking would have been in a spirit better for the State and for the hope of his own future life: "I owe them, under God, to my own industry, to the sacrifices of my father and mother, and to the sympathy of good men." Nor was the boy's self-respect lessened, for the aid was given by loans, to be repaid when possible. The times have changed, and it is no longer the ambition of a promising boy to go to college. They are taught to think that a common-school education is good enough for all practical purposes. And so perhaps it is, but not for all ideal purposes. Our public schools teach too little or too much: too little if education is to go no further, too many things if what is taught is to be taught thoroughly; and the more they *seem* to teach, the less likely is education to go further, for it is one of the prime weaknesses of a democracy to be satisfied with the second-best if it appear to answer the purpose tolerably well, and to be cheaper,— as it never is in the long run.

Our ancestors believed in education, but not in making it wholly eleemosynary. And they were wise in this, for men do not value what they get for nothing, any more than they value air and light till deprived of them. It is quite proper that the cost of our public schools should be paid by the rich, for it is their interest, as Lord Sherbrooke said, "to educate their rulers." But it is to make paupers of the pupils to furnish them, as is now proposed, with text-books, slates, and the like at public cost. This is an advance towards that State Socialism which, if it ever prevail, will be deadly to certain homespun virtues far more precious than most of the book-knowledge in the world. It is to be hoped that our higher institutions of learning may again be brought to bear, as once they did, more directly on the lower, that they may again come into such closer and graduated relation with them as may make the higher education the goal to which all who show a clear aptitude shall aspire. I know that we cannot have ideal teachers in our public schools for the price we pay, or in the numbers we require. But teaching, like water, can rise no higher than its source; and, like water again, it has a lazy aptitude for running down-hill unless a constant impulse be applied in the other direction. Would not this impulse be furnished by the ambition to send on as many pupils as possible to the wider sphere of the University? Would not this organic relation to the higher education necessitate a corresponding rise in the grade of intelligence, capacity, and culture demanded in the teachers?

Harvard has done much by raising its standard to force upwards that also of the preparatory schools. The leaven thus infused will, let us hope, filter gradually downwards till it raise a ferment in the lower grades as well. What we need more than anything else is to increase the number of our highly cultivated men and thoroughly trained minds; for these, wherever they go, are sure to carry with them, consciously or not, the seeds of sounder thinking and of higher ideals. The only way in which our civilization can be maintained even at the level it has reached, — the only way in which that level can be made more general and be raised higher, — is by bringing the influence of the more cultivated to bear with greater energy and directness on the less cultivated, and by opening more inlets to those indirect influences which make for refinement of mind and body. Democracy must show its capacity for producing, not a higher average man, but the highest possible types of manhood in all its manifold varieties, or it is a failure. No matter what it does for the body, if it do not in some sort satisfy that inextinguishable passion of the soul for something that lifts life away from prose, from the common and the vulgar, it is a failure. Unless it know how to make itself gracious and winning, it is a failure. Has it done this? Is it doing this, — or trying to do it? Not yet, I think, if one may judge by that commonplace of our newspapers, that an American who stays long enough in Europe is sure to find his own country unendurable when he comes back. This is not true, if I may judge from some little experience; but it is interesting as implying a certain consciousness, which is of the most hopeful augury. But we must not be impatient; it is a far cry from the dwellers in caves to even such civilization as we have achieved. I am conscious that life has been trying to civilize me for now nearly seventy years, with what seem to me very inadequate results. *We* cannot afford to wait, but the Race can. And when I speak of civilization I mean those things that tend to develop the moral forces of Man, and not merely to quicken his æsthetic sensibility, — though there is often a nearer relation between the two than is popularly believed.

The tendency of a prosperous Democracy — and hitherto we have had little to do but prosper — is towards an overweening confidence in itself and its home-made methods, an overestimate of material success, and a corresponding indifference to the things of the mind. The popular ideal of success seems to be, more than ever before, the accumulation of riches. I say "seems," for it may be only because the opportunities are greater. I am not ignorant that wealth is the great fertilizer of civilization, and of the arts that beautify it. The very names of "civilization" and "urbanity" show that the refinement of manners which made the arts possible is the birth of cities where wealth earliest accumulated because it found itself secure. Wealth may be an excellent thing, for it means power, it means leisure, it means liberty.

But these, divorced from culture, — that is, from intelligent purpose, — become the very mockery of their own essence; not goods, but evils fatal to their possessor, and bring with them, like the Nibelungen Hoard, a doom instead of a blessing. A man rich only for himself, has a life as barren and cheerless as that of the serpent set to guard a buried treasure. I am saddened when I see our success as a nation measured by the number of acres under tillage, or of bushels of wheat exported; for the real value of a country must be weighed in scales more delicate than the "balance of trade." The garners of Sicily are empty now, but the bees from all climes still fetch honey from the tiny garden-plot of Theocritus. On a map of the world you may hide Judea with your thumb, Athens with a finger-tip, and neither of them figures in the "prices current;" but they still lord it in the thought and action of every civilized man. Did not Dante cover with his hood all that was Italy six hundred years ago? And if we go back a century, where was Germany outside of Weimar? Material success is good, but only as the necessary preliminary of better things. The measure of a nation's true success is the amount it has contributed to the thought, the moral energy, the intellectual happiness, the spiritual hope and consolation, of mankind. There is no other, let our candidates flatter us as they may. We still make a confusion between huge and great. I know that I am repeating truisms, but they are truisms that need to be repeated in season and out of season.

The most precious property of Culture, and of a college as its trustee, is to maintain higher ideals of life and its purpose; to keep trimmed and burning the lamps of that pharos, built by wiser than we, which warns from the reefs and shallows of popular doctrine. In proportion as there are more thoroughly cultivated persons in a community will the finer uses of prosperity be taught and the vulgar uses of it become disreputable. And it is such persons that we are commissioned to send out, with such consciousness of their fortunate vocation and such devotion to it as we may. We are confronted with unexampled problems. First of all is democracy, and that under conditions in great part novel; with its hitherto imperfectly tabulated results, whether we consider its effect upon national character, on popular thought, or on the functions of law and government. We have to deal with a time when the belief seems to be spreading, that truth not only can but should be settled by a show of hands rather than by a count of heads, and that one man is as good as another for all purposes, — as, indeed, he is till a real man is needed; with a time when the Press is more potent for good or for evil than ever any human agency was before, and yet is controlled more than ever before by its interests as a business rather than by its sense of duty as a teacher, and must purvey news instead of intelligence; with a time when divers and strange doctrines touching the greatest human interests are allowed to run about unmuzzled in greater number and variety than ever before since the Reformation passed into its stage of putrefactive fermentation; with a time when the idols of the market-place are more devoutly worshipped than ever Diana of the Ephesians was; when the guilds of the Middle Ages are revived among us with the avowed purpose of renewing, by the misuse of universal suffrage, the class-legislation to escape which we left the Old World; when the electric telegraph, by making public opinion simultaneous, is also making it liable to those delusions, panics, and gregarious impulses which transform otherwise reasonable men into a mob; and when, above all, the better mind of the country is said to be growing more and more alienated from the highest of all sciences and services, — the government of it. I have drawn up a dreary catalogue, and the moral it points is this: that the college, in so far as it continues to be still a college, as in great part it does and must, is and should be limited by certain pre-existing conditions, and must consider first what the more general objects of education are, without neglecting special aptitudes more than can be helped. That more general purpose is, I take it, to set free, to supple, and to train the faculties in such wise as shall make them most effective for whatever task life may afterwards set them, for the duties of life rather than for its business, and to open windows on every side of the mind where thickness of wall does not make it impossible.

Let our aim be, as hitherto, to give a good all-round education fitted to cope with as many exigencies of the day as possible. I had rather the college should turn out one of Aristotle's four-square men, capable of holding his own in whatever field he may be cast, than a score of lop-sided ones developed abnormally in one direction. Our scheme should be adapted to the wants of the majority of under-graduates, to the objects that drew them hither, and to such training as will make the most of them after they come. Special aptitudes are sure to take care of themselves, but the latent possibilities of the average mind can be discovered only by experiment in many directions. When I speak of the average mind, I do not mean that the courses of study should be adapted to the average level of intelligence, but to the highest; for in these matters it is wiser to grade upward than downward, since the best is the only thing that is good enough. To keep the wing-footed down to the pace of the leaden-soled, disheartens the one without in the least encouraging the other. "Brains," says Machiavelli, "are of three generations, — those that understand of themselves, those that understand when another shows them, and those that understand neither of themselves nor by the showing of others." It is the first class that should set the stint; the second will get on better than if they had set it themselves; and the third will at least have the pleasure of watching the others show their paces.

In the college proper, I repeat, — for it is the birthday of the college that we are celebrating, it is the college that we love and of which we are proud, — let it continue to give such a training as will fit the rich to be trusted with riches, and the poor to withstand the temptations of poverty. Give to history, give to political economy, that ample verge the times demand, but with no detriment to those liberal arts which have formed open-minded men and good citizens in the past, nor have lost the skill to form them. Let it be our hope to make a gentleman of every youth who is put under our charge; not a conventional gentleman, but a man of culture, a man of intellectual resource, a man of public spirit, a man of refinement, with that good taste which is the conscience of the mind, and that conscience which is the good taste of the soul. This we have tried to do in the past; this let us try to do in the future. We cannot do this for all, at best, — perhaps only for the few; but the influence for good of a highly trained intelligence and a harmoniously developed character is incalculable; for though it be subtile and gradual in its operation, it is as pervasive as it is subtile. There may be few of these, there must be few; but

> "That few is all the world which with a few
> Doth ever live and move and work and stirre."

If these few can best be winnowed from the rest by the elective system of studies; if the drift of our colleges towards that system be general and involuntary, showing a demand for it in the conditions of American life, — then I should wish to see it unfalteringly carried through. I am sure that the matter will be handled wisely and with all forethought by those most intimately concerned in the government of the college.

They who on a tiny clearing pared from the edge of the woods built here (as their Anglo-Saxon ancestors built their first churches), most probably with the timber hewed from the trees they felled, our earliest hall, — with the solitude of ocean behind them, the mystery of forest before them, and all about them a desolation, — must surely (*si quis animis celestibus locus*) share our gladness and our gratitude at the splendid fulfilment of their vision. If we could but have preserved the humble roof which housed so great a future, Mr. Ruskin himself would almost have admitted that no castle or cathedral was ever richer in sacred associations, in pathos of the past, and in moral significance. They who reared it had the sublime prescience of that courage which fears only God, and could say confidently in the face of all discouragement and doubt, "He hath led me forth into a large place; because He delighted in me, He hath delivered me." We cannot honor them too much; we can repay them only by showing, as occasions rise, that we do not undervalue the worth of their example.

Brethren of the Alumni, it now becomes my duty to welcome in your name the guests who have come, some of them so far, to share our congratulations and hopes to-day. I cannot name them all and give to each his fitting phrase. Thrice welcome to them all, — and, as is fitting, first to those from abroad, representatives of illustrious seats of learning that were old in usefulness and fame when ours was in its cradle; and next to those of our own land, from colleges and universities which if not daughters of Harvard are young enough to be so, and are one with her in heart and hope. I said that I could not name them all, but I should not represent you fitly if I gave no special greeting to the gentleman who brings the message of John Harvard's college, Emmanuel. The welcome we give him could not be warmer than that which we offer to his colleagues; but we cannot help feeling that in pressing his hand our own instinctively closes a little more tightly, as with a sense of nearer kindred.

There is also one other name of which it would be indecorous not to make an exception. You all know that I can mean only the President of our Republic. His presence is a signal honor to us all, and to us all I may say a personal gratification. We have no politics here; but the sons of Harvard all belong to the party which admires courage, strength of purpose, and fidelity to duty, and which respects, wherever he may be found, the

"Justum ac tenacem propositi virum,"

who knows how to withstand the

"Civium ardor prava jubentium."

He has left the helm of state to be with us here, and so long as it is intrusted to his hands we are sure that, should the storm come, he will say with Seneca's Pilot, "O Neptune! you may save me if you will; you may sink me if you will; but whatever happen, I shall keep my rudder true!"

## POEM.

### BY OLIVER WENDELL HOLMES,

*Professor Emeritus in the University.*

Twice had the mellowing sun of autumn crowned
The hundredth circle of his yearly round,
When, as we meet to-day, our fathers met:
That joyous gathering who can e'er forget,
When Harvard's nurslings, scattered far and wide,
Through mart and village, lake's and ocean's side,
Came, with one impulse, one fraternal throng,
And crowned the hours with banquet, speech, and song?

Once more revived in fancy's magic glass,
I see in state the long procession pass:
Tall, courtly, leader as by right divine,
Winthrop, — our Winthrop, — rules the marshalled line,
Still seen in front, as on that far-off day
His ribboned baton showed the column's way.
Not all are gone who marched in manly pride
And waved their truncheons at their leader's side:
Gray, Lowell, Dixwell, who his empire shared,
These to be with us envious Time has spared.

Few are the faces, so familiar then,
Our eyes still meet amid the haunts of men;
Scarce one of all the living gathered there,
Whose unthinned locks betrayed a silver hair,
Greets us to-day; and yet we seem the same
As our own sires and grandsires, save in name.

There are the patriarchs, looking vaguely round
For classmates' faces, hardly known if found:
See the cold brow that rules the busy mart;
Close at its side the pallid son of art,
Whose purchased skill with borrowed meaning clothes,
And stolen hues, the smirking face he loathes.
Here is the patient scholar; in his looks

You read the titles of his learned books;
What classic lore those spidery crow's-feet speak!
What problems figure on that wrinkled cheek!
For never thought but left its stiffened trace,
Its fossil foot-print, on the plastic face,
As the swift record of a raindrop stands,
Fixed on the tablet of the hardening sands.
On every face as on the written page
Each year renews the autograph of age;
One trait alone may wasting years defy, —
The fire still lingering in the poet's eye;
While Hope, the siren, sings her sweetest strain, —
*Non omnis moriar* is its proud refrain.


Sadly we gaze upon the vacant chair;
He who should claim its honors is not there, —
Otis, whose lips the listening crowd enthrall
That press and pack the floor of Boston's hall.
But Kirkland smiles, released from toil and care
Since the silk mantle younger shoulders wear, —
Quincy's, whose spirit breathes the self-same fire
That filled the bosom of his youthful sire,
Who for the altar bore the kindled torch
To freedom's temple, dying in its porch.
 Three grave professions in their sons appear,
Whose words well studied all well pleased will hear:
Palfrey, ordained in varied walks to shine,
Statesman, historian, critic, and divine;
Solid and square behold majestic Shaw,
A mass of wisdom and a mine of law;
Warren, whose arm the doughtiest warriors fear,
Asks of the startled crowd to lend its ear;
Proud of his calling, him the world loves best,
Not as the coming, but the parting guest.


Look on that form, — with eye dilating scan
The stately mould of Nature's kingliest man!
Tower-like he stands in life's unfaded prime;
Ask you his name? None asks a second time!
He from the land his outward semblance takes,

Where storm-swept mountains watch o'er slumbering lakes:
See in the impress which the body wears
How its imperial might the soul declares, —
The forehead's large expansion, lofty, wide,
That locks unsilvered vainly strive to hide;
The lines of thought that plough the sober cheek,
Lips that betray their wisdom ere they speak
In tones like answers from Dodona's grove;
An eye like Juno's when she frowns on Jove:
I look and wonder; will he be content, —
This man, this monarch, for the purple meant, —
The meaner duties of his tribe to share,
Clad in the garb that common mortals wear?
Ah, wild Ambition, spread thy restless wings,
Beneath whose plumes the hidden œstrum stings;
Thou whose bold flight would leave earth's vulgar crowds,
And like the eagle soar above the clouds,
What pang like thine can striving mortals know
When the red lightning strikes thee from below?

Less bronze, more silver, mingles in the mould
Of him whom next my roving eyes behold;
His, more the scholar's than the statesman's face,
Proclaims him born of academic race.
Weary his look, as if an aching brain
Left on his brow the frozen prints of pain;
His voice far-reaching, grave, sonorous, owns
A shade of sadness in its plaintive tones,
Yet when its breath some loftier thought inspires,
Glows with a heat that every bosom fires.
Such Everett seems; no chance-sown wild-flower knows
The full-blown charms of culture's double rose:
Alas, how soon, by death's unsparing frost,
Its bloom is faded and its fragrance lost!

Two voices, only two, to earth belong
Of all whose accents met the listening throng:
Winthrop, alike for speech and guidance framed,
On that proud day a two-fold duty claimed.
One other yet, — remembered or forgot, —

He stands before you, — so I name him not.
Can I believe it? I, whose youthful voice
Claimed a brief gamut, — notes not over choice, —
Stood undismayed before that solemn throng,
And *propria voce* sung the saucy song
Which even in memory turns my soul aghast, —
*Felix audacia* was the verdict cast.

What were the glory of those festal days
Shorn of their grand illumination's blaze?
Night comes at last with all her starry train
To find a light in every glittering pane.
From "Harvard's" windows see the sudden flash,
Old "Massachusetts" glares through every sash,
From wall to wall the kindling splendors run
Till all is glorious as the noonday sun.

How to the scholar's mind each object brings
What some historian tells, some poet sings!
The good gray teacher whom we all revered,
Loved, honored, laughed at, and by freshmen feared,
As from old "Harvard" where its light began
From hall to hall the clustering splendors ran,
Took down his well-worn Æschylus and read,
Lit by the rays a thousand tapers shed,
How the swift herald crossed the leagues between
Mycenæ's monarch and his faithless queen;
And thus he read, — my verse but ill displays
The Attic picture, clad in modern phrase: —

> *On Ida's summit flames the kindling pile,*
> *And Lemnos answers from his rocky isle;*
> *From Athos next it climbs the reddening skies,*
> *Thence where the watch-towers of Macistus rise.*
> *The sentries of Mesapius in their turn*
> *Bid the dry heath in high-piled masses burn,*
> *Cithæron's crag the crimsoned smoke-wreaths stain,*
> *Far Ægiplanctus joins the fiery train.*
> *Thus the swift courier through the pathless night*
> *Has gained at length the Arachnæan height,*
> *Whence the glad tidings, borne on wings of flame,*
> *"Ilium has fallen!" reach the royal dame.*

So ends the day; before the midnight stroke
The lights expiring cloud the air with smoke;
While these the toil of younger hands employ,
The slumbering Grecian dreams of smouldering Troy.

As to that hour with backward steps I turn,
Midway I pause; behold a funeral urn!
Ah, sad memorial! known but all too well
The tale which thus its golden letters tell: —

> *This dust, once breathing, changed its joyous life*
> *For toil and hunger, wounds and mortal strife;*
> *Love, friendship, learning's all-prevailing charms,*
> *For the cold bivouac and the clash of arms.*
> *The cause of freedom won, a race enslaved*
> *Called back to manhood, and a nation saved,*
> *These sons of Harvard falling ere their prime*
> *Leave their proud memory to the coming time.*

While in their still retreats our scholars turn
The mildewed pages of the past, to learn
With endless labor of the sleepless brain
What once has been and ne'er shall be again,
We reap the harvest of their ceaseless toil
And find a fragrance in their midnight oil.
But let a purblind mortal dare the task
The embryo future of itself to ask,
The world reminds him, with a scornful laugh,
That times have changed since Prospero broke his staff.
Could all the wisdom of the schools foretell
The dismal hour when Lisbon shook and fell,
Or name the shuddering night that toppled down
Our sister's pride, beneath whose mural crown
Scarce had the scowl forgot its angry lines,
When earth's blind prisoners fired their fatal mines?
New realms, new worlds, exulting Science claims,
Still the dim future unexplored remains;
Her trembling scales the far-off planet weigh,

Her torturing prisms its elements betray;
We know what ores the fires of Sirius melt,
What vaporous metals gild Orion's belt, —
Angels, archangels, may have yet to learn
Those hidden truths our heaven-taught eyes discern,
Yet vain is Knowledge, with her mystic wand,
To pierce the cloudy screen and read beyond;
Once to the silent stars the fates were known,
To us they tell no secrets but their own.

At Israel's altar still we humbly bow,
But where, oh where, are Israel's Prophets now?
Where is the Sibyl with her hoarded leaves?
Where is the charm the weird enchantress weaves?
No croaking raven turns the auspex pale,
No reeking altars tell the morrow's tale;
The measured footsteps of the Fates are dumb,
Unseen, unheard, unheralded, they come, —
Prophet and priest and all their following fail.
Who then is left to rend the future's veil?
  Who but the Poet, he whose nicer sense
No film can baffle with its slight defence,
Whose finer vision marks the waves that stray,
Felt, but unseen, beyond the violet ray;
Who, while the storm-wind waits its darkening shroud,
Foretells the tempest ere he sees the cloud,
Stays not for time his secrets to reveal,
But reads his message ere he breaks the seal?
So Mantua's bard foretold the coming day
Ere Bethlehem's infant in the manger lay;
The promise trusted to a mortal tongue
Found listening ears before the angels sung.
So while his load the creeping pack-horse galled,
While inch by inch the dull canal-boat crawled,
Darwin beheld a Titan form "afar
Drag the slow barge or drive the rapid car;"
That panting giant fed by air and flame,
The mightiest forges task their strength to tame,
Snatched from the grasp of heaven's reluctant sire
As first Prometheus stole its parent fire.

Happy the Poet! him no tyrant fact
Holds in its clutches to be chained and racked;
Him shall no mouldy document convict,
No stern statistics gravely contradict;
No rival sceptre threats his airy throne, —
He rules o'er shadows, but he reigns alone.

Shall I the Poet's broad dominion claim
Because you bid me wear his sacred name
For these few moments? Shall I boldly clash
My flint and steel, and by the sudden flash
Read the fair vision which my soul descries
Through the wide pupils of its wondering eyes?
List then awhile: the fifty years have sped,
The third full century's opened scroll is spread,
Blank to all eyes save his who dimly sees
The shadowy future told in words like these:

How strange the prospect to my sight appears,
Changed by the busy hands of fifty years!
Full well I know our ocean-salted Charles,
Filling and emptying through the sands and marls
That wall his restless stream on either bank,
Not all unlovely when the sedges rank
Lend their coarse veil the sable ooze to hide
That bares its blackness with the ebbing tide.
In other shapes to my illumined eyes
Those ragged margins of our stream arise:
Through walls of stone the sparkling waters flow,
In clearer depths the golden sunsets glow,
On purer waves the lamps of midnight gleam,
That silver o'er the unpolluted stream.
Along his shores what stately temples rise,
What spires, what turrets, print the shadowed skies!
Our smiling Mother sees her broad domain
Spread its tall roofs along the western plain;
Those blazoned windows' blushing glories tell
Of grateful hearts that loved her long and well;
Yon gilded dome that glitters in the sun
Was Dives' gift, — alas, his only one!

These buttressed walls enshrine a banker's name,
That hallowed chapel hides a miser's shame;
Their wealth they left, — their memory cannot fade
Though age shall crumble every stone they laid.

Great lord of millions, — let me call thee great,
Since countless servants at thy bidding wait,—
*Richesse oblige ;* no mortal must be blind
To all but self, or look at human kind,
Laboring and suffering, — all its wants and woe,—
Through sheets of crystal, as a pleasing show
That makes life happier for the chosen few
Duty for whom is something not to do.

When thy last page of life at length is filled,
What shall thine heirs to keep thy memory build?
Will piles of stone in Auburn's mournful shade
Save from neglect the spot where thou art laid?
Nay, deem not thus; the sauntering stranger's eye
Will pass unmoved thy columned tombstone by,
No memory wakened, not a tear-drop shed,
Thy name uncared for and thy date unread.

But if thy record thou indeed dost prize,
Bid from the soil some stately temple rise, —
Some hall of learning, some memorial shrine,
With names long honored to associate thine :
So shalt thy fame outlive thy shattered bust
When all around thee slumber in the dust.
Thus England's Henry lives in Eton's towers,
Saved from the spoil oblivion's gulf devours ;
Our later records with as fair a fame
Have wreathed each uncrowned benefactor's name;
The walls they reared the memories still retain
That churchyard marbles try to keep in vain.
In vain the delving antiquary tries
To find the tomb where generous Harvard lies :
Here, here, his lasting monument is found,
Where every spot is consecrated ground !
O'er Stoughton's dust the crumbling stone decays,
Fast fade its lines of lapidary praise ;
There the wild bramble weaves its ragged nets,
There the dry lichen spreads its gray rosettes, —

Still in you walls his memory lives unspent,
Nor asks a braver, nobler monument.
Thus Hollis lives, and Holden, honored, praised,
And good Sir Matthew, in the halls they raised;
Thus live the worthies of these newer times,
Who shine in deeds, less brilliant, grouped in rhymes.
When o'er our graves a thousand years have past
(If to such date our threatened globe shall last),
These classic precincts myriad feet have pressed
Will show on high, in beauteous garlands dressed,
Those treasured names our later annals know,
While grateful centuries count the debt they owe.

 Once more I turn to read the pictured page
Bright with the promise of the coming age.
Ye unborn sons of children yet unborn,
Whose youthful eyes shall greet that far-off morn,
Blest are those eyes that all undimmed behold
The sights so longed for by the wise of old.
 From high-arched alcoves, through resounding halls,
Clad in full robes majestic Science calls, —
Tireless, unsleeping, still at Nature's feet,
Whate'er she utters fearless to repeat,
Her lips at last from every cramp released
That Israel's prophet caught from Egypt's priest.
 I see the statesman, firm, sagacious, bold,
For life's long conflict cast in amplest mould:
Not his to clamor with the senseless throng
That shouts unshamed, "Our party, right or wrong!"
But in the patriot's never-ending fight
To side with Truth, who changes wrong to right.
 I see the scholar; in that wondrous time
Men, women, children, all can write in rhyme.
These four brief lines addressed to youth inclined
To idle rhyming in his notes I find : —

> *Who writes in verse that should have writ in prose*
> *Is like a traveller walking on his toes;*
> *Happy the rhymester who in time has found*
> *The heels he lifts were made to touch the ground!*

I see gray teachers, — on their work intent,
Their lavished lives, in endless labor spent,
Had closed at last in age and penury wrecked,
Martyrs, not burned, but frozen in neglect,
Save for the generous hands that stretched in aid
Of worn-out servants left to die half paid.
Ah, many a year will pass, I thought, ere we
Such kindly forethought shall rejoice to see :
Monarchs are mindful of the sacred debt
That cold republics hasten to forget.
 I see the priest, — if such a name he bears
Who without pride his sacred vestment wears;
And while the symbols of his tribe I seek
Thus my first impulse bids me think and speak : —

 Let not the mitre England's prelate wears
Next to the crown whose regal pomp it shares,
Though low before it courtly Christians bow,
Leave its red mark on Younger England's brow.
We love, we honor, the maternal dame,
But let her priesthood wear a modest name,
While through the waters of the Pilgrim's bay
A new-launched Mayflower shows her keels the way.
Too old grew Britain for her mother's beads, —
Must we be necklaced with her children's creeds ?
Welcome alike in surplice or in gown
The loyal lieges of the Heavenly Crown!
We greet with cheerful, not submissive mien
A sister Church, but not a mitred Queen!

A few brief flutters, and the unwilling Muse,
Who feared the flight she hated to refuse,
Shall fold the wings whose gayer plumes are shed,
Here where at first her half-fledged pinions spread.
 Well I remember in the long ago
How in the forest shades of Fontainebleau,
Strained through a fissure in a rocky cell
One crystal drop with measured cadence fell.
Still, as of old, forever bright and clear,
The fissured cavern drops its wonted tear;

And wondrous virtue, simple folk aver,
Lies in that tear-drop of *la roche qui pleure*.
   Of old I wandered by the river's side
Between whose banks the mighty waters glide,
Where vast Niagara, crashing down its fall,
Builds and unbuilds its ever-tumbling wall:
Oft in my dreams I hear the rush and roar
Of battling floods, and feel the trembling shore,
As the huge torrent, girded for its leap,
With bellowing thunders plunges down the steep.
   Not less distinct, from memory's pictured urn,
The gray old rock, the leafy woods, return;
Robed in their pride the lofty oaks appear,
And once again with quickened sense I hear,
Through the low murmur of the leaves that stir,
The tinkling tear-drop of *la roche qui pleure*.

So when the third ripe century stands complete,
As once again the sons of Harvard meet,
Rejoicing, numerous as the sea-shore sands,
Drawn from all quarters, — farthest distant lands,
Where through the reeds the scaly saurian steals,
Where cold Alaska feeds her floundering seals,
Where Plymouth, glorying, wears her iron crown,
Where Sacramento sees the suns go down,
Nay, from the cloisters whence the refluent tide
Wafts their pale students to our Mother's side, —
Mid all the tumult that the day shall bring,
While all the echoes shout and roar and ring,
These tinkling lines, oblivion's easy prey,
Once more emerging to the light of day,
Not all unpleasing to the listening ear
Shall wake the memories of this bygone year,
Heard as I hear the measured drops that flow
From the gray rock of wooded Fontainebleau.

Yet, ere I leave, one loving word for all
Those fresh young lives that wait our Mother's call:
   One gift is yours, kind Nature's richest dower, —
Youth, the fair bud that holds life's opening flower,

Full of high hopes no coward doubts enchain,
With all the future throbbing in its brain,
And mightiest instincts which the beating heart
Fills with the fire its burning waves impart.


O joyous youth, whose glory is to dare,
Thy foot firm planted on the lowest stair,
Thine eye uplifted to the loftiest height
Where Fame stands beckoning in the rosy light, —
Thanks for thy flattering tales, thy fond deceits,
Thy loving lies, thy cheerful smiling cheats!
Nature's rash promise every day is broke, —
A thousand acorns breed a single oak,
The myriad blooms that make the orchard gay
In barren beauty throw their lives away;
Yet shall we quarrel with the sap that yields
The painted blossoms which adorn the fields,
When the fair orchard wears its May-day suit
Of pink-white petals, for its scanty fruit?
Thrice happy hours, in hope's illusion dressed,
In fancy's cradle nurtured and caressed,
Though rich the spoils that ripening years may bring,
To thee the dewdrops of the Orient cling, —
Not all the dye-stuffs from the vats of truth
Can match the rainbow on the robes of youth!


Dear unborn children, to our Mother's trust
We leave you, fearless, when we lie in dust:
While o'er these walls the Christian banner waves,
From hallowed lips shall flow the truth that saves;
While o'er these portals *Veritas* you read,
No church shall bind you with its human creed.
Take from the past the best its toil has won,
But learn betimes its slavish ruts to shun.
Pass the old tree whose withered leaves are shed,
Quit the old paths that error loved to tread,
And a new wreath of living blossoms seek,
A narrower pathway up a loftier peak;
Lose not your reverence, but unmanly fear
Leave far behind you, all who enter here!

As once of old from Ida's lofty height
The flaming signal flashed across the night,
So Harvard's beacon sheds its unspent rays
Till every watch-tower shows its kindling blaze.
Caught from a spark and fanned by every gale,
A brighter radiance gilds the roofs of Yale;
Amherst and Williams bid their flambeaus shine,
And Bowdoin answers through her groves of pine;
O'er Princeton's sands the far reflections steal,
Where mighty Edwards stamped his iron heel;
Nay, on the hill where old beliefs were bound
Fast as if Styx had girt them nine times round,
Bursts such a light that trembling souls inquire
If the whole church of Calvin is on fire!
Well may they ask, for what so brightly burns
As a dry creed that nothing ever learns?
Thus link by link is knit the flaming chain
Lit by the torch of Harvard's hallowed plain.

Thy son, thy servant, dearest Mother mine,
Lays this poor offering on thy holy shrine, —
An autumn leaflet to the wild winds tossed,
Touched by the finger of November's frost,
With sweet sad memories of that earlier day,
And all that listened to my first-born lay.
With grateful heart this glorious morn I see, —
Would that my tribute worthier were of thee!

## II.

## The Speeches at the Dinner.

### OPENING ADDRESS.

BY THE HONORABLE CHARLES DEVENS.

*President of the Alumni Association.*

BRETHREN, — Our solemn festival draws to its close. For a few moments we linger still to interchange our mutual sentiments and feelings, and then to part until the three hundredth anniversary summons the sons of Harvard to unite upon a similar occasion. A few may expect to see that distant day, but most of us know that for us it is impossible. But whether we are to join in it or not, those who shall then commemorate are to be our brethren, united by that bond of fraternity whose mystic chords draw together all who have drunk at this fountain. Their voices as our own, when they meet and when they part, will utter their salutation to our beloved University, "Salve, magna Parens!"

It is well in this time of prosperity, when Massachusetts is a wealthy and powerful State and yet but a portion of a mighty nation whose gateways are on the Atlantic and the Pacific seas, to look back to the day when this college was founded, and to the men who made that day great. It was six years only since they had reached these shores. They had contended with the inhospitable climate; the stern soil they had encountered but not subdued. Their settlements were but a fringe along a stormy sea which separated them from the land they had loved so well and had parted from in obedience to a higher call than that of country, to build here their New Jerusalem. Not sustained by any royal favor or power, not disturbed as yet except it might be by a royal frown; exercising boldly the powers of sovereignty even if in nominal obedience to their parent state; fixing definitely the status of citizens, imposing taxes and duties, determining what should be public charges, — that nothing might be wanting to a full and perfect Commonwealth they established this college, endowing it with the magnificent gift equal to a year's revenue.

One great principle they contributed to the science of government, — and the greatest of states and statesmen might well be proud of the contribution. That the education of the people is a public duty; that there is a right in every child and youth in the land to its rudiments, and to the opportunity for a larger and more liberal culture; that the provision for this is a legitimate public expenditure, — are principles of the gravest importance; and for these the world is indebted to them. The monuments to their own just fame which they reared by the establishment of this college and their provision for public schools are not to be found alone in these halls, or in those where similar institutions teach the higher branches of learning and science, but equally in the humblest village schoolhouse wherever in the broad land it nestles in the valley or by the wayside.

In marshalling the degrees of honor, Lord Bacon has assigned the highest place to the *conditores imperiorum*, or founders of states. With other peoples it has been pleasant to invest them with the colors of poetry and romance. It is to the immortal Gods that Romulus traces his ancestry, and the shadowy Arthur who leads the line of Britain's kings is the poetic type of piety, truth, and courage. But the founders of New England we know as they were; nor is there any danger in an age that differs so widely from that in which they lived that their defects will not be pointed out and their shortcomings clearly exposed. These men are revealed to us alike by their acts and their own written words. Learned beyond any body of men who ever went forth to tempt the fortunes of a new world, their habit of self-inspection, and above all that of bearing true witness give them to us in their diaries and their note-books as they were. We see them in their weakness and their strength. In that which they came to do, they were thoroughly in earnest. In the path they had marked out they intended to walk; those who would walk with them were welcome, for others they had no place. If success was theirs they were willing to ascribe all the glory to God; but they knew that in these latter days he works by human means and human agencies, and that it was for them to seek to compass all for which they prayed. They believed in the sword of the Lord and of Gideon; but the sword of Gideon was the good weapon that hung in their own belts and whose hilt was within the grasp of their own strong right hands. They looked for no miracles to be wrought; the ground must be tilled if it was to bring forth bread, the forest must be felled if there were to be fields and pastures, the sea must be vexed by their lines and nets if they would eat of its fish. They had brought with them an educated clergy trained in the great English universities : they did not propose to be separated from the instructions of its knowledge and culture; unless these could grow and increase as wealth and numbers came to them, they that builded the city would have builded it in vain. "Learning," to use their own fine expression, was not " to be buried in the graves of the fathers."

As they sat together in the rude chamber where the General Court met, November 7, 1636, could we have looked upon them they would have seemed to our eyes plain in dress and manners and stern in aspect, for the responsibilities upon them were heavy and solemn ; yet we should have seen also how high resolve, earnest purpose, devoted faith dignified and ennobled their grave and manly features. Henry Vane was there, —

"Vane young in years, yet in sage counsel old,"

as Milton has written of him. Hugh Peters was there, both afterwards to die upon the scaffold for their stern assertion of the liberties of England. John Winthrop was there, and without question, as he is always seen in our Annals, sweet and calm, wise and brave. Of all that was there said nothing is preserved; neither diary, memorandum, nor note-book yield a word, although carefully and lovingly searched. What they did the record tells. Yet the illustrious orator who stood fifty years ago where I most unworthily stand to-day, imagined in words well befitting the occasion the speech which John Winthrop might have made; and we join in the aspiration with which it concludes: "So long as New England or America hath a name on the earth's surface, the fame and the fruit of this day's work shall be blessed."

These men were in many respects, certainly in lofty conception, above the age in which they lived: nowhere can it be said that they fell below it. Yet neither they nor any body of men ever burst through the environment of the temper and thought of the age in which their lot was cast. If they were intolerant of other modes of belief, this was the result of their peculiar political situation rather than indifference to the rights of others. When power fully came to them, as it did come in England, the belief of others was respected. Every sect in its weakness counsels toleration; but Mr. Hume, one of the bitterest of their critics, says of them: "Of all Christian sects this was the first which during its prosperity as well as its adversity always adopted the principle of toleration."

Certainly this college bears no marks of intolerance, if that charge can rightfully be brought elsewhere against the founders of New England. Established primarily for theological instruction; he whose name it bears and whose gift made its existence possible a clergyman; controlled by the ministry at a time when in all the affairs of the colony their influence was little less than paramount,—the liberal spirit of each charter and constitution it has received has been such that its advantages and privileges have been at the disposal of all, irrespective of differences of belief. Let every one that thirsteth come and drink freely. No creed was ever to be signed, no form of faith professed, no catechism answered by student or professor. In reverent faith its founders entertained the then prevalent doctrines of the Protestant Church. Their difference with the Anglican Church had been one of ritual and discipline rather than of doctrine. They must have understood how large an instrument of authority and influence a great seat of learning is in its sway over opinion, but they did not seek to control it by any formulas which should bind the consciences of those who resorted to it.

The quarter of a millennium which has elapsed since the foundation of our college carries us back even more than is indicated merely by the number of its years. It marks the dawn of the present era in literature and science. Shakespeare and Bacon were but a few years dead, Milton was yet in his youth, Newton was still to come. With all the advance of what may be called modern Europe our University is identified, and steadily it must adapt itself in its high office of instruction to the wants of each generation and its growing needs. Firmly fixed, it stands upon the rocks; but the guidance which it shall give to those who look for its light must be such as they can follow through every channel that learning or science may hereafter discover. The control which its Alumni have by electing its overseers imposes on us the duty of ultimately determining what changes shall from time to time be made, and how it shall best fulfil its great office. It is a grave and solemn trust to be administered in reverent gratitude to those who have gone before us, whose labors we have enjoyed, and in the earnest wish that those who may follow us may reap an abundant harvest from the seed we shall sow. Proportions vary, relations change. The mighty march which has been made in physical science; the carefully guarded secrets which Nature, pursued and tortured in a thousand ways, has been compelled to reveal; the powers and forces which have been discovered and applied to the service of man, — have changed the relative position which the arts and sciences must hereafter occupy in any system of general education. The literature of modern Europe, including that of our own English tongue to which our own countrymen have contributed much, could not be said to have had an existence on the day when our college was founded. It necessarily demands and must receive a larger place as it embodies what is best and noblest in modern thought. Yet it does not follow that our obligation to that of the classic ages is to be denied or disowned. Nor need we feel that what has done so much to dignify and elevate the life of man will lose its genial influence, that the language immortalized by "Tully's voice and Virgil's lay and Livy's pictured page" is to be forgotten, or that the mighty instrument of thought and speech with which Demosthenes fulmined over Greece is to be cast aside as broken and useless.

But whatever changes are to come to our University, its faithful spirit in the culture of knowledge is not to change; nor will it ever be discouraged in the attempt to establish the foundations of that noble and high character which makes useful men able in their own persons to exhibit exalted lives. Apart from all direct instruction, religious or moral, there should be an atmosphere which shall impart to those around whom it flows an inspiration to be worthy and true. In the theocracy of the Puritans, those educated here were to be its churchmen, statesmen, and leaders of its people. All this is changed; but it does not therefore follow that leaders are no longer to exist. We have passed out from the age of authority, but the foundations upon which authority should rightfully exist are not therefore destroyed. There was never a time when philanthropic effort met a more generous response, when wise and mature thought met higher appreciation, when carefully considered utterance found larger audience, or when educated men ready to perform the great duties of life could render more efficient service. That this University has fulfilled in a large measure the hopes of its founders in the broad and general aspects in which its anticipated benefits were presented to their minds, we would willingly believe. The list of its scholars, of its lovers of polite literature, of its teachers, its scientists, its statesmen, bears honored and illustrious names. But it is not upon these alone its fame is to rest. Even if it has been said of the majority of men, "They will have perished as though they had never been, and will become as though they had never been born," this when spoken of brave and faithful men such as this college has sent forth by hundreds and even thousands is far from true. Our vision is weak and narrow: it is only when service is marked and peculiar that to our eyes it becomes apparent. The village Hampdens, "the mute, inglorious" Miltons, do not perish as if they had never been. The professional men who in their day have served the communities in which they dwelt, — the schoolmaster, the physician, the clergyman, who has not only taught but led the way to a higher life, — have found here their moral and intellectual training. Those who have found in commerce or its kindred pursuits their appropriate sphere, or those so placed by fortune that it has not been necessary to pursue the gainful callings of life, have been made here men of feeling and culture, dignifying and elevating the world around them. Men like these mould, educate, and control society. They do not look that any laurel wreath of fame shall adorn their brows: it is enough for them that they are brave and steadfast soldiers in the great army by whose fidelity and courage the world advances.

Nor in the great crises of the nation has it been found heretofore that this college has been unworthy of its high purpose. In the struggles by which the English people fought their own way to civil and religious liberty, in the great debate which preceded the conflict of arms with Great Britain herself, the men educated here were ever prominent. All the signers of the Declaration of Independence from Massachusetts were its children. Nor in the great struggle for national life which came to our own generation were its sons wanting. Certainly, standing in this Hall which pious care has reared to their memory, I cannot forget the young, the beautiful, the brave, who nobly perilled or who nobly surrendered life in that terrible conflict. A subject race has been rescued from bondage, a nation has been lifted from the thraldom to which itself had been condemned by its own toleration, and the integrity of the Union has been established forever. Such a cause has consecrated those who have died in its defence.

By these festival rites we surrender to the century that is to follow this University. Adorned, improved, and with greater capacity for the noble work of education it certainly is; nor will we forget the noble spirit by which its founders were actuated. It is not necessary to accept the religious dogmas of the Puritans, or to attach the importance they did to propositions in theology; but we must admire their spirit of self-sacrifice, their sincere desire to elevate their own lives by a faith which lifted them above all that was ignoble in the present, and gilded with a divine light all that was sordid around them. Far below their lofty ideal standards they fell no doubt, yet these were ever above them. Wealth, rank, worldly success were nothing; where truth led the way they were to follow; what duty commanded, that they were to do. To them much that we see around us would appear strange; these splendid edifices, these

> "storied windows richly dight,
> Casting their dim, religious light,"

would seem at variance with the simplicity they loved; but we will not doubt our communion with them so long as we are loyal to truth and duty. Nor if thus faithful, will we doubt that the calm scholar whose figure moulded by a skilful hand sits in perennial youth at our portals, were he to come again in bodily presence, would fail to recognize us as the children for whom his bounty was intended.

The structure that has been reared here contains in itself all the elements of growth and permanence. In each age, those who are to follow us shall repair, restore, and renew it as wisdom and knowledge shall instruct them. The sands of the desert are piled high above the monuments which Egyptian kings have reared to commemorate their conquests and their renown; those of graceful and artistic Greece, and of mighty Rome, crumble and fall into the dust, — but if their sons are faithful, against this edifice of our fathers the waves of time shall beat in vain. No creeping ivy shall throw out its green and flaunting banner from ruined battlements; but above its towers, strengthened by the noblest thought of each coming age, shall float forever our simple word, "VERITAS."

At the conclusion of President Devens's address the chorus sang "Fair Harvard," after which he introduced the President of the University as follows: —

I give you, brethren, our first sentiment: "Our Alma Mater! In grateful memory of her instructions, her sons come to-day by thousands to do her honor." I respectfully request President ELIOT to respond.

## SPEECH OF CHARLES WILLIAM ELIOT.
### President of the University.

MR. PRESIDENT: GRADUATES OF HARVARD COLLEGE:

AT this high festival, in which tender recollections and hopeful anticipations, thanksgivings for the past and aspirations for the future, are mingling, we all think first of our beloved country, —

> "Old at our birth, new as the springing hours,
> Shrine of our weakness, fortress of our powers,
> Consoler, kindler, peerless 'mid her peers," —

and we salute him who here honorably represents her. [Colonel Lee proposed three cheers for the President, which were heartily given.]

Next we give thanks and praises to Massachusetts, colony, province, commonwealth. Hers was the far-seeing and far-reaching act we celebrate; hers the generative deed, done in loneliness and poverty, but in faith. To-day fifty millions of people in wealth and strength and liberty share its fruits.

Then we greet the representatives of other institutions of learning who have come to rejoice with us; and we welcome the men distinguished in the public service and the professions, in letters, science, or art, whose favoring presence adds lustre to our assembly.

To all these guests you, the graduates of Harvard College, bid hearty welcome. But who shall welcome the welcomers? You need no welcome here.

Familiar rooms and paths, hands of comrades and friends, joyous and tender memories and the visions of your youth have welcomed you.

Why has this throng come up, out of the bustle and strife of the forum and the market-place, to our academic seat? What spirit stirs this multitude to-day? You have come to pay homage to the University of your love, and through it to all universities; because in them truth is sought, knowledge increased and stored, literature, science, and art are fostered, and honor, duty, and piety are taught. The spirit in which you come is a spirit of profound and well-grounded hopefulness.

The brief history of modern civilization shows that in backward ages universities keep alive philosophy, and in progressive ages they lead the forward movement, guiding adventurous spirits to the best point of onward departure. They bring a portion of each successive generation to the confines of knowledge, to the very edge of the territory already conquered, and say to the eager youth: "Thus far came our fathers. Now press you on!" The hope of mankind depends on this incessant work of the philosophical pioneer, who may be years, or generations, or centuries in advance of the common march.

And universities are among the most permanent of human institutions. They outlast particular forms of government, and even the legal and industrial institutions in which they seem to be embedded. Harvard University already illustrates this transcendent vitality. Its charter, granted in 1650, is in force to-day in every line, having survived in perfect integrity the prodigious political, social, and commercial changes of more than two centuries. And still, after more than two centuries, do Winthrops, Endicotts, Saltonstalls, Bulkleys, Danforths, Rogerses, Hoars, and Wigglesworths represent at these tables the founders of the college and the Commonwealth. Here, too, by our sides sit Adamses, Quincys, Cushings, Paines, Wards, Warrens, Emersons, and Pickerings, recalling the qualities, and even the features, of our heroes of the Revolutionary period. So may our descendants shout in this very hall, when fifty years hence the President shall recall heroic names of our day, and shall exhort another generation to be worthy of their fathers' fame.

Then, as now, may the graduates of Harvard look backward with exultation and thanksgiving, and forward with confidence and high resolve.

President DEVENS then said: At our tables the Commonwealth of Massachusetts sits alike as a host and as a guest, so that I shall follow the usual custom, even before announcing our most eminent guest, in order that it may join in our welcome to him. I give you: "The Commonwealth of Massachusetts! Our gratitude is due to her as the legitimate successor of the colony which founded Harvard College."

## SPEECH OF GEORGE D. ROBINSON.

### *Governor of Massachusetts.*

MR. PRESIDENT, — The State of Massachusetts delights to join in the celebration of this festival occasion, which marks a great anniversary in the life and career of our ancient University. Our dear Alma

Mater and our honored and progressive Commonwealth have come down the centuries together, intimately allied for the advance of sound learning, for a larger liberty, for a more intelligent and patriotic citizenship, for a sympathetic support of all movements to improve the condition and welfare of the people, and to make universal the blessings of civil and religious freedom.

To-day Massachusetts and Harvard University, receiving with gratitude the congratulations that come from all parts of the civilized world so abundantly, unite in joyful salutations to all the institutions of learning everywhere; to the common schools that stand in our land as the sure bulwark against ignorance and oppression; to the sister States, those contemporaneous in foundation and settlement, and those, too, reared in the later time and established in peace and prosperity upon the virgin soil of our country. And more especially do we regard with tender but exultant veneration the Union of the States, — the mighty republic of America. And so, Mr. President, there is rare felicity that, as we stand here and together contemplate the triumphs of the centuries that have passed, we are in the presence of that grand nation born of the impulses that sprang up here and around us; and we are permitted to signalize this event by our tributes of honor and appreciation to the distinguished, able, patriotic chief magistrate, the President of the United States. [The audience broke into wild cheering, which was again and again renewed, but which was finally quelled by a deprecating wave of the hand from President Cleveland.] And let me say, sir [turning to President Cleveland], what I know is in the hearts of all, — that in whatever of effort he shall make for sound and just government, for the preservation of the liberties of the people, for clean politics, for incorruptible administration of the momentous trusts of his office, he will find himself in close accord with the high aims that actuated the founders of Harvard College and of the fathers who gave us our beloved Commonwealth.

Receiving to-day with abundant gratitude the high honors of the University, I bear to her my renewed allegiance; and I salute her officers and my fellow-graduates with cordial thankfulness and fraternal regard. It is the record of history that in the earlier days when my predecessors in the gubernatorial office visited the college, they held all their conversations with the President for the time being in the Latin language. This delightful custom has latterly fallen quite into disuse; and the present occasion marks its complete abandonment. Indeed, the intercourse between the high officials at the present time is expressed in words quite intelligible and widely current; and the honorary degrees of the great University have to-day, for the first time in her history, been conferred in the welcome vernacular.

But, sir, I know no higher duty at this time than the recognition of the heroic element exemplified in the college life and character. When in 1775 the immortal Washington took command of the assembled forces of New England before the walls of the college, the instructors and the students, exempt from the burdens of military service, repaired to the quieter precincts of Old Concord, and the halls of learning became the barracks for the patriotic soldiery of America. When rebellion threatened the destruction of our Union, another glorious scene was enacted here. The college sent forth her best and her bravest; and their deeds, wrought in blood and in death, were immortalized in glory, and the grateful survivors of the alumni have reared this magnificent temple and placed these monuments here to memorialize their valor and their sacrifice. And though one of our own poets has said, —

> "What's words to him whose faith and truth
> On war's red touchstone rang true metal?
> Who ventured life and love and youth,
> For the great prize of death in battle," —

yet we treasure in our heart of hearts these grand memories of the past as a precious heritage, and we garner them to-day in the lap of our dear old Mother as the rich fruitage of her triumph and her renown.

But, sir, time does not suffice, nor is it for one voice alone when so many more eloquent are awaiting your summons, to recall the grand record of the past, or to express in prophetic language the still greater future that lies before this revered, dignified, and powerful institution. I know there is nothing better for me to bespeak for Harvard University on behalf of the Commonwealth of Massachusetts, than that all her sons in the coming time, standing on the vantage-ground already gained, shall make their lives as honorable, as conspicuous, as beneficent to mankind as those who laid the foundations here in devotion to learning, to pure religion, to sound morals, and to upright citizenship. Venerable Alma Mater! we hail thee as the mother of a mighty race.

> "On thy brow
> Shall sit a nobler grace than now;
> Deep in the brightness of thy skies
> The thronging years in glory rise,
> And as they fleet
> Drop strength and riches at thy feet."

The PRESIDENT said: It has been with the sincerest pleasure, brethren, that we have welcomed here the President of the United States. We welcome him personally for his many merits and high claims to individual consideration. We welcome him politically as the executive head of the great nation of which Massachusetts is a component part. All of us are interested in the success of his administration, and most cordially wish it success. I give you, then, my brethren: "The President of the United States! Wisdom to the head, courage to the heart, strength to the hand always of him who shall bear aloft the shield on which are emblazoned the arms of the American Union."

## SPEECH OF GROVER CLEVELAND.

*President of the United States.*

MR. PRESIDENT AND GENTLEMEN:

I FIND myself to-day in company to which I am much unused; and when I see the alumni of the oldest college in the land surrounding in their right of sonship the maternal board at which I am but an invited guest, the reflection that for me there exists no alma mater gives rise to a feeling of regret, which is only kindly tempered by the cordiality of your welcome and your reassuring friendliness. If the fact is recalled that only twelve of my twenty-one predecessors in office had the advantage of a collegiate or university education, a proof is presented of the democratic sense of our people, rather than an argument against the supreme value of the best and most liberal education in high public positions. There certainly can be no sufficient reason for any space or distance between the walks of a most classical education and the way that leads to political place. Any disinclination on the part of the most learned and cultured of our citizens to mingle in public affairs, and the consequent abandonment of political activity to those who have but little regard for the student and the scholar in politics, are not favorable conditions under a government such as ours. And if they have existed to a damaging extent, very recent events appear to indicate that the education and conservatism of the land are to be hereafter more plainly heard in the expression of popular will.

Surely the splendid destiny which awaits patriotic effort in behalf of our country will be sooner reached, if the best of our thinkers and educated men shall deem it a solemn duty of citizenship actively and practically to engage in political affairs, and if the force and power of their thought and learning shall be willingly or unwillingly acknowledged in party management.

If I am to speak of the President of the United States, I desire to mention, as the most pleasant and characteristic feature of our system of government, the nearness of the people to their President and other high officials. The close view afforded our citizens of the acts and conduct of those to whom they have intrusted their interests, serves as a regulator and check upon temptation and pressure in office, and is a constant reminder that diligence and faithfulness are the measure of public duty.

And such a relation between the President and the people ought to leave but little room in the popular judgment and conscience for unjust and false accusations, and for malicious slanders invented for the purpose of undermining the people's trust and confidence in the administration of their government. No public officer should desire to check the utmost freedom of criticism as to all official acts; but every right-thinking man must concede that the President of the United States should not be put beyond the protection which American love of fair play and decency accords to every American citizen. This trait of our national character would not encourage, if their extent and tendency were fully appreciated, the silly, mean, and cowardly lies that every day are found in the columns of certain newspapers, which violate every instinct of American manliness, and in ghoulish glee desecrate every sacred relation of private life.

There is nothing in the highest office that the American people can confer which necessarily makes their President altogether selfish, scheming, and untrustworthy. On the contrary, the solemn duties which confront him tend to a sober sense of responsibility; the trust of the American people and an appreciation of their mission among the nations of the earth should make him a patriotic man; and the tales of distress which reach him from the humble and lowly and the needy and afflicted in every corner of the land, cannot fail to quicken within him every kind impulse and tender sensibility. After all, it comes to this: the people of the United States have, one and all, a sacred mission to perform; and their President, not more surely than every other citizen who loves his country, must assume a part of the responsibility of demonstrating to the world the success of popular government. No man can hide his talent in a napkin and escape the condemnation his slothfulness deserves, nor evade the stern sentence which his faithlessness invites.

Be assured, my friends, that the privileges of this day so full of improvement, and the enjoyments of this hour so full of pleasure and cheerful encouragement, will never be forgotten; and in parting with you now, let me express the earnest hope that Harvard's alumni may always honor the venerable institution which has honored them, and that no man who forgets or neglects his duty to American citizenship shall find his alma mater here.

PRESIDENT DEVENS said: I would like to remember on this occasion both the founders of the University and all its benefactors. Those of the benefactors who are living have to-day our warmest gratitude; and to-day we would commemorate also those who have gone before us. I am sure there is no one who could more appropriately answer to such a sentiment than one who was the chief marshal of the celebration fifty years ago, and who represents in his own person John

Winthrop. There is no need that I should speak of the esteem in which we who are his brethren hold his learning, eloquence, and patriotism, nor need I speak of the esteem in which he is held by the people of the United States. You will recognize what I mean, when you recall the fact that within the past five years he has been chosen by the unanimous vote of the Congress of the United States to represent its people on two most important anniversaries in the national history. I give you: "The Founders and the Benefactors of Harvard College! May the seed which they have sown be gathered in an abundant harvest." I respectfully ask Mr. WINTHROP to speak a few words.

## SPEECH OF ROBERT C. WINTHROP.

AND they must be a very few words, Mr. President. I almost wish that I could have been spared entirely from this call. Yet I cannot be wholly silent to such a summons. I thank you, I thank you, sir, for the kind compliments with which you have introduced me. I thank you all, fellow-graduates and friends, for your cordial and cheering reception. But I feel that the best way in which I can exhibit my gratitude is to waste none of the precious moments of this afternoon in any vain attempt to give expression to emotions which you know already that I cannot fail to feel.

I am, indeed, most happy, sir, to be recognized here to-day as in some sort the representative of the grand Harvard Jubilee fifty years ago. I remember doing not a little of hard work for that occasion, as Secretary of the Committee of Arrangements; while, as Chief Marshal of the day, it was my privilege to lead off on their winding way more than fifteen hundred Alumni, — the largest number ever assembled here before, or for many years afterwards. I may be pardoned for reminding you that I was then a good deal less than half the age of my excellent friend, Colonel Lee, who has marshalled us so gallantly to-day; and my pride was of course in the inverse ratio of my years.

I look back on that long procession to see now but a host of shadows. Of the Committee of Forty, two only, besides myself, are left among the living, — the pre-eminent lawyer of Boston, Sidney Bartlett, and our illustrious poet, Oliver Wendell Holmes, who gave us a charming little song at that Jubilee, and who has given us so impressive and stirring a poem at this; and who, we all rejoice to perceive, has renewed his youth like the eagle by that brilliant flight across the Atlantic, and by that rapturous reception which awaited him from the wits of Old England.

Sir, it is not for me to dwell too long upon the reminiscences of the past. But it was only a day or two ago that, in glancing over my old files, I found a most touching reminder of that last Jubilee in the original letter, addressed to me as Secretary of the Committee, by the eminent Harrison Gray Otis, announcing the two afflicting bereavements which prevented him from presiding at the banquet. That letter recalled to me most vividly our deep indebtedness to an ever honored and lamented friend for supplying his place so grandly at such short notice, and rescuing us from confusion and discomfiture. No exigency, however sudden or momentous, could ever take Edward Everett by surprise. He was the prince of Harvard scholars and orators of that day and of all days, full of facility and felicity, — to borrow a phrase of Lord Bacon's, — imitating none, and inimitable by any. His bust and portrait are overhanging me at this moment, and his name can never be forgotten when our Alma Mater is counting up her jewels, as she is so proudly to-day.

But I must not linger on such themes, nor indeed on any other topic. I would willingly have said a word or two on some of those Benefactors and Founders in connection with whose memory you have done me the distinguished honor to call me up. I would eagerly have said something in particular about that young graduate of Emmanuel, whose name, originally given to a single college, now gives individuality and oneness to our whole University, *e pluribus unum*. Of his lineaments, alas! we have but a fancy sketch, and even his lineage, having baffled all research for two centuries and a half, has but just been revealed by what one might almost be pardoned for calling a miraculous moving of the Waters. Never, I think, before or since, was such an enduring and wide-spreading fame so unconsciously won as that of John Harvard; nor is there any other name in all the annals of literature and learning so sure to hold its place in the grateful and affectionate remembrance of generation after generation to the last syllable of recorded time.

But there is another still younger man than John Harvard to whom I should have been glad to pay a brief tribute. I refer to that very young man who presided, as Governor, over the little General Court of Massachusetts Bay which first established and endowed this college in 1636. You have named him, sir, and have quoted the familiar line of John Milton's sonnet, —

"Vane, young in years, but in sage counsel old."

But that sonnet of Milton was written sixteen years after Vane was here in Massachusetts, and when he was still only forty years of age. He was but twenty-four years old when he must have approved, and perhaps signed as Governor, the ordinance under which this University was founded and established. It would have given me peculiar pleasure, as a lineal descendant of his old political opponent, to assert and vindicate his claim to share with John Winthrop the honors of this occasion. Whatever other controversies they may have had with each other, they were evidently of one mind and of one heart as to the founding of this institution. They both knew what colleges were. They brought over to New England personal associations with the great universities of Old England. Vane had been a student at Magdalen's, Oxford. Winthrop had been a student of Trinity College, Cambridge. They had united a few months earlier, in that same year 1636, in large subscriptions for the free schools of Boston. Education in all its grades, as a vital necessity of the infant colony, was plainly at the heart of them both alike. Their names may well be joined in all our memories to-day.

The young Henry Vane, afterwards Sir Henry, remained in Massachusetts only two years. He went back to England in 1637, and participated bravely and heroically in the great struggle for English liberty, and left his name at last on that illustrious roll of martyrs on which are to be found the names of Sir Walter Raleigh and William Lord Russell and Algernon Sidney. His name has been absorbed, in later generations, in a title which has a special and most welcome flavor and fragrance for us here to-day, — the ducal title of Cleveland; and I would say, Honor to that name, on both sides of the Atlantic, whether worn by English Dukes or by American Presidents.

I have trespassed on you, sir, far longer than I intended. But I cannot forget, in closing, that except the charming little song of Dr. Holmes, which nothing but his own modesty could have prevented from finding a deserved place in the records, I am the only survivor of those whose voices were heard in the great Jubilee Pavilion fifty years ago. That Pavilion resounded for four or five hours with the eloquence of Quincy and Everett, of Shaw and Story, of Saltonstall and Sprague, and of Daniel Webster, — whose presence alone was enough to give dignity and grandeur to any occasion which he attended. Nor must I omit to mention among those speakers that accomplished and eloquent scholar and orator of South Carolina, who, only seven years later, at the early age of forty-six, died so suddenly and sadly at the home of his friend George Ticknor, while visiting Boston as Secretary of State of the United States.

But I forbear from all further remark. It is rarely given to any one to speak as he would like to speak at two such Jubilees, half a century apart from each other. I feel sincerely and deeply that I had my turn fifty years ago, and that others are fairly entitled to their turn to-day, more especially the distinguished guests from other colleges and from other climes, whom we are all so impatient to hear and welcome. Need I add, sir, that I am but too conscious of infirmities of age and health and voice, which incapacitate me for doing justice to the occasion or to myself? Let me only, as I resume my seat, offer to my beloved Alma Mater, on this auspicious birthday and in presence of so many of her assembled sons, my earnest and affectionate hopes and wishes and prayers for her long continued and ever increasing prosperity and honor *in sæcula sæculorum!*

The PRESIDENT said: Brethren, I give you, "Emmanuel College, Cambridge, England! — united to us forever by the memory of John Harvard." I will ask the Rev. Dr. CREIGHTON to address us.

## SPEECH OF MANDELL CREIGHTON.

*Professor in the University of Cambridge, England; and delegate from Emmanuel College.*

Two years ago Emmanuel College celebrated the three hundredth anniversary of its foundation in some such way as you are doing to-day. On that occasion

two distinguished alumni of Harvard, — Professor
Lowell and Professor Norton, — no less by the dignity
of their presence than by the eloquence of their speech,
almost succeeded in converting our festival into a celebration of Harvard College in its ancestral soil of England. And we Emmanuel men were glad that it should
be so; for the story of the activity of Emmanuel
College is merged in the larger history of the University of Cambridge, and forms part of the annals of
England in church and state, in society and literature.
But the connection of Emmanuel College with Harvard University is an episode of unique picturesqueness in academic annals, and sets Emmanuel College
in a conspicuous place in the intellectual history of
mankind. For the connection between Emmanuel
and Harvard was not due merely to accident. Emmanuel owed its origin to the same movement of
thought which produced your Commonwealth, and the
ideas which found expression on the coast of Massachusetts Bay were fostered in Sir Walter Mildmay's
new college at Cambridge. Emmanuel College was
founded to be a stronghold of the Puritan party in
the days when they were waging a stubborn and
determined war for the possession of the English
Church. The fortunes of the fight turned against
them in the days of Laud and Charles I.; and in
the hour of their discouragement a scanty band of
resolute men set their faces towards this shore, that
they might set up here that form of society which
they despaired of establishing at home. It was not
the fault of Emmanuel men that the Puritans were

vanquished in England; and I trust that I am not unduly influenced by college sentiment if I say that Emmanuel men were the intellectual leaders of the New England colonists.

The pathetic dignity of the act which you commemorate to-day, the resolution of the General Court to found a college, has been eloquently put before you. Let me carry your thoughts a little further to the pathos of the life of him whom you have agreed to recognize as your founder. I would not for a moment be supposed to disparage research of any kind, and I fully recognize the industry and patriotism which has led one of your graduates to search the records of John Harvard's life. But I cannot help feeling a little glad that he has not discovered too much. To me the solitary figure of the unknown scholar, from whom you take your name, has a special significance through its very indistinctness. To some it is given to work out their ideas through a long course of intellectual production or of public service; others can only express themselves in some one decisive act. We know enough of John Harvard's character to justify our admiration; we know that he was devoted to the spread of learning and the promotion of the public welfare. His munificence was applied to further the object of popular aspiration. What the scanty revenues of the community could scarcely compass was accomplished by the example which his hopefulness set forth. He was at once a scholar, a statesman, a philanthropist; a man whom Emmanuel may be proud to have trained, and Harvard may be proud to recognize as her founder. It matters not that John Harvard cannot be shown to have been a man of social or of intellectual distinction. It may be that John Harvard's teachers shook their heads sadly over an awkward lad who sat silent in their lecture-rooms; but the names of John Harvard's teachers are, I fear, forgotten, while John Harvard's name lives and is venerated to-day, and judging from to-day's enthusiasm is likely to live through the long future of this great University. For John Harvard learned a lesson beyond what his teachers could impart; his fine sense caught the spirit of the institution which had inspired his intellectual life, and with the strength of that spirit he could inspire others.

It is true that learning is cosmopolitan, and knows no distinction of place or clime; but we who dwell by the banks of the sluggish Cam rejoice that we can see in John Harvard, ours and yours alike, a bodily symbol of the link that unites us with you who have called into being a new Cambridge where the Charles River broadens into the Atlantic. Our efforts as teachers can have no higher aim than to send forth into the world young men such as was John Harvard, "a godly gentleman and a great lover of learning." To both of us there are "new worlds to conquer not a few," new places which the light of knowledge may illumine. The good wishes which through me Emmanuel College tenders for the prosperity of this great University are warm and heartfelt; and every Emmanuel man will feel himself strengthened for our common work when I tell him how cordial is the welcome which you have to-day given to the memory of his college.

"God save the Queen" was played by the band; then the PRESIDENT said: Brethren, we have here represented to-day, not only Emmanuel College, but the great University of which it forms a part. The careful historian has estimated that in the early period of our colony there were among its teachers one hundred men who were scholars from the two universities of Cambridge and Oxford. Of these, seventy came from Cambridge and twenty from Emmanuel College. We desire to remember Cambridge, Oxford, and all the other universities of Europe. I will invite Rev. Dr. TAYLOR, master of St. John's College of Cambridge University, to address you.

## SPEECH OF CHARLES TAYLOR.

*Master of St. John's College, Cambridge, England.*

MR. PRESIDENT AND GENTLEMEN:

I AM deeply grateful for the manifest tokens of your good-will toward the universities and colleges of Europe, and I deem it a high privilege to be your guest and the delegate of my own University on this historic occasion. The University of Cambridge has been represented at congresses and anniversary celebrations in the Old World. She has sent her delegates to the heart of Europe and to its Eastern verge, to the land of the Northmen and to the South; but I can truly say, speaking for the whole body corporate which I represent, that of all such gatherings there has never been one that could vie in interest for us with this vast and brilliant concourse of scholars and statesmen from all quarters of the Western Continent, to celebrate the two hundred and fiftieth anniversary of its first and foremost University. Cambridge is proud to see her name perpetuated in this intellectual focus of the New World; to see its most ancient college named after an alumnus of one of her own colleges; to be able to count among her graduates some of the most eminent of your own, as Lowell, Cooke, Goodwin, Norton, and Holmes.

Speaking for myself, if time permitted, I might point to features in the surroundings of this place which make me, an Old World Cambridge man, feel at once almost at home here. But above all I find myself among a people whose essential character has never changed since their forefathers crossed the sea to find a new home and found a New England on these shores. They were men wholly devoted to the truth as they apprehended it, and resolved to hand down their light unimpaired to the generations to come. It was this that impelled them to plant the flag of freedom in a New World.

As I entered New York harbor a few days ago, I saw a colossal statue of the Goddess of Liberty, bearing in her hand a torch, which (I was told) was to be lighted for the first time on the evening of the following day. I went to see the spectacle, and the thought occurred to me that there was a point of view from which the symbol of liberty enlightening the world was inadequate and open to criticism. It did not seem to me to do justice to the self-asserting power of the truth, to which the record of all human progress testifies, *Magna est veritas et praevalet.* Liberty herself

is the outcome of enlightenment. It is the truth that
makes men free. And therefore you have done well
to set *Veritas* at the centre of your college seal, as on
the badges that we wear to-day.

But I must be sparing of my words when so many
are still to be called upon to address you. May Harvard live on to keep many such jubilees as this; and
may the Cambridge of the East and the Cambridge of
the West remain ever one in heart and mind as they
are one in name.

The PRESIDENT said: Brethren, I have the pleasure of
informing you that we have most kind messages from the
University of Oxford and from the University of Heidelberg,
which you will see in our published proceedings. The University of Edinburgh is present by a delegate, whom you will
all most gladly welcome. I have the pleasure of introducing
the Right Hon. Sir LYON PLAYFAIR.

## SPEECH OF LYON PLAYFAIR.

*Delegate from the University of Edinburgh.*

I AM sure that the University of Edinburgh, which
I have the honor to represent on this occasion, will be
pleased to learn that you have thought its delegate
worthy to receive an honorary degree from your
University. There has long been a friendly feeling
between the two universities. In 1771, when your
great Bostonian, Benjamin Franklin, visited Edinburgh, he drew attention to the remarkable progress
which Harvard University was then making. At his
recommendation, the University of Edinburgh conferred honorary degrees on Dr. Cooper and Professor

Winthrop of Harvard, as well as on Dr. Stiles of Yale. Ever since then there has been a loving sympathy between Harvard and Edinburgh. In some points they are alike in the character of their studies, but in others they are as different as the two countries in which they are placed.

In America you have a boundless extent of territory, with every variety of climate and produce. That is not the case in Scotland. We are a small country, with high mountain ranges, having an arid soil and bleak climate. Our coasts are inhospitable, and washed by an ocean always melancholy, but often rendered tempestuous by the keen northern winds. Coal and iron exist in only one corner of the country, in quantity insufficient to give to it a manufacturing character. Nevertheless, Scotland is a prosperous nation; and its contentment and prosperity are due to its schools and four universities. For many years it was thought to be a pious duty of the Scotch Church to find out boys of talent, or in the language of my countrymen, "laddies of pregnant pairts," who were sent up to the universities from the farthest parts of Scotland if their mental pregnancy was assured, and they were maintained by church collections, bursaries, or subscriptions. Thus our universities got a practical character very different from those of England, and are in actual touch with its whole population. Oxford and Cambridge could carry on education for its own sake; but the Scotch universities based their instruction on the learned professions, which have been liberalized by academic teaching and academic influences. The English universities are attended by rich students; the Scotch universities by poor students. The difference as to the result was that English universities aimed at teaching its graduates to *spend* a thousand pounds a year with dignity and intelligence, while the Scotch universities taught men to *make* a thousand pounds a year with dignity and intelligence.

If I read the history and practice of Harvard University aright, you stand midway between these two systems. You have many men of wealth in this country, and you are trying to impress upon their sons the dignity of learning and the duty of advancing knowledge by research and original investigations. Your museums, your laboratories, your observatories are admirably calculated to give instruction and to assist in advancing the boundaries of science. But your country is at the same time characterized by its industrial activities, and you have not lost sight of your duty to give sound experimental knowledge to those who are to engage in them, leaving detailed instruction to such institutions as the remarkable Technological College of Boston. This combination of teaching knowledge for itself with a view to high purposes of human development, and at the same time of showing how it may be applied to the useful purposes of life, especially in the learned professions, is a wise conception of a university in a country of such remarkable progress as the United States.

I am proud, by the degree which you have conferred upon me, now to belong to Harvard University, which is so remarkable for its fulfilment in the past, and which has so much promise of development in the future. Bacon calls universities sometimes the eyes, sometimes the lanthorns of a nation. May Harvard University long be a lanthorn, — a Pharos founded on the rock of democracy, — clearly burning and brightly shining, so as to indicate to a country of wonderful growth and prosperity that the expansion of its public intellect and the advancement of the boundaries of knowledge for its own sake and not merely for its applications, are the highest duty and highest boast of modern civilization.

The PRESIDENT said: Brethren, we have received from San Francisco a most kind message, that all our graduates on the Pacific coast propose to dine together this evening at 7 o'clock. I assumed that I had your authority to say to them that the brethren assembled in these college halls sent them their most cordial congratulations.

And now, brethren, I propose to you: "Our Sister Universities, Colleges, and Schools! Wherever in the broad land their temples rise, we send them salutation and greeting, with earnest wishes for their prosperity and usefulness." And I will ask, as the first response to that toast, that we may hear from the Rev. Dr. DWIGHT, of Yale University.

## SPEECH OF TIMOTHY DWIGHT.

*President of Yale University.*

MR. PRESIDENT AND GENTLEMEN:

IT is in accordance with a most interesting custom which has come down to us from earlier days, that in the sentiment just expressed you speak of our universities as "sisters." They are sisters in one family, for they are daughters of a common mother, — the Truth. Although as they move onward through the course of their life they are separated in their dwelling-places, they are yet bound together by a sacred bond; and while they carry the same inheritance along different pathways, they ever look for the blessing which the common mother would bestow upon all alike.

Of these university sisters in America, Harvard is the oldest; and this is her birthday, her most memorable birthday. Through your kind courtesy I am here as the representative of the one next younger than Harvard in the sisterhood. By a somewhat singular coincidence, it chances to be the fact that the oldest university except your own sends to you in my person the youngest in office among the presidents of all these collegiate institutions. It would seem not unfitting that it should be so, for when the younger daughters come to greet the eldest on her festive day, a beautiful custom often followed in our households places the youngest of all the children in the whole circle of the family at the head of the procession which is to bear the greeting and congratulation. As the youngest of these officers in term of service, I present myself before you in the name of all, that I may offer to you our common salutation, and may give expression to the wish that Harvard University may go forward in a prosperous career for the next two hundred and fifty years, and far beyond that period, and may find continually increasing success and honor as the years and generations pass away.

And now, sir, let me say a word or two for myself. Of the graduates of Harvard College in its first class, 1642, two have an ancestral connection with me, although I am not a lineal descendant of either of them. One of these first graduates was John Wilson, who married a daughter of the Rev. Thomas Hooker, the first minister of Hartford, Connecticut. Thomas Hooker was a direct ancestor of mine. The other was George Downing, whose father, Emanuel Downing, married the sister of John Winthrop; and the daughter of Emanuel Downing and Lucy Winthrop I may claim as a direct ancestress of mine. I may take to myself, therefore, some share in the inheritance which belongs to the family of Governor Winthrop. And as I find, in looking into the history of Harvard College, that when it was first founded a provision was made that no meeting of the corporation should carry on its business unless Governor Winthrop, or the lieutenant-governor, or the treasurer of the State should be present, I feel that I have also a sort of hereditary claim upon Harvard College itself. Certainly I have a present claim upon it, for I discover to-day, to my great surprise, that I have become a graduate of Harvard College. Let me say, sir, without offence to my friend President Eliot, that I have obtained my degree according to the provisions of the elective system, and that during the course which has terminated in this degree I have adopted that method which some of the enemies of the elective and voluntary system charge upon it as one of its evils, — namely, I have absented myself from the exercises during the whole period. But notwithstanding this, sir, the President declared to you in the morning exercises that I had graduated with the highest honors which the University can bestow. I wish, sir, to acknowledge my obligations to the elective system.

As President Eliot and myself are now both of us graduates of Harvard College and also of Yale College, what reason, let me ask, can there be why Yale College and Harvard College shall not move onward side by side into the university life of the future, each rejoicing in the other's prosperity? So far as my efforts and work are concerned, I am sure that there will be no want of generous sympathy and friendship between these two oldest universities, for the names of honored men of the olden time in the history of both — Winthrop and Edwards, in union with that which came to me by inheritance — are borne by one of my children, a sweet spirit that came to my household from the unseen realm a few years ago, and thus are familiar to me as words in the daily use and conversation of the family life. The name of Winthrop speaks of this ancient college; that of Edwards is representative of Yale, and also of a benediction which Yale gave to Princeton; and my own ancestral name bears witness for Yale College. I cannot better close these few words of greeting, therefore, than by offering, as the sentiment which I personally bring to you, this hearty wish: May these universities, these two oldest universities of our country, be closely united together; and may the blessing of God rest upon them as the blessing of God rested upon my household when the honored names of which I have spoken were united in one within it.

The PRESIDENT said: Brethren, I shall call up in response to the same sentiment the President of the University of Michigan, who represents not only the colleges of the West, but the great system of instruction which is carried on in those universities that are supported, almost if not entirely, by the States. I present to you President ANGELL, of the University of Michigan.

## SPEECH OF JAMES B. ANGELL.
### *President of the University of Michigan.*

MR. PRESIDENT, — As a delegate from the young West, having travelled further, I think, than any other delegate except our distinguished friends from beyond the sea to be here, I feel a certain hesitancy in accepting the very honorable and very pleasing duty to which you have called me; for these sister universities, a numerous and learned constituency, are many of them venerable with years and with honors, and we in the West are so very young. Why, sir, our modesty, our self-depreciating spirit, has been growing only about fifty years. Even the modesty of our Duluth and Chicago, which have attained such colossal proportions, have had only half a century in which to bring their product to its bright consummate flower and fruit. But, sir, I am sure that I worthily represent the sister colleges when I say that there is not one of them, from the eldest to the very youngest, which does not delight to recognize their obligations to this elder sister, on whose model we all have builded, and at whose shrine we all have kindled our lamps.

We are thankful that we are permitted by your hospitality to come up here to-day and to join with you in expressions of gratitude to the early benefactors of this institution; for we are their debtors hardly less than you. The glowing words in which your great master of classic eloquence, Edward Everett, when fifty years ago he was occupying the chair which you adorn to-day, celebrated the first appropriation of the General Court to the infant college as the earliest example in history of a people voluntarily taxing themselves for the support of education, are every year recited with unction to the legislators of the Western States, and, I am happy to say, not without stimulating them to imitation of your first legislative assembly. The splendid gifts of your Hollises and Holworthys from beyond the sea, and of your Harvards and Winthrops and Saltonstalls and the whole glorious company of their associates on this side of the sea, have, like the widow's mite, and like all other hallowed gifts, been endowed by God with the blessed power of indefinite reproduction in all sections of the land. The familiar story of the heroic self-denial with which your ancestors, while yet in their new settlement, unfurnished with many of the essential comforts of civilized life, shared their scanty harvests of corn with your treasury, and stripped their meagrely-furnished tables of their heirlooms of silver and porcelain to aid the college, has now these two hundred years been melting the hearts and kindling the enthusiasm and unloosing the purse-strings of thousands of men on whom the American colleges have depended for their very existence.

The gospel which, we are told, has been preached and accepted in these streets, that no Bostonian may cherish a reasonable hope of future felicity until he has provided in his will for a generous gift to Harvard, all the rest of us have been proclaiming, *mutatis mutandis*, in the neighborhood of our various colleges. And as those of us, out of Massachusetts at least, are very orthodox, we have given no man any ground for hoping that on this question there is any second probation.

Yet further, — not to speak of your high service to us all in holding up the best standard of culture, since the limit of time forbids, — we are all under obligations to Harvard for her brave experimentations on college and university problems. Many here can recall the apathy on such subjects which prevailed in the third and fourth decades of this century. Even the iconoclastic attacks of my old teacher, Dr. Wayland (*clarum et venerabile nomen!*), when he came thundering down as with the hammer of Thor on old beliefs and old ways, hardly startled college circles from the traditional belief that the old-fashioned college curriculum must be as unchangeable as a Buddhist liturgy. But here the movement which George Ticknor started long ago finally brought forth results. Especially under the present vigorous administration there have been such exhaustive study and such courageous experimenting, that the excitement and stir have reached even the remotest country college and the most secluded village academy; and the discussion of college problems divides with the discussion of tariffs, civil service reform, and party politics the columns of the secular newspapers. This has made an epoch. Never before did the college and the people get so near together. Those who do not accept the doctrines in favor here and those who do are alike indebted to you, for we have all been stirred. In college life as in all life, anything is better than stagnation. Those who differ from you have had the profound, the delicious satisfaction of showing even Harvard that she can be in error. Those of us who agree with you in the main have had the yet higher satisfaction of enjoying your companionship in the new ways. It is simple justice to you to say that it is largely due to you that educational problems are studied afresh in the light of the facts and news of to-day as they never were studied before.

Now, finally, as you have done so much for us in the past, we beg you, fresh in your eternal youth, to push forward toward that bright goal which ever draws us on, — the full development of the American university. You have many advantages for marching in the van. Be assured no petty jealousies on our part shall check you in the race. On the contrary we beg you to push on; we bid you God-speed!

The PRESIDENT said: Brethren, we hope to hear from the colleges of the South, and, above all, from that most interesting of universities, — the University of Virginia, connected so intimately with the name of Thomas Jefferson; and it is with great pleasure that I announce that Mr. FRANCIS R. RIVES is present as delegate from the University of Virginia, and I hope we may hear a few words from him.

## SPEECH OF FRANCIS ROBERT RIVES.

MR. PRESIDENT, — The University on whose behalf I am present is but a child beside the venerable antiquity of Harvard and other institutions of learning here represented; and it is a proverb, you know, that children should be seen and not heard. But, sir, the cordial kindness with which you have called upon me leads me to speak, — at least for a moment.

The author of the Declaration of Independence was the father of the University of Virginia, and the high estimation in which he held Harvard is attested by his earnest efforts, unsuccessful though they were, to have among its first professors your Bowditch and your Ticknor. He then turned to that fruitful source of inspiration to your early founders, — the Cambridge of Old England. That far-seeing philosopher provided that every student of the University of Virginia should be free to attend the schools of his choice. He did this more than sixty years ago; and in some respects at least you of Harvard have of late adopted his provision, by giving a wider election in academic studies. He also, as naturally became the author of the statutes of Virginia for religious freedom, guarded against any obligatory attendance upon public worship; and I think I may say to you in reference to your recent regulation on this subject, that, from our experience, it will conduce to the cause of true religion.

Mr. President, I shall go back to Virginia and tell with what joy I saw Harvard to-day confer the degree of Doctor of Laws upon one who was for a long time a most honored professor in the University of Virginia. That University would have performed the same office for him, but that Mr. Jefferson, in the rules he prescribed for its government, had absolutely prohibited the conferring of any honorary degree; and I note with interest that within the past fortnight a distinguished University of the North has decided in future to prohibit, for itself, the granting of honorary degrees.

I hope, sir, with ardent hope, that Harvard may live in prosperity to celebrate with ever increasing glory its full millennial anniversary; and that between Harvard and the University which I have the honor to represent the ties of friendship may grow closer and closer as time flies on.

The PRESIDENT said: Brethren, I desire to call your attention not only to our scholars, but to those of our graduates and of our friends from other colleges who have rendered public service in the halls of legislation and in other of its most important transactions. I give you: "The public service! The contribution of true, wise, and learned men which Harvard has heretofore made to its needs has been large and generous. It will not be diminished hereafter." And I respectfully ask Senator HOAR to respond to this sentiment.

## SPEECH OF GEORGE F. HOAR.
*United States Senator from Massachusetts.*

YOUR courtesy, Mr. President, which never fails, finds many devices to justify the exercise of your authority. But I wish to speak here, to-day, only by my most honorable and precious title, — that of a son and a lover of Harvard. For the last fifty years the college has made few contributions, in number, to the public life of the country. There have been but three of her graduates in the Senate of the United States since Mr. Everett left it in 1854. There have been but five for fifty years. Whether this be bad for her or not, I will not undertake to say. It has been in my judgment bad for the public service.

But, after all, Harvard has contributed her full share of those things by which the generations are remembered. We have had lessons enough to make us cautious of accepting contemporary judgments. But as they recede, the time comes when the generations of men are compared with each other. What is accidental and passing disappears. The world makes its permanent and commonly final estimate of the great forces and the great men who determine the current of history.

I think it must be admitted that whenever, from the beginning of our history, Massachusetts has had a primacy or leadership in the country, Harvard has furnished leadership to Massachusetts. In the day of the Puritans, when the foundations of empire were laid, the college was not so much the child of the Commonwealth as part of the Commonwealth itself. The church, the general court, the town, the college, were the four voices by which the State spoke.

If you come to the great debate of liberty which decided the Revolution before a gun was fired, the six men, with whom no other Massachusetts name of that generation is mentioned — John Hancock and Sam Adams, Joseph Warren and James Otis, John Adams and Josiah Quincy — were all Harvard men.

Massachusetts divides with Virginia the foremost honors of the Revolution. She has no rivals for the greater honor of forming and instructing that popular sentiment which gave freedom to the slave. Here, perhaps, the leadership of Harvard men is less exclusive. But she contributed to that cause Dr. Channing, John Quincy Adams, President Quincy, Charles Sumner, Richard Dana, Wendell Phillips, the Muse of Longfellow, the wit of Hosea Biglow, — that brave little king-bird who used to drive the buzzards from the sky, — the pen of Palfrey, who attacked slavery with a vigor that Junius never reached, and with a moral purpose of which he was incapable.

It is hazardous, for me I am afraid it is presumptuous, to undertake to say what posterity will regard as the glory of Harvard and of Massachusetts for the generation which is now passing from the stage. As we look back upon mediæval Italy, four laurelled heads come out upon the canvas. So it seems to me that when almost everything else that we are doing or saying is forgotten, our group of six famous poets, — all of them sons of Massachusetts, three of them sons of Harvard by nurture, and one, yes, now two by adoption, — will still be shining in the sky. Science will remember Agassiz. She will not forget Peirce, the inhabitant without a companion of the lofty domain of higher mathematics, —

> "A privacy of glorious light is thine."

But still, and above all, the blessing shall be theirs and the eternal praise —

> "Who gave us nobler loves and nobler cares, —
> The Poets, who on earth have made us heirs
> Of truth and pure delight by heavenly lays."

One of the best things about these eminent men of letters of our time is their cordial and affectionate relation with one other. They do not seem to have descended from the genus *irritabile vatum*. Each of them is at his best when he is speaking of the others. If I were to select the finest specimen of Campbell's genius, it would be a passage of matchless prose. If of our brother Dr. Holmes, it would be his tributes to Longfellow and Emerson. When our brother left off the poet and took on the prophet this morning at the close of his poem, in contemplating the glories of Harvard at the end of the next fifty years, I noticed even he did not venture to predict that they would get a better poem or a better oration than we have had to-day.

So I think, my friends, we may fairly claim, when we come to compare the generations with each other, that there is something which has come from the college, a certain unmistakable Harvard leaven, which in

Massachusetts and in the country has leavened the whole lump. There is one thing that can be said, and should be said, about this Harvard leaven, — that is that it holds out, and keeps fresh, and lasts through. We hear a good deal nowadays about young men's movements, and young men's parties, and what young men want and feel. I have noticed it is commonly said by men who are getting well on to fifty, and whose hair is growing thin on the top. I can speak, and I have a right to speak, now forty years out of college, for the old men among the sons of Harvard. I think the old Harvard men, of any period, might without vanity invite their younger brethren to a friendly comparison either of service or character, where the test shall be any one of the qualities — courage, enthusiasm, energy, generosity, faith — of which youth sometimes claims the monopoly. That is a pretty poor style of character, that is a pretty poor style of instruction, which does not make men grow better as they grow old. The love of liberty, the love of justice, the sense of duty, the sense of honor cannot have been deeply planted, they find no congenial element in the soul where they do not brighten as they burn, — *clarescunt urendo*. It was the gray-haired clergy of Massachusetts at whose knees the patriots of the Revolution learned the lesson of constitutional liberty. It was the gray-haired John Quincy Adams who breasted the stormy waves of the House of Representatives at eighty-three. The Josiah Quincy who saw the beginning and who foresaw the end of the Revolution, and died at thirty; the Josiah Quincy who saw the beginning and who foresaw the end of the Rebellion, and died at ninety, — were of the same spirit, though, if anything, the man of ninety was the younger of the two. It may be that age cools the hearts of common men. But for men tempered by the best Harvard training the saying of Pericles is still true: "The love of honor alone is ever young; and not riches, as some say, but honor, is the delight of men when they are old."

Another lesson we may draw from the birthday of this vigorous life which spans so large a part of what is remembered of the world's history. It is a lesson which men of wealth who desire an honest usefulness or an honorable fame may well heed. That is, that the one safest and most permanent thing in this world is an institution of learning, wisely founded. Whatever perish, that shall endure. There is no memory more pleasant among men than that of its benefactors. There is no monument like a portrait upon its walls. There is no gratitude better worth having than that felt by successive generations toward those to whom they owe their education. There is scarcely an exception in England, and none in America. I do not forget the College of William and Mary in Virginia, next to Harvard in age, once not behind her in influence, — the college of Jefferson and Marshall and Monroe and Winfield Scott; mother of three presidents; to whom, as her chancellor, Washington gave his last public service, and which was destroyed in the Civil War. The stout-hearted old President still rings the morning bell and keeps the charter alive. I would salute him to-day from Harvard, not knowing any act of fidelity more delightful to gaze upon; and I would rejoice more than in any public honor or private good fortune which could come to me, if I might live to see the old historic college of Virginia endowed anew with the liberal aid of the sons of Harvard.

But I ought not to speak any longer. The lesson of this hour is hope, not retrospect. May Harvard continue to send forth her manly children to wrestle with the new centuries as they have with the old, until time shall be no more. May she continue as ever to train them for leadership in the Commonwealth in all noble and lofty paths. May she continue to teach them reverence for the Republican life of which they are to form a part, and for the great history of whose glory they are inheritors.

Here followed the playing of Keller's "American Hymn" by the Cadet Band, after which the PRESIDENT said: Brethren, I am sure that if you remember the earlier portion of the remarks of Senator Hoar, who has just sat down, you will know that the names which now first rush to my lips must be those of the orator and poet of to-day. They have added heavily to the obligation which we have heretofore been under to them. I hope that Professor LOWELL will be kind enough to say a few words.

## SPEECH OF JAMES RUSSELL LOWELL.

MR. PRESIDENT, AND BRETHREN OF THE ALUMNI:

You, sir, have alluded to the phrase with which Senator Hoar began his speech. You will allow me to allude to the phrase with which he closed; namely, that this occasion is rather one for hope than retrospect. You cannot expect me, at this time of the afternoon, and after a certain amount of fatigue this morning, to detain you long. But I wish to be allowed to indulge in one moment of retrospect, which combines in itself also the element of hope. I think it was just fifty years ago that I received the honor from the Faculty of Harvard College of first addressing the University. Four minutes were assigned to me, in which I was to define to the best of my ability the relative merits of Homer and Virgil as epic poets. I have no doubt that a great many of the important things that I said in that dissertation are fresh in the memory of my classmate, our President, and they probably influenced his thought to a certain extent; but I cannot help thinking that this morning was the first time that I really had an opportunity offered me to revenge myself for that parsimony of fifty years ago, and I have some apprehension that I revenged myself a little too amply. But I beg you to believe that I omitted all the best part of my address.

That has always been associated in my mind, — not the dissertation assigned me, but I mean the period of fifty years ago is most intimately associated in my mind with my first literary sensation, certainly my first genuine one. That was at the Phi Beta in 1836, when a young gentleman, fresh from Europe and from the study of medicine there, delivered a poem. I can see him as if it were but yesterday. I was then, I believe, just ending my Sophomore year. I was one of the delighted throng that heard him. I remember with what wonderful spirit and precision that poem was delivered. I can still repeat some of the admirable verses I then heard. I remember how they brought down the house. Dear me! they don't bring down houses now as they did then. How well I remember the alert figure, the brown hair, the bright gray eyes of the poet! Since that time my friend Dr. Holmes seems to have gone out incautiously into a snowstorm without his hat,—an imprudence which a medical man would forbid to anybody else; but I could not help thinking this morning that the poem was delivered with nearly all of the old spirit, with the same force and the same precision and clearness of speech as fifty years ago. I allude to it, not to compliment him,— for I am sure he does not need it,—but simply, as I say, because it points to a certain hope connected with a certain retrospect, that some of us may attain in full vigor the next jubilee of Harvard. But I shall not detain you any longer now, because, as I told you, I am not quite so fresh as I was this morning, and I am largely to blame if you also are not quite so fresh. So you will allow me to yield to my friend Dr. Holmes, who will entertain you much better than I can.

## SPEECH OF OLIVER WENDELL HOLMES.

Dr. Holmes said that he had been writing in verse so much of late that he found it hard to say anything in prose. He was like a sailor just landed, with his sea-legs on. He would content himself with a few words respecting his own share in the centennial of

1836. "It was suggested to me," he said, "by the late Dr. Jacob Bigelow, himself the writer of the capital Latin song beginning —

'Qui alicujus gradûs laureâ donati estis,'

that I should write a song to the tune, then a very familiar one, of 'The Poachers.' This I did, and sung it myself, though a vocalist of very limited power. You may be willing to hear a verse or two from this production, which was sent too late for insertion to the publishing committee of the celebration of 1836."

Dr. Holmes then repeated two or three verses which he happened to remember; among them were the three which follow : —

>When the Puritans came over,
>  Our hills and swamps to clear,
>The woods were full of catamounts,
>  And Indians red as deer,
>With tomahawks and scalping-knives
>  That make folks' heads look queer;
>Oh, the ship from England used to bring
>  A hundred wigs a year!
>
>. . . . . .
>
>And who was on the Catalogue
>  When College was begun?
>Two nephews of the President,
>  And *the* Professor's son
>(They turned a little Indian by,
>  As brown as any bun);
>Lord! how the Seniors knocked about
>  The freshman class of one!
>
>. . . . . .
>
>God bless the ancient Puritans!
>  Their lot was hard enough;
>But honest hearts make iron arms,
>  And tender maids are tough;
>So love and faith have formed and fed
>  Our true-born Yankee stuff,
>And keep the kernel in the shell
>  The British found so rough!

The PRESIDENT said: Our next sentiment is, "A learned and pious clergy, — at all times and everywhere the most efficient friends of education." The Rev. Dr. Hitchcock, who was to respond, has been compelled to retire. We hope, however, that he will furnish the speech for our memorial report which he would have made.[1]

I give you now: "Progress in literature has brought to the many the refined enjoyment of letters which once were the property of a limited class." I invite Professor GILDERSLEEVE of Johns Hopkins University to say a word.

## SPEECH OF BASIL LANNEAU GILDERSLEEVE.

*Professor in Johns Hopkins University.*

IF there is one thing more perplexing to the mind of the after-dinner speaker than another, it is the problem of his special fitness for the part that has been assigned to him. At least this is what they all say in words or in effect; and being myself a reluctant and infrequent intruder into this peculiar province of

---

[1] The following note was later received:

UNION THEOLOGICAL SEMINARY, 1200 PARK AVENUE,
NEW YORK CITY, Feb. 1, 1887.

DEAR SIR, — I should be very sorry to seem to be at all disloyal to an occasion of so much interest to me personally as your Quarter-Millennial Commemoration.

As I told Judge Devens, I had a brief of what I proposed to say after dinner, but as usual it was only a brief; and I got the impression that, on the whole, you found it best to report only what was actually said. So I let the nascent birds — whether owls or eagles — fly away. I was intending to say something about the relative rank of the so-called learned professions as affected by the growth, and by the changes, of our civilization. But as you have so much to report, I think you had better accept simply the assurance of my most cordial good-will.

Yours very truly, ROSWELL D. HITCHCOCK.

MR. JUSTIN WINSOR.

oratory, I cannot do better than to follow the example of more practised men, and wonder why I should be called on to respond to the sentiment of the progress of literature. To many my chief recommendation will be the character of my special studies; for the votary of the dead languages is popularly supposed to be subdued to what he works in, until he becomes a dead thing, until he turns to a manner of stake or milestone or finger-post, or some such conservative fixture, so that he may well answer as a point of reference for more progressive studies, — just as a fetich-worshipper might be chosen as a point of departure for the development of the religious idea. But to some besides myself, if I may judge by what I have heard to-day, the value of classical study as the measure of literary progress is not that of the milestone which is left behind, but that of the vernier that follows the sweep of the telescope through the heavens; and the words of a great master of letters are still ringing in our ears: "Only those languages can properly be called dead in which nothing living has been written." With this comforting reassurance, I should approach my task with greater confidence if I were not appalled by the lateness of the hour, and with the reflection that I can have nothing to add to what has been better said in your hearing.

When the progress of literature is spoken of, we mean, of course, the progress of literature during the last two hundred and fifty years, — for we measure everything to-day by the standard of Harvard; we mean the period that nearly touches Bacon's essays at one end and overlaps Emerson's essays at the other; the period that spans the youth of the satirist Dryden and the maturity of the satirist Lowell; that laughs in its first half-century at the wit of Butler and is radiant in its last half-century with the wit of Holmes. Now, you will not expect me to work out the history of literature for the last two hundred and fifty years at the rate of fifty years a minute for the past, with no margin at all for the boundless future; and you will be more than satisfied with the simple statement of my thesis, which has been abundantly proved and abundantly illustrated by others to-day.

The history of the literature in which we are most vitally interested is the history of the constant adjustment of the modern to the antique. That this adjustment is to end in the elimination of the antique I do not in the least believe. There will always be a corner left somewhere for Greek (there will always be a corner left here), from which Greek will continue to govern our world, even if it ceases to reign over so large a number of titular subjects, and there is to be a new renaissance, very unlike externally to the old renaissance, yet not less potent nor less formative. What that earlier renaissance was, with all its glowing acceptance of antique literature as a fair creation restored from the dead; what the glorious Elizabethan period was, with its unrivalled opulence and splendor of achievement,— does not enter into the scope of our vision to-day. All this was over when Harvard came into being; and it is not necessary to ask what the classics were to Valla, to Politian, or what the classics were to Shakespeare. But what they were to the generations that have followed Shakespeare is faithfully recorded in the register of your University; for the power of Harvard lies in discerning the signs of the times, and in a wise adaptation to the changing relations of the world in which men live. Now, no one can claim a special charm for the transition period in which Harvard was founded. It was, as we know, a period of sobering down from the intoxication of thought and fancy in which the long symposium of the Elizabethan age had culminated. The classics were to be no longer an inspiration but a corrective; and generation after generation had to pass before English literature felt the stirrings of the true life of Greece. Of learning there was no lack in the seventeenth century; but in the beginning of the eighteenth Greek studies languished, and your classical scholar garnished his essays with scraps from Latin poets whom a robust genius like Scaliger despised. On the breaking up of the fountains of the great deep, towards the close of the last century, the pent-up streams of Greek poetry brought their crystal clearness and their refreshing coolness to brighten and sweeten the current of our literature. No pseudo-classicism this, but a real classicism; not a mechanical rule, but a vital principle, — a principle for which we should be the better if every Greek book were chained up and the study of Greek permitted only by special license.

How profoundly our recent literature is penetrated by Greek influence, how steadily Greek laws of artistic work are finding their way to practical acceptance, I need not say here, where that influence, where those laws, have been and are so fully felt, so admirably exemplified. I will only say that if the progress of literature is distinctly in the direction of subtile and refined workmanship; if the excellence of American literature lies in the fine outline and the delicate tint, — we owe this progress, we owe this excellence, to the deeper and truer study, not of all the various nationalities with which the universality of the nineteenth century has brought us into sympathy: we owe this progress, this excellence, directly or mediately to the deeper and truer study of the great classic masters of form. The grandsons of the men that studied the politics of Greek states, of Greek federations, when they were laying the foundations of the republic that was to be, have sought the eternal principles of art on the same soil; and the American literature that is, and that is to be, owes to Harvard and the sons of Harvard a debt which a stranger can record more emphatically than those who cannot praise Harvard without praising themselves.

Here, then, thanks to the permeation of all serious work with the spirit of that serious play which is the cultivation of artistic form, — here, then, wherever else we may have had our training, the man of letters finds a second home; and when Harvard stands, where Heidelberg stood the other day, at the end of her semi-millennium, may lineal hands still uphold her standard, which has led thus far in the line of true literary progress.

The PRESIDENT said: There is a gentleman at our table who is not of our graduates, but one of our honorarii, over whom I claim to exercise the authority you have given me as your President; and I invite Mr. GEORGE WILLIAM CURTIS to give us a few words.

## SPEECH OF GEORGE WILLIAM CURTIS.

I HAVE never been more impressed than to-day with the truth of the saying, "To him who hath shall be given." Everybody knows that to be a son of Harvard is in itself good fortune. But whoever is happy enough to be here to-day must acknowledge that to all other good fortunes must now be added, not only the felicity of coming here to salute the Mother upon her two hundred and fiftieth anniversary, but of finding her two hundred and fifty times fairer and stronger and more beloved than ever before. Still more, while he walks about this Zion, telling her towers, marking her bulwarks, and counting her palaces, if he catches a glimpse of the modest Annex he is still happier in knowing that as his ever-young Mother starts to complete her third century, the spell of old tradition which commanded her to bring forth men children only is broken forever.

But who shall dare to speak now that Harvard herself has spoken by two of the most illustrious among her living voices, which are endeared to every generous heart wherever our language is spoken, — voices sweet and true to the old English faith and spirit which hummed "God save the King" from Plymouth Rock to Lexington Green, and "Yankee Doodle" from Concord Bridge to the Appomattox apple-tree; one of which has steadily helped the world to go right by "hollerin' out, Gee!" at the proper time, and never more clearly than to-day; while the other has set our flag to music, and, victorious over circumstances, has sung itself into immortality in a "one-hoss shay."

No toast could be more suggestive than your toast, but happily there is no need of my speaking. The orator and the poet of the day are its happiest living illustrations. Yet I remember that these are the Academic groves in which the earliest notes of our literature were heard, and here in his Φ B K address in 1809 Buckminster predicted its glorious dawn. Here too, in 1821, Bryant spoke his Φ B K poem, and led the voices which broke into the chorus that filled our spacious air " with sounds which echo still." In the morning light of our literature in which we live you may judge the part of Harvard if you remember that Dana and Everett, and Sparks and Channing, and Bancroft and Prescott, Motley and Ticknor, Palfrey and Parkman and Emerson, Holmes and Lowell were her sons; that here Longfellow taught, and, that nothing may be wanting, she has to-day twined into her chaplet of unfading flowers the pure white rose of Whittier's fame.

It is pleasant, coming from the State and city and river of Washington Irving, to pay tribute to an institution in which so many of our chiefs in literature were trained. But you will not forget that while the characteristic earnestness and sober harmonies of that literature are due to New England, its gay allegro movement began in New York. The sombre "Thanatopsis" of Bryant was contemporary with the rollicking glee of "Knickerbocker's History." But in the "Last Leaf" of Holmes the sparkle of humor began to play on the shadowy surface of the New England stream. In the "Biglow Papers" the old Puritanic genius, mellowed and disenthralled, brought up laughter and remorseless wit as the resistless ally of the public conscience. The smiling Irving had suddenly great and significant co-laborers, who played on his sweet pipe an unwonted tune. The Hudson and the Charles flowed at a level, —

> "And Jura answered from her misty shroud
> Back to the joyous Alps, that called to her aloud!"

New York, Mr. President, — your mighty imperial neighbor, with her immense population, resources, and prosperity, — has been always careless of her own renown, and like one of the old Dutch burghers who settled New Amsterdam, she has been content to sit smoking upon her stoop, looking kindly upon her great neighbors to the right and left, — Pennsylvania and Ohio and New England, — hearing the story of their greatness without malice, without envy, and with hearty sympathy and good cheer. She is very sure that the voice of Columbia, — the college of Hamilton and Jay, of Livingston and Gouverneur Morris, — must awaken a kindred echo in the college of Samuel Adams, of James Otis, and of Josiah Quincy. She listens to the Revolutionary legends of Middlesex, not unmindful of Saratoga or of the city of New York where the national government began. She acknowledges with gratitude that Boston first taught the young New-Yorker his Latin grammar, and that Harvard was nearly one hundred and twenty years old when her first college was founded; and her Dutch heart remembers with pride that the settlers of New England brought a great treasure from Dutch Leyden, and that Holland gave to New England one of the chief guarantees of liberty in giving her the common school.

Mr. President, you see before you a multitude of alumni from many colleges, to each of whom his own *alma mater* is as dear as Harvard to you and your associates. But as all our great days in this country are national days; as they are great because they make us greater, and bind more closely and indissolubly the common American brotherhood, so that we say with Patrick Henry, "I am not a Virginian, a New-Yorker, a Massachusetts man, but I am an American," — so on the day which commemorates the original establishment of the higher education in this country, the education which in every age and country has been the crown of its civilization, and here in the actual benignant presence of the original American *alma mater*, they do not say, "I am a son of Yale or Princeton, of Brown or Columbia, of Michigan or Pennsylvania," but proudly and fondly they declare, "I am a grandson, or great-grandson, or great-great-grandson of old Harvard, the common Mother of us all."

The PRESIDENT proposed as a sentiment, "The advancement of Science," which was responded to as follows:

## SPEECH OF ALEXANDER AGASSIZ.

*Curator of the Museum of Comparative Zoölogy.*

MR. PRESIDENT, AND BRETHREN OF THE ALUMNI:

WHILE all the Alumni unite in the commemoration of our two hundred and fiftieth anniversary, it has a special interest for the men of science, because in the last fifty years — the half-century we celebrate to-day — the greater number of the scientific departments of Harvard have sprung into existence.

Forty years ago two departments of science, now developed into the Botanic Garden and the Observatory, had already taken root here. With the establishment of the Lawrence Scientific School, founded in 1847, a wider scheme of scientific activity was initiated, represented to-day by the Chemical and Physical Laboratories and by the Museums of Natural History, each one greater than the modest structure which first comprised them all. In fact, science at Harvard, on its present basis, has grown up within the memory of her yet living sons. Antiquated we may be, it is true, for many of us have reached the age when, according to the President of the University, our usefulness is nearly over; but we are still young in devotion to our Alma Mater.

We well remember the time when the struggling scientific departments were good-naturedly tolerated as the harmless amusements of enthusiastic fanatics, if they were not more harshly criticised as costly excrescences. But those times are past, and we rejoice to believe that the scientific departments are now admitted as an integral part of the University, becoming ever more identified with her progress. The men who founded them — most of whom have now passed away — would themselves be surprised to-day to see the far-reaching results of their work. Truly, "they builded better than they knew."

In nothing has the American method been so plainly exhibited as in the growth of seats of learning all over this country. It is true that the multiplying of such institutions may go too far, and may tend to scatter the intellectual force of the country. But, on the other hand, they take a strong hold upon local sentiment; and not one of the well-directed individual efforts that have dotted the country over with colleges and technical schools has failed to be sustained by the spontaneous action of enlightened communities.

In our meeting of to-day we cannot but feel that Harvard, with her ever-widening scope, has been the centre from which this national intellectual activity has spread. Although science recognizes no local limits, yet every country must develop its own educational centres. They cannot be imported; they must be the growth of the soil, in harmony with the best spirit of the nation and of its institutions. It is in this sense that the highest seats of learning now growing up among us, relying entirely upon the affection and appreciation of the people about them, seem to me more truly national than any single institution could be which was under the patronage of our central government. Such protection is given only at the cost of intellectual independence. It is true that the well-organized German Universities, so influential in the development of science, are based upon government support; but they owe their success less to this official patronage than to their system of decentralization, combined with well-directed concentration; while the even more powerful influence of England upon the growth of science has been due to the genius of individuals rather than to her wealthy universities. Borrowing what is best from each of these examples, but adapting their methods to our own national conditions, so different from those of Europe, this, the oldest University of the land, may now challenge her transatlantic sisters to a friendly rivalry in the development of the highest scientific culture.

The PRESIDENT said: We have remembered the clergy. We would not part without remembering our two other great schools. I give you therefore, "The Science of Medicine and Surgery!" and I call upon DR. WEIR MITCHELL, of Philadelphia, to say a word.

## SPEECH OF WEIR MITCHELL.

MR. PRESIDENT, AND GENTLEMEN:

I HAVE been desired to say a word. If I had been limited to this, I should perhaps be rather happier.

The doctor, however, is accustomed to come when he is called on, and in the expiring hours of a dinner like this he is very liable to be brought to the front. You can hardly expect when you call upon a practising physician like myself on an occasion like this, when you bring him from the bedside and the laboratory, to hear from him such eloquent words as you have heard to-night from some of the immortals, from the best of our statesmen, the most brilliant of our orators, and the ablest of professors. I shall limit myself therefore to a few words, remembering that although the doctor is very gladly seen when he makes his first appearance, when the time comes for his final exit he is much more properly thanked.

Nothing would be easier for me than to answer from my heart for my profession, if that is the call upon me; but to reply in words which befit the occasion I find much more difficult. Yet nowhere should it be more easy than in Boston to answer for my professional brethren. Some notable medical memories are always present for me as I cross its historic Common, and think of it anew as a rarely beautiful and, in places, a picturesque city. Yet whatever charm of the æsthetic it may have for me, it has a nobler when I remember that it is also the birthplace of the anæsthetic.

While to you men of Boston it is dear for one good reason or another, I think of it as the home of that illustrious line of physicians the Warrens; as the city of the Bowditches; as the place where James Jackson lived and was honored; as to-day the home of the greatest living American surgeon, Henry Bigelow. As I came through your outer hall to-day I saw many names of physicians written upon those tablets which record your peerage of the true and brave who died that we might politically live.

The thought of these men brings back to me what an eloquent speaker said here to-night, that every Massachusetts signer of the Declaration of Independence was a son of Harvard. Let me remind my brethren in this hall that the only physician whose name is on that strong arraignment of the Crown was perhaps of all of us the most famous, — Benjamin Rush, a Pennsylvanian.

There is one great reason why our profession throughout the land owes to Harvard a heavy debt. You have shown that it was possible to remodel in the highest sense medical education. It had got into grooves where it rolled along quietly for many a year. It was due to President Eliot chiefly, I think, that the Harvard Medical School reformed its course of education, and set an example for all the medical schools throughout the land, — an example which, I am glad to say, my own University of Pennsylvania immediately followed.

I have also personally, as a physician, to thank Boston for another thing. It is that one of your graduates, Oliver Wendell Holmes, a man of science and a doctor, — for through his long career as poet and literary man, he has still kept his position as in some sense a doctor, — has emancipated us from the idea that the physician is only a person to write prescriptions and get up in the night when called upon; and has given us abundant proof that there are many other things that he can do without doing any less well his special life-work.

I am not going to say any more about Wendell Holmes. I think I have observed that at Boston dinners it is quite the custom to say something about Holmes, and perhaps about Lowell, and one or two other Boston men. But these two gentlemen have been buttered on both sides, — I mean on both sides of the Atlantic, — and perhaps not even Philadelphia butter would add to the esteem in which you hold them. We are accustomed to be told that you chiefly regard and think of Boston men. I, for one, wish in a certain sense to contradict this. You will allow me, therefore, in parting with you, to say one or two fervent words as to a personal matter. The first letter that I ever received in recognition of any scientific work I had done, came to me when I was a young fellow from Oliver Wendell Holmes. He will never know how much good it did me. The first honor received by me from a society was from the Boston Natural History Society. The second was from the American Academy of Sciences in your city. The chances of a grave illness deprived me when young of the privilege of graduation in arts at my own University; and thus it happens that I receive my first academic degree from this great school of learning. I wish frankly to say that I like it well, and that it is doubtful whether any one who received this honor to-day is more proud of it than I am.

The PRESIDENT said: With so many Doctors of Laws it would be quite unpardonable if we forgot the Law. I give you, "The Law! May its administrators, professors, and students fully realize that justice founded upon reason is its only life." And I will ask Professor THAYER to respond.

## SPEECH OF JAMES B. THAYER.
*Professor in the Law School.*

MR. PRESIDENT, AND GENTLEMEN:

IT was a remarkable step to begin the breeding of lawyers at Harvard College. If there was anything that the founders of this institution did not wish to promote, it was the study and practice of English law.

A certain sort of lawyer — what may be called a reformed lawyer, like Governor Winthrop or the Rev. Nathaniel Ward of Ipswich — our ancestors did indeed value. Such men were useful in the very careful steering that was necessary in working their semi-Judaic ship of State along an English coast; for, in a legal point of view, that vessel drew a good deal too much water. At the very time which we celebrate, the people were clamoring for some laws to regulate the almost absolute discretion of their magistrates; and the Rev. John Cotton was put upon a committee to prepare a code. Dr. Creighton may perhaps remember that Mr. Cotton was some time a Fellow of Emmanuel College. He sent in to the General Court, in this very year of 1636, certain thorough-paced propositions, mentioned by Governor Winthrop as being "a copy of Moses, his judicials, compiled in an exact method;" and they bore for a motto this significant passage: "Jehovah is our Judge, Jehovah is our Lawgiver, Jehovah is our King; He will save us." The reformed lawyers no doubt did their full share in saving our fathers from adopting that; and a far more sagacious compilation was produced by Nathaniel Ward, with some assistance from Lechford,—a lawyer who had not reformed, and who soon vanished from these shores.

Well, how has it come about that so incongruous a topic as law was introduced among the studies of this cherished school of the prophets?

Let me say, before explaining this, that it is not altogether strange that our law at that time should seem to a plain Puritan to be a dark and knavish business; for it was still heavily encumbered with the formalism of the Middle Ages. It was, indeed, already, like Milton's lion, " pawing to get free its hinder parts;" and there was a sort of truth in Coke's dithyrambic praise of it, then but recently published, that "reason is the life of the law, — nay, the common law itself is nothing else but reason;" but it was the truth of prophecy, and not the truth of fact. The law also was then mainly hidden away from laymen and wrapped in a foreign tongue; and it was taught at the Inns of Court in the rudest way, — "hanc rigidam Minervam," said Sir Henry Spelman, a contemporary of our founders, "ferreis amplexibus coercendam." "My mother," says Spelman, "sent me to London to begin upon our law." "Cujus vestibulum salutassem reperissemque linguam peregrinam, dialectum barbarum, methodum inconcinnam, molem non ingentem solum sed perpetuis humeris sustinendam, excidit mihi (fateor) animus." As regards this circumstance, that the law was then mostly written in a foreign tongue, it is interesting to notice that King James, while promoting our English version of the Bible, was also urging the Englishing of the law. "I wish," he said in a printed speech in 1609, when the Bible was nearly ready to be published, "the law written in our vulgar language; for now it is an old, mixt, and corrupt language, only understood by lawyers." It was the English Puritans mainly that brought about this reform; the first book of law reports in English, other than a translation, was printed in the time of the Commonwealth. And when our General Court, in 1647, ordered thirteen volumes of law from England, nine of them existed only in a foreign language, — eight in Norman-French, and one in Latin.

But to come back to my question. It was not until a century and a quarter ago — half way back in that long tract of time which we have been contemplating at this anniversary — that the rude but noble fabric of our English law was first made the subject of university study. "We thus," said Blackstone, the first professor of our law at Oxford, in 1758, "extend the pomoeria of university learning, and adopt a new tribe of citizens within these philosophical walls." That event marked an era in our law; all the world knows the brilliant results that immediately attended it. Blackstone did not accomplish everything, — there was, indeed, much in his lectures that was trivial; but he performed a work which, whether considered in relation to the intractable nature of his material, or, without reference to that, upon its own merits alone, has always excited the admiration of those who were competent to judge of it. It will long survive as a monument to his own powers and to the wisdom of those who perceived that English law deserved to be scientifically studied, — studied by the same methods which belong to all other important parts of human knowledge. The contagion of this example spread to Cambridge, where, by the charter of Downing College in 1800, a similar chair was established, and the acute and learned Edward Christian was appointed to fill it.

It happened that a citizen of Massachusetts was living in London while Blackstone was still wearing his honors, at a period when seven editions of his lectures had been published within ten years. This man — Isaac Royall, of Medford — having died in 1781, the year after Blackstone's death, left to Harvard College a gift of land " towards the endowing a professor of law, . . . or of physic or anatomy." But it was not until 1815 that his purpose was carried out, and the Royall professorship, the earliest chair of law at any American seat of learning, was established. I do not speak now of the private law schools at Litchfield, founded in 1784, or of other later establishments of a like sort. It was here, at Cambridge, seventy years ago, that the pomoeria of university learning were first made to include a new American tribe of citizens within them.

And now, what shall I say of the methods and results of the teaching of law at this University for these seventy years? Why should I say anything? The law has had its day of celebration already. Let me, however, say one thing. If I were asked to name the thing that has characterized the recent efforts of this department of the University, I should say that it is simply a keener perception of the special function of a university school of law, and a stricter effort to apply here, in ways suited to the subject-matter, the same methods of historical research, of careful comparison, analysis, and deduction which are used in other branches of university study. Among the present officers of the School there are different methods in matters of detail, as there must needs be where there are diversities of gifts; but there is entire unity in the general aim and in the desire to do in this great and secular institution, as well as they can, the work that belongs to their generation. That is not quite the same work which fell to their predecessors; it is a quieter work, though full of labor. But it is one in which it is a great happiness to engage; for we know, with an absolute conviction, that we are helping to lay a better foundation for those who will follow us. We need no better assurance that our aims are right than the altogether admirable spirit of study which prevails at the School, and the character, the progress, and the intellectual ardor of the young men that have left it.

# REGISTRATION.

# REGISTRATION

OF

## GRADUATES, NON-GRADUATE OFFICERS, HOLDERS OF HONORARY DEGREES, AND GUESTS

ATTENDING THE COMMEMORATION.

---

ABBE, Cleveland . . . . . . . . . . . . . Washington, D.C.
Abbot, Edwin Hale, A.B. 1855 . . . . . . . Milwaukee, Wis.
Abbot, Everett Vergnies, A.B. 1886 . . . . . Cambridge.
Abbot, Francis Ellingwood, A.B. 1859 . . . . Cambridge.
Abbot, George, A.B. 1864 . . . . . . . . Cambridge.
Abbot, Henry Larcom, *Col. of Eng., U.S. Army* . New York, N.Y.
Abbot, Henry Ward, A.B. 1886 . . . . . . Boston.
Abbot, Julian, A.B. 1826 . . . . . . . . . Lowell.
Abbot, Samuel Leonard, A.B. 1838 . . . . . Boston.
Abbot, William Fitzhale, A.B. 1874 . . . . . Worcester.
Abbott, Benjamin Rush, A.B. 1886 . . . . . Bloomington, Ill.
Abbott, Gordon, A.B. 1884 . . . . . . . . Boston.
Abbott, Samuel Warren, M.D. 1862 . . . . . Wakefield.
Abercrombie, Daniel Webster, A.B. 1876 . . . Worcester.
Abercrombie, Otis Putnam, A.B. 1858 . . . . Lunenburg.
Adams, Charles Francis, Jr. A.B. 1856 . . . . Quincy.
Adams, Charles Kendall, LL.D., *President of Cornell University* . . . . . . . . . . Ithaca, N.Y.
Adams, George Caspar, A.B. 1886 . . . . . Quincy.
Adams, George Everett, A.B. 1860 . . . . . Chicago, Ill.
Adams, George Huntington, A.B. 1870 . . . . New York, N.Y.
Adams, Theodore Parker, A.B. 1867 . . . . . Boston.
Agassiz, Alexander, A.B. 1855 . . . . . . . Cambridge.
Agassiz, George Russell, A.B. 1884 . . . . . Cambridge.
Aldrich, Albert Clinton, A.B. 1879 . . . . . Somerville.
Alexander, William Pomeroy, A.B. 1870 . . . Springfield.
Alger, Alpheus Brown, A.B. 1875 . . . . . . Cambridge.
Allen, Alexander Viets Griswold, D.D., *Professor of Ecclesiastical History in Epis. Theol. School* . Cambridge.
Allen, Arthur Lincoln, A.B. 1885 . . . . . . Arlington.
Allen, Francis Bellows, A. B. 1881 . . . . . New York, N.Y.

Allen, Frederic De Forest, Ph.D . . . . . . Cambridge.
Allen, Frederick Hobbs, A.B. 1880 . . . . . New York, N.Y.
Allen, Gardner Weld, A.B. 1877 . . . . . . Boston.
Allen, Henry Freeman, A.B. 1860 . . . . . . Boston.
Allen, Joseph Henry, A.B. 1840 . . . . . . Cambridge.
Allen, Justin, M.D. 1856 . . . . . . . . . Topsfield.
Allen, Nathaniel Glover, A.B. 1842 . . . . . Auburndale.
Allen, William, A. B. 1837 . . . . . . . . Allston.
Allen, William Ethan, A.B. 1878 . . . . . . Worcester.
Allen, William Hall, A.B. 1878 . . . . . . Saybrook, Conn.
Allen, William Lothrop, A.B. 1886 . . . . . Boston.
Almy, Charles, A.B. 1872 . . . . . . . . Cambridge.
Almy, Francis, A.B. 1879 . . . . . . . . Buffalo, N.Y.
Almy, Frederic, A.B. 1880 . . . . . . . . Buffalo, N.Y.
Amen, Harlan Page, A.B. 1879 . . . . . . . Poughkeepsie, N.Y.
Ames, Fisher, A.B. 1858 . . . . . . . . . West Newton.
Ames, Frederick Lothrop, A.B. 1854 . . . . . North Easton.
Ames, James Barr, A.B. 1868 . . . . . . . Cambridge.
Ames, Oliver, *Lt.-Gov. of Mass.* . . . . . . North Easton.
Amory, Arthur, A.B. 1862 . . . . . . . . Boston.
Amory, Augustine Heard, A.B. 1877 . . . . . Lawrence.
Amory, Charles Walter, A.B. 1863 . . . . . Brookline.
Amory, Francis Inman, A.B. 1871 . . . . . Boston.
Amory, Harcourt, A.B. 1876 . . . . . . . . Boston.
Amory, Robert, A.B. 1863 . . . . . . . . Boston.
Amory, Thomas Coffin, A.B. 1830 . . . . . . Boston.
Anderson, Elbert Ellery, A.B. 1852 . . . . . New York.
Anderson, Luther Stetson, A.B. 1882 . . . . Quincy.
Anderson, Nicholas Longworth, A.B. 1858 . . Washington, D C.
Andrew, John Forrester, A.B. 1872 . . . . . Boston.
Andrew, Brainard Alger, A.B. 1884 . . . . . Charlestown.
Andrews, Clement Walker, A.B. 1879 . . . . Boston.
Andrews, Edward Reynolds, A.B. 1853 . . . . Boston.
Andrews, William Shankland, A.B. 1880 . . . Syracuse, N.Y.
Angell, Elgin Adelbert, A.B. 1873 . . . . . Cleveland, O.
Angell, James Burrill, LL.D., *President of University of Michigan* . . . . . . . . . Ann Arbor, Mich.
Appleton, Edward, A.B. 1835 . . . . . . . Reading.
Appleton, Francis Henry, A.B. 1869 . . . . Peabody.
Appleton, Francis Parker, A.B. 1845 . . . . Dorchester.
Appleton, John Henry, A.B. 1875 . . . . . . Cambridge.
Appleton, William Hyde, A.B. 1864 . . . . . Swarthmore, Pa.
Arnold, Alfred Colburn, A.B. 1884 . . . . . Concordville, Pa.
Arnold, Francis Rose, A.B. 1856 . . . . . . New York, N.Y.
Arnold, Horace David, A.B. 1885 . . . . . . Newton.
Arnold, Howard Payson, A.B. 1852 . . . . . Boston.
Arnold, Louis, A.B. 1855 . . . . . . . . . West Roxbury.
Aspinwall, William, A.B. 1838 . . . . . . . Brookline.
Aspinwall, William Henry, A.B. 1883 . . . . Brookline.

Atherton, Edward Herbert, A.B. 1870 . . . . Roxbury.
Atherton, Frederic William, A.B. 1886 . . . . Boston.
Atherton, Walter, S.B. 1885 . . . . . . . . Stoughton.
Atkinson, Edward Ernest, A.M. 1886 . . . . Cambridge.
Atkinson, Edward Williams, A.B. 1881 . . . . Brookline.
Atkinson, William Parsons, A.B. 1838 . . . . Jamaica Plain.
Atwood, Hartley Frederic, A.B. 1884 . . . . Boston.
Atwood, Luther, A.B. 1883 . . . . . . . . Exeter, N.H.
Austin, Amory, A.B. 1871 . . . . . . . . Boston.
Austin, William Russell, A.B. 1879 . . . . . Charlestown.
Ayars, Henry Morton, A.B. 1886 . . . . . . Cleveland, O.
Ayer, Clarence Walter, A.B. 1885 . . . . . South Byfield.
Ayer, Frederick Fanning, A.B. 1873 . . . . . New York, N.Y.
Ayer, James Bourne, A.B. 1869 . . . . . . Boston.
Ayer, James Cook, A.B. 1886 . . . . . . . Lowell.
Ayers, George David, A.B. 1879 . . . . . . Malden.
Ayers, Howard, S.B. 1883 . . . . . . . . . Cambridge.
Ayres, Marshall, Jr. A.B. 1863 . . . . . . . New York, N.Y.

BABBITT, George Franklin, A.B. 1872 . . . . Boston.
Babcock, James Woods, A.B. 1882 . . . . . Somerville.
Babcock, Lemuel Hollingsworth, A.B. 1873 . . New York, N.Y.
Babcock, William Gustavus, A.B. 1841 . . . . Dorchester.
Babson, Robert Edward, A.B. 1856 . . . . . Boston.
Babson, Robert Tillinghast, A.B. 1882 . . . . Gloucester.
Bachelder, Thomas Cogswell, A.B. 1883 . . . South Boston.
Backus, Henry Clinton, A.B. 1871 . . . . . . New York, N.Y.
Bacon, Charles Franklin, A.B. 1882 . . . . . Newton.
Bacon, Charles William, A.B. 1879 . . . . . Natick.
Bacon, Francis McNeil, Jr, A.B. 1884 . . . . New York, N.Y.
Bacon, Gorham, A.B. 1875 . . . . . . . . New York, N.Y.
Bacon, Grenville, A.B. 1857 . . . . . . . . Roxbury.
Bacon, John William, A.B. 1843 . . . . . . Natick.
Bacon, Jonas Edward, A.B. 1875 . . . . . . Brockton.
Bacon, Robert, A.B. 1880 . . . . . . . . . Boston.
Bacon, William Benjamin, A.B. 1841 . . . . Jamaica Plain.
Bacon, William Francis, A.B. 1885 . . . . . Newton.
Bailey, Hollis Russell, A.B. 1877 . . . . . . Boston.
Baird, Spencer Fullerton, LL.D., *Secretary Smith-*
    *sonian Institution* . . . . . . . . . . Washington, D.C.
Baker, Amos Prescott, A.B. 1867 . . . . . . Newport, R.I.
Baker, Charles Francis, A.B. 1872 . . . . . . Fitchburg.
Baker, Edward Wild, A.B. 1882 . . . . . . Brookline.
Baker, Ezra Henry, A.B. 1881 . . . . . . . Boston.
Baker, James Eliot, A.B. 1883 . . . . . . . Brookline.
Baker, Lucas Lee, A.B. 1883 . . . . . . . . East Templeton.
Baker, Wendell, A.B. 1886 . . . . . . . . New York, N.Y.
Balch, Francis Vergnies, A.B. 1859 . . . . . Jamaica Plain.
Baldwin, Thomas Tileston, A.B. 1886 . . . . Jamaica Plain.

Baldwin, Thomas Williams. A.B. 1873 . . . . Bangor, Me.
Ball, George Homer, A.B. 1869 . . . . . . Worcester.
Bancroft, Charles Parker, A.B. 1874 . . . . . Concord, N.H.
Bancroft, Jacob, A.B. 1884 . . . . . . . . Cambridge.
Bancroft, John Chandler, A.B. 1854 . . . . . Milton.
Bangs, Elisha Dillingham, A.B. 1866 . . . . Boston.
Banker, Benson Beria, A.B. 1866 . . . . . . Boston.
Banks, Nathaniel Prentice, LL.D. 1858 . . . . Waltham.
Barker, William Torrey, A.B. 1873 . . . . . Boston.
Barlow, George Francis, A.B. 1882 . . . . . Brooklyn, N.Y.
Barnard, Frederick Augustus Porter, S.T.D., LL.D., L.H.D., *President of Columbia College* . . . New York, N.Y.
Barnard, George Middleton, A.B. 1857 . . . . Boston.
Barnes, Albert Mallard, A.B. 1871 . . . . . Cambridge.
Barnes, Charles Maynard, A.B. 1877 . . . . . Boston.
Barnes, Walter Saunders, Jr., A.B. 1884 . . . Somerville.
Barnes, William, S.B. 1883 . . . . . . . . Boston.
Barnes, William Sanford, A.B. 1886 . . . . . San Francisco, Cal.
Barrett, George Campbell, A.B. 1856 . . . . Boston.
Barrett, Harry Hudson, A.B. 1874 . . . . . Malden.
Barrett, Luther Gustavus, A.B. 1862 . . . . . South Boston.
Barrett, William, A.B. 1859 . . . . . . . . St. Paul, Minn.
Barrows, Charles Henry, A.B. 1876 . . . . . Springfield.
Barrows, Samuel June, B.D. 1875 . . . . . . Dorchester.
Barstow, Henry Taylor, A.B. 1880 . . . . . . Boston.
Bartlett, Frederick Carew Smythe, A.B. 1875 . . New Bedford.
Bartlett, Henry, A.B. 1885 . . . . . . . . Lowell.
Bartlett, John, A.M. 1871 . . . . . . . . . Cambridge.
Bartlett, Nathaniel Cilley, A.B. 1880 . . . . Haverhill.
Bartlett, Nelson Slater, A.B. 1871 . . . . . . Boston.
Bartlett, Samuel Colcord, D.D., LL.D., *President of Dartmouth College* . . . . . . . . Hanover, N.H.
Bartlett, Stephen Smith, A.B. 1885 . . . . . Boston.
Batchelder, Charles Edwin, A.B. 1873 . . . . Portsmouth, N.H.
Batchelder, Samuel, A.B. 1851 . . . . . . . Cambridge.
Batchelor, George, A.B. 1866 . . . . . . . Wellesley Hills.
Bates, Benjamin Edward, A.B. 1884 . . . . . New York, N.Y.
Bates, Waldron, A.B. 1879 . . . . . . . . Boston.
Bates, William Clinton, A.B. 1877 . . . . . Canton.
Baxter, George Lewis, A.B. 1863 . . . . . . Somerville.
Bayard, Thomas Francis, *Secretary of State* . . Washington, D.C.
Baylies, Edmund Lincoln, A.B. 1879 . . . . . New York, N.Y.
Baylies, Walter Cabot, A.B. 1884 . . . . . . Taunton.
Beach, John Wesley, *President of Wesleyan University* . . . . . . . . . . . . . . . Middletown, Ct.
Beal, Thomas Prince, A.B. 1869 . . . . . . Boston.
Beale, Joseph Henry, Jr., A.B. 1882 . . . . . Dorchester.
Beals, Joshua Gardner, A.B. 1858 . . . . . . Boston.
Beaman, Charles Cotesworth, A.B. 1861 . . . New York, N.Y.

Beaman, Harry Clayton, A.B. 1885 . . . . . Princeton.
Beaman, William Stacy, A.B. 1872 . . . . . New York, N.Y.
Beane, Samuel Collins, A.B. 1861 . . . . . . Salem.
Beatley, James Augustus, A.B. 1873 . . . . Chelsea.
Beckwith, Loring Everett, A.B. 1864 . . . . Cambridge.
Bellows, Russell Nevins, A.B. 1864 . . . . . New York, N.Y.
Belmont, Raymond Rodgers, A.B. 1886 . . . . New York, N.Y.
Bemis, Charles Vose, A.B. 1835 . . . . . . Medford.
Bemis, John Wheeler, A.B. 1885 . . . . . . Cambridge.
Bemis, Jonathan Wheeler, A.B. 1830 . . . . Cambridge.
Bendelari, George Anacletus Conrad, A.B. 1874 . New Haven, Conn.
Bennett, Samuel Crocker, A.B. 1879 . . . . . Boston.
Bent, Samuel Arthur, LL.B. 1865 . . . . . . Boston.
Berry, John King, A.B. 1876 . . . . . . . Roxbury.
Bettens, Edward Detraz, A.B. 1873 . . . . . New York, N.Y.
Bettens, Thomas Simms, A.B. 1874 . . . . . New York, N.Y.
Bickford, Robert, A.B. 1851 . . . . . . . Somerville.
Bickford, Robert Sloan, A.B. 1885 . . . . . Somerville.
Bicknell, Edward, A.B. 1876 . . . . . . . Boston.
Bierwirth, Heinrich Conrad, A.B. 1884 . . . Andover.
Bigelow, Alanson, A.B. 1858 . . . . . . . Cambridge.
Bigelow, Frank Winthrop, A.B. 1854 . . . . Charlestow.
Bigelow, George Brooks, A.B. 1856 . . . . . Boston.
Bigelow, Marshall Train, A.M. 1864 . . . . . Cambridge.
Bigelow, Melville Madison, Ph.D. 1879 . . . Cambridge.
Bigelow, William Sturgis, A.B. 1871 . . . . Boston.
Billings, John Shaw, M.D., *Surgeon-General's Office* Washington, D.C.
Binney, Amos, A.B. 1879 . . . . . . . . Walpole.
Binney, John, A.B. 1864 . . . . . . . . Middletown, Conn.
Bird, Charles Sumner, A.B. 1877 . . . . . East Walpole.
Birtwell, Charles Wesley, A.B. 1885 . . . . Boston.
Bishop, Robert Roberts, Jr., A.B. 1880 . . . Newton Centre.
Bishop, Thomas Wetmore, A.B. 1863 . . . . Salem.
Bissell, Herbert Porter, A.B. 1880 . . . . . Buffalo, N.Y.
Bixby, James Thompson, A.B. 1864 . . . . . Arlington.
Blagden, George, A.B. 1856 . . . . . . . New York, N.Y.
Blair, Lafayette Gilbert, A.B. 1878 . . . . Cambridge.
Blake, Harrison Gray Otis, A.B. 1835 . . . Worcester.
Blake, Samuel Parkman, Jr., A.B. 1855 . . . Boston.
Blake, William Payne, A.B. 1866 . . . . . Boston.
Blanchard, Andrew Delaval, A.B. 1842 . . . North Andover.
Blanchard, Henry, A.B. 1834 . . . . . . . Neponset.
Blanchard, Herbert Wheeler, A.B. 1884 . . . Concord.
Blinn, George Richard, A.B. 1885 . . . . . Bedford.
Bliss, Edward Penniman, A.B. 1873 . . . . Lexington.
Bliss, Henry Warren, A.B. 1884 . . . . . . Boston.
Blodgett, William Ashley, A.B. 1882 . . . . Cambridge.
Boardman, Waldo Elias, D.M.D. 1886 . . . Boston.
Boardman, William Elbridge, A.B. 1865 . . . Boston.

Bodge, George Madison, B.D. 1878 . . . . . East Boston.
Boit, Edward Darley, Jr., A.B. 1863 . . . . . Boston.
Boit, Robert Apthorp, A.B. 1868 . . . . . . Brookline.
Bolan, Joel Carleton, A.B. 1876. . . . . . . Roxbury.
Bolles, Frank, LL.B. 1882 . . . . . . . Cambridge.
Bolles, William Palmer, M.D. 1871 . . . . . Roxbury.
Bolster, Percy Gardner, A.B. 1886 . . . . . Roxbury.
Bombaugh, Charles Carroll, A.B. 1850 . . . Baltimore, Md.
Bonaparte, Charles Joseph, A.B. 1871 . . . . Baltimore, Md.
Bond, George William, A.M. 1874 . . . . . Jamaica Plain.
Bond, Lawrence, A.B. 1877 . . . . . . . . West Newton.
Bond, William Sturgis, A.B. 1859 . . . . . Jamaica Plain.
Booth, William Ferris, S.B. 1884 . . . . . . Poughkeepsie, N.Y.
Borland, William Gibson, A.B. 1886 . . . . New London, Conn.
Bouvé, Walter Lincoln, LL.B. 1879 . . . . . Hingham.
Bowditch, Alfred, A.B. 1876 . . . . . . . Jamaica Plain.
Bowditch, Charles Pickering, A.B. 1863 . . . Jamaica Plain.
Bowditch, Edward, A.B. 1869 . . . . . . . Albany, N.Y.
Bowditch, Henry Ingersoll, A.B. 1828 . . . . Boston.
Bowditch, Henry Pickering, A.B. 1861 . . . . Jamaica Plain.
Bowditch, Jonathan Ingersoll, A.M. 1849 . . . Jamaica Plain.
Bowditch, Vincent Yardley, A.B. 1875 . . . . Boston.
Bowen, Charles Stuart, A.B. 1871 . . . . . . Cambridge.
Bowen, Francis, A.B. 1833 . . . . . . . . Cambridge.
Bowen, James Williams, A.B. 1882 . . . . . Boston.
Boyd, Alexander, Jr. A.B. 1882 . . . . . . . Philadelphia, Pa.
Boyd, William Willard, A.B. 1871 . . . . . . St. Louis, Mo.
Boyden, Roland William, A.B. 1885 . . . . . Beverly.
Boyden, William Cowper, A.B. 1886 . . . . . Sheffield, Ill.
Bradbury, William Howard, A.B. 1881 . . . . Cambridge.
Bradford, Charles Frederick, A.M. 1860 . . . . Roxbury.
Bradford, Edward Hickling, A.B. 1869 . . . . Boston.
Bradford, Gamaliel, A.B. 1849 . . . . . . . Cambridge.
Bradford, George Gardner, A.B. 1886 . . . . Dorchester.
Bradford, George Hillard, A.B. 1876 . . . . . Roxbury.
Bradford, George Partridge, A.B. 1825 . . . . Cambridge.
Bradford, Russell, A.B. 1880 . . . . . . . Cambridge.
Bradish, Frank Eliot, A.B. 1878 . . . . . . Boston.
Bradlee, Josiah, A.B. 1858 . . . . . . . . Boston.
Bradley, Charles Smith, A.B. 1833 . . . . . Providence, R.I.
Bradley, Frederick, D.M.D. 1886 . . . . . . Dedham.
Bradley, John Dorr, A.B. 1886 . . . . . . . Boston.
Bradley, Richards Merry, A.B. 1882 . . . . . Boston.
Bradley, Robert Stow, A.B. 1876 . . . . . . Boston.
Brainerd, Ezra, *President of Middlebury College* . Middlebury, Vt.
Braman, Grenville Davies, A.B. 1885 . . . . Boston.
Brandegee, Edward Deshon, A.B. 1881 . . . . Utica, N.Y.
Brannan, John Winters, A.B. 1874 . . . . . New York, N.Y.
Breed, Amos Franklin, Jr., A.B. 1880 . . . . Lynn.

Brett, Henry, A.B. 1869 . . . . . . . . . . Calumet, Mich.
Brewer, William Augustus, Jr., S.B. 1854 . . . South Orange, N.J.
Brewer, William Dade, Jr., A.B. 1886 . . . . Boston.
Brewster, Frank, A.B. 1879 . . . . . . . . Roxbury.
Brewster, William, A.B. 1881 . . . . . . . Boston.
Bridge, John Ransom, A.B. 1884 . . . . . . LeRoy, N.Y.
Bridge, Josiah, A.B. 1884 . . . . . . . . Cambridge.
Bridge, Samuel James, A.M. 1880 . . . . . Dresden, Me.
Bridgman, Lewis Jesse, A.B. 1881 . . . . . No. Andover Depot.
Briggs, George Ware, B.D. 1834 . . . . . . Cambridge.
Briggs, LeBaron Russell, A.B. 1875 . . . . Cambridge.
Brigham, Clifford, A.B. 1880 . . . . . . . Salem.
Brigham, Lincoln Flagg, LL.B. 1844, *Chief Justice*
    *of the Superior Court* . . . . . . . . . Salem.
Brigham, William Tufts, A.B. 1862 . . . . . Boston.
Brimmer, Martin, A.B. 1849 . . . . . . . . Boston.
Brinsmade, William Gold, A.B. 1881 . . . . Washington, Conn.
Brooks, Arthur, A.B. 1867 . . . . . . . . . New York, N.Y.
Brooks, Arthur Anderson, A.B. 1879 . . . . Greenfield.
Brooks, Francis Augustus, A.B. 1842 . . . . Boston.
Brooks, Francis Boott, LL B. 1846 . . . . . Boston.
Brooks, Frederick, A.B. 1868 . . . . . . . Boston.
Brooks, George Merrick, A.B. 1844 . . . . . Concord.
Brooks, George Wolcott, *Pastor of the First*
    *Church, Charlestown* . . . . . . . . . Charlestown.
Brooks, James Willson, LL.B. 1858 . . . . . Cambridge.
Brooks, John, A.B. 1856 . . . . . . . . . Cambridge.
Brooks, John Cotton, A.B. 1872 . . . . . . Springfield.
Brooks, Phillips, A.B. 1855 . . . . . . . Boston.
Brooks, Stephen Driver, M.D. 1882 . . . . . Evansville, Ind.
Broughton, Henry White, A.B. 1875 . . . . . Jamaica Plain.
Brown, Addison, A.B. 1852 . . . . . . . . New York, N.Y.
Brown, Benjamin Graves, A.B. 1858 . . . . . College Hill.
Brown, Charles Albert, A.B. 1886 . . . . . Framingham.
Brown, Charles Rufus, A.B. 1877 . . . . . . Newton Centre.
Brown, Crawford Richmond, A.B. 1886 . . . . Cambridgeport.
Brown, Edward Jackson, A.B. 1855 . . . . . Boston.
Brown, Edward Wyeth, A.B. 1851 . . . . . . Belmont.
Brown, Francis Henry, A.B. 1857 . . . . . . Boston.
Brown, Frederick Tilden, A.B. 1877 . . . . New York, N.Y.
Brown, George William, A B. 1884 . . . . . Concord.
Brown, Henry Hobart, A.B. 1876 . . . . . . Philadelphia, Pa.
Brown, Henry William, A.B. 1852 . . . . . Worcester.
Brown, Howard Kinmonth, A.B. 1879 . . . . Framingham.
Brown, John Freeman, A B. 1872 . . . . . . Boston.
Brown, John Murray, A.B. 1863 . . . . . . Belmont.
Brown, John Patrick, A.B. 1861 . . . . . . East Boston.
Brown, Melvin, A.B. 1863 . . . . . . . . . Brooklyn, N.Y.
Brown, Romeo Green, A.B. 1884 . . . . . . Montpelier, Vt.

Brown, William Reynolds, LL.B. 1871 . . . . New York, N.Y.
Browne, Edward Ingersoll, A.B. 1855 . . . . Boston.
Browne, George Henry, A.B. 1878 . . . . . . Cambridge.
Browne, Henry Rossiter Worthington, A.B. 1881 Jamaica Plain.
Browne, John Kittredge, A.B. 1869 . . . . . Harpoot, E. Turkey.
Brownell, Thomas Franklin, A.B. 1865 . . . . New York, N.Y.
Brownlow, William Albert, A.B. 1876 . . . . Cambridge.
Bruce, Edward Pierson, A.B. 1877 . . . . . Salem.
Brush, Abraham Stevens, LL.B. 1885 . . . . Boston.
Brush, George Jarvis, *Professor of Mineralogy at Yale College* . . . . . . . . . . . . New Haven, Conn.
Bryant, George Butler, A.B. 1886 . . . . . . Boston.
Bryant, John Duncan, A.B. 1853 . . . . . . Boston.
Bryant, John Sweeney, A.B. 1882 . . . . . . Buffalo, N.Y.
Bryant, Louis Lincoln, M.D. 1874 . . . . . . Cambridge.
Bryant, William Sohier, A.B. 1884 . . . . . Cohasset.
Buckham, Matthew Henry, D.D., *President of the University of Vermont* . . . . . . . . . Burlington, Vt.
Buckingham, John Albert, B.D. 1839 . . . . Newton.
Buckingham, Edgar, A.B. 1831 . . . . . . . Deerfield.
Buckley, Philip Townsend, A.B. 1880 . . . . South Boston.
Buell, George Clifford, A.B. 1882 . . . . . . Rochester, N Y.
Buffum, Charles Thomas, A.B. 1874 . . . . . New York, N.Y.
Buffum, Walter Nutting, LL.B. 1883 . . . . Boston.
Bulkeley, Benjamin Reynolds, B.D. 1882 . . . Concord.
Bullard, John Lincoln, A.B. 1861 . . . . . . New York, N.Y.
Bullard, John Richards, LL.B. 1866 . . . . . Dedham.
Bullard, Stephen, A.B. 1878 . . . . . . . . Boston.
Bullock, Augustus George, A.B. 1868 . . . . Worcester.
Bullock, Rufus Augustus, A.B. 1871 . . . . . Boston.
Bunker, Frederic Story, A.B. 1884 . . . . . Boston.
Bunton, George Wadley, A.B. 1870 . . . . . North Cambridge.
Bunton, William Augustus, A.B. 1867 . . . . Boston.
Burch, James Merrill, A.B. 1883 . . . . . . Necedah, Wis.
Burdett, George Albert, A.B. 1881 . . . . . Brookline.
Burdett, Herbert Channing, A.B. 1878 . . . . Brookline.
Burgess, Edward Phillips, LL.B. 1854 . . . . Dedham.
Burlingham, Charles Culp, A.B. 1879 . . . . New York, N.Y.
Burnett, Harry, A.B. 1873 . . . . . . . . Boston.
Burnham, Arthur, A.B. 1870 . . . . . . . Roxbury.
Burr, Charles Henry, S.B. 1879 . . . . . . Roxbury.
Burr, Heman Merrick, A.B. 1877 . . . . . . Chestnut Hill.
Burr, Isaac Tucker, Jr., A.B. 1879 . . . . . Boston.
Burrage, Albert Cameron, A.B. 1883 . . . . Boston.
Burrage, George Dixwell, A.B. 1883 . . . . . Chestnut Hill.
Burrage, Walter Lincoln, A.B. 1883 . . . . . Boston.
Burrage, William Wirt, A.B. 1856 . . . . . . Cambridge.
Burt, Charles Dean, A.B. 1882 . . . . . . . Taunton.
Burt, Frank Leslie, M.D. 1885 . . . . . . . Boston.

## REGISTRATION.

Burt, John Otis, A.B. 1858 . . . . . . . . . Syracuse, N.Y.
Bush, Samuel Dacre, A.B. 1871 . . . . . . Boston.
Bush, Solon Wanton, B.D. 1848 . . . . . . Boston.
Buswell, Henry Foster, A.B. 1866 . . . . . Canton.
Butler, Harry, A.B. 1879 . . . . . . . . . Portland, Me.
Butler, Prescott Hall, A.B. 1869 . . . . . New York, N.Y.
Butler, Sigourney, A.B. 1877 . . . . . . . Quincy.
Butterfield, Horatio Quincy, A.B. 1848, *President of Olivet College* . . . . . . . . . . . Olivet, Mich.
Buxton, William Albert, A.M. 1886 . . . . Cambridge.
Byerly, William Elwood, A.B. 1871 . . . . Cambridge.
Byrne, James, A.B. 1877 . . . . . . . . . New York, N.Y.
Byrnes, Michael Joseph, S.J. . . . . . . . Boston.

CABOT, Edward Twisleton, A.B. 1883 . . . Brookline.
Cabot, Francis Elliot, A.B. 1880 . . . . . Mattapan.
Cabot, Godfrey Lowell, A.B. 1882 . . . . . Cambridge.
Cabot, Henry Bromfield, A.B. 1883 . . . . Brookline.
Cabot, James Elliot, A.B. 1840 . . . . . . Brookline.
Cabot, John Higginson, A.B. 1850 . . . . . Brookline.
Cabot, Thomas Handasyd, A.B. 1886 . . . Brookline.
Cabot, Walter Channing, A.B. 1850 . . . . Brookline.
Cadbury, Richard Tupper, A.B.1877 . . . . Boston.
Calhoun, Arthur Langmaid, A.B. 1885 . . . Boston.
Cammann, Henry Lorillard, A.B. 1886 . . . New York, N.Y.
Campbell, William Taylor, A.B. 1875 . . . Quincy.
Canfield, Charles Taylor, A.B. 1852 . . . . Cambridge.
Capen, Edward, A.B. 1842 . . . . . . . . . Haverhill.
Capen, Elmer Hewitt, D.D., *President of Tufts College* . . . . . . . . . . . . . . . College Hill.
Capen, Francis Lemuel, A.B. 1839 . . . . . Boston.
Capen, John, A.B. 1840 . . . . . . . . . . Boston.
Carll, Walter Edward, M.D. 1885 . . . . . Greenfield.
Carnochan, Gouverneur Morris, A.B. 1886 . New York, N.Y.
Carpenter, Frank Oliver, A.B. 1880 . . . . Boston.
Carpenter, Frederic Ives, A.B. 1885 . . . . Chicago, Ill.
Carret, James Russell, A.B. 1867 . . . . . Boston.
Carret, José Francisco, S.B. 1856 . . . . . Cambridge.
Carroll, Royal Phelps, A.B. 1885 . . . . . New York, N.Y.
Carter, Frank, A.B. 1875 . . . . . . . . . North Woburn.
Carter, Franklin, Ph.D., LL.D., *President of Williams College* . . . . . . . . . . Williamstown.
Carter, James Coolidge, A.B. 1850 . . . . New York, N.Y.
Cary, Walter, A.B. 1879 . . . . . . . . . Buffalo. N.Y.
Casas, William Beltran de las, A.B. 1879 . Malden.
Casey, John Francis, A.B. 1868 . . . . . . Boston.
Cate, Martin Luther, A.B. 1877 . . . . . . Boston.
Chace, George Frederic, A.B. 1866 . . . . Taunton.
Chadbourne, Thomas Lincoln, A.B. 1862 . . Houghton, Mich.

Chadwick, James Read, A.B. 1865 . . . . . Boston.
Chamberlain, Allen Howard, A.B. 1885 . . . . Foxcroft, Me.
Chamberlain, David Blaisdell, A.B. 1886 . . . W. Hingham.
Chamberlain, Eugene Tyler, A.B. 1878 . . . . Albany, N.Y.
Chamberlain, Nathan Henry, A.B. 1853 . . . . East Boston.
Chamberlaine, Augustus Porter, A.B. 1847 . . . Concord.
Chamberlayne, Charles Frederick, A.B. 1878 . . East Boston.
Chandler, Alfred Dupont, A.B. 1868 . . . . . Brookline.
Chandler, Horace Parker, A.B. 1864 . . . . . Jamaica Plain.
Chandler, John, A.B. 1883 . . . . . . . . Dorchester.
Chandler, Thomas Henderson, A.B. 1848 . . . Boston.
Chanler, Winthrop Astor, A.B. 1885 . . . . . Barrytown, N.Y.
Channing, Edward, A.B. 1878 . . . . . . . Cambridge.
Channing, Francis Allston, M. P. . . . . . . London, Eng.
Chapin, Frank Woodruff, A.B. 1876 . . . . . New York, N.Y.
Chapin, Henry Bainbridge, A.B. 1880 . . . . Boston.
Chapin, Henry Gardner, A.B. 1882 . . . . . Springfield.
Chapin, Herbert Allen, A.B. 1871 . . . . . . Somerville.
Chaplin, Heman White, A.B. 1867 . . . . . Boston.
Chaplin, Winfield Scott, West Point, 1870 . . . Cambridge.
Chapman, John Jay, A.B. 1884 . . . . . . New York, N.Y.
Chase, Charles Augustus, A.B. 1855 . . . . . Worcester.
Chase, Daniel La Forest, A.B. 1864 . . . . . West Somerville.
Chase, George Bigelow, A.B. 1856 . . . . . . Boston.
Chase, George Colby, A. M., *Professor of English
    Literature in Bates College* . . . . . . Lewiston, Me.
Chase, Heman Lincoln, A.B. 1882 . . . . . . Boston.
Chase, Theodore, A.B. 1853 . . . . . . . . Boston.
Chase, Thomas Herbert, A.B. 1885 . . . . . Haverford Coll., Pa.
Chase, Walter Greenough, A.B. 1882 . . . . . Brookline.
Chatard, Thomas Marean, S.B. 1871 . . . . . Washington, D.C.
Chauncey, Charles, A.B. 1859 . . . . . . . Philadelphia, Pa.
Chauncey, Elihu, A.B. 1861 . . . . . . . . New York, N.Y.
Cheever, Clarence Alonzo, S.B. 1881 . . . . . Mattapan.
Cheever, David Williams, A.B. 1852 . . . . . Boston.
Chenery, Winthrop Louis, A.B. 1867 . . . . . Belmont.
Cheney, Edwards, A.B. 1882 . . . . . . . . Lowell.
Cheney, William Franklin, A.B. 1873 . . . . Walnut Hill, Dedham.
Child, Francis James, A.B. 1846 . . . . . . Cambridge.
Child, Linus Mason, LL.B. 1859 . . . . . . Boston.
Childs, Nathaniel, A.M. 1869 . . . . . . . Charlestown.
Choate, Charles Francis, A.B. 1849 . . . . . Southborough.
Choate, Joseph Hodges, A.B. 1852 . . . . . New York, N.Y.
Choate, William, A. B. 1881 . . . . . . . . Beverly.
Churchill, Asaph, A.B. 1831 . . . . . . . . Boston.
Churchill, Charles Marshall Spring, A.B. 1845 . Milton.
Churchill, Frank Spooner, A.B. 1886 . . . . . Milton.
Churchill, John Maitland Brewer, A.B. 1879 . . Dorchester.
Churchill, John Wesley, A.B. 1865 . . . . . Andover.

REGISTRATION. 337

Claflin, Adams Davenport, A.B. 1886 . . . . . Newtonville.
Claflin, William, LL.D. 1869 . . . . . . . Newtonville.
Clapp, Channing, A.B. 1855. . . . . . . . Boston.
Clapp, Clift Rogers, A.B. 1884 . . . . . . . South Boston.
Clapp, Robert Parker, A.B. 1879 . . . . . . Lexington.
Clark, David Crawford, A.B. 1886 . . . . . New York, N.Y.
Clark, Frank Haven, A.B. 1884 . . . . . . Boston.
Clark, Joseph Payson, A.B. 1882 . . . . . . Boston.
Clark, George Faber, B.D. 1846 . . . . . . Hubbardston.
Clark, Horace, A.B. 1885. . . . . . . . . Somerville.
Clark, Leonard Brown, A.B. 1885 . . . . . . Weston.
Clark, Louis Monroe, A.B. 1881 . . . . . . Dorchester.
Clark, Walter Thomas, A.B. 1886 . . . . . . Cambridgeport.
Clarke, Augustus Peck, M.D. 1862 . . . . . Cambridge.
Clarke, Eliot Channing, A.B. 1867 . . . . . Boston.
Clarke, Frank Wigglesworth, S.B. 1867 . . . . Washington, D.C.
Clarke, James Freeman, A.B. 1829 . . . . . Jamaica Plain.
Clarke, Samuel Belcher, A.B. 1874 . . . . . New York, N.Y.
Cleaves, James Edwin, A.B. 1876. . . . . . Medford.
Cleveland, Clement, A.B. 1867 . . . . . . . New York, N.Y.
Cleveland, Grover, *President of United States* . . Washington, D.C.
Clifford, Charles Warren, A.B. 1865 . . . . . New Bedford.
Clifford, Walter, A.B. 1871 . . . . . . . . New Bedford.
Clymer, William Branford Shubrick, A.B. 1876 . Cambridge.
Coale, George Oliver George, A.B. 1874 . . . Jamaica Plain.
Cobb, Charles Henry, M.D. 1881 . . . . . . Boston.
Cobb, Frederic Codman, A.B. 1884 . . . . . Boston.
Coburn, George Albert, M.D. 1873 . . . . . Cambridge.
Codman, Benjamin Storer, M.D. 1845 . . . . Boston.
Codman, Charles Russell, A.B. 1849 . . . . . Cotuit.
Codman, Edmund Dwight, A.B. 1886 . . . . Boston.
Codman, James Macmaster, Jr., A.B. 1884 . . Brookline.
Codman, John, A.B. 1885 . . . . . . . . Boston.
Coffey, John Augustine, LL.B. 1871 . . . . . Boston.
Cogan, Joseph Ambrose, A.B. 1884 . . . . . Cambridge.
Coggeshall, Frederic, A.B. 1886 . . . . . . Cambridge.
Cogswell, Edward Russell, A.B. 1864 . . . . Cambridge.
Cogswell, Francis, A.M. 1881 . . . . . . . Cambridgeport.
Cohn, Adolphe, A.M. *École des Chartes, Paris*, 1874 Cambridge.
Coit, Robert, A.B. 1883 . . . . . . . . . Winchester.
Colburn, Theodore Edson, A.B. 1854 . . . . Boston.
Cole, Charles D'Urban Morris, A.B. 1883 . . . New York, N.Y.
Cole, Frank Nelson, A.B. 1882 . . . . . . . Marlborough.
Cole, John Hanun, A.B. 1870 . . . . . . . New York, N.Y.
Collier, Hiram Price, B.D. 1882 . . . . . . Hingham.
Collins, Edward Lyon, A.B. 1885 . . . . . . West Newton.
Collins, Frederic Kelley, A.B. 1874 . . . . . Cambridge.
Colony, John Joslin, A.B. 1885 . . . . . . Keene, N.H.
Comey, Arthur Messinger, A.B. 1882 . . . . Somerville.

22

Conant, Ernest Lee, A.B. 1884 . . . . . . . Webster.
Conant, William Merritt, A.B. 1879 . . . . . Boston.
Converse, Charles Henry, A.B. 1884 . . . . . Newton.
Cook, Frank Gaylord, A.B. 1882 . . . . . . Cambridge.
Cook, Robert George, A.B. 1886 . . . . . . Rochester, N.Y.
Cook, Silas Parsons, A.B. 1867 . . . . . . . Chelsea.
Cooke, Josiah Parsons, A.B. 1848 . . . . . . Cambridge.
Cooley, Thomas McIntyre, LL.D., *Professor of Constitutional Law and American History in Michigan University.* Ann Arbor, Mich.
Coolidge, Austin Jacobs, A.B. 1847 . . . . . Watertown.
Coolidge, David Hill, A.B. 1854 . . . . . . Boston.
Coolidge, David Hill, Jr., A.B. 1886 . . . . . Boston.
Coolidge, James Ivers Trecothick, A.B. 1838 . . Cambridge.
Coolidge, John Gardner, A.B. 1884 . . . . . Boston.
Coolidge, John Templeman, A.B. 1879 . . . . Boston.
Coolidge, Joseph Swett, A.B. 1849 . . . . . Boston.
Coolidge, Louis Arthur, A.B. 1883 . . . . . Springfield.
Coolidge, Sumner, A.B. 1883 . . . . . . . Mt. Auburn.
Coolidge, Thomas Jefferson, A.B. 1850 . . . . Boston.
Coolidge, Thomas Jefferson, Jr., A.B. 1884 . . . Manchester.
Coolidge, William Henry, A.B. 1881 . . . . . Natick.
Coolidge, William Williamson, A.B. 1879 . . . Salem.
Corey, Arthur Deloraine, A.B. 1886 . . . . . Malden.
Cotting, Benjamin Eddy, A.B. 1834 . . . . . Roxbury.
Couch, Joseph Daniel, M.D. 1883 . . . . . . Somerville.
Coverly, George Todd, Jr., A.B. 1879 . . . . Malden.
Cowdin, John Elliot, A.B. 1879 . . . . . . New York, N.Y.
Cox, Henry Joseph, A.B. 1884 . . . . . . . Boston.
Cox, Wilmot Townsend, A.B. 1879 . . . . . New York, N.Y.
Coxe, Henry Brinton, A.B. 1885 . . . . . . Philadelphia, Pa.
Crafts, George Inglis, A.B. 1833 . . . . . . Charleston, S.C.
Craigin, George Arthur, A.B. 1885 . . . . . Boston.
Cranch, Christopher Pearse, B.D. 1836 . . . . Cambridge.
Crawford, Frank Lindsay, A.B. 1879 . . . . . New York, N.Y.
Creesy, Frank Leonard, A.B. 1882 . . . . . Brookline.
Creighton, Mandell, M.A., *Senior Fellow of Emmanuel College, and Professor of Ecclesiastical History in the University of Cambridge, Eng.; Canon of Worcester* . . . . . . . . . Cambridge, Eng.
Crocker, Adams, A.B. 1885 . . . . . . . . Fitchburg.
Crocker, George Glover, A.B. 1864 . . . . . Boston.
Crocker, George Uriel, A.B. 1884 . . . . . . Boston.
Crocker, Henry Horace, Jr., A.B. 1874 . . . . New York, N.Y.
Crocker, Uriel Haskell, A.B. 1853 . . . . . . Boston.
Crocker, William Tufts, A.B. 1884 . . . . . Fitchburg.
Crosby, George Washington, A.B. 1858 . . . . Newton.
Croswell, James Greenleaf, A.B. 1873 . . . . Cambridge.
Croswell, Simon Greenleaf, A.B. 1875 . . . . . Cambridge.

Crowninshield, Benjamin William, A.B. 1858 . . Boston.
Cruft, Samuel Breck, A.B. 1836 . . . . . . Boston.
Cummings, Edward, A.B. 1883 . . . . . . . Lynn.
Cummings, Prentiss, A B. 1864 . . . . . . . Brookline.
Cummins, Thomas Kittredge, Jr., A.B. 1884 . . Boston.
Cunningham, Henry Winchester, A.B. 1882 . . Boston.
Cunningham, Horace, A.B. 1846 . . . . . . New York, N.Y.
Cunningham, Stanley, A.B. 1877 . . . . . . Boston.
Curtis, Allen, A.B. 1884 . . . . . . . . . Boston.
Curtis, Charles Pelham, A.B. 1845 . . . . . Boston.
Curtis, Charles Pelham, Jr., A.B. 1883 . . . . Boston.
Curtis, George William, LL.D. 1881 . . . West New Brighton, N.Y
Curtis, Hall, A.B. 1854 . . . . . . . . . Boston.
Curtis, Hamilton Rowan, A.B. 1885 . . . . . Boston.
Curtis, Horatio Greenough, A.B. 1865 . . . . Boston.
Curtis, Laurence, A.B. 1870 . . . . . . . . Boston.
Curtis, Louis, A.B. 1870 . . . . . . . . . Boston.
Curtis, Rest Fenner, A.B. 1870 . . . . . . . Boston.
Cushing, Ernest Watson, A.B. 1867 . . . . . Boston.
Cushing, Grafton Dulaney, A.B. 1885 . . . . Boston.
Cushing, Hayward Warren, A.B. 1877 . . . Boston.
Cushing, Hon. Henry Greenwood, *Sheriff of Middlesex County* . . . . . . . . . . . Lowell.
Cushing, Joseph Mackenzie, A.B. 1855 . . . . Baltimore, Md.
Cushing, Livingston, A.B. 1879 . . . . . . Weston.
Cushing, Louis Thomas, A.B. 1870 . . . . . Cohasset.
Cushing, Marshall Henry, A.B. 1883 . . . . . Hingham.
Cushing, Thomas, A.B. 1834 . . . . . . . . Boston.
Cushman, Archibald Falconer, LL.B, 1852 . . New York, N.Y.
Cushman, Lysander William, A.B. 1886 . . . Newville, Cal.
Cushman, Rufus Cutler, A.B. 1869 . . . . . Cambridge.
Cutler, Elbridge Gerry, A.B. 1868 . . . . . . Boston.
Cutler, Samuel Newton, A.B. 1877 . . . . . Somerville.
Cutter, Charles Ammi, A.B. 1855 . . . . . . Boston.
Cutter, Charles Kimball, M.D. 1876 . . . . . Charlestown.
Cutter, Frederick Spaulding, A.B. 1874 . . . Cambridge.
Cutter, Leonard Francis, A.B. 1867 . . . . . Andover.
Cutter, Marshall Munroe, A.B. 1864 . . . . . Brookline.
Cutter, William Everett, A.B. 1869 . . . . . Worcester.

DABNEY, Alfred Stackpole, A.B. 1871 . . . . Boston.
Dabney, George Stackpole, A.B. 1863 . . . . Boston.
Dabney, Louis Stackpole, A.B. 1861 . . . . Boston.
Dabney, Ralph Pomeroy, A.B. 1882 . . . . . Fayal, Azores.
Daland, Edward Francis, A.B. 1856 . . . . . Boston.
Daland, Tucker, A.B. 1873 . . . . . . . . Brookline.
Dale, William Johnson, A.B. 1837 . . . . . North Andover.
Dalzell, John Whitney, A.B. 1879 . . . . . . Cambridge.
Dame, Walter Reeves, A.B. 1883 . . . . . . Clinton.

Dana, George Eames, A.B. 1854 . . . . . . Syracuse, N.Y.
Dana, James, A.B. 1830 . . . . . . . . . Boston.
Dana, James, Jr., A.B. 1875 . . . . . . . Dorchester.
Dana, James Dwight, Ph.D., LL.D., *Professor of Geology and Mineralogy at Yale College* . New Haven, Ct.
Dana, Richard Henry, A.B. 1874 . . . . . . Boston.
Dana, William Franklin, A.B. 1884 . . . . . Boston.
Danforth, Allen, A.B. 1866 . . . . . . . . Plymouth.
Danforth, Henry Gold, A.B. 1877 . . . . . . Rochester, N.Y.
Danforth, William Henry, A.B. 1882 . . . . Worcester.
Daniell, Moses Grant, A.B. 1863 . . . . . . Roxbury.
Daniels, Frank Herbert, A.B. 1879 . . . . . New York, N.Y.
Darling, Frederick Homer, A.B. 1884 . . . . North Cambridge.
Davenport, Bennett Franklin, A.B. 1867 . . . Boston.
Davenport, Francis Henry, M.D. 1874 . . . . Boston.
Daves, Edward Graham, A.B. 1854 . . . . . Baltimore, Md.
Davis, Andrew McFarland, S.B. 1851 . . . . Cambridge.
Davis, Bancroft Gherardi, A.B. 1885 . . . . Cambridge.
Davis, Charles Gideon, A.B. 1840 . . . . . . Plymouth.
Davis, Charles Stevenson, A.B. 1880 . . . . Plymouth.
Davis, Charles Thornton, A.B. 1884 . . . . . Newton.
Davis, George Alonzo, A.B. 1845 . . . . . . Boston.
Davis, James Clarke, A.B. 1858 . . . . . . Boston.
Davis, John Francis, A.B. 1881 . . . . . . San Francisco, Cal.
Davis, Joseph Edwin, A.B. 1883 . . . . . . Lynn.
Davis, Robert Thompson, M.D. 1847 . . . . Fall River.
Davis, Samuel Warren, A.B. 1877 . . . . . . West Newton.
Davis, Simon, A.B. 1876 . . . . . . . . . Boston.
Davis, William Morris, S B. 1870 . . . . . . Cambridge.
Dawes, Henry Laurens, *U. S. Senator* . . . . Pittsfield.
Day, Arthur Kehew, A.B. 1886 . . . . . . . Concord, N.H.
Dean, Clarence Randall, A.B. 1882 . . . . . Taunton.
Dean, Francis Winthrop, S.B. 1875 . . . . . Cambridge.
Dean, Louis Bailey, A.B. 1878 . . . . . . . Brooklyn, N.Y.
Deane, Charles, A.M. 1856 . . . . . . . . Cambridge.
Deane, Walter, A.B. 1870 . . . . . . . . Cambridge.
Dearing, Thomas Haven, M.D. 1861 . . . . . Braintree.
Delano, Samuel, A.B. 1879 . . . . . . . . Boston.
Deming, Horace Edward, A.B. 1871 . . . . . New York, N.Y.
Denègre, Walter Denis, A.B. 1879 . . . . . New Orleans, La.
Denniston, Arthur Clark, A.B. 1883 . . . . . Philadelphia, Pa.
Denny, Arthur Briggs, A.B. 1877 . . . . . . Brookline.
Denny, Clarence Holbrook, A.B. 1863 . . . . Boston.
Denny, Daniel, A.B. 1854 . . . . . . . . . Boston.
Denny, Henry Gardner, A.B. 1852 . . . . . Boston.
De Normandie, James, B.D. 1862, *Pastor of the First Religious Society, Roxbury* . . . . . Roxbury.
Denton, Myron Preston, A.B. 1884 . . . . . Saratoga, N.Y.
Derby, Richard Henry, A.B. 1864 . . . . . . New York, N.Y.

Devens, Arthur Lithgow, A.B. 1874 . . . . . Boston.
Devens, Charles, A.B. 1838 . . . . . . . . Boston.
Devens, Samuel Adams, A.B. 1820 . . . . . Boston.
Dewey, William Richardson, A.B. 1886 . . . . Roxbury.
Dexter, Charles, A.B. 1851 . . . . . . . . Cambridge.
Dexter, George, A.B. 1855 . . . . . . . . Boston.
Dexter, George, B.D. 1864 . . . . . . . . Dorchester.
Dexter, Julius, A.B. 1860 . . . . . . . . . Cincinnati, O.
Dexter, William Sohier, A.B. 1816 . . . . . Boston.
Dickerman, Frank Elliot, A.B. 1886 . . . . . Somerville.
Dickey, Charles Denston, A.B. 1882 . . . . . New York, N.Y.
Dickinson, Hon. John Woodbridge, *Secretary Mass.*
   *Board of Education* . . . . . . . . . . Boston.
Dike, Harrison, A.B. 1880 . . . . . . . . Brooklyn, N.Y.
Dillaway, George Wales, A.B. 1865 . . . . . New York, N.Y.
Dillingham, Pitt, B.D. 1876 . . . . . . . Charlestown.
Dimmock, George, A.B. 1877 . . . . . . . Cambridge.
Dixon, Lewis Seaver, A.B. 1866 . . . . . . Boston.
Dixwell, Epes Sargent, A.B. 1827 . . . . . Cambridge.
Dixwell, John, A.B. 1870 . . . . . . . . . Boston.
Dodd, Edward Merrick, A.B. 1880 . . . . . Worcester.
Dodge, Edward Sherman, A.B. 1873 . . . . . Cambridge.
Dodge, Frank Faden, A.B. 1880 . . . . . . Woburn.
Dodge, Frederic, A.B. 1867 . . . . . . . . Belmont.
Dodge, William Walter, A.B. 1870 . . . . . Cambridge.
Doe, Charles Henry, A.M. 1860 . . . . . . Worcester.
Doggett, Frederick Fobes, A.B. 1877 . . . . . South Boston.
Dole, Charles Fletcher, A.B. 1868 . . . . . Jamaica Plain.
Donaldson, Frank, Jr., A.B. 1879 . . . . . Baltimore, Md.
Dorcey, James Edmund, M.D. 1878 . . . . . Boston.
Dorr, Benjamin Humphrey, A.B. 1878 . . . . Boston.
Dorr, Jonathan, A.B. 1864 . . . . . . . . Boston.
Dorr, Joseph, Jr., A.B. 1883 . . . . . . . . Boston.
Dow, Edmond Scott, A.B. 1883 . . . . . . . Brookline.
Dow, Harry Robinson, A.B. 1884 . . . . . . Lawrence.
Downes, Nathaniel, M.D. 1846 . . . . . . . East Boston.
Dowse, William Bradford Homer, A.B. 1873 . . Boston.
Drake, Herbert Hamilton, A.B. 1877 . . . . . New York, N.Y.
Draper, Frank Winthrop, M.D. 1869 . . . . . Boston.
Draper, William Kinnicutt, A B. 1885 . . . . New York, N.Y.
Drew, Charles Acton, A.B. 1870 . . . . . . Newton.
Drisler, Henry, LL.D., *Jay Professor of Greek in*
   *Columbia College, N.Y.* . . . . . . . . . New York, N.Y.
Driver, Stephen William, A.B. 1860 . . . . . Cambridge.
DuBois, Loren Griswold, A.B. 1876 . . . . . Boston.
Dudley, Sanford Harrison, A.B. 1867 . . . . Cambridge.
Dudley, Warren Preston, LL.B. 1877 . . . . Cambridge.
Duff, William Frederic, A.B. 1876 . . . . . Boston.
Dumaresq, Francis, A.B. 1875 . . . . . . . Boston.

Dunbar, Charles Franklin, A.B. 1851 . . . . . Cambridge.
Dunbar, Frank Asaph, A.B. 1878 . . . . . . Cambridge.
Dunham, Howard Cary, A.B. 1877 . . . . . Portland, Me.
Dunham, Theodore, A.B. 1885 . . . . . Irvington-on-Hudson, N.Y.
Dunn, Francis De Maurice, A.B. 1879 . . . . Needham.
Dunster, Edward Swift, A.B. 1856 . . . . . Ann Arbor, Mich.
Dupee, Horace, A.B. 1832 . . . . . . . . Dorchester.
Durant, Thomas, A.B. 1884 . . . . . . . . Washington, D.C.
Durant, William Bullard, A.B. 1865 . . . . . Cambridge.
Dwight, Edmund, A.B. 1844 . . . . . . . . Boston.
Dwight, John Sullivan, A.B. 1832 . . . . . Boston.
Dwight, Thomas, A.B. 1866 . . . . . . . . Boston.
Dwight, Timothy, A.B. 1849. Yale, S.T.D., *President of Yale University* . . . . . . . . New Haven, Ct.
Dwyer, Richard Joseph, A.B. 1877 . . . . . Medford.
Dyer, Ezra, A.B. 1857 . . . . . . . . . . . Newport, R.I.
Dyer, Louis, A.B. 1874 . . . . . . . . . . Cambridge.

EASTMAN, Edmund Tucker, A.B. 1846 . . . . Boston.
Easton, James Hamlet Bolt, A.B. 1883 . . . . Rochester, Minn.
Eaton, Arthur Wentworth Hamilton, A.B. 1880 . Chestnut Hill.
Eaton, George Herbert, A.B. 1882 . . . . . . Boston.
Eaton, Percival James, A.B. 1883 . . . . . . Maplewood.
Eaton, William Lorenzo, A.B. 1873 . . . . . Concord.
Eayrs, Norman Wilder, A.B. 1871 . . . . . . Newport, R.I.
Eckfeldt, Thomas Hooper, A.B. 1881, *Wesleyan* . Cambridge.
Edgerly, Walter Howard, A.B. 1886 . . . . . Boston.
Edmands, Albert William, A.B. 1862 . . . . . Somerville.
Edmands, John Rayner, S.B. 1869 . . . . . . Cambridge.
Edmands, Moses Grant, A.B. 1879 . . . . . . Brookline.
Edmands, Thomas Sprague, A.B. 1867 . . . . Newton.
Edson, William Bostwick, A.B. 1848 . . . . . Phelps, N.Y.
Ela, Richard, A.B. 1871 . . . . . . . . . . Cambridge.
Ela, Walter, A.B. 1871 . . . . . . . . . . . Cambridge.
Eliot, Amory, A.B. 1877 . . . . . . . . . . Boston.
Eliot, Charles, A.B. 1882 . . . . . . . . . Cambridge.
Eliot, Charles William, A.B. 1853 . . . . . . Cambridge.
Eliot, Christopher Rhodes, B.D. 1881, *Pastor of the First Parish, Dorchester* . . . . . . . Dorchester.
Eliot, Samuel, A.B. 1839 . . . . . . . . . . Boston.
Eliot, Samuel Atkins, A.B. 1884 . . . . . . Cambridge.
Elliot, John Wheelock, A.B. 1874 . . . . . . Boston.
Elliot, Silas Haynes, A.B. 1884 . . . . . . . Cambridge
Elliot, William Henry, A.B. 1872 . . . . . . Keene, N.H.
Elliott, Aaron Marshall, A.B. 1868 . . . . . Baltimore, Md.
Ellis, Arthur Blake, A.B. 1875 . . . . . . . Boston.
Ellis, Bertram, A.B. 1881 . . . . . . . . . Keene, N.H.
Ellis, Edward Clarke, A.B. 1868 . . . . . . Boston.
Ellis, Frederick Hamant, A.B. 1879 . . . . . Framingham.

Ellis, George Edward, A.B. 1833 . . . . . . Boston.
Ellis, Ralph Waterbury, A.B. 1879 . . . . . Springfield.
Ellis, William Rogers, A.B. 1867 . . . . . . New York, N.Y.
Elting, Irving, A.B. 1878 . . . . . . . . . Poughkeepsie, N.Y.
Ely, Philip Van Rensselaer, A.B. 1878 . . . . Boston.
Emerson, Frederick Ware, A.B. 1882 . . . . Newton.
Emerson, Thomas, A.B. 1856 . . . . . . . Newtonville.
Emerton, Ephraim, A.B. 1871 . . . . . . . Cambridge.
Emery, Samuel Hopkins, Jr., LL.B. 1882 . . . Concord.
Emery, Woodward, A.B. 1864 . . . . . . . Cambridge.
Endicott, Hon. William Crowninshield, A.B. 1847,
    *Secretary of War* . . . . . . . . . . Salem.
Ensign, Charles Sidney, LL.B. 1863 . . . . . Newton.
Ernst, Harold Clarence, A.B. 1876 . . . . . Jamaica Plain.
Estabrooks, John Albert, A.B.1873 . . . . . Boston.
Esté, William Miller, A.B. 1852 . . . . . . New York, N.Y.
Eustis, Frank Izard, A.B. 1868 . . . . . . . Cambridge.
Eustis, Herbert Hall, A.B. 1880 . . . . . . Cambridge.
Evans, George William, A.B. 1883 . . . . . Boston.
Evans, William Henry, A.B. 1855 . . . . . . Ashburnham.
Evarts, Prescott, A.B.1881 . . . . . . . . New York, N.Y.
Everett, Charles Carroll, B.D. 1859 . . . . . Cambridge.
Everett, Edward Franklin, A.B. 1860 . . . . Cambridge.
Everett, Oliver Hurd, A.B. 1873 . . . . . . Worcester.
Everett, William, A.B. 1859 . . . . . . . . Quincy.
Everett, William Abbot, A.B. 1849 . . . . . Cambridge.

FAIRCHILD, Charles, A.B. 1858 . . . . . . . Boston.
Farley, Charles Andrews, A.B. 1827 . . . . . Boston.
Farley, James Phillips, Jr., A.B. 1868 . . . . Beverly Farms.
Farlow, John Woodford, A.B. 1874 . . . . . Boston.
Farlow, William Gilson, A.B. 1866 . . . . . Cambridge.
Farnham, Edwin, A.B. 1866 . . . . . . . . Cambridge.
Farnsworth, George Bourne, A.B. 1847 . . . . Roxbury.
Farnsworth, William, A.B. 1877 . . . . . . Boston.
Farrar, Jacob Hamilton, A B. 1874 . . . . . Chicago, Ill.
Faulkner, John Charles, A.B. 1886 . . . . . Keene, N.H.
Faxon, Walter, A.B. 1871 . . . . . . . . . Lexington.
Faxon, William, Jr., A.B. 1883 . . . . . . . Boston.
Fay, Charles Norman, A.B. 1860 . . . . . . Chicago, Ill.
Fay, Clement Kelsey, A.B. 1867 . . . . . . Brookline.
Fay, Francis Britain, A.B. 1883 . . . . . . . Cambridge.
Fay, James Harrison, A.B. 1859 . . . . . . New York, N.Y.
Fechheimer, Samuel Marcus, A.B. 1886 . . . . Cincinnati, O.
Fellows, William Gordon, A.B. 1882 . . . . . Schaghticoke, N.Y.
Fenn, William Wallace, A.B. 1884 . . . . . Somerville.
Fenno, Edward Nicoll, A.B. 1866 . . . . . . Boston.
Fenollosa, Ernest Francisco, A.B. 1874 . . . . Tokio, Japan.
Fernald, Benjamin Marvin, A.B. 1870 . . . . Melrose.

# REGISTRATION.

Fernald, Frederick Atherton, A.B. 1882 . . . . Everett.
Fernald, Orlando Marcellus, A.B. 1864 . . . . Williamstown.
Ferry, Ebenezer Hayward, A.B. 1886 . . . . Hyde Park.
Fessenden, Sewall Henry, Jr., A.B. 1886 . . . . Boston.
Fette, William Eliot, A.B. 1858 . . . . . . . Boston.
Fewkes, Jesse Walter, A.B. 1875 . . . . . . Cambridge.
Field, Walbridge Abner, A.B. Dartmouth, 1855,
   *Justice of the Supreme Court of Massachusetts* . Boston.
Fillebrown, Thomas, D.M.D. 1869 . . . . . Boston.
Fincke, Frederick Getman, A.B. 1873 . . . . Utica, N.Y.
Fish, Charles Everett, A.B. 1880 . . . . . . Chicopee.
Fish, Frederick Perry, A.B. 1875 . . . . . . Boston.
Fisher, Edward Thornton, A.B. 1856 . . . . . Berkshire.
Fisher, George Huntington, A.B. 1852 . . . . Brooklyn, N.Y.
Fisher, George Park, A.M., S.T.D., LL.D.,
   *Professor of Eccl. History at Yale College* . . New Haven, Ct.
Fisher, Horace Newton, A.B. 1857 . . . . . Boston.
Fisher, Theodore Willis, M.D. 1861 . . . . . Boston.
Fisk, Frederic Daniell, A.B. 1886 . . . . . . Cambridge.
Fisk, James Lyman, A.B. 1885 . . . . . . . Cambridge.
Fisk, Lyman Beecher, A.B. 1873 . . . . . . Charlestown.
Fiske, Andrew, A.B. 1875 . . . . . . . . . Weston.
Fiske, Arthur Irving, A.B. 1860 . . . . . . Boston.
Fiske, Charles Henry, A.B. 1860 . . . . . . Weston.
Fiske, Frederic Augustus Parker, A.B. 1881 . . Somerville.
Fiske, George, A.B. 1872 . . . . . . . . . Weston.
Fiske, George Alfred, A.B. 1862 . . . . . . Dorchester.
Fiske, Joseph Emery, A.B. 1861 . . . . . . Wellesley Hills.
Fiske, William Boyd, A.B. 1882 . . . . . . Cambridge.
Fitz, Daniel Francis, A.B. 1859 . . . . . . Boston.
Fitz, Reginald Heber, A.B. 1864 . . . . . . Boston.
Flagg, George Augustus, A.B. 1866 . . . . . Millbury.
Flanders, Frank Byron, A.B. 1874 . . . . . . Lawrence.
Fletcher, Charles Ruel, A.B. 1886 . . . . . East Cambridge.
Flint, Albert Stowell, A.B. 1875 . . . . . . Washington, D.C.
Flint, Charles Louis, A.B. 1849 . . . . . . Boston.
Flint, John Sydenham, A.B. 1843 . . . . . . Roxbury.
Folsom, Charles Follen, A.B. 1862 . . . . . Boston.
Folsom, Charles William, A.B. 1815 . . . . . Cambridge.
Foote, Arthur William, A.B. 1874 . . . . . . Boston.
Foote, Henry Wilder, A.B. 1858 . . . . . . Boston.
Foss, George Edmond, A.B. 1885 . . . . . . St. Albans, Vt.
Foster, Alfred Dwight, A.B. 1873 . . . . . . Boston.
Foster, Charles Chauncy, A.B. 1880 . . . . . Cambridge.
Foster, Charles Henry Wheelwright, A.B. 1881 . Brookline.
Foster, Francis Charles, A.B. 1850 . . . . . Cambridge.
Foster, Samuel Lynde, A.B. 1885 . . . . . . San Francisco, Cal.
Fowler, Harold North, A.B. 1880 . . . . . . Cambridge.
Fox, Austen George, A.B. 1869 . . . . . . . New York, N.Y.

Fox, Jabez, A.B. 1871 . . . . . . . . . . Cambridge.
Fox, William Henry, A.B. 1858 . . . . . . Taunton.
Francis, George Hills, A.B. 1882 . . . . . . Brookline.
Francis, Laurens Norris, A.B. 1870 . . . . . Taunton.
Francke, Kuno, Ph.D., Munich, 1879 . . . . . Cambridge.
French, Amos Tuck, A.B. 1885 . . . . . . New York, N.Y.
French, Francis Ormond, A.B. 1857 . . . . New York, N.Y.
French, George Morrill, M.D. 1884 . . . . Malden.
French, Henry Cormerais, A.B. 1882 . . . . . Chicago, Ill.
French, John Davis Williams, A.B. 1863 . . Boston.
French, William Abrams, A.B. 1865 . . . . . Boston.
Frost, Edward, A.B. 1850 . . . . . . . . . Littleton.
Frost, George Seward, A.B. 1865 . . . . . . Dover, N.H.
Frost, Lewis Pierce, A.B. 1886 . . . . . . . Arlington.
Frothingham, Benjamin Thompson, A.B. 1863 . New York, N.Y.
Frothingham, Octavius Brooks, A.B. 1843 . . Boston.
Frothingham, Paul Revere, A.B. 1886 . . . . Jamaica Plain.
Frothingham, Theodore Longfellow, A.B. 1884 . New York, N.Y.
Fuller, Arthur Ossoli, A.B. 1877 . . . . . . Exeter, N.H.
Fullerton, William Morton, A.B. 1886 . . . . Boston.
Furness, Dawes Eliot, A.B. 1868 . . . . . . Foxburg, Pa.
Furness, William Eliot, A.B. 1860 . . . . . Chicago, Ill.

Gage, Homer, A.B. 1882 . . . . . . . . . . Worcester.
Gage, James Arthur, A.B. 1870 . . . . . . . Lowell.
Gage, Thomas Hovey, Jr., A.B. 1886 . . . . Worcester.
Gage, William Leonard, A.B. 1853 . . . . . Hartford, Ct.
Gale, Justin Edwards, A.B. 1866 . . . . . . Cambridge.
Gallagher, William, A.B. 1869 . . . . . . . Easthampton.
Galloupe, Charles William, A.B. 1879 . . . . Lynn.
Gannett, William Channing, A.B. 1860 . . . Chicago, Ill.
Gardiner, John Hays, A.B. 1885 . . . . . . . Brookline.
Gardiner, Robert Hallowell, A.B. 1876 . . . . Chestnut Hill.
Gardner, Augustus Peabody, A.B. 1886 . . . Boston.
Gardner, George Peabody, A.B. 1877 . . . . Boston.
Gardner, John Edward, A.B. 1856 . . . . . Exeter, N.H.
Gassett, Henry, A.B. 1834 . . . . . . . . . Dorchester.
Gaston, William Alexander, A.B. 1880 . . . Boston.
Gates, Charles Horatio, A.B. 1835 . . . . . Boston.
Gates, George Wellesley, M.D. 1884 . . . . Chelsea.
Gates, Lewis Edwards, A.B. 1884 . . . . . . Cambridge.
Gay, Ebenezer, LL.B. 1841 . . . . . . . . . Boston.
Geddes, James, Jr. A.B. 1880 . . . . . . . Brookline.
Gerould, Charles Walter, A.B. 1883 . . . . . Stoughton.
Gerry, Edwin Peabody, M.D. 1874 . . . . . Jamaica Plain.
Gibbons, Joseph McKean, A.B. 1881 . . . . Boston.
Gibbs, Wolcott, A.B. 1841, Columbia, LL.D. . Newport, R.I.
Gibson, Charles Langdon, A.B. 1886 . . . . Boston.
Gibson, George Alonzo, A.B. 1872 . . . . . Medford.

Giddings, Edward Leach, A.B. 1856 . . . . . Beverly.
Gifford, William Logan Rodman, A.B. 1881 . . New Bedford.
Gilbert, Horatio James, A.B. 1858 . . . . . Milton.
Gildersleeve, Basil Lanneau, Ph.D., LL.D., *Professor of Greek at Johns Hopkins University* . Baltimore, Md.
Gilley, Frank Milton, A.B. 1880 . . . . . . Chelsea.
Gillingham, Thomas Clarence, D.M.D. 1879 . . Boston.
Gilman, Daniel Coit, LL.D., *President of Johns Hopkins University* . . . . . . . . . . Baltimore, Md.
Gilman, Henry Hale, A.B. 1882 . . . . . . Haverhill.
Gilman, John Henry, M.D. 1863 . . . . . . Lowell.
Gilman, Nicholas Paine, B.D. 1871 . . . . . West Newton.
Gilman, Stephen, A.B. 1848 . . . . . . . . Lynnfield.
Gleason, Albert Augustus, A.B. 1886 . . . . Milford.
Gleason, Charles Bertie, A.B. 1885 . . . . . Duxbury.
Gleason, Daniel Angell, A.B. 1856 . . . . . West Medford.
Glover, Horatio Nelson, Jr., A.B. 1884 . . . Dorchester.
Goddard, Farley Brewer, A.B. 1881 . . . . . Malden.
Goddard, Warren Norton, A.B. 1879 . . . . . New York, N.Y.
Godkin, Edwin Laurence, A.M. 1871 . . . . . New York, N.Y.
Goldmark, Henry, A.B. 1878 . . . . . . . . New York, N.Y.
Gooch, Frank Austin, A.B. 1872 . . . . . . New Haven, Ct.
Goodale, George Lincoln, M.D. 1863 . . . . Cambridge.
Goodale, John McGregor, A.B. 1885 . . . . Utica, N.Y.
Gooding, Alfred, A.B. 1877 . . . . . . . . Portsmouth, N.H.
Goodnough, Benjamin Franklin, A.B. 1883 . . Brookline.
Goodnough, Xanthus Henry, A.B. 1882 . . . . Brookline.
Goodrich, Arthur Lewis, A.B. 1874 . . . . . Salem.
Goodrich, Charles Newton, A.B. 1873 . . . . Medford.
Goodridge, James Lawrence, A.B. 1835 . . . . Boston.
Goodwin, James Wells, A.B. 1877 . . . . . . Haverhill.
Goodwin, Wendell, A.B. 1874 . . . . . . . . Jamaica Plain.
Goodwin, William Hobbs, Jr., A.B. 1884 . . . Jamaica Plain.
Goodwin, William Watson, A.B. 1851 . . . . Cambridge.
Gordon, George Angier, A.B. 1881 . . . . . . Boston.
Gorham, Arthur, A.B. 1864 . . . . . . . . . Kinsley, Kan.
Gorham, Robert Stetson, A.B. 1885 . . . . . Northampton.
Goss, Francis Webster, A.B. 1862 . . . . . . Roxbury.
Gould, Benjamin Apthorp, A.B. 1844 . . . . . Cambridge.
Gove, William Henry, A.B. 1876 . . . . . . Salem.
Grandgent, Charles Hall, A.B. 1883 . . . . . Cambridge.
Grannis, Herman Wheaton, A.B. 1870 . . . . Chicago, Ill.
Grant, George Franklin, D.M.D. 1870 . . . . Arlington Heights
Grant, Robert, A.B. 1873 . . . . . . . . . Boston.
Grant, Patrick, A.B. 1828 . . . . . . . . . Boston.
Grant, Percy Stickney, A.B. 1883 . . . . . . Brookline.
Gray, Asa, A.M. 1844 . . . . . . . . . . . Cambridge.
Gray, Edward, A.B. 1872 . . . . . . . . . Boston.
**Gray, Edward Borden, A.B. 1886** . . . . . . New Bedford.

Gray, Francis Calley, A.B. 1866 . . . . . . Boston.
Gray, George Zabriskie, D.D., *Dean of Episcopal*
   *Theological School, Cambridge* . . . . . . Cambridge.
Gray, John Chipman, A.B. 1859 . . . . . . Boston.
Gray, Morris, A.B. 1877 . . . . . . . . . Chestnut Hill.
Gray, Reginald, A.B. 1875 . . . . . . . . Boston.
Gray, Thomas Herbert, A.B. 1867 . . . . . . Walpole.
Green, Charles Montraville, A.B. 1874 . . . Boston.
Green, George Walton, A.B. 1876 . . . . . . New York, N. Y.
Green, James, A.B. 1862 . . . . . . . . . Worcester.
Green, John, A.B. 1855 . . . . . . . . . St. Louis, Mo.
Green, Samuel Abbott, A.B. 1851 . . . . . . Boston.
Greene, Frederick Lewis, A.B. 1876 . . . . Greenfield.
Greene, Herbert Eveleth, A.B. 1881 . . . . Garden City, L.I., N.Y.
Greene, James Sumner, M.D. 1863 . . . . Milton.
Greenhalge, Frederic Thomas, A.B. 1863 . . . Lowell.
Greenleaf, Eugene Douglass, A.B. 1866 . . . . Boston.
Greenman, Walter Folger, A.B. 1885 . . . . . Chelsea.
Greenough, Charles Pelham, A.B. 1864 . . . . Brookline.
Greenough, David Stoddard, A.B. 1865 . . . . Boston.
Greenough, Francis Boott, A.B. 1859 . . . . . Boston.
Greenough, James Bradstreet, A.B. 1856 . . . Cambridge.
Greenough, James Jay, A.B. 1882 . . . . . . Cambridge.
Greenough, Malcolm Scollay, A.B. 1868 . . . . Boston.
Greenough, William Whitwell, A.B. 1837 . . . Boston.
Gregory, Charles Augustus, A.B. 1855 . . . . Chicago, Ill.
Greve, Charles Theodore, A.B. 1884 . . . . . Cincinnati, O.
Griffin, Henry Arthur, A.B. 1886 . . . . . . New York, N.Y.
Grinnell, Charles Edward, A.B. 1862 . . . . Boston.
Griswold, Loren Erskine, A.B. 1884 . . . . . Boston.
Guild, Curtis, Jr., A.B. 1881 . . . . . . . Boston.
Guild, Charles Eliot, A.B. 1846 . . . . . . Boston.
Guild, Samuel Eliot, A.B. 1872 . . . . . . . Boston.
Guitéras, Ramon Benjamin, M.D. 1883 . . . . New York, N.Y.
Gummere, Francis Barton, A.B. 1875 . . . . New Bedford.
Gunnison, Binney, A.B. 1886 . . . . . . . Roxbury.
Gurnee, Augustus Coe, A.B. 1878 . . . . . . New York, N.Y.

Hackett, Frank Warren, A.B. 1861 . . . . . Washington, D.C.
Hagar, Eugene Bigelow, A.B. 1871 . . . . . Boston.
Hagen, Hermann August, Ph.D. 1836, Königsberg Cambridge.
Hale, Abraham Garland Randall, LL.B. 1871 . Stow.
Hale, Albert, A.B. 1861 . . . . . . . . . Dedham.
Hale, Arthur, A.B. 1880 . . . . . . . . . Philadelphia, Pa.
Hale, Edward, A.B. 1879 . . . . . . . . . Boston.
Hale, Edward Everett, A.B. 1839 . . . . . . Roxbury.
Hale, Edwin Blaisdell, LL.B. 1875 . . . . . Cambridge.
Hale, George Silsbee, A.B. 1844 . . . . . . Boston.
Hale, William Gardner, A.B. 1870 . . . . . . Ithaca, N.Y.

Hall, Arthur Lawrence, A.B. 1880 . . . . . Revere.
Hall, Asaph, A.M. 1879; LL.D. Yale. *Professor of Mathematics, U. S. Navy* . . . . . . Washington, D.C.
Hall, Asaph, Jr., A.B. 1882 . . . . . . . . . New Haven, Ct.
Hall, Benjamin Homer, A.B. 1851 . . . . . Troy, N.Y.
Hall, Edward Henry, A.B. 1851, *Pastor of the First Parish, Cambridge* . . . . . . . . . . Cambridge.
Hall, Edwin Herbert, A.B. 1875, *Bowdoin* . . . Cambridge.
Hall, Frank Rockwood, A.B. 1872. . . . . . Brookline.
Hall, Frederic Bound, A.B. 1880 . . . . . . Somerville.
Hall, James, S.B., Rensselaer Polytechnic Institute, 1832, *State Geologist, N.Y.* . . . . . Albany, N.Y.
Hall, James Milton, A.B. 1883 . . . . . . . Haverhill.
Hall, Robert Sprague, A.B. 1872 . . . . . . Charlestown.
Hall, Thomas Bartlett, A.B. 1843 . . . . . . Brookline.
Hall, William Stickney, A.B. 1869 . . . . . Cambridge.
Hallowell, Norwood Penrose, A.B. 1861 . . . West Medford.
Halsey, Frederic Robert, A.B. 1868 . . . . . New York, N.Y.
Halstead, Thomas, A.B. 1856 . . . . . . . New York, N.Y.
Hamilton, Charles Albert, A.B. 1878 . . . . Medford.
Hamlin, Charles Sumner, A.B. 1883 . . . . Roxbury.
Hamlin, Cyrus, D.D. 1861; LL.D. *Ex-President of Robert College* . . . . . . . . . . Lexington.
Hamlin, Edward Everett, A.B. 1886 . . . . . Roxbury.
Hamlin, Frank, A.B. 1884 . . . . . . . . . Bangor, Me.
Hammond, Samuel, Jr., A.B. 1881 . . . . . Boston.
Hammond, Walter Whitney, A.B. 1863 . . . Philadelphia, Pa.
Hanks, Charles Stedman, A.B. 1879 . . . . Cambridge.
Hansen, Otto Reinhardt, A.B. 1885 . . . . . Milwaukee, Wis.
Hapgood, Asa Gustavus, A.B. 1872 . . . . . Boston.
Harding, Emor Herbert, A.B. 1876 . . . . . Boston.
Harding, George Franklin, A.B. 1849 . . . . Chicago, Ill.
Harding, Louis Brauch, A.B. 1879 . . . . . Stamford, Ct.
Harding, Selwin Lewis, A.B. 1886 . . . . . Cambridge.
Harding, William Penn, A.B. 1853 . . . . . Cambridge.
Hardon, Henry Winthrop, A.B. 1882 . . . . New York, N.Y.
Hardon, Joseph Bradford, A.B. 1861 . . . . Jamaica Plain.
Hardwick, Charles Theodore, A.B. 1884 . . . Quincy.
Hardy, Alpheus Holmes, A.B. 1861 . . . . . Boston.
Harlow, Edwin Augustus Warren, A.B. 1841 . . Quincy Point.
Harlow, Robert Henry, A.B. 1841 . . . . . . Quincy Point.
Harrington, Charles, A.B. 1878 . . . . . . . Boston.
Harrington, Francis Bishop, M.D. 1881 . . . Boston.
Harris, Charles Nathan, LL.B. 1884 . . . . . Boston.
Harris, George Balmer, A.B. 1886 . . . . . Salem.
Harris, Thaddeus William, A.B. 1884 . . . . Cohasset.
Harris, Thomas Robinson, A.B. 1863 . . . . New York, N.Y.
Hart, Albert Bushnell, A.B. 1880 . . . . . . Cambridge.
Hartshorn, George Trumbull, A.B. 1882 . . . Taunton.

## REGISTRATION. 349

Hartshorne, James Mott, Jr., A.B. 1885 . . . New York, N.Y.
Hartwell, Alfred Stedman, A.B. 1858 . . . . South Natick.
Hartwell, Shattuck, A.B. 1844 . . . . . . . Littleton.
Harwood, Herbert Joseph, A.B. 1877 . . . . Littleton.
Haskell, Augustus Mellen, A.B. 1856 . . . . West Roxbury.
Haskins, David Greene, A.B. 1837 . . . . . Cambridge.
Haskins, David Greene, Jr., A.B. 1866 . . . Cambridge.
Hassam, John Tyler, A.B. 1863 . . . . . . Boston.
Hastings, Edward Rogers, A.B. 1878 . . . . South Weymouth.
Hastings, George Russell, A.B. 1848 . . . . Boston.
Hastings, Leslie, A.B. 1871 . . . . . . . . Cambridge.
Hastings, William Henry Howe, M.D. 1868 . . Boston.
Hatch, Arthur Gillespie, A.B 1884 . . . . . Cambridge.
Hathaway, Francis, A.B. 1849 . . . . . . . New Bedford.
Hathaway, Horatio, A.B. 1850 . . . . . . . New Bedford.
Hauteville, Frederic Sears Grand d', A.B. 1850 . Boston.
Hawes, Edward Southworth, A.B. 1880 . . . Boston.
Hawes, Nathaniel Ware, D.M.D. 1879 . . . . Boston.
Hawkins, Eugene Dexter, A.B. 1881 . . . . New York, N.Y.
Hay, Gustavus, A.B. 1850 . . . . . . . . Boston.
Hayden, Edward Daniel, A.B. 1854 . . . . Woburn.
Hayden, Horace John, A.B. 1860 . . . . . New York, N.Y.
Hayes, Alexander Ladd, A.B. 1863 . . . . Cambridge.
Hayes, Augustus Allen, A.B. 1857 . . . . . Washington, D.C.
Hayes, Hammond Vinton, A.B. 1883 . . . . Cambridge.
Hayes, William Allen, Jr., A B. 1881 . . . . Cambridge.
Hayes, William Allen, 2d., A.B. 1866 . . . . Cambridge.
Haynes, Henry Harrison, A.B. 1873 . . . . Tilton, N.H.
Haynes, Henry Williamson, A.B. 1851 . . . Boston.
Hayward, Charles Latham, Jr., A.B. 1869 . . Boston.
Hayward, Lemuel, A.B. 1845 . . . . . . . Keene, N.H.
Hazard, Daniel Lyman, A.B. 1885 . . . . Narragansett Pier, R.I.
Hedge, Frederic Henry, A.B. 1825 . . . . . Cambridge.
Hedge, Frederic Henry, Jr., A.B. 1851 . . . Lawrence.
Heilbron, George Henry, A.B. 1883 . . . . Boston.
Hemenway, Augustus, A.B. 1875 . . . . . Boston.
Hemenway, Charles Morrison, A.B. 1881 . . Somerville.
Hemmenway, Horace Pierce, M.D. 1862 . . . East Somerville.
Henry, Bertram Curtis, A.B. 1886 . . . . . Brookline.
Henshaw, Henry Arnold, A.B. 1886 . . . . Montvale.
Henshaw, John Andrew, A.B. 1847 . . . . Cambridge.
Herrick, Edwin Hayden, A.B. 1877 . . . . Philadelphia, Pa.
Heywood, John Healy, A.B. 1836 . . . . . Melrose.
Hickox, Ralph W., A.B. 1872 . . . . . . . Cleveland, O.
Hidden, William Henry, Jr., A.B., 1885 . . . Cambridgeport.
Higginson, Edward, A.B. 1874 . . . . . . Fall River.
Higginson, Francis Lee, A.B. 1863 . . . . . Boston.
Higginson, Henry Lee, A.M. 1882 . . . . . Boston.
Higginson, James Jackson, A.B. 1857 . . . . New York, N.Y.

## REGISTRATION.

Higginson, Thomas Wentworth, A.B. 1841 . . . Cambridge.
Higginson, Waldo, A.B. 1833 . . . . . . . Boston.
Hight, LeRoy Lincoln, A.B. 1886 . . . . . . Portland, Me.
Hill, Adams Sherman, A.B. 1853 . . . . . . Cambridge.
Hill, Benjamin Thomas, A.B. 1886 . . . . . Worcester.
Hill, Edward Bruce, A.B. 1874 . . . . . . . New York, N.Y.
Hill, Edwin Newell, A.B. 1872 . . . . . . . Haverhill.
Hill, Hamilton Alonzo, A.B. 1853 . . . . . Boston.
Hill, Henry Barker, A.B. 1869 . . . . . . . Cambridge.
Hill, Henry Eveleth, A.B. 1872 . . . . . . . Worcester.
Hill, Thomas, A.B. 1843 . . . . . . . . . . Portland, Me.
Hill, William Bancroft, A.B. 1879 . . . . . Athens, N.Y.
Hilliard, Samuel Haven, A.B. 1859 . . . . . Boston.
Hillis, John, A.B. 1868 . . . . . . . . . . Maynard.
Hills, William Barker, A.B. 1871 . . . . . Cambridge.
Hills, William Henry, A.B. 1880 . . . . . . Roxbury.
Hinckley, Henry, A.B. 1860 . . . . . . . . Lynn.
Hinkley, Holmes, A.B. 1876 . . . . . . . . Boston.
Hitchcock, Edward, M.D. 1853 . . . . . . . Amherst.
Hitchcock, James Ripley Wellman, A.B. 1877 . New York, N.Y.
Hitchcock, Roswell Dwight, D.D., LL.D., *President of Union Theological Seminary, N.Y. City* New York, N.Y.
Hoar, David Blakely, A.B. 1876 . . . . . . Brookline.
Hoar, Ebenezer Rockwood, A.B. 1835 . . . . Concord.
Hoar, George Ebenezer, A.B. 1883 . . . . . Vernon, Vt.
Hoar, George Frisbie, A.B. 1846, *U. S. Senator for Massachusetts* . . . . . . . . . . . Worcester.
Hoar, Rockwood, A.B. 1876 . . . . . . . . Worcester.
Hoar, Samuel, A.B. 1867 . . . . . . . . . Concord.
Hoar, Sherman, A.B. 1882 . . . . . . . . . Waltham.
Hobart, George Burnap, A.B. 1875 . . . . . Plymouth.
Hobbs, Charles Cushing, A.B. 1855 . . . . South Berwick, Me.
Hobbs, George Miller, A.B. 1850 . . . . . . Boston.
Hobbs, Marland Cogswell, A.B. 1885 . . . . Brookline.
Hochdörfer, Richard, Ph.D. Leipzig . . . . . Cambridge.
Hodges, Amory Glazier, A.B. 1874 . . . . . New York, N.Y.
Hodges, Archie Livingstone, A.B. 1883 . . . Taunton.
Hodges, George Clarendon, D.B. 1879 . . . . Boston.
Hodges, Richard Manning, A.B. 1847 . . . . Boston.
Hodges, William Donnison, A.B. 1877 . . . . Boston.
Hodgkins, William Candler, S.B. 1877 . . . . Washington, D.C.
Hoffman, Edward Fenno, A.B. 1869 . . . . . Philadelphia, Pa.
Holden, Harry, A.B. 1885 . . . . . . . . . Haverhill.
Holder, Frederic Blake, A.B. 1881 . . . . . Boston.
Holland, Arthur, A.B. 1872 . . . . . . . . New York, N.Y.
Holland, Frederic May, A.B. 1859 . . . . . Concord.
Holland, Frederic West, A.B. 1831 . . . . . Concord.
Hollingsworth, Amor Leander, A.B. 1859 . . . Milton.
Holman, John Charles, A.B. 1876 . . . . . . Brookline.

# REGISTRATION. 351

Holman, William Henry, A.B. 1875 . . . . . Southport, Ct.
Holmes, Artemas Henry, A.B. 1870 . . . . . New York, N.Y.
Holmes, Howland, A.B. 1843 . . . . . . . Lexington.
Holmes, John, A.B. 1832 . . . . . . . . . Cambridge.
Holmes, John Parker, A.B. 1884 . . . . . . Philadelphia, Pa.
Holmes, Nathaniel, A.B. 1837 . . . . . . . Cambridge.
Holmes, Oliver Wendell, A.B. 1829, M.D., D.C.L.,
  LL.D. . . . . . . . . . . . . . . . Boston.
Holmes, Oliver Wendell, Jr., A.B. 1861 . . . . Boston.
Holt, Jacob Farnum, A.B. 1857 . . . . . . Philadelphia, Pa.
Homans, John, A B. 1858 . . . . . . . . . Boston.
Homer, Charles Savage, S.B. 1855 . . . . . . New York, N.Y.
Homer, Thomas Johnston, A.B. 1879 . . . . Roxbury.
Honeywell, Thomas Miller, A.B. 1874 . . . . Oil City, Pa.
Hood, Frederic Clark, A.B. 1886 . . . . . Chelsea.
Hooker, Edward Dwight, M.D. 1883 . . . . . Cambridge.
Hooper, Edward William, A.B. 1859 . . . . . Cambridge.
Hooper, Nathaniel Leech, A.B. 1846 . . . . . Boston.
Hooper, Sewall Henry, A.B. 1875 . . . . . . Hingham.
Hooper, William, A.B. 1880 . . . . . . . . Boston.
Hopkins, Abram Duane, A.B. 1879 . . . . . New York, N.Y.
Hopkins, Adoniram Judson, A.B. 1874 . . . . East Boston.
Hopkins, James Hughes, A.B. 1882 . . . . . Provincetown.
Hopkins, Mark, A.M., M.D., S.T.D., LL.D, *Professor of Moral and Intellectual Philosophy at
  Williams College* . . . . . . . . . . . Williamstown
Hopkinson, John Prentiss, A.B. 1861 . . . . Cambridge.
Hornbrooke, Francis Bickford, D.B. 1877 . . . Newton.
Horne, Edwin Temple, A.B. 1864 . . . . . . Dorchester.
Horsford, Eben Norton, A.M. 1847 . . . . . Cambridge.
Horton, Charles Paine, A.B. 1857 . . . . . . Bourne.
Horton, Edwin Johnson, A.B. 1860 . . . . . Pomeroy, O.
Horton, Henry Kenney, A.B. 1870 . . . . . . Boston.
Horton, Samuel Dana, A.B. 1864 . . . . . . Pomeroy, O.
Hosmer, Alfred, A.B. 1853 . . . . . . . . Watertown.
Hosmer, Samuel Dana, A.B. 1850 . . . . . . Auburn.
Houghton, Henry Oscar, A.B. 1877 . . . . . Cambridge.
Houston, Frank Augustine, A.B. 1879 . . . . Haverhill.
Howard, Albert Andrew, A.B. 1882 . . . . . Boston.
Howard, Charles Tasker, A.B. 1856 . . . . . Boston.
Howard, Edwin, A.B. 1885 . . . . . . . . Chelmsford.
Howard, William DeCreet, A.B. 1879 . . . . Chicago, Ill.
Howe, Archibald Murray, A.B. 1869 . . . . . Cambridge.
Howe, Henry Marion, A.B. 1869 . . . . . . Boston.
Howe, Henry Saltonstall, A.B. 1869 . . . . . Biddeford, Me.
Howe, John Edward, A.B. 1884 . . . . . . . Cambridgeport.
Howe, Octavius Thorndike, A B. 1873 . . . . Lawrence.
Howe, Walter Henry, A.B. 1886 . . . . . . Lowell.
Howes, George Edwin, A.B. 1886 . . . . . . Stamford, Ct.

Howland, Francis, A.B. 1849 . . . . . . . . New York, N.Y.
Howland, William Russell, LL.B. 1885 . . . . Cambridge.
Hubbard, Charles Wells, A.B. 1878 . . . . . Weston.
Hubbard, Harry, A.B. 1884 . . . . . . . . . Malden.
Hubbard, William Hammond, A.B. 1879 . . . Chicago, Ill.
Huddleston, John Henry, A.B. 1886 . . . . . Boston.
Hudson, Charles Henry, A.B. 1846 . . . . . Somerville.
Hudson, John Elbridge, A.B. 1862 . . . . . Boston.
Hudson, Woodward, A.B. 1879 . . . . . . . Concord.
Huidekoper, Edgar, A.B. 1868 . . . . . . . Meadville, Pa.
Hulme, Peter, A B. 1872 . . . . . . . . . . Poughkeepsie, N.Y.
Hulse, Samuel Vaughn, LL B. 1872 . . . . . Newark, N.J.
Humason, William Lawrence, A.B. 1877 . . . New Britain, Ct.
Humphrey, James Ellis, S.B. 1886 . . . . . . North Weymouth.
Humphreys, Charles Alfred, A.B. 1860 . . . . Framingham.
Hunt, Edward Browne, A.B. 1878 . . . . . . Boston.
Hunt, Frederick Thayer, A.B. 1882 . . . . . Weymouth.
Hunt, Freeman, A.B. 1877 . . . . . . . . . North Cambridge.
Hunting, Nathaniel Stevens, A.B. 1884 . . . . Des Moines, Ia.
Huntington, Oliver Whipple, A.B. 1881 . . . . Cambridge.
Huntington, William Edwards, *Dean of College of
   Liberal Arts, Boston University* . . . . . . Newton Centre.
Hurley, Frank Edward, A.B. 1886 . . . . . . Farmington, N.H.
Hutchins, Herbert Bacon, A.B. 1886 . . . . Tivoli-on-Hudson, N.Y.
Hutchins, William Everett, A.B. 1879 . . . . North Cambridge.
Hutchinson, Gardiner Spring, LL.B. 1858 . . . New York, N.Y.
Hutchinson, Marcello, A.B. 1872 . . . . . . Taunton.
Hyatt, Alpheus, S.B. 1862 . . . . . . . . . Cambridge.
Hyde, George Smith, A.B. 1853 . . . . . . . Boston.
Hyde, Thomas Alexander, A.B. 1881 . . . . . Cambridge.
Hyde, William, A.B. 1881 . . . . . . . . . Weymouth.
Hyde, William DeWitt, A.B. 1879, *President of
   Bowdoin College* . . . . . . . . . . . Brunswick, Me.

INCHES, Charles Edward, A.B. 1861 . . . . . Boston.
Ingalls, Edmond Cunningham, A.B. 1873 . . . Saco, Me.
Ingalls, William, A B. 1835 . . . . . . . . Boston.
Ingalsbe, Grenville Mellen, LL.B. 1872 . . . . Sandy Hill, N.Y.
Ireland, Frederick Guion, A.B. 1868 . . . . . New York, N.Y.
Irish, Cyrus Wendell, A.B. 1885 . . . . . . Lowell.
Isham, Charles, A.B. 1876 . . . . . . . . . New York, N.Y.
Ives, David Otis, A.B. 1879 . . . . . . . . Salem.

JACK, Edwin Everett, A.B. 1884 . . . . . . Boston.
Jackson, Alton Atwell, M.D. 1883 . . . . . . E. Jefferson, Me.
Jackson, Charles Cabot, A.B. 1863 . . . . . Boston.
Jackson, Charles Loring, A.B. 1867 . . . . . Cambridge.
Jackson, Edward, A.B. 1849 . . . . . . . . Boston.
Jackson, Ernest, A.B. 1878 . . . . . . . . Boston.

REGISTRATION. 353

Jackson, Frank, A.B. 1871 . . . . . . . . Boston.
Jackson, George West, A.B. 1879 . . . . . . Boston.
Jackson, Henry, A.B. 1880 . . . . . . . . Boston.
Jackson, James Frederick, A.B. 1873 . . . . . Fall River.
Jackson, Louis Lincoln, A.B. 1885 . . . . . . Brighton.
Jackson, Patrick Tracy, Jr., A.B. 1865 . . . . Cambridge.
Jackson, Robert Tracy, S.B. 1884 . . . . . . Boston.
Jacob, Lawrence, A.B. 1878 . . . . . . . . New York, N.Y.
Jacobs, Francis Wayland, LL.B. 1861 . . . Boston.
Jacobs, George Edward, A.B. 1876 . . . . . Dorchester.
Jacobs, Henry Barton, A.B. 1883 . . . . . . West Scituate.
Jacobs, Justin Allen, A.B. 1839 . . . . . . Cambridge.
James, William, M.D. 1869 . . . . . . . . Cambridge.
Jaques, Henry Percy, A.B. 1876 . . . . . . Milton.
Jaretzki, Alfred, A.B. 1881 . . . . . . . . New York, N.Y.
Jaynes, Julian Clifford, D.B. 1884 . . . . . West Newton.
Jeffries, Benjamin Joy, A.B. 1854 . . . . . . Boston.
Jeffries, Walter Lloyd, A.B. 1875 . . . . . . Boston.
Jeffries, William Augustus, A.B. 1875 . . . . Boston.
Jenks, Charles William, A.B. 1871 . . . . . Boston.
Jenks, Henry Fitch, A.B. 1863 . . . . . . . Canton.
Jennings, Charles Herbert, A.B. 1884 . . . . Cambridge.
Jennings, Edward Borden, A.B. 1886 . . . . Fall River.
Jennison, Frank Elwood, A.B. 1883 . . . . . New York, N.Y.
Jewett, George Frank, A.B. 1886 . . . . . . Cambridge.
Jillson, Franklin Campbell, M.D. 1886 . . . . Malden.
Johnson, Amos Howe, A.B. 1853 . . . . . . Salem.
Johnson, Arthur Stoddard, A.B. 1885 . . . . Boston.
Johnson, Charles Rensselaer, A.B. 1875 . . . Worcester.
Johnson, Edward Crosby, A.B. 1860 . . . . . Boston.
Johnson, Francis Howe, A.B. 1856 . . . . . Andover.
Johnson, John Warren, A.B. 1873 . . . . . . Woburn.
Johnson, Laurence Henry Hitch, A.B. 1880 . . . Boston.
Jones, Arthur Earl, A.B. 1867 . . . . . . . Cambridge.
Jones, Claudius Marcellus, A.B. 1866 . . . . Boston.
Jones, George Warren, M.D. 1872 . . . . . . Cambridgeport.
Jones, Gilbert Norris, A.B. 1884 . . . . . . Bangor, Me.
Jones, Henry Champion, A.B. 1880 . . . . . Boston.
Jones, Henry Olmstead, A.B. 1881 . . . . . Columbus, O.
Jones, Henry Walter, A.B. 1885 . . . . . . Cambridge.
Jones, Jesse Henry, A.B. 1856 . . . . . . . North Abington.
Jones, Leonard Augustus, A.B 1855 . . . . . Boston.
Jones, Samuel Cleaves, A.B. 1886 . . . . . . Roxbury.
Jones, Walter Ingersoll, A.B. 1874 . . . . . Boston.
Jordan, Frederic Dolbier, A.B 1880 . . . . . Lawrence.
Jordan, James Clark, A.B. 1870 . . . . . . Boston.
Joy, Frederic, A.B. 1881 . . . . . . . . . Winchester.
Joyce, George Frederic, A.B. 1881 . . . . . Merrimac.
Judkins, Benjamin, A.B. 1848 . . . . . . . Concord.

23

KAAN, Frank Warton, A.B. 1883 . . . . . . Somerville.
Keasbey, Edward Quinton, LL.B. 1870 . . . . Newark, N.J.
Keating, Patrick Michael, A.B. 1883 . . . . . Boston.
Keegan, Dermot Warburton, A.B. 1862 . . . . New York, N.Y.
Keegan, Vincent Elijah, M.D. 1865 . . . . . . Boston.
Keene, Francis Bowler, A.B. 1880 . . . . . . Milwaukee, Wis.
Keener, William Albert, LL.B. 1877 . . . . . Cambridge
Keith, Arthur, A.B. 1885 . . . . . . . . . . Wollaston.
Keith, George Paul, A.B. 1883 . . . . . . . Wollaston.
Keith, Merton Spencer, A.B. 1872 . . . . . . Quincy.
Kelley, Clarence Erskine, A.B. 1873 . . . . . Haverhill.
Kelley, Webster, A.B. 1879 . . . . . . . . Boston.
Kellner, Maximilian Lindsay, A.B. 1885 . . . . Cambridge.
Kelly, George Reed, A.B. 1880 . . . . . . . Boston.
Kelsey, Ambrose Parsons, Ph.D., *Professor of Natural History in Hamilton College* . . . . . . Clinton, N.Y.
Kendall, Charles Grant, A.B. 1847 . . . . . . New York, N.Y.
Kendall, Frank Alexander, A.B. 1886 . . . . . Framingham.
Kendall, Joshua, A.B. 1853 . . . . . . . . Cambridgeport.
Kenison, Nehemiah Samuel, A.B. 1886 . . . . Allenstown, N.H.
Kennedy, George Golding, A.B. 1864 . . . . . Readville.
Kent, Edward, A.B. 1883 . . . . . . . . . . New York, N.Y.
Kent, John Bryden, M.D. 1869 . . . . . . . Putnam, Ct.
Kent, John Fuller, A.B. 1875 . . . . . . . . Concord, N.H.
Kettell, Charles Willard, A.B. 1870 . . . . . Cambridge.
Kettell, George Adams, A.B. 1866 . . . . . . Charlestown.
Keyes, John Shepard, A.B. 1841 . . . . . . . Concord.
Keyes, Prescott, A.B. 1879 . . . . . . . . . Concord.
Kidder, Camillus George, A.B. 1872 . . . . . New York, N.Y.
Kidder, Edward Hartwell, A.B. 1863 . . . . . Brooklyn, N.Y.
Kidder, Frederic Henry, A.B. 1876 . . . . . . Medford.
Kidder, Jerome Henry, A.B. 1862 . . . . . . Washington, D.C.
Kidner, Reuben, A.B. 1875 . . . . . . . . . Boston.
Kilby, Henry Sherman, A.B. 1873 . . . . . . No. Attleborough.
Kimball, David Pulsifer, A.B. 1856 . . . . . . Boston.
Kimball, Henry Colman, A.B. 1840 . . . . . . Stoughton.
Kimball, Marcus Morton, A.B. 1886 . . . . . Boston.
Kimball, Wallace Lowe, A.B. 1875 . . . . . . Bradford.
Kimball, William Frederick, A.B. 1875 . . . . Chelsea.
King, Charles Carroll, A.B. 1885 . . . . . . Montpelier, Vt.
King, Edward, A.B. 1853 . . . . . . . . . . New York, N.Y.
King, Moses, A.B. 1881 . . . . . . . . . . Newton.
King, Stephen Henry, M.D. 1872 . . . . . . Providence, R.I.
Kingsbury, Edward Phipps, A.B. 1879 . . . . Holliston.
Kinney, Henry Nason, A.B. 1879 . . . . . . Winsted, Ct.
Kirby, Edward Napoleon . . . . . . . . . . Cambridge.
Knapp, Arthur Mason, A.B. 1863 . . . . . . Boston.
Knapp, Arthur May, A.B. 1860 . . . . . . . Watertown.
Knapp, Frederick Newman, A.B. 1843 . . . . Plymouth.

Knapp, Philip Coombs, A.B. 1878 . . . . . . Boston.
Knowles, Arthur Jacob, A.B. 1881 . . . . . Boston.
Knowlton, Thomas Oaks, LL.B. 1871 . . . . New Boston, N.H.

LADD, Babson Savilian, A.B. 1870 . . . . . Boston.
Lamar, Hon. Lucius Quintius Curtius, *Secretary of the Interior* . . . . . . . . . . . Washington, D.C.
Lamb, Charles Estus, A.B. 1886 . . . . . . Providence, R.I.
Lamb, Horatio Appleton, A.B. 1871 . . . . . Boston.
Lambert, William Bartlett, A.B. 1867 . . . . Cambridge.
Lamson, Artemas Ward, A.B. 1849 . . . . . Dedham.
Lamson, Charles Dudley, S.B. 1865 . . . . . Boston.
Lamson, Gardner Swift, A.B. 1877 . . . . . Boston.
Lancaster, Walter Moody, A.B. 1879 . . . . Worcester.
Lanciani, Rodolfo. *Professor of Archæology in University of Rome* . . . . . . . . . . Rome, Italy.
Lane, Edward Binney, A.B. 1881 . . . . . . Boston.
Lane, Gardiner Martin, A.B. 1881 . . . . . Cambridge.
Lane, George Martin, A.B. 1846 . . . . . . Cambridge.
Lane, John Chapin, A.B. 1875 . . . . . . . Norwood.
Lane, William Coolidge, A.B. 1881 . . . . . Cambridge.
Langdell, Christopher Columbus, A.B. 1851 . . Cambridge.
Langley, Samuel Pierpont, *Director of the Observatory at Allegheny City, Pa.* . . . . . . . . Allegheny, Pa.
Langmaid, Samuel Wood, A.B. 1859 . . . . . Boston.
Lanman, Charles Rockwell, A.B. 1871, *Yale* . . Cambridge.
Lapeyre, George Fortuné, A.B. 1886 . . . . . New Orleans, La.
Latham, Aaron Hobart, A.B. 1877 . . . . . . Brookline.
Lathrop, Andrew Janes, A.B. 1859 . . . . . Waltham.
Lathrop, William Henry, A.B. 1863 . . . . . Lowell.
Latimer, George Dimmick, D.B. 1886 . . . . Cambridge.
Laughlin, James Laurence, A.B. 1873 . . . . Cambridge.
Lawrance, William Irvin, D.B. 1885 . . . . . Dorchester.
Lawrence, Amory Appleton, A.B. 1870 . . . . Boston.
Lawrence, Arthur, A.B. 1863 . . . . . . . . Stockbridge.
Lawrence, George Porter, LL.B. 1860 . . . . Cambridge.
Lawrence, James, A.B. 1874 . . . . . . . . Groton.
Lawrence, Rosewell Bigelow, A.B. 1878 . . . Medford.
Lawrence, Samuel Crocker, A.B. 1855 . . . . Medford.
Lawrence, William, A.B. 1871 . . . . . . . Cambridge.
Lawrence, William Badger, A.B. 1879 . . . . Medford.
Lawton, Alexander Robert, LL.B. 1842 . . . Savannah, Ga.
Lawton, Frederick, A.B. 1874 . . . . . . . Lowell.
Lawton, William Cranston, A.B. 1873 . . . . Cambridge.
Learned, William Pollock, A.B. 1880 . . . . Pittsfield.
Learoyd, Charles Henry, A.B. 1858 . . . . . Taunton.
Leatherbee, George Henry, A.B. 1882 . . . . Parkersburg, W. Va.
Ledlie, George Hees, A.B. 1884 . . . . . . . Cambridge.
Lee, Daniel David, D.V.S. 1886 . . . . . . . Jamaica Plain.

Lee, Edward Thomas, A.B. 1886 . . . . . . . Hartford, Ct.
Lee, Elliot Cabot, A.B. 1876 . . . . . . . . . Brookline.
Lee, Frederick Schiller, A.B., *St. Lawrence University*, 1878 . . . . . . . . . . . . . . Canton, N.Y.
Lee, Henry, A.B. 1836 . . . . . . . . . . . Brookline.
Lee, Joseph, A.B. 1883 . . . . . . . . . . Brookline.
Lee, Thomas, A.B. 1879 . . . . . . . . . . Washington, D.C.
Leeds, Albert Ripley, A.B. 1865 . . . . . . Hoboken, N.J.
Lefavour, Edward Brown, A.B. 1876 . . . . Beverly.
Legate, Burton John, A.B. 1877 . . . . . . Boston.
Leidy, Joseph, M.D., LL.D., *Director of the Biological Department, and Professor of Anatomy, University of Pennsylvania* . . . . . . . Philadelphia, Pa.
Leland, Willis Daniels, A.B. 1876 . . . . . North Weymouth.
Le Moyne, Francis Julius, A.B. 1877 . . . . Chicago, Ill.
Leonard, Amos Morse, A.B. 1866 . . . . . . Boston.
Leonard, Frederick Moses, A.B. 1879 . . . . Philadelphia, Pa.
Leverett, George Vasmer, A.B. 1867 . . . . Cambridge.
Lewis, Edwin Creswell, A.B. 1859 . . . . . Laconia, N.H.
Lewis, Henry Foster, A.B. 1885 . . . . . . Chicago, Ill.
Lewis, Isaac Newton, A.B. 1873 . . . . . . Walpole.
Lighthipe, Charles Francis, A.B. 1875 . . . Orange, N.J.
Lilienthal, Howard, A.B. 1883 . . . . . . . Saratoga Springs, N.Y.
Lincoln, Albert Lamb, Jr., A.B. 1872 . . . . Brookline.
Lincoln, Arthur, A.B. 1863 . . . . . . . . Boston.
Lincoln, Charles Sprague, A.B. 1850 . . . . Somerville.
Lincoln, Charles Jairus, A.B. 1865 . . . Aspinwall Hill, Brookline.
Lincoln, Francis Henry, A.B. 1867 . . . . . Hingham.
Lincoln, Francis Newhall, A.B. 1871 . . . . Boston.
Lincoln, Frederic Walker, A.M. 1853 . . . Mt. Everett, Dorchester.
Lincoln, Nathan, A.B. 1842 . . . . . . . . Cambridgeport.
Lincoln, Solomon, A.B. 1857 . . . . . . . Boston.
Lincoln, Waldo, A.B. 1870 . . . . . . . . Worcester.
Littauer, Lucius Nathan, A.B. 1878 . . . . . New York, N.Y.
Littauer, William, A.B. 1886 . . . . . . . New York, N.Y.
Littlefield, George Emery, A.B. 1866 . . . . North Cambridge.
Livermore, Joseph Perkins, A.B. 1875 . . . Cambridge.
Livingood, Frank Shalter, A.B. 1876 . . . . Reading, Pa.
Lloyd, Alfred Henry, A.B. 1886 . . . . . . Montclair, N.J.
Locke, Warren Andrew, A.B. 1869 . . . . . Cambridge.
Lodge, Henry Cabot, A.B. 1871 . . . . . . Nahant.
Loeser, Charles Alexander, A.B. 1886 . . . New York, N.Y.
Lombard, Josiah, A.B. 1863 . . . . . . . . New York, N.Y.
Lombard, Warren Plimpton, A.B. 1878 . . . New York, N.Y.
Lombard, William Alden, A.B 1883 . . . . . Boston.
Long, Joseph Mansfield, A.B. 1885 . . . . . Brookline.
Longfellow, Alexander Wadsworth, Jr., A.B. 1876 Portland, Me.
Longfellow, Samuel, A.B. 1839 . . . . . . Cambridge.
**Longfellow, William Pitt Preble, A.B. 1855** . . Boston.

Lord, Arthur, A.B. 1872 . . . . . . . . . . Plymouth.
Lord, Augustus Mendon, A.B. 1883 . . . . . Cambridge.
Lord, Eliot, A.B. 1873 . . . . . . . . . Boston.
Lord, William Tyler, A.B. 1883 . . . . . . Boston.
Loring, Augustus Peabody, A.B. 1878 . . . . Boston.
Loring, Caleb William, A.B. 1839 . . . . . Beverly Farms.
Loring, Francis Caleb, A.B. 1863 . . . . . Boston.
Loring, George Bailey, A.B. 1838 . . . . . Salem.
Loring, William Caleb, A.B. 1872 . . . . . Boston.
Lothrop, Arthur Prescott, A.B. 1882 . . . . Taunton.
Loud, John Jacob, A.B. 1866 . . . . . . . . Weymouth
Lounsbury, Edward Haskell, A.B. 1884 . . . Woburn.
Lovering, Charles Taylor, A.B. 1868 . . . . Boston.
Lovering, Ernest, A.B. 1881 . . . . . . . . Cambridge.
Lovering, James Walker, A.B. 1866 . . . . . Cambridge.
Lovering, Joseph, A.B. 1833 . . . . . . . . Cambridge.
Lovett, Robert Williamson, A.B. 1881 . . . . Boston.
Lovejoy, Charles Averill, A.B. 1868 . . . . Lynn.
Lowe, Fred Messenger, M.D. 1884 . . . . . . Boston.
Lowell, Abbott Lawrence, A.B. 1877 . . . . Boston.
Lowell, Edward Jackson, A.B. 1867 . . . . . Boston.
Lowell, Francis Cabot, A.B. 1876 . . . . . Boston.
Lowell, James Russell, A.B. 1838, D.C.L., LL.D. . Southborough.
Lowell, John, A.B. 1843 . . . . . . . . . . Chestnut Hill.
Lowell, John, Jr., A.B. 1877 . . . . . . . . Chestnut Hill.
Lowell, Percival, A.B. 1876 . . . . . . . . Boston.
Lowman, Jesse, A.B. 1884 . . . . . . . . . Cincinnati, O.
Luce, Robert, A.B. 1882 . . . . . . . . . . Somerville.
Ludlow, James Bettner, A.B. 1881 . . . . . New York, N.Y.
Lull, Herbert Warren, A.B. 1874 . . . . . . Milford.
Lunt, Edward Clark, A.B. 1886 . . . . . . . Malden.
Lyman, Arthur, A.B. 1883 . . . . . . . . . Boston.
Lyman, Arthur Theodore, A.B. 1853 . . . . . Boston.
Lyman, Benjamin Smith, A.B. 1855 . . . . . Northampton.
Lyman, Charles Parker, F.R.C.V.S. . . . . . Chestnut Hill.
Lyman, George Hinckley, Jr., A.B. 1873 . . . Boston.
Lyman, Theodore, A.B. 1855 . . . . . . . . Brookline.
Lyon, David Gordon, A.B. 1875 . . . . . . . Cambridge.
Lyon, Henry, A.B. 1835 . . . . . . . . . . Charlestown.
Lyon, William Henry, D.B. 1873 . . . . . . Roxbury.

MCALLISTER, Hall, Jr., A.B. 1886 . . . . . San Francisco, Cal.
McArthur, John R., A.B. 1885 . . . . . . . Chicago, Ill.
McCagg, Louis Butler, A.B. 1884 . . . . . . New York, N.Y.
McCleary, Samuel Foster, A.B. 1841 . . . . Brookline.
McCook, Robert Latimer, A.B. 1885 . . . . . New York, N.Y.
McCosh, James, D.D., LL.D., *President of College of New Jersey* . . . . . . . . . . Princeton, N.J.
McCoy, Walter Irving, A.B. 1882 . . . . . . Troy, N.Y.

McDaniel, Benjamin Franklin, D.B. 1869 . . . Salem.
McDaniel, Samuel Walton, LL.B. 1878 . . . . Cambridge.
Macdonald, Loren Benjamin, A.B. 1886 (B.D. 1881) Shirley.
McDuffie, John, Jr., A.B. 1884 . . . . . . . . Greenfield.
McGrath, Thomas, LL.B. 1865 . . . . . . . . St. Andrews, N.B.
McGrew, Gifford Horace Greeley, A.B. 1874 . . Wareham.
Machado, José Antonio, A.B. 1883 . . . . . . Salem.
Machen, Arthur Webster, LL.B. 1851 . . . . Baltimore, Md.
McInnes, Edwin Guthrie, A.B. 1883 . . . . . Malden.
McInnes, William Morrow, A.B. 1885 . . . . Roxbury.
McIntire, Farrington, A.B. 1843 . . . . . . . Wollaston Heights.
Mack, Alfred, LL.B. 1883 . . . . . . . . . . Cincinnati, O.
Mack, Charles Samuel, A.B. 1879 . . . . . . Boston.
Mack, Henry W., LL.B. 1884 . . . . . . . Dakota Flats, N.Y.
Mackay, William, A.B. 1855 . . . . . . . . Cambridge.
McKeever, Henry Francis, LL.B. 1871 . . . Boston.
McKelvey, John Jay, A.B. 1884, *Oberlin* . . . Sandusky, O.
McKenzie, Alexander, A.B. 1859 . . . . . . Cambridge.
McKim, Haslett, Jr., A.B. 1866 . . . . . . . Navesink, N.J.
Mackintosh, William Davis, A.B. 1869 . . . Arlington Heights.
McLennan, Francis, A.B. 1879 . . . . . . . Montreal, Can.
Macvane, Silas Marcus, A.B. 1873 . . . . . Cambridge.
MacVeagh, Charles, A.B. 1881 . . . . . . . New York, N.Y.
Magoun, Thatcher, A.B. 1858 . . . . . . . Boston.
Mahoney, John Francis, A.B. 1885 . . . . Waltham.
Mallory, Frank Burr, A.B. 1886 . . . . . . Cleveland, O.
Mandell, Henry Fauntleroy, A.B. 1884 . . . Boston.
Mann, George Combe, A.B. 1867 . . . . . . Jamaica Plain.
Manning, Leonard Jarvis, A.B. 1876 . . . . College Hill.
Mansfield, Ex-Sumner, A.B. 1868 . . . . . Brookline.
Marden, Francis Alexander, A.B. 1863 . . . Stamford, Ct.
Marden, Orrison Swett, M.D. 1882 . . . . . Boston.
Mark, Edward Laurens, A.B. 1871, *Univ. Mich.* , Cambridge.
Marsh, Francis, A.B. 1863 . . . . . . . . . Dedham.
Marsh, Othniel Charles, A.B. Yale, 1860, *Professor
of Palæontology in Yale College* . . . New Haven, Ct.
Marsters, John Marshall, A.B. 1847 . . . . North Cambridge.
Martin, Alfred Wilhelm, D.B. 1885 . . . . Montreal, Can.
Martin, Austin Agnew, A.B. 1873 . . . . . Boston.
Mason, Amos Lawrence, A.B. 1863 . . . . Boston.
Mason, Atherton Perry, A.B. 1879 . . . . . Fitchburg.
Mason, Charles, A.B. 1834 . . . . . . . . . Fitchburg.
Mason, Charles Frank, A.B. 1882 . . . . . Revere.
Mason, Harry White, A.B. 1878 . . . . . . Newton Centre.
Mason, John James, A.B. 1866 . . . . . . . Newport, R.I.
Mason, William Castein, A.B. 1874 . . . . Bangor, Me.
Mason, William Powell, A.B. 1856 . . . . Walpole, N.H.
Matthews, Albert, A.B. 1882 . . . . . . . . Boston.
Matthews, Nathan . . . . . . . . . . . . . Boston.

## REGISTRATION. 359

Matthews, Nathan, Jr., A.B. 1875 . . . . . . Boston.
May, Henry Farnham, A.B. 1881 . . . . . . Boston.
May, James Rundlet, A.B. 1861 . . . . . . Portsmouth, N.H.
May, Samuel, A.B. 1829 . . . . . . . . . Leicester.
Mead, Julian Augustus, A.B. 1878 . . . . . . Watertown.
Melledge, James Harold, A.B. 1881 . . . . . Lawrence.
Melledge, Robert Job, A.B. 1877 . . . . . . Cambridge.
Memminger, Robert Withers, A.B. 1859 . . . . Charleston, S.C.
Meriam, Horatio Cook, D.M.D. 1874 . . . . . Salem.
Merriam, Frank, A.B. 1871 . . . . . . . . Boston.
Merriam, John McKinstry, A.B. 1886 . . . . South Framingham.
Merrill, Moses, A.B. 1856 . . . . . . . . Boston.
Merritt, Edward Percival, A.B. 1882 . . . . . Boston.
Metcalf, Eliab Wight, A.B. 1859 . . . . . . North Cambridge.
Metcalf, Simeon McCausland, M.D. 1881 . . . Los Angeles, Cal.
Métivier, James, A.B. 1877 . . . . . . . . Cambridge.
Meyer, George von Lengerke, A.B. 1879 . . . . Boston.
Mifflin, George Harrison, A.B. 1865 . . . . . Boston.
Millingen, Alexander van, M.A., *Edinburgh, Scotland, Professor in Robert College* . . . . . Constantinople, Tur.
Mills, Arthur, A.B. 1872 . . . . . . . . . Brookline.
Mills, Ezra Palmer, A.B. 1885 . . . . . . . New York, N.Y.
Mills, Hiram Roberts, A.B. 1876 . . . . . . Hartford, Ct.
Milton, Henry Slade, A.B. 1875 . . . . . . Waltham.
Minot, Charles Henry, Jr., A.B. 1886 . . . . . Boston.
Minot, Charles Sedgwick, S.D. 1878 . . . . . Boston.
Minot, George Richards, A.B. 1871 . . . . . Boston.
Minot, Robert Sedgwick, A.B. 1877 . . . . . Jamaica Plain.
Mitchell, Charles Andrews, A.B. 1881 . . . . Concord, N.H.
Mitchell, James William, A.B. 1879 . . . . . Boston.
Mitchell, Silas Weir, 1850, *Univ. Pennsylvania* . . Philadelphia, Pa.
Mitchell, Walter, A.B. 1846 . . . . . . . . New York, N.Y.
Mixter, George, A.B. 1863 . . . . . . . . Boston.
Mixter, Samuel Jason, M.D. 1879 . . . . . . Boston.
Monks, George Howard, A.B. 1875 . . . . . Boston.
Monroe, William Ingalls, A.B. 1879 . . . . . Boston (Highlands).
Montague, Frazer Livingston, A.B. 1884 . . . Chelsea.
Montague, Henry Watmough, A.B. 1878 . . . Chelsea.
Montgomery, William, Jr., A.B. 1867 . . . . . New York, N.Y.
Moore, Edward Cook, Jr., A.B. 1878 . . . . . Yonkers, N.Y.
Moors, Arthur Wendell, A B 1880 . . . . . . Boston.
Moors, Francis Joseph, A.B. 1886 . . . . . . Boston.
Moors, John Farwell, A.B. 1842 . . . . . . Greenfield.
Moors, John Farwell, A.B. 1883 . . . . . . Boston.
Morgan, Charles, A.B. 1880 . . . . . . . . Bordentown, N.J.
Morgan, Morris Hicky, A B. 1881 . . . . . . Cambridge.
Morison, George Burnap, A.B. 1883 . . . . . Boston.
Morison, George Shattuck, A.B. 1863 . . . . . New York, N.Y.
Morison, John Holmes, A.B. 1878 . . . . . . Boston.

Morison, John Hopkins, A.B 1831 . . . . . . . Boston.
Morison, Robert Swain, A.B. 1869 . . . . . . Cambridge.
Morisou, Samuel Lord, A.B. 1873 . . . . . . New York, N.Y.
Morong, Arthur Bennett, M.D. 1876 . . . . . Boston.
Morrell, George Dallas, A.B. 1877 . . . . . . Philadelphia, Pa.
Morrill, George, A.B. 1846 . . . . . . . . Boston.
Morris, Alfred Hennen, A.B. 1885 . . . . . . West Chester, N.Y.
Morris, George Patrick, A.B. 1883 . . . . . . South Boston.
Morris, John Gavin, A.B. 1879 . . . . . . . South Boston.
Morris, William Radcliff, A.B. 1877 . . . . . Omaha, Neb.
Morse, Charles Francis, A.B. 1883 . . . . . . Boston.
Morse, Edwin Wilson, A.B. 1878 . . . . . . New York, N.Y.
Morse, Godfrey, A.B. 1870 . . . . . . . . Boston.
Morse, Henry Lee, A.B. 1874 . . . . . . . Boston.
Morse, Robert McNeil, A.B. 1857 . . . . . . Jamaica Plain.
Morse, William Lambert, A.B. 1874 . . . . . Marlborough.
Morse, William Russell, A.B. 1876 . . . . . Roxbury.
Morss, Charles Henry, A.B. 1880 . . . . . . Portsmouth, N.H
Morss, John Wells, A.B. 1884 . . . . . . . Boston.
Morton, Johnson, A.B. 1886 . . . . . . . . Pawtucket, R.I.
Motley, George Storer, A.B. 1879 . . . . . . Lowell.
Motte, Ellis Loring, A.B. 1859 . . . . . . . Boston.
Mullen, Thomas Aloysius, A B. 1884 . . . . . South Boston.
Mullett, Alfred Edgar, D.B. 1873 . . . . . . Charlestown.
Mumford, James Gregory, A.B. 1885 . . . . Rochester, N.Y.
Mumford, William Woolsey, A.B. 1884 . . . New York, N.Y.
Munro, John Cummings, A.B. 1881 . . . . . Lexington.
Munroe, Charles Edward, S.B. 1871 . . . . . Newport, R.I.
Munroe, Charles William, A.B. 1847 . . . . . Cambridge.
Munroe, Nathan Watson, A.B. 1830 . . . . . Greenfield.
Munroe, William Adams, A.B. 1864 . . . . . Boston.
Murkland, Charles Sumner, D.B. 1883 . . . . Manchester, N.H.
Murphy, William Stanislaus, A.B. 1885 . . . . Boston.
Murray, John Archibald, A.B. 1878 . . . . . New York, N.Y.
Muzzey, Artemas Bowers, A.B. 1824 . . . . . Cambridge.
Muzzey, David Patterson, D.B. 1869 . . . . . Cambridgeport.
Myers, James Jefferson, A.B. 1869 . . . . . Cambridge.

Nash, Bennett Hubbard, A.B. 1856 . . . . . Boston.
Nash, George Miner, A.B. 1877 . . . . . . . Everett.
Nash, Henry Sylvester, A.B. 1878 . . . . . . Cambridge.
Nash, Nathaniel Cushing, A.B. 1884 . . . . . Cambridge.
Nason, Rufus William, A.B. 1873 . . . . . . Boston.
Neal, George Benjamin, A.B. 1846 . . . . . Charlestown.
Nelson, Edward Beverly, A.B. 1873 . . . . . Rome, N.Y.
Nelson, Henry David, A B. 1884 . . . . . . Milford.
Nelson, Thomas, A.B. 1866 . . . . . . . . Boston.
Nesmith, Joseph Aaron, A.B. 1881 . . . . . Lowell.
Nesmith, Thomas, A.B. 1871 . . . . . . . . Lowell.

Newcomb, Simon, S.B. 1858 . . . . . . . . Washington, D.C.
Newell, Otis Kimball, M D. 1882 . . . . . . Boston.
Newell, Samuel, A.B. 1857 . . . . . . . . Great Barrington.
Newell, William Wells, A.B. 1859 . . . . . . Cambridge.
Newhall, Herbert William, A.B. 1879 . . . . Lynn.
Newhall, John Breed, A.B. 1885 . . . . . . Lynn.
Nichols, Arthur Howard, A.B. 1862 . . . . . Boston.
Nichols, Benjamin White, A.B. 1842 . . . . . Boston.
Nichols, Charles Corbett, A.B. 1883 . . . . . Everett.
Nichols, Edgar Hamilton, A.B. 1878 . . . . . Cambridge.
Nichols, Frederick, A.B. 1883 . . . . . . . Boston.
Nichols, Frederick Spelman, A.B. 1849 . . . . Boston.
Nichols, George Henry, A.B. 1833 . . . . . . Boston.
Nichols, Harry Peirce, A.B. 1871 . . . . . . New Haven, Ct.
Nichols, Henry Gilman, A.B. 1877 . . . . . . Boston.
Nichols, John Loring, A.B. 1879 . . . . . . Somerville.
Nichols, John Taylor Gilman, A.B. 1836 . . . Saco, Me.
Nichols, John Taylor Gilman, M.D. 1859 . . . Cambridge.
Nichols, Seth, A.B. 1885 . . . . . . . . . Boston.
Nichols, William Ichabod, A.B. 1874 . . . . Littleton.
Nickerson, George Augustus, A.B. 1876 . . . . Boston.
Noble, George Washington Copp, A.B. 1858 . . Cambridge.
Noble, John, A.B. 1850 . . . . . . . . . Roxbury.
Nolen, William Whiting, A.B. 1884 . . . . . Philadelphia, Pa.
Noonan, John Andrew, A.B. 1884 . . . . . . South Boston.
Norcross, Grenville Howland, A.B. 1875 . . . Boston.
Norcross, Otis, A.B. 1870 . . . . . . . . . Boston.
Norris, Albert Lane, M.D. 1865 . . . . . . Cambridge.
Norris, Samuel, Jr., A.B. 1883 . . . . . . . Bristol, R.I.
Norton, Charles Eliot, A.B. 1846 . . . . . . Cambridge.
Norton, Eliot, A.B. 1885 . . . . . . . . . Cambridge.
Noyes, Charles, A.B. 1856 . . . . . . . . North Andover.
Noyes, Edward Isaac Kimbal, A.B. 1885 . . . Cambridge.
Noyes, Ernest Henry, M.D. 1880 . . . . . . Boston.
Noyes, George Dana, A.B. 1851 . . . . . . Brookline.
Noyes, James Atkins, A.B. 1883 . . . . . . Brooklyn, N.Y.
Noyes, Samuel Bradley, A.B. 1844 . . . . . Canton.
Noyes, William, A.B. 1881 . . . . . . . . New York, N.Y.
Nunn, Charles Peirce, A.B. 1879 . . . . . . Lexington.
Nutter, George Read, A.B. 1885 . . . . . . Boston.

O'BRIEN, Hon. Hugh, *Mayor of Boston* . . . . Boston.
O'Brien, Hon. John Bernard, *Sheriff of Suffolk County* . . . . . . . . . . . . . . . . Boston.
Okakura, Kakuyo, *Tokio University* . . . . . Tokio, Japan.
O'Keefe, John Aloysius, A.B. 1880 . . . . . Lynn.
Oliver, Henry Kemble, A.B. 1852 . . . . . . Boston.
Olmstead, James Monroe, A.B. 1873 . . . . . Boston.
Olmsted, Frederick Law, A.M. 1864 . . . . . Brookline.

Olney, George Washington, LL.B. 1855 . . . . New York, N.Y.
Olney, Peter Butler, A.B. 1864 . . . . . . . New York, N.Y.
Orcutt, William Hunter, A.B. 1869 . . . . . Cambridgeport.
Ordronaux, John, LL.B. 1852 . . . . . . . . Roslyn, N.Y.
Ordway, Herbert Ingersoll, A.B. 1873 . . . . Newton Centre.
Osborne, Louis Shreve, A.B. 1873 . . . . . . Chicago, Ill.
Osborne, Thomas Mott, A.B. 1884 . . . . . . Auburn, N.Y
Osgood, Edmund Quincy Sewall, A.B. 1875 . . Grafton.
Osgood, George, D.B. 1847 . . . . . . . . . Kensington, N.H.
Osgood, George Laurie, A.B. 1866 . . . . . Cambridge.
Osgood, Henry Blanchard, A.B. 1878 . . . . . Roxbury.
Osgood, Joseph Barlow Felt, A.B. 1846 . . . Salem.
Osgood, William Fogg, A.B. 1886 . . . . . . Milton.
Otis, Charles Harrison, A.B. 1873 . . . . . Brooklyn, N.Y.
Otis, Edward Osgood, A.B. 1871 . . . . . . Boston.
Otis, James, A.B. 1881 . . . . . . . . . . . Roxbury.
Owen, Roscoe Palmer, A.B. 1863 . . . . . . Boston.
Oxnard, Henry Ernest, A.B. 1886 . . . . . . Portland, Me.

PAGE, Henry Deeley, A.B. 1878 . . . . . . . Boston.
Page, Rolla Oscar, A.B. 1845 . . . . . . . Brooklyn, N.Y.
Page, William Hussey, Jr., A.B. 1883 . . . . New York, N.Y.
Paine, James Leonard, A.B. 1881 . . . . . . Cambridge.
Paine, John Knowles, A.M. 1869 . . . . . . Cambridge.
Paine, Robert Treat, A.B. 1855 . . . . . . . Boston.
Palfray, Charles Warwick, A.B. 1835 . . . . Salem.
Palfrey, Cazneau, A.B. 1826 . . . . . . . . Cambridge.
Palmer, Charles Dana, A.B. 1868 . . . . . . Lowell.
Palmer, Franklin Sawyer, A.B. 1886 . . . . Roslindale.
Palmer, George Herbert, A.B. 1864 . . . . . Cambridge.
Palmer, Joseph Newell, A.B. 1886 . . . . . . Cambridge.
Palmer, William Henry, A.B. 1863 . . . . . New York, N.Y.
Park, Edwards Amasa, A.M. 1844, S.T.D., *Emeritus Professor of Christian Theology at Andover Theological Seminary* . . . . . . . . . Andover.
Park, John Gray, A.B. 1858 . . . . . . . . Worcester.
Parker, Charles Henry, A.B. 1835 . . . . . . Boston.
Parker, Charles Pomeroy, A.B. 1876, *Oxford* . . Cambridge.
Parker, Chauncey Goodrich, A.B. 1885 . . . . Newark, N.J.
Parker, Edmund Morley, A.B. 1877 . . . . . Cambridge.
Parker, George Howard . . . . . . . . . . Philadelphia, Pa.
Parker, Henry Ainsworth, A.B. 1864 . . . . . Cambridge.
Parker, Henry Boynton, A.B. 1867 . . . . . Oswego, N.Y.
Parker, James Cutler Dunn, A.B. 1848 . . . Brookline.
Parker, W. Stevens, A.B. 1850 . . . . . . . Stonington, Ct.
Parker, Wilbur Bates, D.M.D. 1875 . . . . . Boston.
Parkman, Charles McDonogh, A.B. 1846 . . . Rahway, N.J.
Parkman, Francis, A.B. 1844 . . . . . . . . Boston.
Parkman, Henry, A.B. 1870 . . . . . . . . Boston.

Parks, Gorham, A.B. 1854 . . . . . . . . . Albany, N.Y.
Parmenter, James Parker, A.B. 1881 . . . . . Arlington.
Parmenter, William Ellison, A.B. 1836 . . . . Arlington.
Parrish, Samuel Longstreth, A.B. 1870 . . . . New York, N.Y.
Parsons, Charles Chauncy, A.B. 1860 . . . . . Hempstead, N.Y.
Parsons, Charles William, A.B. 1840 . . . . . Providence, R.I.
Parsons, Theophilus, A.B. 1870 . . . . . . . Brookline.
Partridge, George Fairbanks, A.B. 1885 . . . . Caryville.
Paton, James Morton, A.B. 1881 . . . . . . . Cambridge.
Patten, Francis Bartlett, A.B. 1879 . . . . . Roxbury.
Patterson, George Herbert, LL.B. 1863 . . . . Providence, R.I.
Patton, Jacob Cansler, A.B. 1877 . . . . . . . Cambridge.
Patton, John Sidney, A.B. 1874 . . . . . . . . Allston.
Paul, Walter Everard, A.B. 1883 . . . . . . . Auburn, Me.
Paulding, James Kirke, A.B. 1885 . . . . . . Cold Spring, N.Y.
Payne, James Henry, Jr. A.B. 1886 . . . . . . Boston.
Payson, Edward Payson, LL.B. 1871 . . . . . Boston.
Peabody, Andrew Preston, A.B. 1826 . . . . . Cambridge.
Peabody, Francis Greenwood, A.B. 1869 . . . . Cambridge.
Peabody, Joseph, A.B. 1844 . . . . . . . . . Boston.
Peabody, Robert Swain, A.B. 1866 . . . . . . Boston.
Pearce, Edward Douglas, A.B. 1871 . . . . . Providence, R.I.
Pearmain, Sumner Bass, A.B. 1883 . . . . . . Boston.
Pease, Theodore Claudius, A.B. 1875 . . . . . Malden.
Peckham, William Gibbs, A.B. 1867 . . . . . New York, N.Y.
Peirce, Benjamin Osgood, A.B. 1876 . . . . . Cambridge.
Peirce, James Mills, A.B. 1853 . . . . . . . Cambridge.
Peirce, Joshua Rindge, A.B. 1851 . . . . . . Dorchester.
Peirson, Edward Lawrence, A.B. 1884 . . . . Salem.
Peirson, Horatio Perry, A.B. 1885 . . . . . . Salem.
Pellew, George, A.B. 1880 . . . . . . . . . Boston.
Penhallow, Charles Sherburne, A.B. 1874 . . . Jamaica Plain.
Pepper, George Dana Boardman, D.D., LL.D.,
    *President of Colby University* . . . . . . Waterville, Me.
Perkins, Edward Cranch, A.B. 1866 . . . . . Milton.
Perkins, Gilman Nichols, A.B. 1886 . . . . . Rochester, N.Y.
Perkins, John Walter, A.B. 1882 . . . . . . Hyde Park.
Perkins, John Wright, A.B. 1865 . . . . . . South Byfield.
Perkins, Maurice, A.M. 1865 . . . . . . . . Schenectady, N.Y.
Perkins, Robert Patterson, A.B. 1884 . . . . Philadelphia, Pa.
Perrin, Arthur, A.B. 1877 . . . . . . . . . Cambridge.
Perrin, Frank, D.M.D. 1877 . . . . . . . . Cambridge.
Perrin, Willard Taylor, A.B. 1870 . . . . . Worcester.
Perry, Frederick Gardiner, A.B. 1879 . . . . Weston.
Perry, Herbert Mills, A.B. 1880 . . . . . . New Ipswich, N.H.
Perry, Oscar Edward, A.B. 1883 . . . . . . Worcester.
Peters, Christian Henry Frederick, Ph.D. Berlin,
    1836, *Professor of Astronomy, Director of Observatory, Hamilton College* . . . . . . . Clinton, N.Y.

Peterson, Ellis, A.B. 1853 . . . . . . . . . Jamaica Plain.
Peterson, Reuben, A.B. 1885 . . . . . . . . East Boston.
Pevey, Gilbert Abiel Abbott, A.B. 1873 . . . . Cambridge.
Pfeiffer, Oscar Joseph, M.D. 1884 . . . . . . Denver, Col.
Phelps, Francis, A.B. 1837 . . . . . . . . . Boston.
Philbrick, Edward Southwick, A.B. 1846 . . . Brookline.
Philbrick, William Dean, A.B. 1855 . . . . . Newton Centre.
Phillips, Walter Brigham, A.B. 1886 . . . . . Boston.
Phillips, Willard Quincy, A.B. 1855 . . . . . Paris, France.
Phippen, Hardy, A.B. 1884 . . . . . . . . . Salem.
Pickering, Arthur Howard, A.B. 1874 . . . . . Roxbury.
Pickering, Edward Charles, S.B. 1865 . . . . Cambridge.
Pickering, Henry, A.B. 1861 . . . . . . . . Boston.
Pickering, Henry Goddard, A.B. 1869 . . . . Boston.
Pickman, Dudley Leavitt, A.B. 1873 . . . . . Boston.
Pierce, Edward Lillie, LL.B. 1852 . . . . . . Milton.
Pierce, Edward Peter, LL.B. 1877 . . . . . . Fitchburg.
Pierce, George Winslow, A.B. 1864 . . . . . Boston.
Pike, Robert Gordon, A.B. 1843 . . . . . . . Middletown, Ct.
Pilsbury, Ernest Henry, A.B. 1880 . . . . . . Brooklyn, N.Y.
Pine, George Stevenson, A.B. 1876 . . . . . Roxbury.
Pingree, David, A.B. 1863 . . . . . . . . . Salem.
Pinney, George Miller, Jr., A.B. 1878 . . . . New York, N.Y.
Piper, George Fiske, D.B. 1862 . . . . . . . Bedford.
Piper, George Frederick, A.B. 1867 . . . . . Cambridge.
Piper, William Taggard, A.B. 1874 . . . . . Cambridge.
Pitkin, Charles Alfred, A.B. 1873 . . . . . . Braintree.
Playfair, Rt. Hon. Sir Lyon, M.P., *Delegate from
Edinburgh University* . . . . . . . . . . London, Eng.
Pollard, Alonzo Wilder, A.B. 1883 . . . . . . Roxbury.
Poole, Jerome Bonaparte, A.B. 1867 . . . . . Rockland.
Poor, Albert, A.B. 1879 . . . . . . . . . . Boston.
Porter, Charles Burnham, A.B. 1862 . . . . . Boston.
Porter, Edward Griffin, A.B. 1858 . . . . . . Lexington.
Potter, Silas Allen, A.B. 1876 . . . . . . . Roxbury.
Potter, William Henry, A.B. 1878 . . . . . . Roxbury.
Potter, William James, A.B. 1854 . . . . . . New Bedford.
Pousland, Charles Fitz, A.B. 1872 . . . . . . Salem.
Powell, John Wesley, *Director U. S. Geol. Survey* Washington, D.C.
Pratt, Charles Augustus, A.B. 1886 . . . . . East Somerville.
Pratt, Frank Gustine, A.B. 1884 . . . . . . . Keene, N.H.
Pratt, George Greenleaf, A.B. 1866 . . . . . Boston.
Preble, Henry, A.B. 1875 . . . . . . . . . Portland, Me.
Preble, Wallace, A.B. 1879 . . . . . . . . . Cambridge.
Preble, William Pitt, LL.B. 1843 . . . . . . Portland, Me.
Prentiss, Henry Conant, A.B. 1854 . . . . . Roxbury.
Prentiss, John, A.B. 1884 . . . . . . . . . Keene, N.H.
Presbrey, Palmer Ellis, A.B. 1885 . . . . . . Cambridge.
Presbrey, Silas Dean, A.B. 1860 . . . . . . . Taunton.

Preston, Frank Whipple, S.B. 1858 . . . . . New Ipswich, N.H.
Preston, James Faulkner, A.B. 1883 . . . . . Boston.
Preston, John, A.B. 1882 . . . . . . . . . New Ipswich, N.H.
Preston, William Arthur, A.B. 1854 . . . . . New Ipswich, N.H.
Priest, George Eaton, A.B. 1862 . . . . . . . Watertown.
Prince, Morton Henry, A.B. 1875 . . . . . . Boston.
Proctor, Thomas Parker, A.B. 1854 . . . . . Boston.
Pudor, Gustav Adolph, A.B. 1886 . . . . . . Portland, Me.
Putnam, Alfred Porter, D.B. 1855 . . . . . . Concord.
Putnam, Allen, A.B. 1825 . . . . . . . . . Boston.
Putnam, Charles Pickering, A.B. 1865 . . . . Boston.
Putnam, George, A.B. 1854 . . . . . . . . Cambridge.
Putnam, Henry Ware, A.B. 1869 . . . . . . Roxbury.
Putnam, Herbert, A.B. 1883 . . . . . . . . Minneapolis, Minn.
Putnam, James Jackson, A.B. 1866 . . . . . Boston.
Putnam, William Lowell, A.B. 1882 . . . . . Boston.

QUINCY, Henry Parker, A.B. 1862 . . . . . . Dedham.
Quincy, Josiah, A.B. 1880 . . . . . . . . Quincy.
Quincy, Josiah Phillips, A.B. 1850 . . . . . Quincy.
Quincy, Samuel Miller, A.B. 1852 . . . . . . Boston.

RAND, Benjamin, A.B. 1879 . . . . . . . . Canning, N.S.
Rand, Edward Lathrop, A.B. 1881 . . . . . . Cambridge.
Randall, Charles Lawrence, M.D. 1872 . . . . Brighton.
Randall, Samuel Haskell, LL.B. 1859 . . . . . New York, N.Y.
Rankin, Edward Everett, A.B. 1886 . . . . . Deerfield.
Ranlet, Charles, A.B. 1883 . . . . . . . . Holyoke.
Ranlett, David Dodge, A.B. 1857 . . . . . . St. Albans, Vt.
Ranlett, Frederick Jordan, A.B. 1880 . . . . Auburndale.
Rantoul, Robert Samuel, A.B. 1853 . . . . . Salem.
Rathbone, John Henry, A.B. 1886 . . . . . . Albany, N.Y.
Rawle, Francis, A.B. 1869 . . . . . . . . Germantown, Phila., Pa.
Raymond, Manley Amsden, A.B. 1875 . . . . New York, N.Y.
Read, Charles Coolidge, A.B. 1864 . . . . . . Cambridge.
Read, Edward, A.B. 1869 . . . . . . . . . Cambridge.
Read, John, A.B. 1862 . . . . . . . . . . Cambridge.
Read, Nathaniel Goodwin, A.B. 1871 . . . . Cambridge.
Reeby, William Henry, D.B. 1876 . . . . . . Harvard.
Reed, Arthur, A.B. 1862 . . . . . . . . . Boston.
Reed, Charles Montgomery, LL.B. 1870 . . . Boston.
Reed, Frederick, A.B. 1881 . . . . . . . . Boston.
Reed, James, A B. 1853 . . . . . . . . . Boston.
Reed, Joseph Wheeler, A.B. 1867 . . . . . . Maynard.
Reed, Milton, A.B. 1868 . . . . . . . . . Fall River.
Renouf, Edward Augustus, A.B. 1838 . . . . Keene, N.H.
Reynolds, John, A.B. 1871 . . . . . . . . Brooklyn, N.Y.
Reynolds, John Phillips, A.B. 1815 . . . . . Boston.
Reynolds, Thomas Walter, A.B. 1886 . . . . Brooklyn, N.Y.

Rice, Alexander Hamilton, LL.D. 1876 . . . . Boston.
Rice, Nathan Payson, A.B. 1819 . . . . . . New York, N.Y.
Rich, James Rogers, A.B. 1870 . . . . . . . Boston.
Richards, Henry Augustus, A.B. 1886 . . . . Weymouth.
Richards, Theodore William, A.B. 1886 . . . Sadsburyville, Pa.
Richards, William Phillips, A B. 1876 . . . . West Somerville.
Richards, William Reuben, A.B. 1874 . . . . Boston.
Richards, William Whitlock, A.B. 1868 . . . New York, N.Y.
Richardson, Daniel Merchant, A.B. 1883 . . . Lowell.
Richardson, Daniel Samuel, A.B. 1836 . . . . Lowell.
Richardson, Hazen Kimball, A.B. 1886 . . . . Middleton.
Richardson, Herbert Augustus, A.B. 1882 . . . South Framingham.
Richardson, Homer Bartlett, A.B. 1875 . . . . New York, N.Y.
Richardson, Horace, A.B. 1852 . . . . . . . Boston.
Richardson, Maurice Howe, A.B. 1873 . . . . Boston.
Richardson, Myron Wallace, A.B. 1886 . . . . Wilmington.
Richardson, William King, A.B. 1880 . . . . . Boston.
Richardson, William Lambert, A.B. 1864 . . . Boston.
Richardson, William Minard, A.B. 1879 . . . . Cambridge.
Ricketson, John Howland, A.B. 1859 . . . . . Pittsburg, Pa.
Riddle, George, A.B. 1874 . . . . . . . . . Cambridge.
Ripley, Fred Jerome, M.D. 1883 . . . . . . . Brockton.
Ritchie, John, A.B. 1861 . . . . . . . . . . Boston.
Rives, Arthur Landon, A.B. 1874 . . . . . . Newport, R.I.
Rives, Francis Robert, A.M. 1841, *University of
   Virginia* . . . . . . . . . . . . . . . . New York, N.Y.
Rix, Francis Reader, A.B. 1875 . . . . . . . Lowell.
Robbins, Elliott Daniel, M.D. 1879 . . . . . . Charlestown.
Roberts, Herbert Howard, A.B. 1878 . . . . . Reading.
Roberts, Odin Barnes, A.B. 1886 . . . . . . Boston.
Roberts, Walter Hill, A.B. 1877 . . . . . . . Melrose.
Roberts, Waters Dewees, A.B. 1885 . . . . . Riverton, N.J.
Robeson, William Rotch, A.B. 1835 . . . . . Lenox.
Robins, Edward Blake, A.B. 1864 . . . . . . Boston.
Robinson, Charles Prosser, A.B. 1885 . . . . Parker's Landing, Pa.
Robinson, Edward, A.B. 1879 . . . . . . . . Boston.
Robinson, Ezekiel Gilman, D.D., LL.D., *President
   of Brown University* . . . . . . . . . . . Providence, R.I.
Robinson, Frank Walcott, A.B. 1870 . . . . . Jamaica Plain.
Robinson, George Dexter, A.B. 1856, *Governor of
   Massachusetts* . . . . . . . . . . . . . Chicopee.
Robinson, Nelson Lemuel, A.B. 1881 . . . . . Canton, N.Y.
Robinson, Warren Merton, A.B. 1878 . . . . Lynn.
Roby, Eben Willard, A.B. 1877 . . . . . . . New York, N.Y.
Rodman, Samuel William, A.B. 1834 . . . . Burlington.
Rogers, Edmund Law, A.B. 1839 . . . . . . Baltimore, Md.
Rogers, Henry Bromfield, A.B. 1822 . . . . . Boston.
Rogers, Henry Munroe, A.B. 1862 . . . . . . Boston.
Rogers, Isaac Lothrop, A.B. 1881 . . . . . . New York, N.Y.

Rolfe, William James, A.M. 1859 . . . . . . Cambridge.
Rollins, Eben William, A.B. 1841 . . . . . . Boston.
Rollins, Frank Waldron, A.B. 1877 . . . . . Abington.
Rollins, William Henry, A.B. 1841 . . . . . Portsmouth, N.H.
Ropes, John Codman, A.B. 1857 . . . . . . Boston.
Ropes, William Ladd, A.B. 1846 . . . . . . Andover.
Rotch, Arthur, A.B. 1871 . . . . . . . . Boston.
Rotch, Morgan, A.B. 1871 . . . . . . . . New Bedford.
Rotch, Thomas Morgan, A.B. 1870 . . . . . Boston.
Rotch, William, A.B. 1865 . . . . . . . . Boston.
Rotch, William James, A.B. 1838 . . . . . . New Bedford.
Rousmaniere, Edmund Swett, A.B. 1883 . . . Pontiac, R.I.
Royce, Josiah, A.B. 1875, *University of California* Cambridge.
Ruddick, William Henderson, M.D. 1868 . . . South Boston.
Ruggles, John, A.B. 1836 . . . . . . . . . Brookline.
Rumrill, James Augustus, A.B. 1859 . . . . . Springfield.
Russell, Charles Francis, D.B. 1884 . . . . . Weston.
Russell, Charles Howland, A.B. 1872 . . . . New York, N.Y.
Russell, Charles Theodore, A.B. 1837 . . . . Cambridge.
Russell, Charles Theodore, Jr., A.B. 1873 . . . Boston.
Russell, Edward Baldwin, A.B. 1872 . . . . . Boston.
Russell, Elliott, A.B. 1848 . . . . . . . . Boston.
Russell, Eugene Dexter, A.B. 1880 . . . . . Wakefield.
Russell, Francis Henry, A.B. 1853 . . . . . Brookline.
Russell, Henry Sturgis, A.B. 1860 . . . . . Milton.
Russell, John, A.B. 1882 . . . . . . . . . Plymouth.
Russell, LeBaron, A.B. 1832 . . . . . . . Boston.
Russell, Thomas Hastings, A.B. 1843 . . . . Boston.
Russell, William Eustis, A.B. 1877, *Mayor of Cambridge* . . . . . . . . . . . . Cambridge.

SAFFORD, Nathaniel Morton, A.B. 1869 . . . Milton.
Salisbury, Edward Elbridge, A.M., LL.D., *Ex-Professor of Arabic and Sanskrit at Yale College* . . . . . . . . . . . . . . New Haven, Ct.
Salisbury, Henry Edward, A.B. 1886 . . . . . New York, N.Y.
Salisbury, Stephen, A.B. 1856 . . . . . . . Worcester.
Saltonstall, Leverett, A.B. 1844 . . . . . . Chestnut Hill.
Saltonstall, Richard Middlecott, A.B. 1880 . . . Chestnut Hill.
Sampson, Alden, A.B. 1876 . . . . . . . . New York, N.Y.
Sampson, Calvin Proctor, A.B. 1874 . . . . . Charlestown.
Sampson, Junius, A.B. 1871 . . . . . . . . New Iberia, La.
Sanborn, Franklin Benjamin, A.B. 1855 . . . Concord.
Sanborn, Thomas Parker, A.B. 1886 . . . . . Springfield.
Sanborn, William Delano, A.B. 1871 . . . . . Winchester.
Sanderson, Robert . . . . . . . . . . . Cambridge.
Sanford, Edward Terry, A.B. 1885 . . . . . Knoxville, Tenn.
Sanger, Chester Franklin, A.B. 1880 . . . . . Cambridge.
Sanger, George Partridge, A.B. 1840 . . . . . Cambridge.

Sanger, George Partridge, Jr., A.B. 1874 . . . Boston.
Sanger, John White, A.B. 1870 . . . . . . Cambridge.
Sanger, Sabin Pond, A.B. 1883 . . . . . . . Boston.
Sargent, Charles Sprague, A.B. 1862 . . . . . Brookline.
Sargent, Dudley Allen, *Bowdoin*, 1875 . . . . Cambridge.
Sargent, Edwin Lawrence, A.B. 1868 . . . . Cambridge.
Sargent, George Amory, A.B. 1876 . . . . . Boston.
Sargent, John Osborne, A.B. 1830 . . . . . . New York, N.Y.
Sargent, Joseph, A.B. 1834 . . . . . . . . . Worcester.
Sargent, Lucius Manlius, A.B. 1870 . . . . . Boston.
Saunders, Charles Gurley, A.B. 1867 . . . . . Boston.
Saunders, Charles Robertson, A.B. 1884 . . . Cambridge.
Saunders, William Elmer, A.B. 1871 . . . . . Cambridge.
Savage, Charles Wesley, A.B. 1874 . . . . . Lowell.
Savage, Henry Wilson, A.B. 1880 . . . . . . Boston.
Savage, William Henry, *Pastor of the First Congregational Society of Watertown* . . . . . Watertown.
Savary, William Henry, D.B. 1860 . . . . . South Boston.
Sawin, Charles Austin, A.B. 1885 . . . . . . Cambridge.
Sawin, George William, A.B. 1884 . . . . . Cambridge.
Sawtell, James Andrew, A.B. 1859 . . . . . Newton.
Sawyer, Arthur Brown, A.B. 1885 . . . . . . Chelsea.
Sawyer, Fred Leland, A.B. 1883 . . . . . . Cumberland Centre, Me.
Sawyer, George Augustus, A.B. 1877 . . . . . Cambridge.
Sawyer, George Carleton, A.B. 1855 . . . . . Utica, N.Y.
Schofield, William, A.B. 1879 . . . . . . . Cambridge.
Schouler, James, A.B. 1859 . . . . . . . . Boston.
Schurz, Carl, LL.D. 1875 . . . . . . . . . New York, N.Y.
Scott, Henry Edwards, A.B. 1881 . . . . . . Middlebury, Vt.
Scott, James Patterson, A.B. 1871 . . . . . . Philadelphia, Pa.
Scudder, Samuel Hubbard, S.B. 1862 . . . . . Cambridge.
Scudder, Winthrop Saltonstall, A.B. 1870 . . . Brookline.
Seamans, William Shepard, A.B. 1877 . . . . New York, N.Y.
Searle, Arthur, A.B. 1856 . . . . . . . . . Cambridge.
Sears, Edmund Hamilton, A.B. 1874 . . . . . Boston.
Sears, Henry Francis, A.B. 1883 . . . . . . Boston.
Sears, Philip Howes, A.B. 1844 . . . . . . . Boston.
Sears, Richard Dudley, A.B. 1883 . . . . . . Boston.
Seaver, Edwin Pliny, A.B. 1864 . . . . . . Newton Highlands.
Sedgwick, Henry Dwight, A.B. 1843 . . . . . New York, N.Y.
Sewall, Samuel Edmund, A.B. 1817 . . . . . Melrose.
Seward, Josiah Lafayette, A.B. 1868 . . . . . Lowell.
Sexton, Lawrence Eugene, A.B. 1884 . . . . New York, N.Y.
Shackford, Charles Chauncy, A.B. 1835 . . . . Brookline.
Shaler, Nathaniel Southgate, S.B. 1862 . . . . Cambridge.
Sharples, Stephen Paschall, S.B. 1866 . . . . Cambridge.
Shattuck, Frederick Cheever, A.B. 1868 . . . Boston.
Shattuck, George Brune, A.B. 1863 . . . . . Boston.
Shattuck, George Cheyne, A.B. 1831 . . . . . Boston.

## REGISTRATION.

| | |
|---|---|
| Shattuck, George Otis, A.B. 1851 | Boston. |
| Shaw, Francis, A.B. 1875 | New Braintree. |
| Shaw, George Shattuck, A.B. 1849 | Cambridge. |
| Shaw, Harry Clay, A.B. 1884 | Rockland. |
| Shaw, Samuel Savage, A.B. 1853 | Boston. |
| Shea, Daniel William, A.B. 1886 | Greenland, N.H. |
| Sheafe, William, A.B. 1879 | Boston. |
| Sheldon, Edward Stevens, A.B. 1872 | Cambridge. |
| Shepard, Harvey Newton, A.B. 1871 | Boston. |
| Shepard, Luther Dimmick, D.M.D. 1879 | Dorchester. |
| Sherburne, Edward Child, A.B. 1872 | Boston. |
| Sherman, Thomas Foster, A.B. 1877 | Boston. |
| Sherwin, Thomas, A.B. 1860 | Jamaica Plain. |
| Shorey, George Langdon, A.B. 1873 | Lynn. |
| Shurtleff, Hiram Smith, A.B. 1861 | Dorchester. |
| Shute, Charles Bailey, A.B. 1865 | Malden. |
| Silsbee, Arthur Boardman, A.B. 1875 | Boston. |
| Silsbee, Nathaniel Devereux, A.B. 1852 | Cohasset. |
| Silsbee, William, A.B. 1832 | Trenton, N.Y. |
| Sim, Arthur Wesley, A.B. 1885 | Salem. |
| Simes, Robert Fields, A.B. 1885 | Portsmouth, N.H. |
| Simmons, John Franklin, A.B. 1873 | Abington. |
| Simmons, Walter Willard, A.B. 1886 | Allston. |
| Simpkins, John, A.B. 1885 | Yarmouth Port. |
| Simpson, Frank Ernest, A.B. 1879 | Boston. |
| Sinclair, Albert Thomas, A.B. 1864 | Boston. |
| Sinclair, Alexander Doull, M.D. 1857 | Boston. |
| Sinnott, Joseph Edward, A.B. 1886 | Philadelphia, Pa. |
| Skillings, William Edward, A.B. 1866 | Bethel, Me. |
| Slack, William Dudley, A.B. 1851 | Pittsburg, Pa. |
| Slade, Daniel Denison, A.B. 1844 | Chestnut Hill. |
| Slade, James Fulton, A.B. 1878 | New York, N.Y. |
| Slade, Marshall Perry, A.B. 1881 | New York, N.Y. |
| Slater, William Strutt, A.B. 1854 | Webster. |
| Sleeper, Frank Henry, A.B. 1876 | West Newton. |
| Slocum, William Henry, Jr., A.B. 1886 | Jamaica Plain. |
| Smith, Charles Gilman, A.B. 1847 | Chicago, Ill. |
| Smith, Clement Lawrence, A.B. 1863 | Cambridge. |
| Smith, Edward Irving, A.B. 1885 | Lincoln. |
| Smith, Edward Sutton, A.B. 1853 | Boston. |
| Smith, Ernest Charles, D.B. *Bowdoin*, 1884 | Cambridge. |
| Smith, Frank Warren, A.B. 1886 | Dorchester. |
| Smith, Frank Webster, A.B. 1877 | Westfield. |
| Smith, Frederick Mears, A.B. 1880 | Cambridge. |
| Smith, Frederic Warren, A.B. 1879 | Cambridge. |
| Smith, George Williamson, D.D. *President of Trinity College* | Hartford, Ct. |
| Smith, Hamilton Irving, A.B. 1875 | East Boston. |
| Smith, Henry Augustus, LL.B. 1871 | Roxbury. |

Smith, Henry St. John, A.B. 1872 . . . . . . Portland, Me.
Smith, Herbert Massey, M.D.V. 1886 . . . . Haverhill.
Smith, James Beebe, A.B. 1883 . . . . . . Springfield.
Smith, Jeremiah, A.B. 1856 . . . . . . . . Dover, N.H.
Smith, Jonathan Jason, M.D. 1879 . . . . . Boston.
Smith, Nathaniel Stevens, A.B. 1869 . . . . New York, N.Y.
Smith, Ormond Gerald, A.B. 1883 . . . . . . New York, N.Y.
Smith, Robert Dickson, A.B. 1857. . . . . . Boston.
Smith, Robert Dickson Weston, A.B. 1886 . . . Boston.
Smith, Samuel Francis, A.B. 1829. . . . . . Newton Centre.
Smith, Theophilus Gilman, A.B. 1871 . . . . Cambridge.
Smith, Walter Bugbee, A.B. 1870 . . . . . . Philadelphia, Pa.
Smith, Walter Edward Clifton, A.B. 1883 . . . Boston.
Smith, Willard Everett, A.B. 1879 . . . . . Boston.
Smith, William Christopher, A.B. 1885 . . . . Chatham.
Smith, William Henry Leland, LL.B. 1848 . . Boston.
Smith, William Lord, A.B. 1886 . . . . . . Boston.
Smith, William Wharton, A.B. 1885 . . . . . Philadelphia, Pa.
Smyth, Egbert Coffin, D.D., *Professor of Ecclesiastical History in Andover Theological Seminary* . . . . . . . . . . . . . . Andover.
Snell, Arthur Lincoln, A.B. 1886 . . . . . . Lawrence.
Snow, Charles Armstrong, A.B. 1882. . . . . Boston.
Snow, George Andrew, A.B. 1885 . . . . . . Cambridge.
Snow, Herman, D.B. 1843 . . . . . . . . Cambridgeport.
Somerby, Samuel Ellsworth, A.B. 1879 . . . . South Framingham.
Somers, George Burbank, A.B. 1886 . . . . . San Francisco, Cal.
Soren, George Wales, A.B. 1851 . . . . . . New York, N.Y.
Soule, Charles Carroll, A.B. 1862 . . . . . . Brookline.
Southworth, Robert Alexander, A.B. 1874 . . . Charlestown.
Sowdon, Arthur John Clark, A.B. 1857 . . . . Boston.
Spalding, George Frederick, A.B. 1882 . . . . Brookline.
Sparhawk, Clement Willis, M.D. 1884 . . . . West Roxbury.
Sparhawk, Edward Epps, A.B. 1878 . . . . . Roxbury.
Spaulding, Henry George, A.B. 1860 . . . . . Newton.
Spaulding, John, LL.B. 1850 . . . . . . . Boston.
Spelman, Henry Munson, A.B. 1884 . . . . . Cambridge.
Spelman, Israel Munson, A.B. 1836 . . . . . Cambridge.
Spooner, John Winthrop, A.B. 1867 . . . . . Hingham.
Sprague, Charles Franklin, A.B. 1879 . . . . Boston.
Sprague, Edward Everett, A.B. 1868 . . . . . New York, N.Y.
Sprague, Henry Harrison, A.B. 1864 . . . . . Boston.
Sprague, Richard, A.B. 1881 . . . . . . . Boston.
Sproat, James Crossman, A.B. 1871 . . . . . Taunton.
Spuller, Eugène, A.B. 1857, Dijon, *Member of the French Chamber of Deputies* . . . . . . . Paris, France.
Squire, John Adams, A.B. 1884 . . . . . . Arlington.
Stackpole, Frederick Dabney, A.B. 1873 . . . . Boston.
Stackpole, Joseph Lewis, A.B. 1857 . . . . . Boston.

| | |
|---|---|
| Stacy, Melville, A.B. 1867 | Somerville. |
| Standish, Myles, M.D. 1879 | Boston. |
| Stanton, Benjamin Irving, LL.B. 1881 | Albany, N.Y. |
| Stanton, Jere Edmund, D.M.D. 1884 | Boston. |
| Stanton, Nathaniel Greene, M.D. 1866 | Newport, R.I. |
| Starbuck, Henry Pease, A.B. 1871 | New York, N.Y. |
| Starr, Benjamin Charles, A.B. 1877 | Cleveland, O. |
| Stearns, Charles Onslow, A.B. 1867 | Boston. |
| Stearns, Elijah Wyman, A.B. 1838 | Bedford. |
| Stearns, George Andrew, Jr. A.B. 1881 | Worcester. |
| Stearns, George Hermon, A.B. 1878 | Mansfield. |
| Stebbins, James Hervey, S.B. 1878 | New York, N.Y. |
| Stebbins, Richard, A.B. 1846 | Omaha, Neb. |
| Stebbins, Roderick, A.B. 1881 | Milton. |
| Stedman, Charles Ellery, A.B. 1852 | Dorchester. |
| Stetson, Edward, A.B. 1876 | Bangor, Me. |
| Stetson, Eliot Dawes, A.B. 1882 | New Bedford. |
| Stevens, Charles Herbert, A.B. 1882 | Cambridge. |
| Stevens, Charles Wistar, A.B. 1860 | Charlestown. |
| Stevens, Daniel Waldo, A.B. 1846 | Vineyard Haven. |
| Stevens, Edmund Horace, M.D. 1867 | Cambridge. |
| Stevens, Edward Knights, A.B. 1882 | Newport, R.I. |
| Stevens, George Blanchard, A.B. 1866 | Gloucester. |
| Stevens, Henry James, A.B. 1857 | North Andover. |
| Stevens, William Stanford, A.B. 1880 | Boston. |
| Stewart, George Andrew, A.B. 1884 | South Boston. |
| Stewart, Samuel Barrett, D.B. 1862 | Lynn. |
| Stimson, Frederic Jesup, A.B. 1876 | New York, N.Y. |
| Stockbridge, John Calvin, D.D. 1859 | Providence, R.I. |
| Stocker, Alfred Augustus, M.D. 1852 | Cambridge. |
| Stoddard, Francis Russell, A.B. 1866 | Boston. |
| Stoddard, William Prescott, A.B. 1866 | Plymouth. |
| Stone, Arthur Kingsbury, A.B. 1883 | Framingham. |
| Stone, Charles Wellington, A.B. 1874 | Boston. |
| Stone, Eben Francis, A.B. 1843 | Newburyport. |
| Stone, Edwin Palmer, A.B. 1874 | Boston. |
| Stone, Henry, D.B. 1860 | South Boston. |
| Stone, Lincoln Ripley, M.D. 1854 | Newton. |
| Stone, Livingston, A.B. 1857 | Charlestown, N.H. |
| Stone, Philip Sidney, A.B. 1872 | Cambridge. |
| Stone, Ralph, A.B. 1872 | Buffalo, N.Y. |
| Stone, Richard, A.B. 1861 | Boston. |
| Stone, William Abbott, A.B. 1886 | Cambridge. |
| Storer, John Humphreys, A.B. 1882 | Boston. |
| Storer, Malcolm, A.B. 1885 | Newport, R.I. |
| Storrow, Charles, A.B. 1861 | Brookline. |
| Storrow, Charles Storer, A.B. 1829 | Boston. |
| Storrow, James Jackson, Jr., A.B. 1885 | Boston. |
| Stowell, George Leverett, A.B. 1871 | Portsmouth, N.H. |

Stratton, Charles Edwin, A.B. 1866 . . . . . Boston.
Strong, Charles Pratt, A.B. 1876 . . . . . . Boston.
Stuart, Frederic William, A.B. 1881 . . . . . South Boston.
Studley, John Butler, A.B. 1881 . . . . . . Concord.
Sturgis, Richard Clipston, A.B. 1881 . . . . . Boston.
Sturgis, Roger Faxton, A.B. 1884 . . . . . . Boston.
Sturgis, William Codman, A.B. 1884 . . . . . Brookline.
Sullivan, Cornelius Patrick, LL.B. 1885 . . . . Boston.
Sullivan, Jeremiah Henry, LL.B. 1872 . . . . Cambridge.
Sullivan, William, A.B. 1878 . . . . . . . Boston.
Sullivan, William Dunning, A.B. 1883 . . . . Somerville.
Sumner, Allen Melancthon, S.B. 1865 . . . . Boston.
Suter, Hales Wallace, A.B. 1850 . . . . . . Boston.
Suter, John Wallace, A.B. 1881 . . . . . . Winchester.
Sutro, Theodore, A.B. 1871 . . . . . . . . New York, N.Y.
Sutton, Eben, Jr., A.B. 1885 . . . . . . . . North Andover.
Swaim, Joseph Skinner, A.B. 1873 . . . . . . Providence, R.I.
Swan, Charles Herbert, A.B. 1870 . . . . . . Boston.
Swan, William Willard, A.B. 1850 . . . . . Brookline.
Swayze, Francis Joseph, A.B. 1879 . . . . . Newton, N.J.
Swift, Lindsay, A.B. 1877 . . . . . . . . . West Roxbury.
Swift, Robert, S.B. 1881 . . . . . . . . . Boston.
Swift, William Nye, A.B. 1877 . . . . . . . New Bedford.
Swinburne, George Knowles, A.B. 1881 . . . . New York, N.Y.
Swinscoe, Henry Kirkland, A.B. 1885 . . . . Clinton.
Sylvester, William Henry, A.B. 1879 . . . . . Newtonville.

TAFT, Charles Hutchins, A.B. 1881 . . . . . Cambridge.
Taft, Stephen Swift, A.B. 1870 . . . . . . . Palmer.
Tallmadge, Hiram Ewers, A.B. 1854 . . . . . New York, N.Y.
Tappan, Lewis William, A.B. 1860 . . . . . Milton.
Tarbell, George Grosvenor, A.B. 1862 . . . . Boston.
Tarbell, John Parker, A.B. 1828 . . . . . . Boston.
Taussig, Frank William, A.B. 1879 . . . . . Cambridge.
Taylor, Arthur, A.B. 1880 . . . . . . . . . Boston.
Taylor, Charles, D.D., *Master of St. John's College,
Cambridge, England* . . . . . . . . . Cambridge, Eng.
Taylor, Edward Randolph, S.B. 1868 . . . . . Cleveland, O.
Taylor, Frank Hendrickson, A.B. 1877 . . . . Philadelphia, Pa.
Taylor, Frederic Weston, A.B. 1878 . . . . . North Cambridge.
Taylor, James Brainerd, A.B. 1867 . . . . . Newton.
Taylor, John Bunker, M.D. 1847 . . . . . . East Cambridge.
Taylor, John Doe, A.B. 1849 . . . . . . . . New York, N.Y.
Taylor, Nelson, Jr., A.B. 1875 . . . . . . . South Norwalk, Ct.
Taylor, Percy Hayes, A.B. 1886 . . . . . . Cambridge.
Temple, Frederick Henry, A.B. 1879 . . . . . Charlestown.
Thacher, Thomas Chandler, A.B. 1882 . . . . Boston.
Thayer, Albert Smith, A.B. 1875 . . . . . . New York, N.Y.
Thayer, Charles French, A.B. 1846 . . . . . Boston.

Thayer, James Bradley, A.B. 1852 . . . . . . . Cambridge.
Thayer, John Eliot, A.B. 1885 . . . . . . . . Lancaster.
Thayer, Joseph Henry, A.B. 1850 . . . . . . Cambridge.
Thayer, Nathaniel, A.B. 1871 . . . . . . . . Boston.
Thayer, Nathaniel Niles, A.B. 1878 . . . . . Boston.
Thayer, William Sydney, A.B. 1885 . . . . . Cambridge.
Thissell, Joseph Abbott, M.D. 1885 . . . . . Beverly.
Thomas, Flavel Shurtleff, M.D. 1874 . . . . Hanson.
Thomas, James Bourne Freeman, A.B. 1860 . . Boston.
Thomas, James Eames, A.B. 1879 . . . . . . Rockland.
Thomas, Theodore . . . . . . . . . . . . New York, N.Y.
Thomas, Washington Butcher, A.B. 1870 . . . Boston.
Thompson, Albert Harris, A.B. 1873 . . . . . Boston.
Thompson, Charles Miner, A.B. 1886 . . . . . Burlington, Vt.
Thompson, John McQuaid, A.B. 1886 . . . . Boston.
Thompson, Lucian Bisbee, LL.B. 1867 . . . . Boston.
Thorndike, Albert, A.B. 1881 . . . . . . . Cambridge.
Thorndike, Augustus, A.B. 1884 . . . . . . Brookline.
Thorndike, Charles, A.B. 1854 . . . . . . . Brookline.
Thorndike, George Quincy, A.B. 1847 . . . . Boston.
Thorndike, Samuel Lothrop, A.B. 1852 . . . . Cambridge.
Thorp, Joseph Gilbert, Jr., A.B. 1879 . . . . Cambridge.
Thurber, James Danforth, A.B. 1858 . . . . . Plymouth.
Thurlow, John Howard, M.D. 1881 . . . . . . Roxbury.
Ticknor, Benjamin Holt, A.B. 1862 . . . . . Boston.
Ticknor, Howard Malcom, A.B. 1856 . . . . . Jamaica Plain.
Tiffany, Francis, A.B. 1847 . . . . . . . . West Newton.
Tiffany, Francis Buchanan, A.B. 1877 . . . . Boston.
Tiffany, William Shaw, A.B. 1845 . . . . . . Roxbury.
Tileston, John Boies, A.B. 1855 . . . . . . Brookline.
Tillinghast, William Hopkins, A.B. 1877 . . . Cambridge.
Tilton, Edward James, A.B. 1885 . . . . . . Andover.
Tomkins, Floyd Williams, Jr., A.B. 1872 . . . New York, N.Y.
Tomlinson, George Samuel, A.B. 1863 . . . . Roxbury.
Toppan, Robert Noxon, A.B. 1858 . . . . . . Cambridge.
Torrey, Henry Warren, A.B. 1833 . . . . . . Cambridge.
Tower, Augustus Clifford, A.B. 1877 . . . . New York, N.Y.
Tower, Benjamin Lowell Merrill, A.B. 1860 . . Boston.
Towne, Trueman Benjamin, LL.B. 1870 . . . . Boston.
Townsend, Charles Wendell, A.B. 1881 . . . . Boston.
Townsend, Edward Mitchell, Jr., A.B. 1884 . . New York, N.Y.
Townsend, Howard, A.B. 1880 . . . . . . . New York, N.Y.
Townsend, Stephen Van Rensselaer, A.B. 1882 . New York, N.Y.
Toy, Crawford Howell, A.B., *University of Virginia*,
  1856 . . . . . . . . . . . . . . . . Cambridge.
Trask, Jabez Nelson, A.B. 1862 . . . . . . . New Salem.
Trask, William Ropes, A.B. 1885 . . . . . . Cambridge.
Treat, John Harvey, A.B. 1862 . . . . . . . Lawrence.
Treat, Samuel, A.B. 1837 . . . . . . . . . St. Louis, Mo.

Trowbridge, John, S.B. 1866 . . . . . . . Cambridge.
Tubbs, Alfred Stewart, A.B. 1870 . . . . . . . San Francisco, Cal.
Tuck, Henry, A.B. 1863 . . . . . . . . . New York, N.Y.
Tucker, Alanson, A.B. 1872 . . . . . . . . Boston.
Tucker, William Lawrence, A.B. 1865 . . . . Boston.
Tuckerman, Gustavus, A.B. 1882 . . . . . . Plymouth.
Tuckerman, Leverett Saltonstall, A.B. 1868 . . Salem.
Tudor, Frederic, A.B. 1867 . . . . . . . . Boston.
Tufts, James Arthur, A.B. 1878 . . . . . . Exeter, N.H.
Turner, Samuel Epes, A.B. 1869 . . . . . . Cambridge.
Turpin, Bradford Strong, A.B. 1880 . . . . . Dorchester.
Tuttle, William Henry Harrison, LL.B. 1877 . . Arlington.
Tweed, Benjamin Franklin, A.M. 1853 . . . . Cambridgeport.
Twombly, William Lance Dow, A.B. 1877 . . . Watertown.
Tyler, John Ford, A.B. 1877 . . . . . . . . Boston.
Tyler, William Seymour, D.D., 1857, *Professor of Greek in Amherst College* . . . . . . . Amherst.

UNDERWOOD, Henry Oliver, A.B. 1870 . . . . Belmont.
Underwood, Melvin Augustus, A.B. 1866 . . . Dorchester.
Underwood, William Orison, A.B. 1884 . . . . Boston.
Upham, Henry Lauriston, D.M.D. 1886 . . . . Boston.
Upham, William Phineas, A.B. 1856 . . . . . Salem.
Upton, George Bruce, A.B. 1849 . . . . . . Boston.

VAN BRUNT, Henry, A.B. 1854 . . . . . . . . Cambridge.
Van Cleef, Frank Louis, A.B. 1885 . . . . . Wellington, O.
Van Duzer, Henry Sayre, A.B. 1875 . . . . . New York, N.Y.
Van Nest, George Willett, A.B. 1874 . . . . . New York, N.Y.
Van Rensselaer, William Bayard, A.B. 1879 . . Albany, N.Y.
Van Slyck, Cyrus Manchester, LL.B. 1878 . . . Providence, R.I.
Vaughan, Charles Everett, A.B. 1856 . . . . Cambridge.
Vaughan, Francis Wales, A.B. 1853 . . . . . Cambridge.
Vaughan, William Warren, A. B. 1870 . . . . Boston.
Vaughn, John, A.B. 1879 . . . . . . . . . New York, N.Y.
Viaux, Frederic Henry, A.B. 1870 . . . . . . Boston.
Vickery, Herman Frank, A.B. 1878 . . . . . Boston.
Vinson, Cornelius Marchant, A.B. 1839 . . . . Boston.
Vinton, Charles Henry, A.B. 1878 . . . . . . Boston.

WADE, Winthrop Howland, A.B. 1881 . . . . Boston.
Wadsworth, Alexander Fairfield, A.B. 1860 . . Boston.
Wadsworth, Charles David, A.B. 1867 . . . . New York, N.Y.
Wadsworth, Hiram Warren, A.B. 1885 . . . . Cambridge.
Wadsworth, Oliver Fairfield, A.B. 1860 . . . . Boston.
Wagar, Mars Edward, A.B. 1881 . . . . . . Cleveland, O.
Wait, William Cushing, A.B. 1882 . . . . . . Medford.
Waitt, Joseph Ellsworth, D.M.D. 1883 . . . . Roxbury.
Wakefield, John Lathrop, A.B. 1880 . . . . . Dedham.
Walcott, Charles Folsom, A.B. 1857 . . . . . Cambridge.

Walcott, Charles Hosmer, A.B. 1870 . . . . . Concord.
Walcott, Henry Pickering, A.B. 1858 . . . . . Cambridge.
Waldo, Leonard, S.D. 1879 . . . . . . . . New Haven, Ct.
Waldock, James, A.B. 1845 . . . . . . . . Roxbury.
Wales, Benjamin Read, A.B. 1863 . . . . . Dorchester.
Wales, Joseph Howe, A.B. 1861 . . . . . . Brookline.
Walker, George, A.B. 1844 . . . . . . . . Portland, Me.
Walker, Grant, A.B. 1873 . . . . . . . . Boston.
Walker, Henry, A.B. 1855 . . . . . . . . Boston.
Walker, James Putnam, A.B. 1861 . . . . . Bangor, Me.
Walker, John Baldwin, A.B. 1884 . . . . . Boston.
Wallace, Herbert Ingalls, A.B. 1877 . . . . . Fitchburg.
Ward, David Henshaw, A.B. 1853 . . . . . . Oakland, Cal.
Ware, Charles, A.B. 1880 . . . . . . . . . New York, N.Y.
Ware, Charles Eliot, A.B. 1834 . . . . . . . Boston.
Ware, Charles Eliot, Jr., A.B. 1876 . . . . . Fitchburg.
Ware, Charles Pickard, A.B. 1862 . . . . . . Brookline.
Ware, Darwin Erastus, A.B. 1852 . . . . . . Boston.
Ware, George Washington, Jr., LL.B. 1861 . . Boston.
Ware, Horace Everett, A.B. 1867 . . . . . . Milton.
Ware, Loammi Goodenow, A.B. 1850 . . . . Burlington, Vt.
Ware, Thornton Kirkland, A.B. 1842 . . . . Fitchburg.
Ware, William Robert, A.B. 1852 . . . . . . New York, N.Y.
Waring, William Henry, A.B. 1852 . . . . . Brooklyn, N.Y.
Warner, Henry Eldridge, A.B. 1882 . . . . . Cambridge.
Warner, Joseph Bangs, A.B. 1869 . . . . . . Cambridge.
Warner, William Pearson, A.B. 1874 . . . . Cambridge.
Warren, Charles Everett, A.B. 1860 . . . . . Boston.
Warren, Fiske, A.B. 1884 . . . . . . . . . Boston.
Warren, John Collins, A B. 1863 . . . . . . Boston.
Warren, Joseph Weatherhead, A.B. 1871 . . . Boston.
Warren, Winslow, A.B. 1858 . . . . . . . . Dedham.
Warren, William Ross, A.B. 1883 . . . . . . New York, N.Y.
Washburn, Alexander Calvin, A.B. 1839 . . . Norwood.
Washburn, Alfred Foster, A.B. 1873 . . . . . Cambridge.
Washburn, Andrew, A.B. 1852 . . . . . . . Hyde Park.
Washburn, Charles Grenfill, A.B. 1880 . . . . Worcester.
Washburn, Frank Booth, A.B. 1881 . . . . . Boston.
Washburn, John Bell, A.B. 1886 . . . . . . Plymouth.
Washburn, John Davis, A.B. 1853 . . . . . . Worcester.
Washburn, Philip Moen, A.B. 1882 . . . . . Worcester.
Waterhouse, Frank Shepard, LL.B. 1876 . . . Portland, Me.
Waterman, Thomas, A.B. 1864 . . . . . . . Boston.
Waters, Henry Fitz-Gilbert, A.B. 1855 . . . . Salem.
Waters, Thomas Franklin, A.B. 1872 . . . . Ipswich.
Watson, Benjamin Marston, A.B. 1839 . . . . Plymouth.
Watson, Robert Clifford, A.B. 1869 . . . . . Milton.
Watson, William, S.B. 1857 . . . . . . . . Boston.
Weaver, Gerrit Elias Hambleton, A.B. 1881 . . Cambridge.
Webb, John Sidney, A.B. 1882 . . . . . . . Washington, D.C.

Webb, Nathan, A.B. 1816 . . . . . . . . . Portland, Me.
Webber, Alonzo Carter, M.D. 1849 . . . . . Cambridge.
Webster, Hollis, A.B. 1884 . . . . . . . . Dorchester.
Webster, Joseph Rowe, A.B. 1854 . . . . . Dorchester.
Weed, George Marston, A.B. 1886 . . . . . Newton.
Weed, George Standish, A.B. 1886 . . . . Plattsburgh, N.Y.
Weld, Aaron Davis, Jr., A.B. 1853 . . . . Boston.
Weld, Charles Stuart Faucheraud, A.B. 1863 . . Hyde Park.
Weld, Christopher Minot, A.B. 1880 . . . . . Boston.
Weld, Francis Minot, A.B. 1860 . . . . . . New York, N.Y.
Weld, George Walker, A.B. 1860 . . . . . . Boston.
Weld, James Edward, A.B. 1882 . . . . . . New York, N.Y.
Welling, Richard Ward Greene, A.B. 1880 . . . New York, N.Y.
Wellington, James Lloyd, A.B. 1838 . . . . . Swansea.
Wellington, William Williamson, A.B. 1832 . . Cambridgeport.
Wells, Benjamin Williams, A.B. 1884 . . . . Boston.
Wells, Charles Luke, A.B. 1879 . . . . . . . Gardiner, Me.
Wells, Frank, A.B. 1864 . . . . . . . . . . Brookline.
Wells, James Lee, M.D. 1883 . . . . . . . . Boston.
Wells, John Doane, A.B. 1854 . . . . . . . Cambridge.
Wells, Stiles Gannett, A.B. 1886 . . . . . . Boston.
Wendell, Barrett, A.B. 1877 . . . . . . . . Boston.
Wendell, Evert Jansen, A.B. 1882 . . . . . . New York, N.Y.
Wendell, Frank Thaxter, A.B. 1874 . . . . . Boston.
Wentworth, Alonzo Bond, LL.B. 1863 . . . . Dedham.
Wentworth, Elmer Ellsworth, A.B. 1882 . . . Chelsea.
Wentworth, George Albert, A.B. 1858 . . . . Exeter, N.H.
Wentworth, Samuel Hidden, A.B. 1858 . . . Boston.
Wenzell, Henry Burleigh, A.B. 1875 . . . . . St. Paul, Minn.
Wesselhoeft, William Fessenden, A.B. 1884 . . Boston.
West, Benjamin Hussey, A.B. 1835 . . . . . Neponset.
West, Edward Graeff, A.B. 1877 . . . . . . Roxbury.
Weston, Melville Moore, A.B. 1870 . . . . . Boston.
Wetherbee, Albion Otis, A.B. 1885 . . . . . Charlestown.
Wetherbee, Roswell, M.D. 1882 . . . . . . . Cambridgeport.
Wetmore, Edmund, A.B. 1860 . . . . . . . . New York, N.Y.
Wharton, William Fisher, A.B. 1870 . . . . . Boston.
Wheatland, George, A.B. 1824 . . . . . . . Salem.
Wheatland, Henry, A.B. 1832 . . . . . . . Salem.
Wheeler, Frank Sumner, A.B. 1872 . . . . . Chicago, Ill.
Wheeler, Henry, A.B. 1878 . . . . . . . . . Boston.
Wheeler, Henry Nathan, A.B. 1871 . . . . . Cambridge.
Wheeler, Horace Leslie, A.B. 1881 . . . . . Newton Centre.
Wheeler, Increase Sumner, A.B. 1826 . . . . Framingham.
Wheeler, Jesse Franklin, A.B. 1868 . . . . . Boston.
Wheeler, John Henry, A.B. 1871 . . . . . University of Virginia, Va.
Wheeler, Leonard, A.B. 1866 . . . . . . . . Worcester.
Wheelock, George Rogers, A.B. 1873 . . . . Boston.
Wheelwright, Andrew Cunningham, A.B. 1847 . Brookline.
Wheelwright, Charles Chapin, A.B. 1885 . . . Roxbury.

Wheelwright, Edmund March, A.B. 1876 . . . Jamaica Plain.
Wheelwright, John Tyler, A.B. 1876 . . . . Boston.
Wheelwright, Josiah, A.B. 1843 . . . . . . Boston.
Whiston, Edward Andem, M.D. 1861 . . . . Newtonville.
White, Charles Joyce, A.B. 1859 . . . . . . Cambridge.
White, Franklin Davis, A.B. 1880 . . . . . . Milton.
White, George Rantoul, A.B. 1886 . . . . . Wellesley Hills.
White, George Warner, A.B. 1874 . . . . . . Boston.
White, James Clarke, A.B. 1853 . . . . . . Boston.
White, John Allison, A.B. 1884 . . . . . . Williamsport, Pa.
White, John Silas, A.B. 1870 . . . . . . . New York, N.Y.
White, John Williams, Ph.D. 1877 . . . . Cambridge.
White, McDonald Ellis, A.B. 1885 . . . . . Boston.
White, Moses Perkins, A.B. 1872 . . . . . . Cambridge.
White, William Augustus, A.B. 1863 . . . . New York, N.Y.
White, William Howard, A.B. 1880 . . . . . Brookline.
White, William Orne, A.B. 1840 . . . . . . Brookline.
Whitehouse, Edward Lawrence, A.B. 1874 . . . Augusta, Me.
Whiteside, Julian Lincoln, A.B. 1885 . . . . Lowell.
Whiting, Charles Hoover, A.B. 1879 . . . . Boston.
Whiting, Frederick Erwin, A.B. 1880 . . . . Auburndale.
Whiting, Harold, A.B. 1877 . . . . . . . . Cambridge.
Whiting, Isaac Spalding, A.B. 1882 . . . . . Lexington.
Whiting, John Eaton, A.B. 1862 . . . . . . Boston.
Whitman, Crosby Church, A.B. 1886 . . . . Cambridge.
Whitman, Edmund Allen, A.B. 1881 . . . . . Cambridge.
Whitman, George Luther, A.B. 1857 . . . . . New York, N.Y.
Whitney, Charles Leavitt Beals, A.B. 1871 . . . Brookline.
Whitney, David Rice, A.B. 1848 . . . . . . Boston.
Whitney, Edson Leone, A.B. 1885 . . . . . . Boston.
Whitney, Henry Austin, A.B. 1846 . . . . . Blue Hill.
Whitney, Joseph Cutler, A.B. 1878 . . . . . Milton.
Whitney, Hon. William Collins, *Secretary of the Navy* . . . . . . . . . . . . . . . . Washington, D.C.
Whitney, William Fiske, A.B. 1871 . . . . . Boston.
Whittemore, Charles Alexander, A.B. 1885 . . Cambridgeport.
Whittemore, Fred Webster, M.D. 1878 . . . . Cambridgeport.
Whittemore, George Henry, A.B. 1860 . . . . Cambridge.
Whittemore, John Marshall, A.B. 1866 . . . . Cambridge.
Whittier, Charles Albert, A.B. 1860 . . . . . Boston.
Whittier, Edward Newton, M.D. 1869 . . . . Boston.
Whitwell, Frederick Silsbee, A.B. 1884 . . . . Boston.
Wigglesworth, Edward, A.B. 1861 . . . . . . Boston.
Wigglesworth, George, A.B. 1874 . . . . . . Boston.
Wight, Daniel, A.B. 1837 . . . . . . . . . Natick.
Wigmore, John Henry, A.B. 1883 . . . . . . San Francisco, Cal.
Wilbur, Hubert Granville, A.B. 1886 . . . . Fall River.
Wilbur, Joshua Green, M.D. 1862 . . . . . . Brooklyn, N.Y.
Wilder, Enos, A.B. 1865 . . . . . . . . . Madison, N.J.
Wilds, Judson Boardman, A.B. 1871 . . . . . New York, N.Y.

Wilkinson, Alfred, A.B. 1880 . . . . . . . Syracuse, N.Y.
Willard, Joseph, A.B. 1855 . . . . . . . . Boston.
Willard, Robert, A.B. 1860 . . . . . . . . Boston.
Williams, Charles Herbert, A.B. 1871 . . . . Boston.
Williams, David Weld, A.B. 1873 . . . . . . Boston.
Williams, Francis Charles, A.B. 1843 . . . . Roxbury.
Williams, Francis Henry, M.D. 1877 . . . . . Boston.
Williams, Francis Smith, A.B. 1881 . . . . . New York, N.Y.
Williams, Francis Stanton, A.B. 1837 . . . . Boston.
Williams, George Henry, A.B. 1881 . . . . . Boston.
Williams, Henry, A.B. 1837 . . . . . . . . Boston.
Williams, Henry Bigelow, A.B. 1865 . . . . . Boston.
Williams, Henry Jules, A.B. 1884 . . . . . . Boston.
Williams, Henry Morland, A.B. 1885 . . . . Boston.
Williams, Henry Willard, M.D. 1849 . . . . . Boston.
Williams, John Bertram, A.B. 1877 . . . . . Cambridge.
Williams, John Davis, A.B. 1866 . . . . . . Boston.
Williams, Otho Holland, Jr., A.B. 1880 . . . Baltimore, Md.
Williams, Pelham, A.B. 1853 . . . . . . . Troy, N.Y.
Williams, Rufus Phillips, A.M. 1878 . . . . Boston.
Williams, Sydney Augustus, A.B. 1858 . . . Boston.
Williams, Theodore Chickering, A.B. 1876 . . New York, N.Y.
Williams, William Hall, A.B. 1883 . . . . . Wakefield.
Williamson, William Cross, A.B. 1852 . . . . Boston.
Williston, Samuel, A.B. 1882 . . . . . . . Cambridge.
Willson, Edmund Russell, A.B. 1875 . . . . . Providence, R.I.
Willson, Robert Wheeler, A.B. 1873 . . . . . Cambridge.
Willson, Samuel Stearns, LL.B. 1865 . . . . Dedham.
Wilson, Charles, D.M.D. 1870 . . . . . . . Boston.
Wilson, Charles Abbot, A.B. 1886 . . . . . . Washington, D.C.
Wilson, Daniel Munro, D.B. 1872 . . . . . . Quincy.
Wilson, Frank, LL.B. 1878 . . . . . . . . Sanford, Me.
Wilson, John Brainerd, A.B. 1884 . . . . . . Peabody.
Wilson, John Thomas, LL.B. 1868 . . . . . Winchester.
Winkley, Henry William, A.B. 1881 . . . . . St. Stephen, N.B.
Winlock, George Lane, A.B. 1885 . . . . . . Cambridge.
Winlock, William Crawford, A.B. 1880 . . . . Washington, D.C.
Winn, William Adams, A.B. 1872 . . . . . . Arlington.
Winslow, John, LL.B. 1852 . . . . . . . . Brooklyn, N.Y.
Winslow, Kenelm, S.B. 1883 . . . . . . . Jamaica Plain.
Winslow, Samuel Ellsworth, A.B. 1885 . . . . Worcester.
Winslow, William Warren, A.B. 1885 . . . . Punxsutawney, Pa.
Winslow, Winthrop Church, A.B. 1883 . . . Boston.
Winsor, Frederick, A.B. 1851 . . . . . . . Winchester.
Winsor, Justin, A.B. 1853 . . . . . . . . Cambridge.
Winsor, Robert, A.B. 1880 . . . . . . . . Weston.
Winsor, Walter Thaxter, A.B. 1870 . . . . . Brookline.
Winthrop, Egerton Leigh, A.B. 1885 . . . . . New York, N.Y.
Winthrop, John, A.B. 1863 . . . . . . . . Stockbridge.
Winthrop, Robert Charles, A.B. 1828 . . . . Boston.

Wister, Owen, A.B. 1882 . . . . . . . . . Philadelphia, Pa.
Wiswell, Charles Henry, A.B. 1877 . . . . . Cambridge.
Withington, Charles Francis, A.B. 1874 . . . . Roxbury.
Withington, David Little, A.B. 1874 . . . . . Newburyport.
Wolcott, Roger, A.B. 1870 . . . . . . . . Boston.
Wolff, John Eliot, A.B. 1879 . . . . . . . Cambridge.
Wood, Alexander Morris, M.D. 1863 . . . . . Somerville.
Wood, Edward Stickney, A.B. 1867 . . . . . Cambridge.
Wood, Frederic, LL.B. 1859 . . . . . . . . Morristown, N.J.
Wood, Horatio, Jr., A.B. 1857 . . . . . . . Lowell.
Wood, Stephen Blake, A.B. 1879 . . . . . . Arlington.
Wood, Stuart, Ph.D. 1875 . . . . . . . . Philadelphia, Pa.
Woodard, Charles Fuller, A.B. 1870 . . . . . Bangor, Me.
Woodberry, George Edward, A.B. 1877 . . . . Beverly.
Woodbury, Arthur Henry, A.B. 1883 . . . . . Beverly.
Woodbury, Frederick Clinton, A.B. 1882 . . . Boston.
Woodbury, George Whittemore, A.B. 1886 . . . Gloucester.
Woodbury, Gordon, A.B. 1886 . . . . . . . New York, N.Y.
Woodbury, John, A.B. 1880 . . . . . . . . Lynn.
Woodbury, Ludovicus Augustus, M.D. 1872 . . Groveland.
Woodman, Edward, A.B. 1877 . . . . . . . Portland, Me.
Woodman, George Sullivan, M.D. 1819 . . . . Newtonville.
Woodman, Walter, A.B. 1875 . . . . . . . Portland, Me.
Woodruff, Thomas Tyson, LL.B. 1884 . . . . Boston.
Woods, Edward Franklin, A.B. 1885 . . . . . Somerville.
Woodward, Samuel Bayard, A.B. 1874 . . . . Worcester.
Woodworth, Herbert Grafton, A.B. 1882 . . . Longwood.
Worcester, Alfred, A.B. 1878 . . . . . . . Waltham.
Worcester, Joseph Ruggles, A.B. 1882 . . . . Waltham.
Worthen, William Ezra, A.B. 1838 . . . . . New York, N.Y.
Wright, Edward Clarence, A.B. 1886 . . . . . Cambridge.
Wright, James Anderson, Jr., A.B. 1879 . . . New York, N.Y.
Wright, James Edward, A.B. 1861 . . . . . . Montpelier, Vt.
Wright, John Allen Collier, A.B. 1881 . . . . Rochester, N.Y.
Wright, Merle St. Croix, A.B. 1881 . . . . . Boston.
Wyeth, Nathaniel Jarvis, A.B. 1850 . New Dorp, Staten Island, N.Y.
Wyman, Alphonso Adelbert, A.B. 1883 . . . . West Acton.
Wyman, Gerald, A.B. 1869 . . . . . . . . Boston.
Wyman, John Palmer, Jr., A.B. 1874 . . . . Cambridgeport.
Wyman, Louis Augustus, A.B. 1872 . . . . . Lynn.
Wyman, Morrill, A.B. 1833 . . . . . . . . Cambridge.
Wyman, Samuel Edwin, A.B. 1874 . . . . . Cambridge.

Yocom, James Reed, A.B. 1885 . . . Richmond, Staten Island, N.Y.
Young, Alexander, LL.B. 1862 . . . . . . . Boston.
Young, Edward James, A.B. 1848 . . . . . . Cambridge.
Young, Ernest, A.B. 1873 . . . . . . . . . Cambridge.
Young, Samuel Lane, M.D. 1852 . . . . . . Cambridgeport.

www.ingramcontent.com/pod-product-compliance
Lightning Source LLC
Chambersburg PA
CBHW032030220426
43664CB00006B/424